Paul's Epistle to the

Romans

Volume 1

Chapters 1 – 8

Notes & Commentary
by
Tim Hegg

TorahResource • 2005

2nd Printing (with minor corrections), 2007

ISBN 0-9759359-0-9 (Volume 1)
ISBN 978-0-9759359-0-3 (Volume 1)

Cover concept & design by
Joshua Hegg

Printed in the United States by Morris Publishing
3212 East Highway 30
Kearney, NE 68847
1-800-650-7888

Table of Contents

Preface

No single epistle in the Apostolic Scriptures commands such a prodigious place as Paul's Epistle to the Romans. It is the Apostle's *magnum opus,* and contains his systematic thought and teaching on the whole matter of how sinners may have a right-standing before God. It stands, therefore, as a focal point of Apostolic teaching, and ought to be received as of central importance for those who claim faith in Yeshua, the Messiah. Its breadth is, at times, overwhelming, not merely by its length, but even more on account of its in-depth treatment of the grand themes of redemption as culminating in the person and work of Yeshua. We do well, then, to apply ourselves to the study of its inspired text, receiving it as a capstone in the progressive revelation of God to His people.

This commentary is the result of several years of teaching within the scope of a weekly study conducted at Beit Hallel, a Torah community in Tacoma, Washington. It was our habit to meet almost every Wednesday evening to study through the epistle, and to make application to our lives, both individual and corporate. The notes which follow are my thoughts as I studied the text, and prepared for our weekly study. It was always with the anticipation of lively dialog that I prepared these notes. I realized early on in our study that the perspectives and input of the group as we met were invaluable for hearing and understanding this ancient text, and for making its eternal truths applicable to our present day and lives. It is with much gratefulness to all who participated in this study that I now offer the notes in their entirety, edited, and in some-cases, updated and changed to reflect the conclusions we reached as we studied together.

Some General Explanations

I have sought to read and study the Epistle of Romans from a "Hebraic" perspective. That is, believing that Paul remained a Pharisee even after his having come to faith in Yeshua, and that he continued to live his life as a Torah observant Jew, it seemed to me only proper that we should attempt to understand this epistle within the framework of 1st Century Judaisms, and within the perspective of a Torah observant Apostle of Yeshua. For this reason, I retained some Hebrew terms in the place of more traditional English labels. For instance, I have consistently referred to Jesus by His Hebrew name, Yeshua, and have used Messiah in place of the Greek "Christ." I have regularly preferred Torah to "Law" when the Greek word νόμος, *nomos,* most likely points to the written Scriptures. I have likewise used the terms "assembly," "congregation," or the Hebrew *kehilah* (קְהִלָּה) in place of the traditional "church" when referring to the assembly of believers in Yeshua. This is because the term "church" (ἐκκλησία, *ekklesia*) has taken on a meaning in our times which I am convinced it did not have in the time of Paul. I also refer to the Tanach rather than to the "Old Testament," and to the Apostolic Scriptures instead of the "New Testament." In Paul's day, the Scriptures consisted of the Torah, Prophets and Writings, and therefore the idea of Old Testament Scriptures as distinct from New Testament Scriptures had not yet occurred.

But I have not opted to use these Hebraic terms (and a few others) merely to be novel or provocative, but because I believe that words are powerful, and that in attempting to view the Epistle to the Romans in a Hebraic context, choosing Hebraic terms for key ideas and for the

Messiah will hopefully remind the reader that he or she is studying a text that must be viewed from a different cultural and sociological perspective, or else it will inevitably be misunderstood.

I have not hesitated to refer to both the Hebrew and Greek texts, as I consider it of vital importance that the originals be consulted in order to understand the author's intention. When the commentary refers to single words, or short phrases, I have transliterated the Hebrew and Greek to give greater useability to those who may not have facility in the biblical languages. However, within a paragraph, once a foreign word is transliterated, it will be expected that the reader will recognize the Hebrew or Greek term under consideration, and thus transliteration is suspended.

I have regularly consulted the rabbinic writings and quoted them throughout the commentary. I recognize the danger in this, and some may think I have used the sources without discernment. Surely we cannot expect that what the rabbis wrote hundreds of years after the time of Paul should necessarily illumine Paul's thoughts and perspective. So quoting later midrashim or talmuds in connection with Paul's writings is tenuous at best. However, it seems to me, as well as to others, that often within the rabbinic literature of the 2nd through the 5th Centuries CE, there are contained those items which did find their beginnings in much earlier times. I think it is patently clear that in some measure, for instance, the early midrashim, the Mishnah, as well as some of the sayings in the Talmud and Targumim, reflect the theology and perspective of 1st Century Judaisms, particularly Pharisaism. For this reason, I have not hesitated to show rabbinic parallels, either to highlight a similar perspective with Paul, or to show how Paul went cross-grain with what might well have been the prevailing theology of his peers.

The reader will notice immediately that I have relied very heavily upon the magisterial commentary of C. E. B. Cranfield (*The Epistle to the Romans*, 2 vols., in *The International Critical Commentary* [T & T Clark, 1975, reprinted with corrections: 1977, 1975]). One might presume that I have fallen prey to the unscholarly habit of relying upon a single reference work, something that inevitably leads to trouble. However, please let me explain my heavy use of Cranfield. In past years I have taught through Romans several times, in various venues. I have preached the epistle to Christians on Sundays, I have taught the epistle at the undergraduate level, and I have studied it through several times for my own edification. During these years of becoming familiar with Paul's work, I utilized numbers of commentaries by a number of well known scholars in the field: John Calvin, John Murray, James D. G. Dunn, Robert Haldane, John Brown, F. Godet, H. C. G. Moule, William G. T. Shedd, William S. Plumer, D. Martin Lloyd-Jones, F. F. Bruce, Sandey and Hendlam, F. B. Meyer, William Hendricksen, Adolph Schalter, Peter Stuhlmacher, and others. When I first obtained Cranfield's two volume commentary, I began to work through it, and realized (as did most who reviewed it) that it was magisterial indeed. Not only had Cranfield managed to keep the whole epistle in mind as he worked through the minutiae of the text, he also had taken great pains to consult the time-tested commentaries and to distill the best thoughts of past scholars, interacting with their conclusions and assessing them against his own understanding of the text. Moreover, Cranfield has given serious consideration to the Judaic background of the Apostle, which is in itself a breath of fresh air in Romans studies. I have not always agreed with Cranfield, and have taken him to task at times. For instance, he, in the tradition of nearly all Christian commentators, has accepted the view that Paul considered the Torah either partially abolished, or at least in many ways replaced with a new "Christian" ethic. I do not hold that view, and as such often (especially in those sections of Romans where Paul is dealing with the place of Torah in the life of the believer) will take exception to Cranfield's viewpoint. However, in the broad strokes of things, I have consistently found his work to be head and shoulders above most of the others. It seemed superfluous, then, for me to constantly refer to other commentaries. In the course of writing these notes, I did consult other commentators, especially Calvin, and at times gleaned from them ideas which I included in my notes. I have attempted to give credit wherever a particular view or interpretation is heavily dependent upon a single author or commentator.

Through the commentary are dispersed several Excursuses or studies on various topics. Some may have wished that I might have gathered those and placed them at the end of the commentary. But my reason for placing them within the text is because they give the necessary data to support the position I took on these subjects within the exegesis of the text itself. I thought it important to ask the reader to consider a fuller treatment of the given subject in order to understand the perspective presented in the notes.

I have dealt with the question of "Paul and the Torah (Law)" in my book, *The Letter Writer* (First Fruits of Zion, 2002). There I have attempted to show that Paul remained a Torah pursuant Pharisee as he served Yeshua as His Apostle. That is to say, Paul did not consider a zealous adherance to the written Torah as in any way incongruous to a sincere and forthright faith in Yeshua. We must consider, however, that in Paul's day, the Oral Torah of the Sages had gained such prestige as to be, in some cases, not only equal in authority to the written, divine Torah, but also eclipsing it in terms of everyday *halachah* (from Hebrew הלך, *halach*, "to walk," thus describing the manner in which one lives out one's beliefs). Yeshua Himself bemoaned this phenomenon (Mk 7:8-9). Since, however, I have written on this subject elsewhere, I have not gone to great lengths to duplicate this work in the commentary. As such, I have taken the point of view that Paul both loved and maintained adherance to the Torah, and expected his disciples to do the same. Some readers may feel that I have not sufficiently supported this viewpoint in the notes themselves. I would refer such readers to my book for a fuller discussion of the matter.

I have divided the notes into two volumes: Volume 1: chapters 1-8; Volume 2: chapters 9-16 (forthcoming). I hope to include Adobe Acrobat files of the entire commentary with the publication of Volume 2. This will allow electronic searching of the text.

In a commentary of this size, one might expect a thorough and detailed critical introduction to Paul's Epistle to the Romans. The few pages alloted to introduction, therefore, will disappoint some. However, I thought it unncessary to reproduce yet another critical introduction to the epistle, when so many exist in our day. I would refer the reader to Cranfield's introduction, as well as the introduction in the recent commentary by Schreiner (see the following bibliography). Likewise, the introduction in Dunn's fine commentary is excellent and well worth consulting. Of course, one might profitably consult the comments in a number of New Testament Introductions available (again, consult the following bibliography).

One might ask why yet another commentary on Romans would even be considered! I doubt that, in recent times, any other book of the Bible has had more written about it than Paul's Epistle to the Romans. A comprehensive bibliography would fill hundreds of pages. My reason, however, for offering these notes is simply that, by-and-large, the commentaries on Romans that fill my shelves almost universally take a negative view of the Torah, and cast Paul's perspective in this light. Few have approached the epistle from the viewpoint that Paul considered the Torah not only viable but necessary for the believer's growth in holiness. Therefore, it seemed warranted to me that an attempt to understand Romans from a Torah perspective was needed, and I have offered these notes with that in mind. However, having said this, I also hope that the Torah perspective through which I have interpreted Paul's letter will only highlight and emphasize the glory of Yeshua as Messiah and Redeemer. It is my firm belief that a correct understanding and living out of the Torah enhances and in every way extols the absolute glory and wonder of the incarnation and the salvific work accomplished for the elect by our Messiah.

The following bibliography is a brief listing of works that I have found helpful in the study of Romans. For full bibliographies, consult Cranfield, Dunn, and Schreiner.

Bibliography

Commentaries & Works on Romans

Barth, Karl. *The Epistle to the Romans.* Oxford, 1933.

Brown, John. *Analytical Exposition of the Epistle of Paul to the Romans.* (Reprint of the 1857 Edition) Baker, 1981.

Bruce, F. F. *The Epistle of Paul to the Romans.* Eerdmans, 1973.

Calvin, John. *Commentaries,* 22 vols. (Baker Book House, 1984 reprint), *Romans* vol. 19.

Cranfield, C. E. B. *A Critical and Exegetical Commentary on The Epistle to the Romans.* 2 vols. T & T Clark, 1975.

Dunn, James D. G. *Word Bible Commentary: Romans* (Vols. 38a & 38b). Word, 1988.

Godet, F. *Commentary on the Epistle to the Romans.* (Reprint of the 1883 Editon) Zondervan, 1956.

Haldane, Robert. *An Exposition of the Epistle to the Romans.* (Reprint of the 1839 Edition) MacDonald Pub., 1958.

Hodge, Charles. *Commentary on the Epistle to the Romans.* Eerdmans, 1974.

Lloyd-Jones, D. Martin. *Romans 1-8.* 7 vols. Zondervan, 1974-1976.

Moule, H. C. G. *Romans* in *The Cambridge Bible for Schools and Colleges.* Cambridge Univ. Press, 1889.

Murray, John. *The New International Commentary on the New Testament – Romans.* Eerdmans, 1973.

Nanos, Mark. *The Mystery of Romans.* Fortress, 1996.

Plumer, William. *A Commentary on Romans.* (Reprint of the 1870 Edition) Kregel, 1971.

Schlatter, Adolf. *Romans: The Righteousness of God.* Hendrickson, 1995.

Schreiner, Thomas R. *Romans* in *The Baker Exegetical Commentary on the New Testament.* Baker, 1998.

Shedd, Willam T. *Critical and Doctrinal Commentary on the Epistle of Paul to the Romans.* (Reprint of the 1879 Edition) Klock and Klock, 1978.

Shulam, Joseph and Lecornu, Hillary. *Romans: A Commentary on the Jewish Roots of Romans.* Lederer, 1997.

Stuhlmacher, Peter. *Paul's Letter to the Romans.* Westminster, 1994.

Introductions

Brown, Raymond E. *An Introduction to the New Testament.* Doubleday, 1997.

Childs, Brevard S. *The New Testament as Canon: An Introduction.* Fortress, 1984.

Guthrie, Donald. *New Testament Introduction.* IVP, 1970.

Pauline Studies & Theology

Akenson, Donald Harman. *Saint Paul.* Oxford, 2000.

Beker, J. Christian. *Paul the Apostle: The Triumph of God in Life and Thought.* Fortress, 1980.

Boyarin, Daniel. *A Radical Jew: Paul and the Politics of Identity.* Univ. of Calif., 1994.

Carson, D. A., O'Brien, Peter T., Seifrid, Mark A., eds. *Justification and Variegated Nomism,* 2 vols. Baker, 2001, 2004.

Das, Andrew A. *Paul, the Law, and the Covenant.* Hendrickson, 2001.

Davies, W. D. *Paul and Rabbinic Judaism.* SPCK, 3rd Edition, 1970.

_____. *Jewish and Pauline Studies.* Fortress, 1984.

Donaldson, Terence L. *Paul and The Gentiles.* Fortress, 1997.

Dunn, James D. G. *The Theology of Paul the Apostle.* Eerdmans, 1998.

_____, ed., *Paul and the Mosaic Law.* Eerdmans, 2001.

Engberg-Pedersen, Troels, ed. *Paul Beyong the Judaism/Hellensim Divide.* WJK, 2001.

Gager, John G. *Reinventing Paul.* Oxford, 2000.

Gathercole, Simon J. *Where is Boasting?* Eerdmans, 2002.

Georgi, Dieter. *The Opponents of Paul in Second Corinthians.* Fortress, 1986.

Hawthorne, Gerald F. and Martin, Ralph P., eds. *Dictionary of Paul and His Letters.* IVP, 1993.

Hengel, Martin and Schwemer, Anna Maria. *Paul Between Damascus and Antioch.* WJK, 1997.

Hooker, M. D. and Wilson, S. G. *Paul and Paulinism.* SPCK, 1982.

Kim, Seyoon. *Paul and the New Perspective: Second Thoughts on the Origin of Paul's Gospel.* Eerdmans, 2002.

Lapide, Pinchas and Stuhlmacher, Peter. *Paul: Rabbi and Apostle.* Augsburg, 1984.

Longenecker, Richard N. *Paul, Apostle of Liberty.* Baker, 1976.

Lüdemann, Gerd. *Paul, Apostle to the Gentiles.* Fortress, 1984.

_____. *Paul: The Founder of Christianity.* Prometheus Books, 2002.

Machen, J. Gresham. *The Origin of Paul's Religion.* Eerdmans, 1925.

McRay, John. *Paul: His Life and Teaching.* Baker, 2003.

Murphy-O'Connor, Jerome. *Paul: A Critical Life.* Oxford, 1966.

Penna, Romano. *Paul the Apostle.* 2 vols. Thomas P. Wahl, transl. Liturgical Press, 1996.

Räisänen, Heikki. *Paul and the Law.* Fortress, 1983.

Reicke, Bo. *Re-examining Paul's Letters.* Trinity Press International, 2001.

Reisner, Rainer. *Paul's Early Period.* Eerdmans, 1998.

Ridderbos, Herman. *Paul: An Outline of His Theology.* Eerdmans, 1975.

Roetzel, Calvin. *Paul: The Man and the Myth.* Fortress, 1999,

Sanders, E. P. *Paul and Palestinian Judaism.* Fortress, 1977.

_____. *Paul, the Law, and the Jewish People.* Fortress, 1983.

Schreiner, Thomas R. *Paul: Apostle of God's Glory in Christ.* IVP, 2001.

Segal, Alan F. *Paul the Convert.* Yale Univ. Press, 1990.

Stendahl, Krister. *Paul Among Jews and Gentiles.* Fortress, 1976.

Stuhlmacher, Peter. *Revisiting Paul's Doctrine of Justification.* IVP, 2001.

Tomson, Peter J. *Paul and the Jewish Law: Halakha in the Letters of the Apostle to the Gentiles.* Van Gorcum/Fortress, 1990.

Trobisch, David. *Paul's Letter Collection.* Fortress, 1994.

Wenham, David. *Paul: Follower of Jesus or Founder of Christianity?* Eerdmans, 1995.

Witherington, Ben III. *The Paul Quest: The Renewed Search for the Jew of Tarsus.* IVP, 1998.

Young, Brad H. *Paul the Jewish Theologian.* Hendrickson, 1997.

Textual Issues

Gamble, Harry Jr. *The Textual History of the Letter to the Romans.* Eerdmans, 1997.

Swanson, Reuben, ed. *New Testament Greek Manuscripts – Romans.* Tyndale House/William Carey International Univ., 2001.

Abbreviations

Apostolic Writings	The New Testament
Avot	The tractate *Pirkei Avot* (Sayings of the Fathers) contained in the Mishnah
Bavli	Babylonian Talmud
BADG	W. Bauer, *A Greek-Lexicon of the New Testament and Other EarlyChristian Literature*, eds. W. F. Arndt and F. W. Gingrich, 2nd ed. revised by F. W. Danker (Chicago: University of Chicago, 1979, 2000)
BDB	F. Brown, S. R. Driver, and C. A. Briggs, *Hebrew and English Lexicon of the Old Testament* (Oxford: Clarendon, 1907)
HaShem	Circumlocution for the Tetragrammaton, "the Name"
Jastrow	M. Jastrow, *Dictionary of the Targumim, the Talmud Bavli and Yerushalmi, and the Midrashic Literature*
JPS	Jewish Publication Society Bible (1976)
KB	Ludwig Koehler and Walter Baumgartner. *The Hebrew and Aramaic Lexicon of the Old Testament*(1999, 2000)
KJV	King James Version Bible
Lxx	Septuagint, the Greek translation of the Tanach
MT	Masoretic Text as per *Biblia Hebraica Stuttgartensia*, UBS
NASB	New American Standard Bible Update
NIV	New International Bible
Sifra	Rabbinic commentary on Leviticus
Sifre	Rabbinic commentary on Numbers and Deuteronomy
Tanach	The Old Testament
Targum / Targumim	The Aramaic translations of the Tanach
TDNT	G. Kittel and G. Friedrich, eds., *Theological Dictionary of the New Testament* (10 vols.; Grand Rapids: Eerdmans: 1964-76)
TDOT	G. J. Botterweck and H. Ringgren, eds. *Theological Dictionary of the Old Testament* (14 vols. to date; Grand Rapids: Eerdmans, 1974-)
UBS	Aland, et al, *The Greek New Testament*, United Bible Society, 3rd Ed.
Yerushalmi	Jerusalem Talmud

Abbreviations for rabbinic literature:

Midrash Rabbah, e.g., Mid. Rab. *Genesis* xiv.5
Bavli, e.g., b.*Sanhedrin* 98a.
Yerushalmi, e.g., y.*Sanhedrin* 1:2, 18d
Mishnah, e.g., m.*Sanhedrin* 10:1
Tosefta, e.g., t.*Sanhedrin* 1.4
Citations of materials from Qumran follow normal conventions: e.g., 4Q285 = Cave 4, Qumran, document number 285.
Citations of Greek manuscripts follow the UBS Greek text, 3rd edition and Swanson (see above, "Textual Issues").

Introduction

It is not my purpose to give an exhaustive introduction to Paul's Epistle to the Romans. These may be found in a number of standard commentaries and reference works. I would suggest C. E. B. Cranfield, *A Critical and Exegetical Commentary on The Epistle to the Romans*, 2 vols. (T & T Clark, 1975), 1:1-30; Donald Guthrie, *New Testament Introduction* (InterVarsiity Press, 1970), pp. 393ff; Gerald F. Howthorne and Ralph P. Martin, eds. *Dictionary of Paul and His Letters* (InterVarsity Press, 1993), pp. 838ff.

However, it will be important for us to have at least some idea of the general background of Paul's Epistle to the Romans.

Authorship: Until modern times, no one doubted that the author of the Epistle to the Romans was Paul. Internally, this is clearly stated: 1:1; 11:13; 15:15-20. Additionally, the themes of the epistle are clearly "Pauline," meaning they match the general themes of other epistles deemed to be written by Paul. As far as external evidence for the Pauline authorship of Romans, the early Church Fathers all ascribe Romans to Paul (Marcion, Irenaeus), and the early fathers quote from Romans in complete sections and quotes, ascribing the work to Paul. In general, both ancient and modern scholarship has affirmed that Paul was the author of Romans.

Date: The historical events that surround the writing of the epistle help narrow its date of composition. Apparently Paul was in the midst of bringing collected funds to the believers in Jerusalem (cf. Rom 15:25-26, cp. 1 Co 16:1-9. 2). He must have stopped at Corinth, as the names Erastus and Gaius, both residents of Corinth, would indicate (cf. Rom 16:23). Additionally, Phoebe was from the neighboring city of Cenchrea. Most scholars have placed the writing of Romans during Paul's 3rd journey to establish and strengthen the congregations of The Way. His first journey began in 47/48 CE; his second journey occurred 49-51 CE, and his final journey was in the years 52-56 CE. Generally it is held that the epistle was written around 55 or 56 CE while Paul stopped in Corinth to visit the believers there.

Recipients: "to all who are beloved of God in Rome" (1:7). But who were these addressed as "beloved?" Did Paul write to a group of believers who viewed themselves as a synagogue within the larger community of 1st Century Judaisms, or did he write to a congregation who considered themselves a breakaway from the synagogue?

We may first question how we should understand the word "church" (ἐκκλησία, *ekklesia*) in the epistle of the Romans (cf. 16:1, 4, 16, 23). The word *ekklesia* did not take on a technical meaning until much later. In the pre-destruction era, *ekklesia* simply was a convenient word to describe any group that formed around common identity and purpose. Thus, in Acts 19:32, the angry mob that gathered at the theater to lynch Paul is called an *ekklesia* by Luke, showing that the word carried no special meaning at this early stage. When the followers of Yeshua, known as the people of "The Way," are called an *ekklesia,* this simply marks them as a group identified by common beliefs and religious practices. Likewise, the word "synagogue" (*sunegoge*) was another Greek term defining an assembly or gathering of people. In the 1st Century, a synagogue was used to define a group of people more than a building. The place where a synagogue met was called a προσευχή, *proseuxe,* "house of prayer." There is every reason to think, then, that Paul was writing to a synagogue community in Rome that saw themselves as within the larger community of Judaism. "The Way" was considered, both by those "inside" and those without, as a sect of Judaism. There is no reason to think that the congregation in Rome to whom Paul wrote was anything but a synagogue community.

According to Nanos (*The Mystery of Romans,* p. 49, n. 32), there have been 11 synagogue structures (some houses used for synagogal purposes) uncovered in Rome dating to the time period of Paul's epistle. That these structures can house 20 minimum, 40 maximum people, it seems obvious that there must have been more than 11 to accommodate the 20,000-50,000 Jews estimated to live in Rome at that time.

The community which Paul addressed in this epistle was made up of both Jew and Gentile, cp. 1:13; 2:14, 17ff ; cp. 11:13. It is therefore a foundational question as to who is the implied audience of his "bold reminder" (15:15). Whom did Paul intend to inform and influence by this "reminder": believing Jews, believing Gentiles, both equally, or perhaps to varying degrees? One's assumptions in this matter are telling; they necessarily and profoundly affect how one reads the text. (cf. the remarks of Nanos, *Mystery,* p. 77).

We may summarize the thoughts of Nanos, *Mystery,* pp. 75ff , as follows:
- if the list in chapter 16 is taken as representative, 5 of the 26 names are surely Jewish, thus making 80% Gentile names. Perhaps this represents the makeup of the congregation in general, 80% Gentile, 20% Jewish.
- 1:1-7, 13; 11:13-14; 15:15-16 all make clear that Paul was writing specifically to believing Gentiles in Rome even though there were also believing Jews in the congregation.

   a) 10:1-3; 10:18-11:11, "your" vs. "them;" "wild olive branch" vs. "natural branch."

   b) 14:1-15:3, 4ff, the "strong" are addressed directly to forego their perceived freedoms from Judaic customs in matters of food, in view of the priorities of the kingdom of God and instead to accommodate the "opinions" of those "stumbling" for whom Messiah died in the pursuit of peace: "For he who in this way serves Messiah is acceptable to God and approved by men" (14:18). Paul wraps up this instruction to Christian Gentiles with a vision of them worshipping the One God in one voice in the midst of the circumcised, thus fulfilling Israel's eschatological aspirations of all the nations one day recognizing Israel's God as the God of all humankind: "Rejoice, O Gentiles, with his people" (15:10; cf. vv. 4-12). [Nanos, p. 81-2]

- Thus, if Paul's intended audience are the believing Gentiles, who comprised the majority of the congregation, the exhortations to the "strong" and how they are to deal with the "weak" must have this group in mind (cf. 14:1f; 15:1f).
- This leads to the general purpose of the epistle.

Purpose: 1) to address the believing Gentiles of the congregation in Rome, and to remind them of their need to follow the Apostolic edict (Acts 15 cf. Rom 15:15) and to maintain the Jewish *halachah* to which they were originally committed (the "obedience of the faith," cf. 1:5) and thus constitute them as "obedient in word and deed," (15:18) i.e., walking according to established *halachah.*

2) to establish in certain terms the means by which God declares a sinner righteous, so that the exhortation to *halachic* matters would not be confused as involving some kind of "righteousness by the works of the Torah," the teaching that people-group status (specifically "Jewish status) was the grounds for covenant membership (cf. 10:3).

3) to help the Gentile believers in their role of making the unbelieving Jewish community jealous through their (i.e., the Gentiles) obvious life of righteousness (cf. 11:13-14).

Romans 1
Commentary

1 Paul, a bond-servant of Messiah Yeshua, called as an apostle, set apart for the gospel of God,

Paul's Hebrew name was Shaul (שָׁאוּל), probably after the first king of Israel who was likewise from the tribe of Benjamin.[1] Since Paul was born a Roman citizen, however, he also would have been given a Roman name as a child, and this was no doubt Paul (παῦλος). At the beginning of his mission to the Gentiles, he apparently decided to use the Roman name rather than his Hebrew name, since from that time on he is only referred to by Paul.[2] Apparently in Paul's mind, his mission to the Gentiles warranted that he use his Roman name. It may also be that the Hebrew Name "Shaul" sounded bad in the ears of Hellenistic Greeks. A Greek word σαῦλος, *saulos*, which sounds very much like "Shaul," means "conceited" especially referring to a "haughty gait," and was used to describe the "loose and wanton gait of prostitutes" (See T. J. Leary, "Paul's Improper Name," *NTS* 38[1992], 467-69). Whatever the case, it is clear that Paul considered his Roman name something that well fit his mission.

I've often been perplexed that many Messianic groups refer to the Apostle as "Rabbi Shaul." I think this misses the mark on two points: (1) it makes it appear that from a Messianic perspective, a Hebrew name is better than a Greek name, and (2) it assumes that Paul sought and received rabbinic ordination (סְמִיכָה, *s'michah*) and that he functioned in this capacity. In reality, nothing whatsover in the biblical record indicates that this was so. On the contrary, that fact that some would attempt to diminish Paul's authority by indicating he had no *bona fide* "papers" (2Cor 3) might tell us that he never did receive his rabbinic ordination. Perhaps his turning to Yeshua preceded his scheduled *s'michah*.

It seems to me that if Paul regularly introduced himself by using his Roman name, we should use it of him as well. The "Hebrew of Hebrews" served God with a Roman name. Perhaps this, as much as anything, tells us about his viewpoint of equality between Jew and Gentile in the body of Messiah.

Bond-servant (δοῦλος, *doulos*) – The term in Greek and Roman culture is fraught with a feeling of abhorrence. No one would have characterized himself as a *doulos* of the king, for such a designation would have been revolting to the king himself. Nor is such language found in the Greek literature to describe a worshipper's relationship to the gods.

The key to Paul's use is mostly to be found in the Tanach (Old Testament), for the Greek translation of the Tanach, (Lxx) uses the δοῦλος (*doulos*) word-group often to translate עֶבֶד, *'eved*, the word meaning "servant." Such expressions as "servant of God" denoted a relationship, and the word-group itself is most often employed in the sense of worship and service to God. Thus, for Paul to use this term in the opening of his epistle connects him with all who, in righteousness and faith, saw themselves as God's servants. And it especially connects him to Israel and ultimately to Yeshua Who is Himself the Servant of the Lord.

Apostle – The Greek word literally means "one who is sent" and translates the Hebrew שְׁלוּחִים / שָׁלִיחַ or the Aramaic שְׁלִיחָא. The Jewish community was not unaccustomed to the idea of an emissary sent out from the synagogue to accomplish a specific task on their behalf. In the rebuke which Yeshua gave to the Pharisees He says:

> Woe to you, scribes and Pharisees, hypocrites, because you travel about on sea and land to make one proselyte; and when he becomes one, you make him twice as much a son of hell as yourselves. Matt 23:15

It is well known that the Sanhedrin was in the habit of sending "apostles" to the outer regions of the diaspora in order to teach the dispersed Jewish people, and to carry *halachic* decisions to those unable to regularly hear the decisions of the Sanhedrin.[3] Those who were sent with such a commission thus came to the people bearing the authority of their sending, and were received accordingly. For Paul, then, his apostleship, stemming as it did from Messiah, suggested the <u>necessity</u> of his reception by those to whom he went.

What is more, since Paul came with the authority of Yeshua as his Master, it is clear from the very nature of his office that he was not at liberty to change or in any way overturn the teaching of the One Who had sent him. As the Apostle of Yeshua, Paul was <u>under obligation</u> to give the clear and unambiguous message of the One Who had commissioned him.

Set apart for the Gospel of God – "Set apart" (ἀφωρισμένος, ἀφορίζω, *aphorismenos, aphorizo*) reminds one of the generally accepted derivation for "Pharisee" (פְּרָשִׁים, *p'rashim,* "to separate from") and in fact on at least one occasion (Ezek 45:4) translates (in the Lxx) the Hebrew קָדַשׁ, "to be separated, holy." Is it possible that Paul, in his mission for Yeshua, now considered himself to be a true "Pharisee" (=separated one) in a way he never was before?

An understanding of the word "gospel" (εὐαγγέλιον, *euangelion*) is impossible apart from recognizing its background in the Hebrew word בְּשַׂר, *basar,* found often in the pi'el form in the Tanach with a meaning "to announce good news" (e.g., 1Ki 1:42; Jer 20:15), especially of victory (e.g., 1Sa 31:9). The in-breaking of God's reign is announced as the "gospel" in such texts as Ps 40:9 [MT: 10; Lxx 39:10]; 96[Lxx: 95]:2; Is 40:9; 41:27; 52:7; 60:6; 61:1.

Note that Paul identifies the gospel as the "gospel of God." This could mean that God is the subject of the gospel, or that God is the source of the gospel. While both are true, it would seem that God being the source of the gospel is Paul's emphasis here, wanting his readers to know that his message was not new or innovative, but that it was the "good news" which God had proclaimed throughout His revelation through the prophets who came before.

2 which He promised beforehand through His prophets in the holy Scriptures,

Promised – Paul teaches that the gospel is the result of God's promise, that is to say, it depends entirely upon God's faithfulness. "Promise" (ἐπαγγελία, *epangelia*) is a key term in Pauline writings and often identifies the unilateral nature of the covenant made with Abraham. God's covenant was a "promise" (for which the Hebrew has no distinct term) since it was dependent entirely upon God and not upon man. Man may sin and reject God, but God will fulfill every aspect of His covenant.

On the word-group "promise" in Pauline literature, note the following:

> Acts 13:32–33 And we preach to you the good news of the promise made to the fathers, that God has fulfilled this *promise* to our children in that He raised up Yeshua, as it is also written in the second Psalm, 'You art My Son; today I have begotten You.'

Acts 26:6–7 And now I am standing trial for the hope of the promise made by God ✓ to our fathers; {the promise} to which our twelve tribes hope to attain, as they ear- · nestly serve {God} night and day. And for this hope, O King, I am being accused by Jews.

Rom 4:13–21 For the promise to Abraham or to his descendants that he would be · heir of the world was not through the Torah, but through the righteousness of faith. ✓ For if those who are of the Torah are heirs, faith is made void and the promise is nullified; for the Torah brings about wrath, but where there is no Torah neither is · there violation. For this reason {it is} by faith, that {it might be} in accordance with ✓ grace, in order that the promise may be certain to all the descendants, not only to · those who are of the Torah, but also to those who are of the faith of Abraham, who · is the father of us all, (as it is written, "A father of many nations have I made you") in the sight of Him whom he believed, {even} God, who gives life to the dead and calls into being that which does not exist. In hope against hope he believed, in · order that he might become a father of many nations, according to that which had been spoken, "So shall your descendants be." And without becoming weak in faith he contemplated his own body, now as good as dead since he was about a hundred years old, and the deadness of Sarah's womb; yet, with respect to the promise of God, he did not waver in unbelief, but grew strong in faith, giving glory to God, and being fully assured that what He had promised, He was able also to perform.

Rom 9:8–9 That is, it is not the children of the flesh who are children of God, but ✓ the children of the promise are regarded as descendants. For this is a word of promise: "At this time I will come, and Sarah shall have a son."

Gal 3:16–22 Now the promises were spoken to Abraham and to his seed. He does · not say, "And to seeds," as {referring} to many, but {rather} to one, "And to your seed," that is, Messiah. What I am saying is this: the Torah, which came four hun- dred and thirty years later, does not invalidate a covenant previously ratified by God, so as to nullify the promise. For if the inheritance is based on Torah, it is no longer based on a promise; but God has granted it to Abraham by means of · a promise. Why the Torah then? It was added because of transgressions, having been ordained through angels by the agency of a mediator, until the seed should come to whom the promise had been made. Now a mediator is not for one {party only}; whereas God is {only} one. Is the Torah then contrary to the promises of God? May it never be! For if a Torah had been given which was able to impart life, then righteousness would indeed have been based on Torah. But the Scripture has shut up all men under sin, that the promise by faith in Yeshua Messiah might be given to those who believe.

Gal 3:29 And if you belong to Messiah, then you are Abraham's offspring, · heirs according to promise.

Eph 2:11–12 Therefore remember, that formerly you, the Gentiles in the flesh, who are called "Uncircumcision" by the so-called "Circumcision," {which is} performed in the flesh by human hands-- {remember} that you were at that time separate from Messiah, excluded from the commonwealth of Israel, and strangers to the covenants of the promise, having no hope and without God in the world.

From the outset of this great epistle, Paul emphasizes that the gospel he is preaching is nothing new or even different from the message of the Prophets. It is more fully revealed now in the coming of Yeshua, but it is not different. The good news which was the possession of Israel for so many years was now to be given, without restraint, to the nations.

We may also note that Paul refers to the "holy Scriptures" (γραφαῖς ἁγίαις, *graphais hagiais*). By the time of Paul, the canon of the Tanach had most likely been solidified into the groupings of the Torah, the Prophets (*Neviim*) and the Writings or Hagiographa (*ketuvim* in Hebrew). Thus, Yeshua refers to Moses, the Prophets, and Psalms (Lk 24:44) as the gathered Scriptures that spoke of Him. For Paul, the foundation of his work and teaching were the inspired Scriptures of the Tanach (2Tim 3:16-17). Obviously, what we now have as the Apostolic Scritpures (New Testament) had not yet been formed in Paul's day.

3 concerning His Son, who was born of a descendant of David according to the flesh

concerning His Son – "Son" terminology was common in the 1st Century, "son of God" and "son of Man" being connected to the prophecies in Daniel (3:25; 7:13). Both were messianic. In recent years, the "son of God" terminology employed by Paul in this text has come under heavy fire. Liberal scholars have claimed that the idea of the "divine man" came into Hellenistic Judaism under the influence of Greco-Roman paganism. However, the "Son of God" text found at Qumran (4Q246) has brought such an interpretation into question. This Dead Sea Scroll text has clear parallels to the Lukian infancy narrative, showing that "son of God" terminology was extant in Judaism before the Christian era, and that it was used to denote messianic figures. We should not shrink back from the obvious fact, here, that Paul uses the phrase "His Son" to denote both the divine nature of the Messiah as well as His Messiahship. For surely a son partakes of the nature of his father.

born of a descendant of David according to the flesh – Not all of the Sages of the 1st Century required that one attribute of Messiah be his lineage to the tribe of Judah. Akiva proclaimed Simeon bar-Kochba to be messiah, a man who never, as far as we know, claimed Davidic ancestry. Nonetheless, the vast majority did believe that Messiah would come from the tribe of Judah, based upon such passages as 2Sa 7:16; Ps 89:3f, 19ff; Is 11:1, 10; Jer 23:5f; 30:9; 33:14-18.

The gospels trace Yeshua's Davidic descent through Joseph (Mt 1:16, 20; Lk 1:27; 2:4; 3:23), though making clear that Joseph was not the natural father (Mt 1:18-25; Lk 1:34ff). Mary may have been of the tribe of Levi, related to Aaron, for Elizabeth, wife of Zacharias, Mary's relative (Lk 1:36) is specifically related to Aaron (Lk 1:5). Legally, from a Jewish perspective in the 1st Century, Yeshua would have registered as the tribe of Judah, since legally His father was so registered. Thus, this legal aspect is taken up by the Gospel writers as well as Paul as a significant fulfillment of the Davidic prophecies (Gen 49:10; 2 Sa 7:11ff; Is 9:7; 16:5; Jer 23:5; 30:9; 33:15, 17, 21; Ezek 34:23; 37:24; Hos 3:5).

The Talmud speaks of Messiah ben Ephraim (or Yoseph) [b.*Sukkah* 52a; cf. Beit HaMidrash 5:187-88; b.*Sanhedrin* 98b; Mid. Rab. *Gen.* 95; Mid. Rab. *Canticles* ii.33] and Messiah ben David [b.*Sukkot* 52b; b.*Sota* 48b]. Messiah ben Yoseph was to be slain, while Messiah ben David would win victory over Israel's enemies and bring in everlasting peace.

It has become more and more clear, as an increasing number of texts have come to light in our times (particularly those from Qumran), that there were at least some within the Judaisms of the Second Temple period who anticipated a suffering Messiah (see Israel Knohl, *The Messiah before Jesus: the Suffering Servant of the Dead Sea Scrolls* [Univ of Calif Press, 2000]; Hegg, *The Letter Writer* [FFOZ, 2002], pp 160ff). Clearly, the prophetic idea that the Messiah would suffer for the transgressions of His people cannot be denied, and Paul stands squarely within this interpretation of the prophets and Judaic tradition.

This opening remark by Paul shows from the outset that his purpose is to extol Yeshua as

Messiah, and to do so within the Jewish framework of Yeshua and His family. Why else would he find it so important to mention His Davidic lineage? We may therefore see that from the beginning Paul is intent upon presenting Yeshua as both Jewish and the long-awaited Jewish Messiah.

4 who was declared the Son of God with power by the resurrection from the dead, according to the Spirit of holiness, Yeshua Messiah our Lord,

who was declared the Son of God with power – The designation "Son of God" was a well-used term in the 1st Century CE, and gained its popularity through the apocalyptic literature which was so prevalent at that time. In Daniel 3:25, the text בַר אֱלָהִין is translated "son of the gods" in the NASB and NIV, while the NRSV has ". . . like the appearance of a god." Grammatically, however, the phrase could equally have been translated "son of God," since the plural (Aramaic) אֱלָהִין, like the Hebrew אֱלֹהִים, can refer either to the true God of Israel, or to the false "gods" of the nations.

In the Latin and Syriac version of 4 Ezra, God refers to the Messiah as "My Son" (7:28-29; 13:32, 37, 52; 14:9 [in some of these texts the Coptic, Ethiopic, and Arabic versions have similar expressions]). Rabbinic texts as well used the phrase to refer to the Messiah (b. *Suk* 52a, commenting on Ps 2:7).

In the Gospels the title Son of God was considered to denote deity (Mt 26:63ff; Lk 22:70ff; Jn 10:36ff; Jn 19:7) and therefore not to be taken upon oneself as a mortal.

We may question where the phrase "with power" should attach itself. Should we understand that Yeshua was declared to be the Son of God, and that in such a declaration He was recognized to be powerful (thus seeing the phrase as modifying "Son of God"), or should we understand the phrase to modify the verb "declared," i.e., the declaration of Yeshua as Son of God, though made by various people at various times, was nonetheless made with special force or power via the resurrection?

There is no grammatical issue which would help us decide, other than the fact that it is most common, particularly in Semitic languages (and Paul's native tongue was Semitic) to put an adjectival or adverbial phrase immediately following the word or words it modifies. This being the case, we might opt for taking the phrase as modifying "Son of God," i.e., that Yeshua was not only declared or shown to be the Son of God, but He was shown to be the Son of God who is powerful, through the resurrection. The enemies of Yeshua knew that His resurrection would certainly substantiate all of His claims, and it was for this reason that they were willing to do anything to see to it that the resurrection never took place. The lie which was afterward manufactured, that His body had been stolen by the disciples, may have made the Temple guard appear as foolish, but at least gave some kind of retort for those who refused to believe the undeniable fact—Yeshua had died and arisen on the third day, just as He had said.

by the resurrection from the dead, according to the Spirit of holiness, Yeshua Messiah our Lord – The NASB capitalizes the word "Spirit," thus referring to the person of the Holy Spirit, but translates according to the order of words in the Greek text. The NIV takes further liberties:

> and who through the Spirit of holiness was declared with power to be the Son of God by his resurrection from the dead: Jesus Christ our Lord,

taking the phrase "through the Spirit of holiness" to refer to the verb "declared" rather than to the preceding clause, "resurrection from the dead.

We may summarize the questions about this text as follows:

1) does the phrase "Spirit of holiness" refer to the Holy Spirit, or should "spirit"

be understood as referring to the human spirit?

2) should the phrase "spirit of holiness" describe the means by which the declaration was made, or should it describe the means by which Yeshua was resurrected?

The normal Hebrew רוּחַ הַקֹּדֶשׁ, *ruach hakodesh*, could easily be translated by the Greek πνεῦμα ἁγιωσύνης (*pneuma hagiosunes*) as a strengthened form of πνεῦμα ἅγιόν (*penuma hagion*), and could, as nearly all the more ancient commentators suggest, refer to the Holy Spirit. What is more, it was the teaching of the Apostles that the Holy Spirit played a pivotal role in the resurrection of Yeshua, cf. 1 Pt 3:18, and Paul specifically teaches this in Romans (cf. 8:11). It is the role of the Spirit to quicken or give life to the dead, both in the physical world as well as in the non-physical.

Further, to have the phrase modify the verb "declared" (as the NIV does) seems a bit far-fetched. That Paul accredits the Holy Spirit with the power which raised Yeshua from the dead only sets the stage for his teaching on the quickening work which the Spirit does in the heart of every sinner who turns to Messiah in faith.

Yeshua Messiah our Lord – The given name was Yeshua, from the Hebrew verb יָשַׁע, *yasha'*, "to save, rescue" (cf. Mt 1:21). Here Paul puts the fact of Yeshua's incarnation first. The Talmud[4] uses the form "Yeshu" (יֵשׁוּ) rather than the current "Yeshua" (יֵשׁוּעַ). "Christ," Χριστός, the Greek equivalent to מָשִׁיחַ, means "anointed one," "Messiah." "Lord," κύριος, may be equivalent to אֲדֹנָי, Adonai, or even יהוה, for the Lxx uses the term for both. At any rate, Paul wants to give His full name at the opening of the epistle, as he intends for us to focus on both the eternal as well as the incarnational aspects of this One who is our Messiah. There is little doubt that by the time of Paul the titles applied to Yeshua (Messiah, Lord) had become standardized, though the order and combination of the titles was fluid (Yeshua the Messiah, Messiah Yeshua, Adonai Yeshua the Messiah, etc.). It is not always certain that the order of the names implies an emphasis, but it certainly may be so. Thus, to put the name Yeshua first may be to emphasize His incarnation and salvific mission, while placing Messiah first may stress His fulfillment of prophecy as the Messiah. "Lord" (Adonai) placed first may emphasize His sovereign position as Creator, etc.

5 through whom we have received grace and apostleship to bring about the obedience of faith among all the Gentiles for His name's sake,

through whom we have received grace and apostleship – "Through whom," i.e., through the risen Messiah, for it was through the direct revelation of Yeshua to Paul as he travelled toward Damascus (Acts 9) that he received his calling to represent Yeshua to the nations.

The plural "we" is most likely simply a "writer's plural," not uncommon in Greek[5] nor in Paul's writings (cf. Rom 3:8-9; 1 Co 9:11ff; 2 Co 1:12ff; 1 Thess 3:1f).

"Grace and apostleship" is most likely a hendiadys (Greek term meaning "one through two"), a literary expression in which a single idea is expressed by a pair of words. In this case the meaning would be "the office of apostle as a gracious gift undeserved by any human worth." The authority which Paul claims as an Apostle to the Gentiles is not an authority which he gained through his own efforts, nor something to which he was personally entitled. The ap-pointment to the office of apostle was entirely a matter of God's grace.

to bring about the obedience of faith among all the Gentiles – Here we have a succinct statement of purpose for Paul's apostleship. Cranfield[6] lists the following possible understandings of this phrase:

1) "obedience to the faith" (i.e., to faith in the sense of the body of accepted doctrine)
2) "obedience to faith" (i.e., to the authority of faith)

3) "obedience to God's faithfulness attested in the gospel"
4) "obedience which faith works"
5) "obedience which faith requires"
6) "a believing kind of obedience"   *see Numbers 20:12*
7) "the obedience which consists in faith"

Cranfield opts for #7 since it is obvious that Paul equates faith and obedience.

Nanos gives a slightly different interpretation of the phrase, though #5 of Cranfield's list is essentially what Nanos teaches. He interprets the phrase to regard the requirements of *halachah* upon the Gentiles who, because of their acceptance of Yeshua as Messiah, had joined themselves with the Jews who had likewise believed in Him. They, as equals in the body of Messiah, were expected to accept upon themselves the righteous *halachah* enjoined upon them by the Jerusalem Council (Acts 15).

This, according to Nanos, was of utmost importance because the demonstration of God as the one God of all the nations depended upon Gentiles worshipping in community with the Jewish community, not existing as a separate entity. In order to be a viable part of the community, it was necessary that they submit to received *halachah* as enjoined upon them by the Jerusalem Council. This submission to the established *halachah* is what Paul termed "obedience of the faith."

This view of the phrase in question takes seriously the emphasis which the 1st Century Jewish community placed upon the issues of purities. The question of what place the God-fearing Gentile could occupy in the Jewish community was a matter of current debate in the time of Paul. Even the status of the proselyte, though generally agreed upon by the Sages, was nonetheless contested by some. The proselyte was generally given an entirely equal status with the native born, proven by the rabbinic ruling that he was allowed to marry a Jewish woman, even the daughter of a priest.[7] A God-fearer, however, was a Gentile who worshipped the One God of Israel, but who never underwent the ritual of the proselyte, and thus remained a Gentile in the eyes of the Sages. The status of this group was debated. What about the righteous Gentile in the world to come? in the afterlife? within the community of the diaspora? (See Hegg, *FellowHeirs* [FFOZ, 2003], chapter 4).

The Apostolic *halachah* had been decided at the Jerusalem Council: the believing Gentiles would be admitted to the congregation as equals without undergoing the ritual of a proselyte, but they were admitted as righteous Gentiles, not as pagans. As such, they were expected to leave paganism and its manner of life and adhere to the *halachah* of the faithful community of Israel. This was not an "entrance requirement" (though some may have construed it as such). It was rather about community with God and His people. The laws of purity to which the Jewish community adhered revolved around the two main sources of impurity: unclean food and sexual impurity. Since the idolatrous practices of the pagan temples were heavily involved with such impurities, it was imperative that the Gentiles entirely cut themselves off from any involvement in the rituals of the pagan temples. It was to this issue that the Apostolic decrees of Acts 15 addressed themselves.

It should also be emphasized that at the time when the decree of Acts 15 was formulated, there was no indication that the Council foresaw that the Gentiles would soon comprise the majority in many of the congregations. It is one thing to require Gentiles to conform to *halachic* measures when in the minority, and quite another thing to do so when they comprise the majority. This latter situation is no doubt what Paul faced as he wrote this epistle.

I am inclined to agree with the assessment of Nanos on this phrase "obedience of faith." Some may argue that obedience of righteous *halachah* for the Gentiles seems less than grand as Paul's primary, apostolic calling. But to this I would stress the pervasive scope of *halachah* in the 1st Century. How one "walked," i.e., conducted one's life, was a direct statement of one's love for God. To neglect *halachah* was to equally deny one's allegiance and submission to the Creator. To confess Yeshua as one's Lord but to continue to live after the manner of the pagans was entirely incongruous in the mind and teaching of Paul.

Pagan lifestyle, however, was not only characterized by the gross sins of immorality and debauchery. From a Jewish perspective, the pagan lived without knowledge of nor care for the Torah. What he ate, what he touched, what he did—all of these placed him in a continual (even if theoretical) state of uncleanness, and therefore without ability to approach the God of Israel Who required purity of all who worshipped Him.

Consider Paul's use of the term "Gentile" in a number of places:

> 1 Cor. 10:20 *No, but I say* that the things which the Gentiles sacrifice, they sacrifice to demons, and not to God; and I do not want you to become sharers in demons.
> Eph. 2:11 Therefore remember, that formerly you, the Gentiles in the flesh, who are called "Uncircumcision" by the so-called "Circumcision," *which is* performed in the flesh by human hands—
> Eph. 4:17 This I say therefore, and affirm together with the Lord, that you walk no longer just as the Gentiles also walk, in the futility of their mind,
> 1 Thess. 4:5 not in lustful passion, like the Gentiles who do not know God;
> 1 Pet. 4:3 For the time already past is sufficient *for you* to have carried out the desire of the Gentiles, having pursued a course of sensuality, lusts, drunkenness, carousals, drinking parties and abominable idolatries.

In these places (and some others), Paul is clearly using the term "Gentile" to mean "pagan." His use of the additional phrase "according to the flesh" (Eph 2:11) shows that for Paul the Gentile who comes to faith in Yeshua is, in some measure, no longer a Gentile at heart, though he still may be according to the flesh. In heart, the obedience of faith has changed the manner of his living to conform to the righteousness required by those who worship the One God of Israel.

Thus, while *halachah*, rules of living, may seem at first blush to comprise only a fraction of Paul's calling and emphasis, it does, from a Jewish perspective, comprise the whole, for righteous *halachah* is the inevitable requirement for consistent worship of God. The impure remain at a distance; the pure are allowed in.

Now while such statements of purity relate primarily and ultimately to one's soul, the outward, physical aspects of *halachah* are the means by which the righteous soul is nourished and maintained. The cooperative nature of sanctification as Paul teaches it fits perfectly into the practice of *halachah*, for the redeemed sinner is in partnership with God Himself in the task of holy living. As such, obedience to the *halachah* becomes the means by which the believer, whether Jew or Gentile, contributes to the pursuit of holiness, all the while recognizing that the Spirit is the One who energizes the child of God to walk as he should.

Thus, Paul recognizes that his apostolic calling is fulfilled when Gentiles, who formerly walked according to the lusts of their flesh, rather now turn to God and accept upon themselves the freeing restraints of righteous living, of the *halachah* which conforms to the Torah of God. Such change in outward behavior bespeaks a true change of heart. Here, then, lies inevitable proof in the apostle's eyes of true conversion. By claiming that his goal in being an apostle was to secure the "obedience of the faith" among the Gentiles, he in essence announced that his goal was the honest and evident conversion of the nations.

6 among whom you also are the called of Yeshua Messiah;

"among whom" (ἐν οἶς, *en hois*), i.e., among the Gentiles referred to in the previous verse. Here it is clearly seen that Paul views the synagogue at Rome as comprised in the majority of Gentiles,[8] even though a sizeable percentage (perhaps 20%) of the congregation were Jewish.

The term "called" (κλητός, *kletos*) is used by Paul in a similar fashion in 8:28, 1 Co 1:24. Note its repetition in this opening section, being used in vv. 1, 6, 7. We may rightly ask what the background of this term is.

The Lxx regularly uses the word κλητός ("called") to translate קֹדֶשׁ, *kodesh,* "holy convocation," the required gathering of the community on Sabbath and the Appointed Times (מוֹעֲדִים) [Ex 12:16; Lev 23:2ff; Num 28:25]. In fact, in these places the terminology matches our text exactly, having κλητός ἅγιός, "holy convocation." Does Paul have this in mind when he employs the term here? The term also is used in the Lxx of "invited guests" (1 Sa 15:11; 1 Ki 1:41, 49; Zeph 1:7). Interestingly, the Qumran documents show that the term "called ones" was to be inscribed upon the trumpets that called the congregation to gather (1QM 3.2), and the "sons of Zadok" (i.e., the true priests) are referred to as "the elect of Israel, the men called by name . . ." (1QM4.3f).

The Pauline use of the term "called" seems to focus upon the effectual working of God in drawing those He has chosen to Himself. The "called" are therefore those who have responded to His summons. But His call is far more than merely an invitation, for His call is effectual. That is to say, even as God's call upon Paul to his office as apostle was effectual, so the call of God upon the elect secures their eventual heeding of the call, and responding. The fact that those who have confessed Yeshua as Messiah alone are designated "the called" emphasizes that Paul's use of the term relates to its effectual nature. Only those who respond are ever designated "the called."

"of Yeshua HaMashiach" may designate either the Name by which they are called or the agent doing the calling. The latter seems most likely, for they, being followers of Yeshua, were heeding His call to take up their crosses and follow Him. Here the Messianic believer is singled out by his or her allegiance to Yeshua as the promised Messiah, and to follow His teachings and *halachah.*

7 to all who are beloved of God in Rome, called as saints: Grace to you and peace from God our Father and the Lord Yeshua Messiah.

The literal order of the Greek is "to all who are in Rome beloved of God" but the NASB attempts to smooth out the sentence by rearranging the word order. NIV has the word order correct but adds an "and," "To all in Rome who are loved by God and called to be saints." Obviously, Paul did not address his letter to everyone who was living in Rome, so the two final clauses of the sentence help define and limit the group to whom he writes: (1) beloved of God, and (2) called saints.

"Beloved of God" (ἀγαπητοῖς Θεοῦ, *agapetois theou*) is a quality possessed by all who are chosen by Him to receive His grace. This same adjective is used of Israel who has still, as a nation, rejected Yeshua (11:28) but whose ultimate salvation is promised, showing that the primary basis for this designation is God's sovereign election. It is significant that at the outset of this epistle Paul wishes to focus, not so much on their love for God, but His love for them. The one must always precede the other, for "we love Him because He first loved us" (1Jn 4:19). It is also interesting that this Greek adjective ("beloved" ἀγαπητός, *agapetos*) is found three times in the Lxx of Gen 22, the Binding of Isaac (22:2, 12, 26). Here, the "beloved" of the father is symbolically sacrificed.

The term is also found in the Lxx in those Psalms of David in which he refers to himself as God's "beloved" (Ps 60:5; 108:6[7]; 127:2). Clearly for the Psalmist this term bespeaks a close, familial relationship, something David was able to balance against his understanding of God's awesomeness, and the holy fear such an understanding brings.

Thus, "called as saints" brings the picture into focus. The grace of God has come, a demonstration of His love, to set those of His choosing apart unto Himself. The word "saints" is nothing more than the word "holy" (ἅγιος, קָדוֹשׁ) which has the root sense of "to be marked off," "separate," "withdrawn from common use." The term is most often used of God in the Tanach, and refers primarily to the will of God in which He claims the absolute allegiance of His people. Thus "holiness" in the world of the Tanach is never void of direct relationship with God, the Holy One. Cranfield writes:

> The 'holiness' of God denotes the absolute authority with which He confronts men. But this authority was the authority of Him who had revealed Himself as merciful and righteous; and under the influence of the prophets the ethical element in 'the holy' was strongly emphasized. The term 'holy,' applied to Israel, expressed the fact that they were God's special people. Their holiness derived from God's gracious choice, and it involved the obligation on their part to seek to be and do what was in accordance with the revealed character of their God by obedience to His law. Paul's use of ἅγιος rests squarely upon this OT foundation. Those who have been called by the holy God are holy in virtue of His calling and are thereby claimed for holiness of life.[9]

8 First,[10] I thank my God through Yeshua Messiah for you all, because your faith is being proclaimed throughout the whole world.

Paul's opening line, after the introductory prologue, follows a set pattern in letter writing of his day, in which the sender's prayer (in Roman culture, to pagan gods) on behalf of the one to whom the epistle is sent, is a standard opening. Though he follows such protocol (note the use of "First"), yet he is not constrained by literary convention as much as he recognizes the need to communicate his deep love and affection for the Roman congregation, a love and affection which was demonstrated by his unceasing prayers on their behalf. We do well to follow Paul's pattern and demonstrate our love for one another through fervent, consistent prayer for each other.

His thanksgiving on their behalf is directed to God "through Yeshua Messiah." Here Paul teaches the mediatorial office of Yeshua, the One through whom the Father may be rightly approached. As our *cohen hagadol* (כֹּהֵן הַגָּדוֹל, high priest) we enter into the presence of God through Him (cf. Heb 8:1, cp. 9:24). Apart from our High Priest, there is no entrance into the "throne of grace" (cf. Heb 2:15, 16). Yet because of His work on our behalf, we may enter "in Him" with our thanksgiving and requests with a bold spirit, knowing we will indeed be received.

because your faith is being proclaimed throughout the whole world – What was apparently being spoken of throughout the then-known-world was that many in Rome had come to faith in Yeshua. This phrase does not imply that the faith of the Roman *kehilah* (קְהִלָּה, "congregation") was particularly deep or extraordinary. What was circulating about them was the simple reality of their dedication to follow Yeshua and to receive Him as Messiah. For there to be an established synagogue of believers in Yeshua in the Imperial Capital was, in itself, an oddity of that day. Here, as we can see if we look at the epistle as a whole, Jew and Gentile together worshiped the One God of Israel as the prophets foretold. Such a phenomenon was newsworthy in the Roman Empire of the 1st Century.

I would note, as well, that here we have a clear indication that "world" (κόσμος, *kosmos*) is a term used in a number of different ways by Paul, and here as a term denoting the inhabited lands generally considered by Paul to be the world in which he lived.

9 For God, whom I serve in my spirit in the preaching of the gospel of His Son, is my witness as to how unceasingly I make mention of you,

For God is my witness – The NASB changes the order of the sentence in its translation: "For God, whom I serve in my spirit in the preaching of the gospel of His Son . . . ." But the order in the Greek text is: "For God is my witness, whom I serve in my spirit in the gospel of His Son, how unceasingly I make mention of you." The point is that Paul uses an oath formula in the opening "For God is my witness."[11] Here is a point he wants his readers to accept, yet it is something that cannot be verified by external witnesses, for it is an inner reality. Such being the case, he invokes the Name of God as witness to his truthfulness through the taking of an oath.

Paul's willingness to take an oath seems to go contrary to the teaching of Yeshua (Mt 5:33-37) and James (5:12) in which they appear to deny (or ban) the use of oaths. It seems to me patently clear that Paul's freedom to engage in oaths nearly rules out any notion that Yeshua had forbidden their use. Yet how do we reconcile the two? The problem disappears when one understands the tangled web of Rabbinic laws which had overshadowed the issue of oaths in the 1st Century. So complicated were the rulings that, if accepted, a person could maintain or annul his covenant with hardly any personal consequences. In other words, the Rabbinic *halachah* had made oath-taking a mere façade for the hypocrite who wanted to look pious but was primarily selfish.

In a paper on Matthew 5:17-20,[12] I noted the following about Yeshua's prohibition of oaths in Matthew 5:33ff:

> One need only read the Mishnah tractate Nedarim to begin to understand the tangle of *halachah* which the Sages had created in attempting to keep the people from hasty vows. So involved were the laws that they could be twisted and used to one's sinful advantage.
> The misuse of korban is what prompted Yeshua's rebuke in Matthew 23, and is clearly attested in the primary sources. Thus, a system of oath-taking which had become useless as to righteousness had lost its value. Note carefully that Yeshua prohibits swearing by things, whether by heaven or earth, Jerusalem or the altar or one's head. The matter of whether a vow was valid and binding depended, in great measure, by what the vow had been attached to, and many other factors. In such a tangle of *halachah*, Yeshua instructed His followers to make their vows simple and honest: "yes, yes" or "no, no."
>
> But Yeshua is not alone in such a stance. In b.*Bava Metzia* 49a we read "Let your nay and yea be both zedek." R. Huna said, "The yea of the righteous is a yea; their no is a no."[13] According to Montefiore, "Yes, yes and no, no may be regarded as equivalent to oaths."[14] He bases this upon Rabbinic statements: R. Elazar said, "Yea is an oath, and nay is an oath": Raba said, "But only then if yea and nay are said twice."[15] According to *Mechilta*, the Israelites answered "Yea, yea and nay, nay to the commands at Sinai."[16]
>
> It seems very possible that what Yeshua demands in this case is a complete avoiding of oaths or vows which required a person to bend to the hopeless web of regulations governing vows in the 1st Century. It was not necessary to take a vow by some object, region, or person. But nothing in the written Torah required the Nazirite vow, for example, to include a mention of a "witness." Such a vow could be strictly between a man and God. The Rabbinic "fences" surrounding vows, however, is yet another example of how the traditions of the elders had set aside the Torah of God, i.e., made it practically impossible to "keep."
> Yeshua's intention was to fulfill the Torah by making it possible for God's people to implement it.

Thus, what Yeshua prohibited was the skillful use of oaths by which the person who took them looked pious, but had no intention of actually keeping the oath that he had sworn. And apparently Paul (and we would assume the Messianic community) understood this, and continued to engage in oath-taking apart from the entaglements of the Rabbinic *halachah*.

whom I serve in my spirit – This clause is not parenthetical in the least, but gives a full reason why Paul should be willing to take an oath in God's name (i.e., with God as his witness) regarding his constant prayers for the Romans. Specifically, Paul's prayer for the Romans is an integral part of his service of God, and therefore it is fitting that God be witness to it.

The Greek term λατρεύω, *latreuo*, "serve" is the common Lxx translation of עֲבֹדָה, *'avodah*, which is everywhere used of the service of the priests in the Tabernacle or Temple. Paul considers the outworking of his calling to evangelize the Gentiles as an act of worship to God, a work which apparently required much prayer. This should be an example to us, for all too often we engage in the proclamation of the gospel without sufficient preparation in prayer.

in my spirit – This has been variously understood by commentators:

1) referring to the Holy Spirit indwelling Paul
2) as indicating a spiritual (as characterized by The Way) service contrasted with a carnal (pagan) service[17]
3) as meaning "wholeheartedly"
4) as meaning "sincerely"
5) as indicating his whole person
6) as indicating his ministry of prayer as being the inward side of his apostolic service contrasted with the outward side consisting of his preaching, etc.

While any of these could technically fit the language, the last (#6) fits the context best and should most likely be accepted as Paul's meaning. As such, an emphasis is put upon the importance of prayer in the service of God, particularly by those who fulfill leadership roles in the *kehilah* or congregation.

in the gospel of His Son – For Paul, the gospel (ἐυαγγελία, *euangelia*) formed the central core of the mission as he served God. This gospel was (and is) Messiah-centered. That is to say, one cannot speak of the gospel apart from Messiah, for the gospel is fulfilled in the person and work of God's Son. Apart from Messiah, there is no "good news." The promised salvation, given soon after the Fall, centered upon this "seed of the woman," and was anticipated on the basis of God's unfailing promise. When Yeshua finally appeared, the good news of the forgiveness of sins was to be found fulfilled in Him, and thus He embodied, as it were, the gospel itself. To attempt to have any gospel apart from Messiah is to have no gospel at all.

This fact, for Paul, was central to His theology and mission. Perhaps nothing is clearer in this grand epistle than the centrality of Messiah in the Divine plan of salvation. To "dethrone" Him through the teaching that one could obtain righteousness through one's own *mitzvot* (good deeds) based upon one's people-group association, was the very antithesis of the gospel for Paul. But it not only formed the antithesis of the gospel, it diminished the glory of the Son, and made such "righteousness" through the "works of the Torah" anathema in Paul's mind.

how unceasingly I make mention of you – Paul's prayer for the Roman congregation was not merely a passing fancy, but a regular (and therefore integral) part of Paul's service to God on their behalf. Here, unmistakenly, is Paul's personal confession in the power and importance of prayer. Apparently he understood and believed that the spiritual success of this strategically placed congregation hinged, in some measure, upon his faithful mention of them in his prayers. One cannot help but surmise that the prayers of Paul were both positive, asking for their growth and maturity in the Scriptures, as well as negative, praying against the advances of Satan and his cohorts who would no doubt have loved to disrupt and splinter the congregation which named the name of Yeshua. Once again, Paul's example is a good one for Messianic leaders today! Our ultimate fight is against the demonic and evil forces who desire our demise. Prayer must therefore be our constant duty.

10 always in my prayers making request, if perhaps now at last by the will of God I may succeed in coming to you.

always in my prayers – Initially we must ask whether this phrase connects with what precedes, or with what follows. While either choice makes sense, it seems somewhat unlikely that Paul intends to convey that every time he prays he asks God to allow him to visit the Romans. As such, it seems more likely that it attaches to what precedes: ". . . unceasingly I make mention of you always in my prayers. (I am) requesting that now at last by the will of God I might succeed in coming to you." But even this is not smooth, and the exact punctuation of the sentence is not clear.[18]

making request, if perhaps now at last by the will of God I may succeed in coming to you – Paul uses a number of different words to describe the activity of prayer in this passage. In v. 8 he uses the verb "I thank" (εὐχαριστέω, *eucharisteo*); in v. 10 he uses the noun "prayer" (προσευχή, *proseuke*). He alludes to intercessory prayer when, in v. 9, he says of the Romans that he "makes mention" of them in prayer. Even from these initial instances of Paul's talking of prayer, it is clear that 1st Century synagogue encompassed a full range of prayers, not rote liturgy.

"By the will of God"—Note the words of James (4:13-15) –

> "Come now, you who say, "Today or tomorrow, we shall go to such and such a city, and spend a year there and engage in business and make a profit." Yet you do not know what your life will be like tomorrow. You are just a vapor that appears for a little while and then vanishes away. Instead, you ought to say, "If the Lord wills, we shall live and also do this or that."

This sense of divine Providence is clearly taught elsewhere in the Apostolic Writings (cf. Rom 15:32; Acts 18:21; 1Co 4:19; 16:7; Heb 6:3). The belief that life is ordained by God's decree is also found in the Rabbinic literature, as for instance, in *Tanchuma* (Buber's Edition) *Devarim* 3a:

> Rest in the Lord and wait patiently for Him (Ps 37:7). By a pun this is said to mean, "Accept God's decree, even if, for His name's sake, thou art made a corpse." As Job said, "Though He slay me, I will hope in Him" (Job 13:15). [The word "rest" in Ps 37:7 דום can also mean "wail," as in mourning the dead.]

The rabbinic view of God's providence is captured in the saying of Akiva in *Avot* 3:15: "All is foreseen, but freedom of choice is given; and the world is judged with goodness, and all is in accordance with works." Similarly, b.*Berchot* 33b has, "Everything is in the hand of heaven except for the fear of heaven." Thus, the rabbis sought to retain the theological tension between God's all controlling hand and the responsibility of man to obey His commandments.

Paul explains in the following verses (11-15) his plans for coming to Rome and the reasons why he feels his visit is urgent. In 15:24 he illucidates further on this subject. Surely he saw Rome as a strategic part of the overall plan to reach the Gentiles with the Gospel of Yeshua. Yet even more strategic, if my assessment is correct, was the need to correct the tendency toward non-observance of the Torah in the Roman church, for if that congregation was to play a central role in the ingathering of the Gentiles, then certainly they must be exemplary in their living out of the *mitzvot*. For only in this way would the world look at Jew and Gentile worshipping together and recognize the phenomenon of the ingathering of the Gentiles to the One God of Israel, rather than seeing the start of a "new religion."

11 For I long to see you in order that I might impart some spiritual gift to you, that you may be established.

Here we come to one of Paul's primary purposes for visiting the Roman community, to "impart some spiritual gift." The word "impart" is μεταδίδωμι, *metadidomi,* and may mean, in addition to "impart," "to share," as in 12:8 (sharing of one's property). Paul wanted to share or impart some "spiritual gift" (χάρισμα, *charisma*). This word is used in Romans in several ways:

1) to denote generally God's gracious gift in Yeshua HaMashiach (5:15, 16; 6:23);
2) in the plural to denote the gracious gifts bestowed upon Israel (11:29);
3) in 12:6, to denote a special gift or endowment bestowed on a member of the body of Yeshua in order that it may be used by that member in His service and in the service of others.

How should we understand χάρισμα, "spiritual gift" in this verse? Some suggest that it has a more general sense here, and that it means simply that by Paul's presence God would bestow a blessing upon the Roman congregation. Some have suggested that Paul was attempting to legitimize himself in the eyes of those who were "spiritual," i.e., who were more "mystical" in their approach to faith and worship. If this were the case, Paul would be intending by these words to convey that his coming would be endowed by the Spirit, and that his ministry among them would be so empowered by the Spirit so as to leave them with a lasting impression of the Spirit's power.

But I would suggest that Paul is here considering the fruit which will be instilled in the Roman believers when he comes to exercise his spiritual gift among them, namely, the calling of the Gentiles to the obedience of faith to which the Jerusalem council had commanded them. This seems to fit best with the idea that by the imparting of the spiritual gift, they would be "established" (στηρίζω, *sterizo*).

> . . . Paul had in mind a far deeper intention than pleasant fellowship and congeniality in his opening and closing address. The language chosen to communicate his expectations upon his planned arrival in Rome, and the immediacy of this letter in view of his unavoidable delay, should be considered in the context of Paul's personal apostolic preaching of the gospel (his "spiritual gift") and his continued commitment, as recorded by Luke, to proclaiming "obedience" to the apostolic decree for gentiles who come to "faith" in Israel's Christ as the Savior of the world (the obedience of faith).[19]

that you may be established – The goal of Paul's mission to the Roman synagogue was that they might be "established" (στηριχθῆναι, *sterichthenai* from στηρίζω, *sterizo* related to ἵστημι, *histemi,* "to stand"), i.e., that they might strengthened in the truth and in their ability to honor God not only in their individual lives but also in their corporate affairs. Thus, the establishing Paul intends for the Romans relates to the "obedience of faith" (v. 5).

The next verse, in fact, details this more specifically.

12 that is, that I might be encouraged together with you while among you, each of us by the other's faith, both yours and mine.

The eschatological vision initially given to Abraham ("in your seed all the nations of the earth shall be blessed") and expanded by the prophets[20] is that of Jew and non-Jew worshipping together before the one true God, the God of Israel. Thus, each would benefit the other, and together they would be the complete family of God. This picture of the eschaton is surely in Paul's mind as he considers the mutual encouragement which his visit to Rome will engender.

What is more, it is clear that this mutual encouragement[21] is dependent upon a singular faith, i.e., a faith which both the Jew and the non-Jew possess and participate in. This faith is not a mental agreement to a body of truth, but an outworking of righteousness in daily living. All must conform to the "obedience of faith" if there should be genuine, mutual encouragement.

13 I do not want you to be unaware, brethren, that often I have planned to come to you (and have been prevented so far) so that I may obtain some fruit among you also, even as among the rest of the Gentiles.

Paul did not himself establish the Roman congregation, though by this strong statement[22] it appears he felt it his obligation to visit them and to see the fruit of his labors among them. Some suggest that he anticipates an accusation of neglect and attempts to ward it off by this early reference to his desires to come and the external forces which prevented him.

Of the three Greek words most often used in the Apostolic Writings for the sense of "wish," "desire," προτίθημι, protithemi used here, is the strongest.[23] What the choice of words implies is that Paul actually made plans to come to Rome but those plans were variously interrupted. 15:22 speaks to this same issue, and there the context may offer the explanation that the work of evangelism in which he was then engaged was considered a higher priority than a visit to Rome.

so that I might obtain some fruit among you also, even as among the rest of the Gentiles – The fruit Paul hoped to obtain was no doubt similar to that referred to in Phil 1:22, "But if I am to live on in the flesh, this will mean fruitful labor for me; and I do not know which to choose." Paul's mission in life was to realize fruit among the Gentiles to whom he had been called. This would have most likely been in conversions as well as in growth in faith and holy living. As the Apostle to the Gentiles (11:13), Paul no doubt saw Rome as a strategic hub of his work, for it was the center of the Gentile world in Paul's time.

This is the second time we encounter the term "Gentile" (ἔθνος, ethnos) in the book of Romans (cf. 1:5), and it would behoove us to consider its use generally in the Apostolic Writings.

The term is used in three different ways:

1) as a term meaning "nations" without reference to any particular nation: Mt 24:7; Ac 8:9; 10:22; 17:26; Rom 2:24;
2) as a term used, particularly in the Tanach (Lxx) and the Apostolic Scriptures, of those nations *other than Israel,* and denoting non-Jewish in contrast to Jewish: Mt 10:5; 12:21; Mk 7:26; Ac 9: 15; 10:45; 11:1, 18; 13:46, 48; 14:2, 5, 27; 15:3, 7; Rom 1:5, 13; 3:29; 15:10-18; Gal 1:16; 2:2.
3) as a term used to denote pagans and paganism: Mt 5:47; 6:32; 10:18; Eph 4:17f; Gal 2:15.

Though only sample verses have been selected for each category, this listing does reflect the reality that "non-Jew" is the most often found meaning for the term *ethnos* in the Apostolic writings. Since the prevailing rabbinic theology of Paul's day had put such paramount importance upon Jewish identity as the grounds for covenant membership, it is understandable that the "nations" (*ethnoi*) would be identified as outside of the covenant, and thus as "other." Indeed, apart from the ingathering of the Gentiles into the faith, the nations were those who "were without hope and without God in this present world" (Eph 2:12).

Yet we must carefully interpret the word *ethnos* whenever we encounter it, allowing the context to determine its meaning. At times, Paul will use the term simply to indicate a person whose lineage was outside that of Jacob. Likewise, he will use the word to mean those nations which were outside of Israel. When he does use the word *ethnos* to mean "pagan," the context will clearly signal this meaning.

What is the "fruit" which Paul expects to obtain among the non-Jews in the Roman synagogue? If this language is similar to that used in Phil 1:22, then surely Paul refers both to conversions among the Gentiles as well as growth in their understanding of the Scriptures and of God's character and work. In specific terms, he no doubt hopes to bear fruit in helping the Gentile converts to appreciate and support the Torah-centered life to which God had called Israel. Since they were now "grafted in," they must come fully to appreciate the *mitzvot* as the path of life, not of bondage. To be able to strengthen them in the resolve of their faith would, for Paul, be the fruit he so much desired.

14 I am under obligation both to the Greeks and to barbarians, both the wise and to the foolish.

Though Paul had not personally founded the congregation in Rome, he nonetheless felt a direct responsibility for them in that he had been called by God as the apostle to the Gentiles. In adding this phrase, he makes it clear that he does not intend to detract from the work of the others which has been on-going at Rome from the congregation's inception, but that he is simply fulfilling the obligations laid upon him in his calling.

The two pairs of terms[24] could either refer to four distinct groups, to two groups, or to one group (if all the terms were simply synonyms). The construction would favor the interpretation that Paul refers to one group, and that he notes a wide variety within that group. The context would lead me to see the Gentiles as that group to which he refers, and the contrasting terms (Greek vs. barbarian, wise vs. fool) denoting the extremes of culture and education within the Gentile world. The Greek considered himself at the height of culture and education, while a great deal of the world's population was uneducated and barbaric.

Paul's obligation was, of course, the divine calling which was upon him. Thus, his obligation was only secondarily to the Gentile world—it was primarily toward God.

15 Thus, for my part, I am eager to preach the gospel to you also who are in Rome.

Paul's eagerness to preach the gospel to the Gentiles who were part of the synagogue community in Rome should not be misconstrued to mean that he was eager to gain converts. For Paul, preaching the gospel was nothing less than preaching Messiah! Far from the modern usage of the term which tends to relegate the "gospel" to evangelism, the "gospel" in Paul's mind is the whole story—the victory which God wins for His people. Paul was anxious to preach the victory of God in Rome, and to encourage all of the Gentile believers to see themselves as fully participating in this gospel.

16 For I am not ashamed of the gospel, for it is the power of God for salvation to everyone who believes, to the Jew first and also to the Greek.

(The addition of "of Messiah" – "For I am not ashamed of the gospel of Messiah," is an addition found in a few later Greek manuscripts and is not attested in the earliest witnesses.)

Paul's eagerness rests not only on the divine calling, something which always presupposes enabling, but also upon the very nature of the gospel within the working of the Holy Spirit.

Why would anyone be ashamed of the gospel? Because this is the natural response to it, for it (1) stands in opposition to the world, and thus attracts the world's hostilities, and (2) the manner in which the gospel comes not in worldly power and majesty, but in the veiled humility of the incarnation which, to the world would certainly look abject and foolish. This is particularly true when one considers the Greek world, with its propensity for displaying human strength and intellect. On the contrary, the gospel calls for the sinner to admit his weakness, indeed, his inability—to reckon all worldly wisdom as foolish in the face of the lowly Messiah!

But Paul (though perhaps even he was at times tempted to hold the gospel with some measure of shame as is true for all believers) had come to know the reality of the gospel, and the manner in which God takes what is foolishness to man and turns it to proclaim and establish His greatness.

for it is the power of God for salvation to everyone who believes – The demonstrative "it" refers to the gospel previously mentioned: "for the gospel is the power of God . . . ." "For salvation" means "resulting in salvation" (εἰς σωτηρίαν, *eis soterian*). Paul has come to realize that the gospel, though often despised by the world, is nevertheless, in spite of all appearances, the very supreme power of God by which He saves sinners.

This statement regarding the gospel and that which immediately follows it form, it seems, the kernel truth about which Paul wraps this entire epistle. All that he intends his readers to know may be summed up in (1) the manner in which God makes a sinner righteous, and (2) the means by which He does this.

The idea that God's word is endowed with power, and that as a result when He speaks there are inevitable results is a clear theme of the Tanach, and one which Paul no doubt draws upon here. The proclamation of the gospel is not merely persuading the mind of men, but it is the sending forth of the divine word which has, in the hands of the Spirit, an efficatiousness to it. Even as the Lord spoke in creation and the worlds were formed (cf. Gen 1:3, 6, etc.; Ps 147:15; Is 40:8; 55:10f; Jer 23:29), so the divine power (δύναμις, *dunamis*) goes forth in the proclamation of the gospel.

Salvation (σώζω, σωτηρία, *sozo, soteria*) while having a general meaning in the everyday Greek of Paul's world is used by him only in the sphere of relationship between God and man. For Paul, to "be saved" is to be rescued from the deserved punishment for sin, i.e., death, and to be given eternal life. The message of Paul in the gospel is that this salvation cannot be merited or purchased, but is the free gift of God to all who through faith receive it. Thus, the gospel is the power of salvation to all who believe. But this belief (πίστις, *pistis*, πιστεύω, *pisteuo*) or faith has one and only one object—the person of Yeshua. Thus, the gospel has always been centered in Yeshua, the Messiah, and always will be. It is therefore impossible to receive and enjoy the gospel apart from receiving and enjoying Yeshua—the gospel and Yeshua are inseparable.

The word translated "gospel" is εὐαγγελία, *euangelia*, which means "good message" or "good news." For sinful man, who, left to his own devices, cannot obtain salvation, the proclamation that another has made the way for him is good news indeed! Only if one sees and understands the helplessness of mankind can the gospel be appreciated for its goodness. Yet the gospel comes with the message of death—death to oneself and death of the innocent One as substitute for the sinner. To discover its goodness one must accept it with eyes of faith, otherwise it looks entirely foolish (cf. 1Co 1:18ff). But must faith precede the hearing of the gospel, or does the gospel produce the faith to hear? This is the mystery within the power of the gospel, for it draws the heart of the seeker to exercise faith in the Messiah Yeshua and in God Who sent Him, a faith which God Himself gives as a gift (Eph. 2:8-10). This faith, as the saving response to the gospel, is not something which man possesses as an attribute of his humaness, nor is it the meritorious work of a few who attain to higher standards than the rest. For Paul, faith is no work of the individual (Rom 4:5) for salvation is altogether—not almost altogether—God's work.

Furthermore, the word "all" in this phrase ("to all who believe") emphasizes a major theme in this epistle and in all of Paul's writings, namely, that the salvation which results from the reception of the gospel by faith is a salvation that knows no ethnic, gender, economic or cultural boundaries. The anti-Gentile bias of the emerging Oral Torah in Paul's day is here clearly rejected by Paul as it was by Yeshua. In fact, nothing characterizes Paul's understanding of the eschaton more than the picture of Jew and Gentile worshipping together as one body of believers, worshipping the God of Abraham, Isaac, and Jacob. This "fellow-heir" concept (cf. Eph. 3:6) permeates Paul's writings, and is introduced at the beginning of Romans, his *magnum opus,* showing the priority he gave to this truth.

to the Jew first and also to the Greek – Here Paul explains the former "all"—the "all" includes both Jew and Gentile. But he also emphasizes something that is at the heart of his understanding of salvation as a whole, and why he is not ashamed of the gospel. Paul's mode of operation was "to the Jew first and also to the Greek," that is to say, for Paul the promises made to the fathers (cf. 11:28) must inevitably be fulfilled, and that apart from its fulfillment there is, indeed, a great deal to be ashamed of with regard to the gospel. Thus, it was Paul's habit to go to the synagogue first, and to proclaim the message of the gospel to his own brothers as a matter of priority. That he would teach that the salvation of the Gentiles would form a jealousy which would draw Israel to Yeshua is, in itself, a demonstration of the priority which he places upon the salvation of Israel as the necessary fulfillment of the gospel message itself. Thus, "first" (πρῶτος, *protos*) should be understood in the sense of first in priority, not first chronologically. Cranfield says of the construction that

> it is suggestive of the fundamental equality of Jew and Gentile in the face of the gospel (the gospel is the power of God unto salvation for believing Jew and believing Gentile alike), while the word πρωτον [first] indicates that within the framework of this basic equality there is a certain undeniable priority of the Jew.[25]

For Paul, the gospel could have no success if it did not contain within its message the power to bring Israel to faith in Yeshua. Thus, this opening but succinct phrase sets the stage for the later exposition of this very theme in chapters 9-11. Paul's understanding of the gospel embraces both an individual as well as a corporate dimension of salvation. It is individual in that everyone who is justified (declared to be just in God's eyes) is personally drawn by God to Himself and specifically redeemed from the penalty of his or her sin. Yet it is corporate because each individual so redeemed automatically becomes a member of the one "family of God," a family whose father is Abraham (4:16, 17). But to neglect the importance of the Jew, even the Jew who had not yet confessed Yeshua to be the Messiah—to overlook these is to miss the heart of the gospel as far as Paul is concerned. His high praise for the gospel comes, not only because it has been so successful among the Gentiles, but also because he knows that it will also be the means by which Israel will be saved. In fact, the salvation of Israel (11:25) will be the ultimate demonstration of the power of the gospel.

What are the implications of this teaching of Paul? Some are obvious! First, the teaching often called "replacement theology," that the church has replaced Israel because God has forsaken her and given her heritage to the Christians—this teaching would, if we take Paul's perspective, portray the gospel as impotent. Rather than being the power of God resulting in salvation, it is shown to be weak and incapable of turning the Jewish heart to Yeshua. Thus replacement theology not only slaps at the face of God for the promises He has made, but it undermines the very nature and power of the gospel.

Secondly by way of implication, if "to the Jew first and also to the Greek" is seen to be God's priority in the realization of the gospel, then it ought to be the priority for the church and for every individual who confesses Yeshua as Savior. This effectively rules out any notion of anti-Semitism within the Christian community, for anti-Semitism, when viewed in this light, is a denial of the gospel itself.

Thirdly, God's priority list, "to the Jew first and also to the Greek" ought to be the priority of the believing community in terms of ministry. To some Jews, such a statement might send shudders up the spine! What I mean by priority in ministry is perhaps best expressed as priority in love and understanding. If, as I said before, anti-Semitism is a denial of the gospel, then the converse is true: a true love for Israel and the Jewish people will be a platform for the establishment of the gospel. Priority in ministry does not mean "how can we make them Christians" but "how can we demonstrate the love and righteous life which we have come to know in Yeshua."

But there is a fourth issue which the phrase "to the Jew first and also to the Greek" raises, and this is the fact that salvation, in all times, and for all peoples is "from the Jews" (Jn 4:22). Never can the gospel be preached rightly while neglecting to acknowledge the essential place Israel has played and continues to play in the outworking of the gospel. This essential place in the gospel includes the fact that God has chosen Israel out of all the nations (Gen 12:1ff; Neh 9:7; Deut 14:2; Amos 3:2; Rom 11:28-29). It also is seen in that God chose Israel to be the one to guard and carry His direct revelation, the Torah (cf. Rom 3:1). Furthermore, the priority of the Jew can be seen in that Yeshua Himself came as a Jew to the Jews (Jn 1:12; Mt 10:5-6; 15:24).

While emphasizing these priorities, it is equally important to note where the Jew does not have priority. In what ways do the Jews not have priority? 1) in righteousness or merit. No one has priority in this realm, for all are on the same level—sinners in need of God's righteousness. Paul's conclusion in 3:9-10 is that "there is none righteous, not even one." 2) in how they are saved. Jew and Gentile are saved exactly the same way. Note 3:29-30, "Is God the God of the Jews only? Is He not the God for the Gentiles also? Yes, of Gentiles also!" Paul's conclusion is that all, both Jew and Gentile, are saved by faith in Yeshua. 3) in participation in God's covenant blessings. There are no "second-class" citizens in the kingdom of God. Paul makes it clear that Gentiles who come to faith in Yeshua have the same standing in the family of God as the Jews who receive Yeshua (Eph 2:12ff; 3:4-6). We are all fellow-heirs and co-inheritors of the covenant promises.

Why the emphasis upon the priority of the Jew in the gospel then? While a number of answers could be given, I think the primary reason Paul so much emphasizes the priority of the Jew is to guard against thinking that the mass conversion of the Gentiles began the formation of something new and separate from the salvific work God had already accomplished among the people of Israel. To the extent that the gospel continues to be tied to its Jewish priority, to that extent it continues to be tied to Torah and to the history of salvation in the history of Israel. It is when the gospel is stripped of its Jewish heritage and used rather in an anti-Semitic way that it produces something new and different, something which has no ties whatsoever to Abraham and the patriarchs. In such a perspective God is no longer the God of Abraham, Isaac, and Jacob, but the God of the Church—a new entity without vital connection to the people of God called "Israel." It is this mindset which breeds arrogance, a trait Paul apparently feared was raising its ugly head among the Gentiles in the Roman synagogue (cp. Rom 11:18-20).

As members of the body of Yeshua we must admit that within our sinful flesh there is every capacity for anti-Semitism, and that in some ways, as our flesh rebels against God, it will also rebel against that which God loves. If Israel is the "apple of His eye" (Zech 2:8), the rebel heart, in its rebellion, is tempted to hate Israel in order to strike a blow at God Himself.

17 For in it the righteousness of God is revealed from faith to faith; as it is written, "BUT THE RIGHTEOUS man SHALL LIVE BY FAITH."

The verse opens with γαρ, "For," linking it to the previous statement. The gospel demonstrates the power of God for through it the righteousness of God is made known. That is to say, the power which the gospel displays is the divine power by which a sinner is made righteous in the eyes of God. Apart from divine power no sinner is ever made righteous.

Secondly, the pronoun αὐτῷ, "it," refers back to the "gospel" of v. 16, meaning that the focal point of God's power for changing the human heart is Yeshua whom the gospel itself proclaims. But further, the God-ordained means by which He desires to display His saving power is nothing less than the preaching of the good news. Though not glorious in and of itself (cf. 1Co 1:21), the preaching of the gospel is the means God has promised to bless.

The actual order of the words in the Greek text is not retained by the English translations, but would be "For the righteousness of God in it is revealed . . . ." Putting the word "righteousness" at the beginning of the sentence would show its proper emphasis.

What is this "righteousness of God" (δικαιοσύνη θεοῦ, *dikaiosune theou*) which, according to Paul, is revealed in the triumph of the gospel? We may first want to ask what the term "righteousness" (δίκη, *dike*, δίκαιος, *dikaios*, δικαιοσύνη, *dikaiosune*) means. Its primary meaning in the classical Greek was that of "custom" and "conforming to the custom." This came to mean "right" or "accepted." The Greek term, however, was greatly nuanced by the Lxx's use of it to translate the Hebrew צֶדֶק, *tzedek*, the word used in the Tanach to describe "actions which fulfill the God-given obligations in the Torah," "the demands of a particular relationship." The adjective, צַדִּיק, *tzadik*, could describe those whose conduct and character conformed to the administration of justice, but could also be used of a particular status within the community, i.e., "innocent," "justified," etc. Thus, in the 1st Century, and still today, there exists a large debate and division between the Roman Catholic and Reformed church as to whether or not Paul is speaking of "righteous character" (i.e., righteous life on this earth) or "right standing before God" (i.e., imputed righteousness) when he speaks of the righteousness which the sinner enjoys as the result of being saved. It seems to me that when taken in the contexts in which the term(s) are found, there is little doubt that what Paul means by using the word "righteous" when describing a saved individual is that such an individual has been acquitted of guilt by the court of Heaven, that God has conferred a righteous status upon that individual. Of course, in biblical theology, and especially in Paul's theology, those who are "declared righteous" by the court of Heaven also are transformed into righteous individuals through the ongoing process of sanctification. "Faith" and "faithfulness" are two sides of the same coin.

A great deal has been written to answer the question of what exactly is meant by "the righteousness of God" in our verse. There are actually two primary ways we may look at the phrase, depending upon whether we take "God" to be a subjective genitive (i.e., righteousness as a description of God and His activity) or objective genitive (i.e., righteousness which has its source in God, or righteousness that God gives). The former view would see that in the salvation of a sinner the righteous acts of God are seen and understood. The latter view would say that when a sinner is saved he is declared righteous, and that this righteousness comes from God, so that the Gospel reveals the kind of righteousness which God gives to sinners who receive the Son. While there are arguments to favor both interpretations (cf. Moule, 1.96-7), I favor the view that the righteousness which Paul is here emphasizing is the activity of God whereby He declares a sinner just. I would thus paraphrase: "for in it (the Gospel) the manner by which God declares a sinner just is revealed." That is to say, the Gospel rightly understood and rightly taught gives the divine method of salvation, which is the imputation of righteousness by God's divine act. On the basis of the sacrifice of Yeshua, God is both just and the justifier, and therefore able to fully declare the sinner "not guilty" because the penalty for his sin has been paid

by Messiah. The Gospel therefore discredits any notion of being able to attain righteousness
through one's own status, or through his own efforts. This is clearly how the phrase "righteousness of God" is used in 10:3, for "righteousness of God" is contrasted with "attempting to establish their own righteousness." This must mean that man's attempt to justify himself stands at
contrast to "God's righteousness," i.e., the method God has ordained to make sinners righteous
in His sight.

from faith to faith – A great number of suggestions have been given through the years for
the interpretation of this phrase:

1) from the faith of the OT to the faith of the NT
2) from the faith of the law to the faith of the gospel
3) from the faith of the preachers to the faith of the hearers
4) from the present faith to the future
5) from the faith of words (whereby we now believe what we do not see)
   to the faith of the things, that is, realities (whereby we shall hereafter
   possess what we now believe in)
6) from God's faithfulness to man's faith
7) indicating a growth in faith

Most of these, however, seem to overlook the fact that Paul is obviously connecting what he
says here to the quote which follows from Hab 2:4: וְצַדִּיק בֶּאֱמוּנָתוֹ יִחְיֶה, "but a righteous one by his
faith will live" (a word for word translation). The use of the ב in בֶּאֱמוּנָתוֹ "by his faith" is most
probably to be understood as "on the basis of," meaning, then, "the righteous one will live on
the basis of his faith." The life which the just man has is a life which is based upon his faith.

The quote from Hab 2:4 –

MT	Lxx	Paul
וְצַדִּיק בֶּאֱמוּנָתוֹ יִחְיֶה	ὁ δὲ δίκαιος ἐκ πίστεώς μου ζήσεται	ὁ δὲ δίκαιος ἐκ πίστεώς ζήσεται
and a righteous one in (on the basis of) his faith shall live	but the righteous one out from my faith shall live	but the righteous one out from faith shall live

The obvious difference between the MT and the Lxx is the possessive pronoun "my" in place of
the Hebrew "his." It seems very likely that the Lxx translators saw a *yod* in the place of the *vav*,
a common interchange in certain orthography. In fact, a number of witnesses of the Romans text
attempt to correct it toward the Lxx, adding the pronoun μου, "my" (vulgate, syriac[h], and a corrector in C).

The Habakkuk pesher (1QpHab, a midrash on the text of Habakkuk) gives this interesting
interpretation of 2:4: "Its prophetic meaning concerns all the doers of the Law in the house of
Judah whom God will deliver from the house of damnation, because of their patient suffering
and their steadfast faith in the Teacher of Righteousness." (Brownlee, *Mid Pesher of Hab.*, p.125).

Habakkuk 2:4 is referred to in Midrash Rabbah several times. In Mid. Rab. *Exodus* xxiii.5
(on the text of S.S. 4:8) a discussion of faith ensues, and the faith of Abraham is referred to, with
reference to Gen 15:6. After this, the text has "This was the faith which Israel had inherited and
concerning which it is written, But the righteous shall live by his faith." Another time, in Mid.
Rabbah *Ecc* iii.9§1, there is extended comment on Hab 2:4—

> R. Isaac b. R. Marion said: But the righteous shall live by his faith (Hab. 2:4) means that
> even the Righteous One who lives for ever lives from His faith. The Holy One, blessed be

He, said: First I slew the firsborn of Egypt (as it is stated, and it came to pass at midnight, that the Lord smote all the firsborn in the land of Egypt, Ex 12:29); therefore every firstborn that is born to you sanctify unto Me, as it is stated, Sanctify unto Me all the firstborn (Ex 13: 2), i.e., sanctify unto Me the firstborn by faith in Me. That is the meaning of But the righteous shall live by his faith.

The Talmud refers to Hab 2:4 in the discussion of how the Torah may be summarized (b. *Makkot* 23b). R. Simlai had asserted that the 613 commandments received by Moses had been summed up by David in eleven commandments (Ps 15), by Isaiah in six (Is 33:15f), by Micah in three (Mic 6:8), by Isaiah again in two (Is 56:1), and finally by Amos in one (Amos 5:4), but that R. Nachman ben Isaac had substituted Hab 2:4b for Amso 5:4 as the summary in one commandment.

That Hab 2:4b gets this kind of attention in the Rabbinic literature shows that it was a commonly utilized text in the Judaisms of the 1st Century.

The context of the Habakkuk text is the conclusion of the prophet's cry of woe, in which he questions God over the use of the Chaldeans to punish the chosen people. For the prophet, this brought into question God's justice and even His holiness (1:13f). In raising the question of how God could use such a wicked nation to punish His people, he awaits God's answer (2:1). The Lord's answer comes in the form of a revelation or vision that Habakkuk was to record and make known. It's application would be for the appointed time, and those who believed in God would await its fulfillment, even though it might appear for the interim that it was not correct. The proud in heart would doubtless refuse to accept the revelation given to the prophet, but the one who had faith (and would thus accept the revelation) would live, i.e., preserve his life on the basis of acting in accordance with the revelation which God would give the prophet. Thus, "the just shall live by faith."

The lack of the article on צַדִּיק, *zadik*, "righteous" leaves us with the possibility that it represents anyone who is righteous, or that it applies to the righteous of the nation of Israel. For either interpretation, the principle is the same. It is an acceptance of and submission to the revelation of God that will yield life. The opposite is likewise true, for rejection of God's revelation is rejection of life itself.

It is obvious that Paul quotes the text in support of his earlier statement that the righteousness of God is revealed in the gospel which begins with faith and depends upon faith. He understands the term "faith" to be in every way bound up with the gospel and its acceptance.

There are a number of questions that confront us as we consider this quote from Habakkuk and Paul's understanding of it. First is to what we should connect the phrase "by faith" (ἐκ πίστεως, *ek pisteos*). Should we read it to mean "the one who is righteous as a result of his faith" (attaching "by faith" to the word "righteous") or "by faith shall live" (attaching "by faith" to the word "live")? There is a sense, of course, in which both are true. One's righteousness comes, as Paul will so directly teaches in these opening chapters, through faith in the Messiah, so it is clearly a "by faith righteousness." But it is equally true that one lives because of one's faith. But while both are true, it seems most likely that Paul understood "by faith" as modifying the manner in which one is able to obtain righteousness before God. Surely the material which immediately follows this quote emphasizes that the righteousness which God gives is a righteousness which must be received through the exercise of faith, and cannot be obtained otherwise.

Some suggest that Paul simply reinterprets the passage for his own purpose, disregarding the context of the prophecy itself. But I rather think that the revelation given to Habakkuk stresses the same truth, namely, that the righteous of Israel will be characterized by a willingness to submit to the word of God, even when it appears to be out of touch with the present circumstances.

A second question that presents itself as we consider this quote from Hab 2:4 is why Paul left out the possessive pronoun "his"—"the righteous one will live by his faith" (assuming he was reading the Hebrew text) or the possessive pronoun "my"—"the righteous one will live by my faith" (if he were reading the Lxx).

First we may note that the Lxx rendering ("the righteous shall live by my faith") interprets the "faith" as God's faithfulness. In the face of the impending Chaldean invasion which God has revealed to Habakkuk, the righteous one need not fear, for God's faithfulness will sustain his life. This must be how the Lxx translators understood the text.

Yet Paul did not quote the Lxx at this point, giving some indication that he did not agree with this understanding of "faith" in the Habakkuk text of the Lxx. Interestingly, the author to the Messianic Jews (Hebrews), when quoting Hab 2:4b, does quote directly from the Lxx ("the righteous shall live by My faith"), for the sense of God's faithfulness fits his admonition in Heb 10:37-38 (where a quote from Is 26:20 is combined with the quote from Hab 2:4).

Secondly, Paul is consistent, for when he quotes Hab 2:4 in Gal 3:11, he quotes it exactly as he does here, without any possessive pronoun following the word "faith." Here, in Galatians, we get a fuller understanding of the Apostle's interpretation of the Habakkuk text, for in quoting Hab 2:4 he does so to establish the fact that "no one is justified by the Torah before God." Here, then, "faith" is put over against "works of the Torah" as the means by which a sinner is justified. (We shall see that this phrase, "works of the Torah," is directly connected with the whole issue of the proselyte ritual to which the Gentiles were being directed.)

This fits perfectly with the emphasis Paul wishes to bring in Rom 1 by quoting the Habakkuk text, for he is substantiating the fact that God's method of declaring a sinner righteous has always been on the basis of faith, something which is itself not a righteous work but the exercise of a God-given gift whereby the sinner is able to submit to God's revealed truth and to live in accordance with it.

We find important clues as to the meaning of "faith" in this quote of Habakkuk by understanding the Hebrew word אֱמוּנָה, 'emunah. The first time we find the word in the Tanach, it refers to the hands of Moses held up by Aaron and Hur (Ex 17:12)—"his hands were אֱמוּנָה until the going down of the sun," i.e., they were raised continually and incessantly. In every other passage where the term אֱמוּנָה is found, it refers to the conduct of persons or of God, sometimes categorizing such actions as attributes ("faithful," "genuine," "reliable," etc.). Jepsen notes:

> Thus 'emunah is not so much an abstract quality . . . but a way of acting which grows out of inner stability, "conscientiousness." Whereas 'emeth [a related word meaning "truth"] is always used in relationship to something (or someone) on which (or whom) one can rely, 'emunah seems more to emphasize one's own inner attitude and the conduct it produces. The frequently suggested translation, "conscientiousness," would seem to come closest to the meaning intended in many passages.[26]

On the basis of the meaning of אֱמוּנָה, 'emunah, it seems warranted that some translations (NEB, JPS, margin of RSV and NRSV) have opted to translate Hab 2:4 along the lines of "the righteous will live on the basis of his faithfulness." Indeed, in *BDB*'s Lexicon (p. 53) Hab 2:4b is translated as "a righteous man by his faithfulness liveth."

How does this affect our interpretation of the text in Romans 1? First, we must understand that for Paul and for all biblical writers, "faith that saves" encompasses one's entire life and is not merely a mental exercise. True saving faith is evident by the deeds which it produces. One is therefore "justified" by how one lives (Jms 2:21ff). Surely there is a "faith" which does not save (cf. Jn 2:23,24; 8:30ff), a "faith" which even the demons have (Jms 2:19). But the faith which produces life in a person, and urges that person to grow in the exercise of faith, is the faith which is God-given and which brings salvation. This genuine faith inevitably produces faithfulness— "from faith to faith," that is, initiated by faith and issuing in faithfulness.

Secondly, understanding that the concepts of "faith" and "faithfulness" are always intertwined, the faith which Paul here speaks of by quoting Hab 2:4 is a faith which lasts. That is to say, a person who possesses true saving faith is a person who will inevitably grow in faithfulness toward God and man. There is no place for a "falling away" in Paul's understanding of faith (Rom 8:29-30). Nor is there any hint of the "carnal Christian," who though genuinely "saved" lives a life characterized by faithlessness and sin. For Paul, the presence of true saving faith is always accompanied by growing faithfulness to God and to His word, and thus his mission among the Gentiles was to bring about the "obedience of faith," a term which no doubt is expanded and interpreted by this quote from Habakkuk.

Thirdly, we must listen carefully to Paul, indeed, to the Scriptures as a whole. For understanding that faith always issues in faithfulness (i.e., a growing in faith toward God) some are always jumping to the illogical and unscriptural conclusion that one is able to produce this "faithfulness" by one's own efforts, and that therefore the faithfulness which characterizes true saving faith is the result of one's own works. From this it is asserted that salvation is earned by working hard at being faithful in one's life and actions. But such reasoning, beyond being entirely illogical from a biblical standpoint, would be rejected out of hand by Paul, for a very fundemental reason: the whole growth in faithfulness toward God begins by the divine planting of the seed of faith into the soul, an event entirely out of the hands of any individual. Indeed, this planting of faith within the soul whereby a sinner turns to trust upon God, seeking His mercy and grace, is manifest by the confession of the sinner that he or she is entirely unable to please God or gain His favor (Rom 3:10ff). From Paul's perspective, saving faith begins, not by mustering one's strength to accomplish a good work, but by undergoing a death to one's self and being made alive in Messiah. Saving faith is therefore characterized by one's own confession of utter helplessness in the face of utter guilt and condemnation. To think that one can earn salvation by mustering faithfulness in life and deed is to put the cart before the horse, the fruit before the root.

18 For the wrath of God is revealed from heaven against all ungodliness and unrighteousness of men who suppress the truth in unrighteousness,

We may rightly say that this verse is the beginning of four main sections in this epistle, the opening verses 1-17 being a thorough introduction to Paul's main themes. The four sections are:

1) 1:18-4:25
2) 5:1-8:39
3) 9:1-11:36
4) 12:1-15:13

This opening section expounds the phrase of v. 17, "from faith to faith," for what Paul goes on to describe in this most dark passage of the epistle is not the immorality of the pagan cultures which surrounded him at the time, but rather the heart of all men in all ages apart from faith. If the righteousness of God is revealed in the gospel, that is to say, the means by which God declares a sinner righteous, and if this grand phenomenon of righteous standing must inevitably begin and issue out of faith, then proof for such a statement would be to see the likewise inevitable heart of man who, apart from faith, attempts to govern his own world and life by his own standards.

It seems most likely that Paul has Gentiles particularly in mind in these verses, but we should consider this more carefully. In using the term "men" (ἄνθρωπος, *anthropos*) and nowhere using the word "Gentile," it may be that while the heart of unregenerate mankind is best portrayed in the immoral passions of the pagan nations, yet the idolatry mentioned in v. 23 echos language of Ps 106:20 and Jer 2:11, passages directed toward the Jewish nation. What is more, the heart of the section 2:1-3:20 teaches precisely that the Jew, who thinks himself entitled to sit in judgment on the Gentiles, does himself the very same things that he condemns in them. We should consider, therefore, the real possibility that Paul describes in these verses not strictly the Gentile heart, but the heart of all who attempt to define and procure their own righteousness apart from faith. While the outward expressions may differ (pagan ritual vs. arrogant self-confidence), the heart is the same. Idolatry, whether projected toward a pagan god represented by statuary, or portrayed in a smug reliance upon one's ethnic status, is still idolatry, and flows from a heart bound up in the darkness of sin.

Paul therefore speaks to this issue from the light of the cross, from the reality of his own confrontation with the risen Messiah, and from his understanding of the Torah as illuminated by the Holy Spirit. The heart with which we are to love God has been overtaken by sin, a sin inherited and a sin encouraged. The only remedy for such a sin-laden heart is the redeeming work of Yeshua and the God-given repentance which accompanies salvation. The righteousness of God, the manner in which God declares a sinner righteous, likewise encompasses practical righteousness, indeed, as the inevitable proof of the divine declaration. For the wrath of God revealed against all ungodliness and unrighteousness is the necessary flipside of the grace of which faith lays hold. Thus, the utter necessity of faith is clear, for apart from faith one is left to his or her own devices, and thus to the utter unrighteousness to which the heart is prone.

"For" (γαρ, gar) connects our verse to the previous, as stated above, in supporting the statement "from faith to faith." That is, there is no doubt that righteousness must come from outside of the sinner, for left to himself he will always grow in unrighteousness.

Wrath (ὀργή, orge) is used both of God's anger against sin and sinners, but also of the future judgment in which He will make His wrath known in the destruction of the unrighteous (cf. 1Thess 1:10). Here, however, the present tense verb ἀποκαλύπτεται, apokaluptetai (from ἀποκαλύπτω, apokalupto, "to reveal," "disclose," "bring to light") indicates that the wrath of God of which Paul speaks is not something reserved entirely for the future, but something that is presently being revealed, being made known.

What is more, the anger spoken of here is not the irrational emotion so often found among sinners, but the righteous indignation against injustice, cruelty and corruption. We cannot therefore understand the wrath of God as analogous to the wrath of men, even when that wrath is righteous, for our righteous anger is always mixed with some measure of corruption and is always compromised (more or less) by the presence of sin in our own beings. God's anger is infinitely pure and without compromise, so that it harmonizes fully with His attributes of love and mercy, even if we are not able in and of ourselves to understand its intersection.

But we will learn more about the wrath of God if we will answer the question of how it is revealed. Some would understand the revelation of God's wrath to be in the effects of the sin itself. The ungodliness (ἀσέβεια, asebeia) and unrighteousness (δικαιοσύνη, dikaiosune) spoken of, and no doubt described in the following verses, carries with it a penalty—disease, hurt, frustrations, futilities, and disasters. Others want to cast an eschatological perspective on the passage and project it into the eschaton where God's judgment will be open and plain. But neither of these take into account the obvious parallelism between v. 17 and 18, in both of which the idea of "revelation" is contained. In v. 17, it is the righteousness of God which is revealed, while in v. 18 it is the wrath of God being revealed. The parallel thought gives the sense that the wrath of God is revealed in the proclamation of the gospel, i.e., in describing the method by which God declares a sinner righteous. In the on-going proclamation of the gospel, the wrath of God against all ungodliness and unrighteousness is revealed, for the gospel is centered in the events of the cross and the tomb. While the consequences of sin may be understood as an indication of God's wrath, or even the apocalyptic events described by the prophets a sure picture of God's righteous wrath, nothing compares to the measure of God's wrath described in the cross itself. Thus, if one should understand the wrath of God in its extreme, then one must look at the cross, and the Messiah there crushed by the wrath of God against ungodliness and unrighteousness. Nothing in all of this world's history can paint the utter fulness of God's wrath against sinners more vividly than the blows He inflicted upon His own Son, Yeshua. For Paul, then, the proclamation of the gospel is at once the revelation of how God declares a sinner righteous, and the revelation of God's wrath against sin in all of its forms.

from heaven – The wrath of God is said to be revealed "from heaven." "Heaven" is found only here and in 10:6 in the epistle of Romans. Its use as a metonym for the name of God is well attested in the Rabbinic literature, and may, in fact, have bearing on the present text. It seems that in light of the understanding of how God's wrath is revealed given above (i.e., in the proclamation of the Gospel), the "from heaven" is to emphasize with utter seriousness that the wrath of God is really God's wrath, i.e., from heaven, and not merely a theological or philosophical concept. In the same way that the righteousness of God is revealed in the gospel, but has its source in heaven, so the wrath of God is proclaimed in the gospel but actually comes directly from the Creator. The current despair and carnage which is the inevitable fruit of sin is, in the final analysis, a display of God's own just wrath against sin and sinners.

against all ungodliness and unrighteousness of men – Ungodliness is ἀσέβεια, *asebeia* and unrighteousness ἀδικία, *adikia,* both words with *alpha privative* (where the Greek α affixed to the beginning of the word functions like our English prefix un- as a negation). Some have suggested that the two terms fit well the transgression of the two tables of the Torah, the first table being sins against God (ungodliness) and the second against man (unrighteousness). Others have suggested simply that this phrase acts as a hendiadys, that is, a two-word expression (like our English "good and plenty" or "well and good") to describe a single thing. (The fact that ἀδικία at the end of the verse stands alone as referring apparently to the whole might favor this second suggestion.) Regardless of Paul's purpose in using both words, it is well for us to be reminded that all sin is sin against God directly, and that it likewise is a violation of God's ordained order.

who suppress the truth in unrighteousness – The word "suppress" (κατέχειν, *katechein*) means "to hold down" and can be used both positively (as to retain what is true, cf. Lk 8:15) as well as negatively. Here we have a Pauline exposition on "sin" at its core, for sin by its very nature is an attempt to suppress the truth, to offer to the naive heart and mind an alternative which is not the truth, but which holds back the truth and thus prevents knowing God as Creator, Judge, and Redeemer. Cranfield writes:

> Sin is always an assault upon the truth, that is the fundamental truth of God as Creator, Judge and Redeemer, (which because it is truth, must be taken into account and come to terms with, if man is not to live in vain), the attempt to suppress it, bury it out of sight, obliterate it from the memory; but it is of the essence of sin that it can never be more than an attempt to suppress the truth, an attempt which is always bound in the end to prove futile. (*Romans* 1.112)

To suppress the truth, then, is the character of the ungodly and the unrighteous. The converse must then be equally true, i.e., that the character of godliness and righteousness is to always be searching for and striving to accept the truth—the truth first and foremost as revealed by God in His Son Yeshua, for it is in the full revelation of Yeshua that we see the full righteousness of God, and His wrath against sin. Thus, the Scriptures remain our foundation, and we strive to know the truth from them.

19 because that which is known about God is evident within them; for God made it evident to them.

Here Paul gives further reason why God is just in displaying His wrath against those who practice ungodliness, by showing that He has indeed revealed Himself to them, so that the conclusion of v. 18, that they "suppress the truth" is further substantiated, for God has made the truth known to them.

"that which is known about God" is understood to mean that which is "knowable" about God, γνωστός (*gnostos*) allowing this meaning in this context.[27] Paul no doubt cast the phrase this way in order to maintain aspects of God which are mysterious, unrevealed, and thus beyond our knowledge. Consider Deut 29:29—

> "The secret things belong to the LORD our God, but the things revealed belong to us and to our sons forever, that we may observe all the words of this Torah.

Paul does not mean by this that God is knowable in the sense of approachable by man apart from grace, for the subsequent chapters will make this clear. What he must mean in this context, then, is that sinful mankind has a certain level of knowledge, an experiential knowledge of God which supports the reality of His existence and power, but does not inevitably lead to repentance and salvation.

This knowledge of God that sinful man cannot escape is true knowledge, for it is "evident" (θανερός, *phaneros*), a word in the Greek which has a base meaning of "visible" or "apparent." Those who deny the existence of God are therefore constantly engaged in denial of what they know to be true. This knowledge is made known "among them" (a better alternative translation than "in them," for God's revelation of Himself is made known through the whole creation, not just in the creation of mankind).

What is more, this knowledge does not exist, as it were, in "brute fact," as though it finds its source in the inevitable fingerprints of the Creator upon His creation. While it is true that God's creative personage has touched every part of our existence, our text stresses the fact that God Himself has taken the initiative to make His existence known. Thus, such knowledge of God of which the Apostle speaks is not a knowledge gained from passive facts, but is the direct effect of God's intended purpose to make Himself known.

20 For since the creation of the world His invisible attributes, His eternal power and divine nature, have been clearly seen, being understood through what has been made, so that they are without excuse.

Paul intends to continue the sense of the mystery of God by using the oxymoron ". . . invisible attributes . . . clearly seen." He is describing the indescribable, and thus uses language which alerts his readers to the obvious fact that God, though revealed through various means, is still infinitely mysterious and wonderful. Mankind, though given a true revelation of God, cannot by this revelation "dissect" God (as it were) and discover all there is to know about Him through a thorough investigation of the created world.

Here, then, we have the crux text on general revelation, or that part of God's revealing Himself through the created world. The importance of this concept cannot be overestimated, for it is through the general revelation (as over against the special revelation of the Scripture and the incarnate Son) that mankind as a whole stands without excuse before the God, the Creator they have rejected.

The attributes which Paul specifically denotes are "His power" (δύναμις, *dunamis*) and "divine nature" (θειότης, *theiotes*). The attribute of power attributed to God is everywhere found in the Scriptures, so much so that ἡ δύναμις ("the power") can be used as a substitute for the Divine Name itself (Mt 26:64=Mk 14:62). The Greek term translated "divine nature" (θειότης) is only found here (cp. θεότης, *theotes* "deity" in Col 2:9) and means "divinity." It is a Hellenistic term found first in Wisdom 18:9 and denotes the divine nature and the properties attached to it. It is no wonder that Paul combines the concept of power and divine nature, for when one looks physically at the created world, one is almost always taken aback with the grandeur and innate power of the world. In fact, the idea that these invisible attributes are "clearly seen" may actually put an emphasis upon the physical act of "seeing" more than the sense of "see with the mind's eye" as this passage is often interpreted. It is as man looks at the created world, seeing that it has been made by One greater, more powerful, indeed infinitely more powerful than himself, that he comes to realize the existence of the Creator. The only way that a person can deny what is evident is to lie both to himself and to others. Thus, Paul pointedly writes "so that they are without excuse." No one will be able to stand before the bar of justice and claim that he or she was not made aware of God's existence. No one will be able to charge God with injustice for meting out the just punishment upon those who have failed to submit to God and receive His Son as Savior. All will be without just excuse because all have been impacted by the created world in such a way as to verify beyond doubt the existence of God who is Creator.

To this may be added the obvious fact that evolution, regardless of its brand or color, is an attempt to diminish or do away with this cardinal reality. To find a way that the creation is, in fact, not a creation, but a tangled mass of probability and random events, is, in the end, a bold attempt to do away with the very witness that will stand at the judgment day against those who have rejected God and His Messiah. This is subtly evident in our day by the appearance of "Darwin" bumpter stickers in protest of the so-called Christian *ichthus* (fish) symbols. Why would a symbol (whether valid or not) that purports to witness to Yeshua as Creator be countered by a "Darwin" icon? The answer is evident.

21-23 For even though they knew God, they did not honor Him as God or give thanks, but they became futile in their speculations, and their foolish heart was darkened. Professing to be wise, they became fools, and exchanged the glory of the incorruptible God for an image in the form of corruptible man and of birds and four-footed animals and crawling creatures.

Verses 21-23 sum up the response of sinful man to the self-revelation of God in the creation. Here Paul addresses the obvious question which his teaching has raised, namely, "if God has so clearly revealed Himself, why hasn't mankind responded to Him in greater numbers?" Paul shows that rather than respond to God in faith, mankind in his sinfulness has rather rebelled against God, choosing to create his own gods or even put himself forward as a god. Paul is beginning His exposition of the wickedness of mankind's heart, and his ultimate inability to respond to God on his own strength and wisdom.

We may note the characteristics of sinful man as listed by Paul here:

Mankind's Actions	Mankind's Inaction
Futile speculations	Did not honor God
Foolish heart darkened	Did not give thanks to God
Professed wisdom	
Became fools	
Exchanged God's glory	

Here we may ask the question of cause and effect. Note carefully how Paul puts mankind's inaction first, and lists his sinful activities second. The principle seems obvious: failure to honor God and give Him thanks leads to all manner of self-centeredness, which finally leads to idolatry.

idolatry. Note as well the principle that to honor God leads naturally to thanksgiving.

What is idolatry at its core? Idolatry is both the failure to give God the honor He deserves as well as giving the honor reserved only for God to another. At the heart of idolatry is the desire to control—to control one's destiny or the outcome of the events of life. All paganism is characterized by attempts to control the gods through ritual and ceremony, or through trickery. The statue which an idolator erects as a point of worship is nothing less than an attempt to bring the invisible god closer by means of the image and ritual connected to it. We ought to examine our worship and walk with God, that we not slip into religious forms of idolatry, thinking that through our practice of worship we can somehow guarantee the outcome of life's events.

Note well the progression: after failing to honor God by acknowledging Him as Creator, and thus failing likewise to thank Him for the creation, sinful man turns to "futile speculation." Being created with the need for God, mankind, after rejecting Him, creates his own god through "futile speculation." Paul no doubt refers to the various cosmogonies forumlated by the ancient pagan civilizations in order to explain the existence of mankind and the world in which he lived. Once the creatorhood of God has been abandoned, the slide into full idolatry has begun. Intellectual pride takes over, and man exists, not as the image-bearer of his Creator, but as even lower than the animal life which God created for his use. He bows to the animals over which he was to rule.

There is a sense then, as v. 21 plainly indicates, that a great part of glorifying God is to give Him thanks as the source of all things which we need and enjoy in this life. The unthankful spirit of rebellion is at home with the deception of idolatry.

24-25 Therefore God gave them over in the lusts of their hearts to impurity, so that their bodies would be dishonored among them. For they exchanged the truth of God for a lie, and worshiped and served the creature rather than the Creator, who is blessed forever. Amen.

This concept of God giving sinners over to their own desires has been bothersome for many as they read this passage. The word translated "gave them over" is παρέδωκεν, an aorist of the verb παραδίδωμι, *paradidomi* "to deliver," "hand over." The exact phrase ("God gave them over") is used two more times in this very section, in vv. 26 and 28, giving an undeniable emphasis upon this activity of God. How should we understand God's action in "giving them up?"

First, the repeated phrase would indicate that this was not a passive response of God to the sin of mankind, but an active one. God, in regard to the rebellious actions of sinful mankind, acted not in mercy and grace (in this instance) but in punishment and retribution by giving sinful mankind over to the very sin he desired, but the sin which would be his final demise.

But in understanding this as an action of God in permitting sinful mankind to go his own sinful way, we could run the risk of concluding that a sinner's approach to God is more or less in his own hands. That is to say, if these spoken of in our text (Gentiles most likely) were allowed to go their own way by the Almighty because they persisted in their sin, it might be easy to conclude that those who come to faith are those who, of their own accord, turn from their sinfulness to seek God. Yet such a conclusion will never stand in the face of Paul's dramatic statements of 3:10ff, that no one seeks after God and that everyone has turned aside and gone straying from God after one's own lusts. How then are we to understand the actions of God in the "giving them over" process?

We must see the actions of God as both just and merciful at the same time. God, in His justice, gives to the sinner what the sinner seeks: the ability to sin and to go further in sin. Yet in the justice of this (since sin carries with it its own temporal penalty) there is also mercy, for the penalty of sin which sin carries may turn the sinner from his ways and to the Lord. Cranfield writes:

> It seems more consistent with what is said elsewhere in the epistle (e.g. in chapter 11) to understand the meaning to be that God allowed them to go their own way in order that they might at last learn from their consequent wretchedness to hate the futility of a life turned away from the truth of God. We suggest then that Paul's meaning is neither that these men fell out of the hands of God . . . nor that God washed His hands of them; but rather that this delivering them up was a deliberate act of judgment and mercy on the part of the God who smites in order to heal (Is 19:22), and that throughout the time of their God-forsakenness God is still concerned with them and dealing with them. (*Romans*, 1:121)

It should also be remarked that the same verb *paradidomi* ("to deliver") is used in 8:32 in reference to the Father "delivering up" the Son to the cross. Thus, the idea of "deliver" or "give over" does not necessarily contain within it the idea of "give up forever," "wash one's hands of it," etc. The fact that God gave up the Son to the cruelties of the cross certainly did not mean He had given Him up forever. Thus, in our present text the idea of "striking" in order to "heal" may be the better interpretation.

The result of God "giving them over" is that they, unfettered, give way to their base passions, and rather than carrying God's image as mankind, descend to the level of animals, dishonoring themselves and God with each other in unnatural sexual acts. Verse 25 describes that they "exchanged the truth of God for a lie," reiterating essentially what has already been stated in v. 23.

The Greek text includes the article before "lie:" "exchange the truth of God for *the* lie." Here, no doubt, idolatry is set as opposite to the worship of God. The truth of God is the reality of His person known through His self-revelation, that He and He alone is God and there is no other, that He alone created the world and all things, and that He alone is deserving of mankind's worship. "The lie," first announced by Satan in the garden, is nothing short of idolatry, i.e., that there are more gods than One, and that mankind can create gods or even make himself into a god equal to or greater than the Creator. This is "the lie" fashioned by the father-of-lies, the Evil one.

When confronted with the stark contrasts of the One true God and the lie of idolatry, Paul, in good Hebrew fashion, pronounces a *brachah*, a blessing upon the Name of God, as approriate for anyone who has dedicated heart and soul to the singular worship of the One true God. It is almost as though Paul could not leave God's name and the mention of idolatry in the same sentence without sanctifying the Name (setting it apart) by means of a blessing. The Hebrew would be בָּרוּךְ יהוה לְעוֹלָם וָעֶד, "blessed is Adonai forever and ever" or even הַקָּדוֹשׁ בָּרוּךְ הוּא, "the Holy One, blessed be He," shortened in the Aramaic liturgy (such as the Kaddish) to בְּרִיךְ הוּא, "blessed be He."

26 For this reason God gave them over to degrading passions; for their women exchanged the natural function for that which is unnatural,

We may infer from this and the entire context that God honors proper sexual relations, and such relations honor Him. I infer this from the fact that in changing the creative order in male/female relationships, the text plainly teaches that mankind dishonors God, and that He gives them over to "degrading" passions. Thus, when proper sexual relations occur between husband and wife, this must both honor God and be honored by God. So the writer to the Messianic Jews (Hebrews) states: "Let marriage *be held* in honor among all, and let the *marriage* bed be undefiled; for fornicators and adulterers God will judge." (Heb. 13:4)

The passions to which God permits sinful and rebellious man to go are labelled as "degrading." ἀτιμία, *atimia*, is simply the Greek word for "honor" with negativing *alpha-privative*. There are passions which honor God and there are those which do not. Here, then, is an important truth, that when our passions align with God's creative purpose, they are honorable. But

32

when they do not, they are "dishonorable" or "degrading." They not only dishonor God, but they also dishonor mankind who were created in His image.

Verses 26 and 27 describe the whole nature of homosexual activity in clear and forthright terms. Note carefully how much emphasis is put upon the "natural " order of things (φυσικός, *phusikos*, "natural," "belonging to nature"). The foundation for Paul's argument is the creative order, for in the creative order Paul, like all the biblical writers, finds a Divine order which signals the Divine intention of His creation. God created the world in such a way so as to reveal Himself, and thus every part of the creation has Divine purpose. As such, to tamper with the creation, to turn it on its head, to exchange the creative order for the chaos of sinful man, is to deny the Creator and His designs.

Thus, the sin of homosexuality is first and foremost a direct sin against God, and only secondarily a sin against mankind. This is, of course, true of all sins, but it may be said particularly of the sin of homosexuality. In no other dimension of human relations has God so clearly revealed His love for us than in the male/female relationship properly held within the covenant of marriage. Here, in marriage, the many-yet-one mystery of God ("Let us make man in our image," Gen 1:18) is seen: "therefore a man shall leave his father and his mother and cleave unto his wife, and the two shall become one" Gen 2:24. It is in the physical union of man and wife that the mysterious multiplicity yet infinite unity of the Godhead is experienced by the image-bearers, for man and woman different and therefore individual, become one. And this unity is further physically portrayed in the children the union produces.

Perhaps, then, homosexuality as no other sin hits at the heart of the very revelation of God, and seeks to eradicate the image of the Creator stamped upon the beings of His pleasure. Yet in the midst of the disgust which the Apostle portrays over such sin, we may once again infer that even as homosexuality destroys the divine picture of unity, so marriage as defined by the Creator extols and magnifies the truth of the One God whose unity is perfect and eternal , who nonetheless exists in three: Father, Son, and Holy Spirit.

27 receiving in their own persons the due penalty of their error.

This may parallel v. 18 and the wrath of God being revealed (though refer to the notes on v. 18 for my own understanding of the wrath of God being revealed in the history of the cross), though it seems most likely that the punishment they receive is the sexual perversion itself, attended with all of its lack of satisfaction and its unquenchable thirst for more.

The Greek and Roman cultures were well known for their tolerance and even glorification of all sorts of sexual perversion. It was common among Semitic cultures as well, though to the Jews it was a grave abomination (Gen 19:1-28; Lev 18:22; 20:13; Deut 23:17f; 1Ki 14:24; 2Ki 23:7; Is 1:9; 3:9; Lam 4:6). Paul speaks of it elsewhere in 1Cor 6:9; 1Ti 1:10 and Peter also in 2Pt 2:6ff. Cf. also Jude 7. One should also not overlook Mt 10:14f; 11:23f.

Surely in our times the same outlook is increasingly gaining a foothold among the majority of our society, and hastens toward being fully ripe for God's wrath.

28 And just as they did not see fit to acknowledge God any longer, God gave them over to a depraved mind, to do those things which are not proper,

This clearly parallels what Paul has already written in verses 22 and 25, bringing the reader to a summary before making additional statements. The Greek term translated "acknowledge" is ἐπίγνωσις, *epignosis*, a compound word made up of the preposition ἐπι, "upon," "over," "on the basis of" and γνῶσις, *gnosis*, one of the common nouns meaning "knowledge," and related to the verb ἐπιγινώσκω, *epiginosko*, "to know." While often the term is simply synonymous with the common "to know," the additonal preposition may indicate knowledge that has been accumulated, i.e., facts upon facts. In classical Greek the term is only used of moral or ethical knowledge (i.e., knowledge learned through repeated circumstances of life). Paul may have chosen to use the word here to emphasize that those who refuse to bow before God have refused to accept multiple revelations of His being and character. They fail to accept fact upon fact that otherwise would render them believers. The literal translation of the Greek would be, "And just as they did not see fit to have God in knowledge. . . ." In other words, they refuse to accept what they know to be true.

God gave them over to a depraved mind . . . . The verse begins with the Greek word καθώς, *kathos*, "just as," "in like manner," so we must understand that God's actions in giving them over is in direct response and character to their own actions. I might say it this way: even as they refused to acknowledge God, so in like manner God refused to acknowledge them. Thus, to "give them over" (cf. vv. 24, 26) is to allow them to go in their own selfish and deluded direction—to be consumed with their false outlook.

The "depraved mind" is ἀδόκιμον νοῦν (*adokimon noun*) in the Greek. Ἀδόκιμος (*adokimos*) is used elsewhere in the Apostolic Writings in 1Cor 9:27; 2Cor 13:5, 6, 7; 2Ti 3:8; Tit 1:16; Heb 6:8 and properly means "failing the test," "disqualified," "unsatisfactory," "useless," disreputable," "reprobate." Thus, its use here is to emphasize that the mind to which these are given over is a mind entirely debilitated and corrupted so as to be a completely untrustworthy guide in moral decisions, as the concluding phrase indicates, "to do those things which are not proper." "Proper," therefore, is clearly defined by Paul as that which agrees with God and His revelation. He alone is the standard of right and wrong.

29-31 being filled with all unrighteousness, wickedness, greed, evil; full of envy, murder, strife, deceit, malice; they are gossips, slanderers, haters of God, insolent, arrogant, boastful, inventors of evil, disobedient to parents, without understanding, untrustworthy, unloving, unmerciful; and although they know the ordinance of God, that those who practice such things are worthy of death, they not only do the same, but also give hearty approval to those who practice them.

Here we have one of Paul's lists of sins, a list comprised of 21 items in the Greek. Many have suggested various groupings, but none are obvious. It may be that Paul, in typical Hebrew style, arranges the words in a chiastic arrangement, something like the following:

```
unrighteousness,
  wickedness,
    greed,
      evil;
        full of envy,
          murder,
            strife,
              deceit,
                malice;
                  they are gossips,
                  slanderers,
                  haters of God,
                insolent,
              arrogant,
            boastful,
          inventors of evil,
        disobedient to parents,
      without understanding,
    untrustworthy,
  unloving,
unmerciful;
```

If Paul had some arrangement like this in mind, then the triad "gossips, slanderers, haters of God" stands at the middle of the chiasm and thus the place of emphasis. From a Hebrew perspective, those who regularly engage in *leshon hara*, (evil speech) are those who show their contempt for God. We may note in parallel to this thought the words of James: "If anyone does not stumble in what he says, he is a perfect man, able to bridle the whole body as well" (James 3:2).

unrighteousness: opposite of Hebrew צְדָקָה, *tzedakah,* which would involve acts of mercy (thus the final word in the list is "unmerciful")

wickedness: all forms of evil

greed: selfish getting without consideration of others ("evil eye")

evil: Greek κακία, *kakia,* a general word for bad actions

envy: perhaps the primary source of all sin; ultimately, the desire to be God

murder: the physical side of envy; taking a life

strife: the opposite of שָׁלוֹם, *shalom,* peace. One who causes division among people

deceit: lying, appearing to be other than one truly is

malice: κακοηθείας, which means "spite" or ill-feelings against another individual

gossips: a person who destroys another person with לָשׁוֹן הָרָע *leshon hara'* evil speech

slanderers: literally to speak evil. This may go beyond gossip to even fabricating evil tales about another person in order to destroy them.

insolent: only here and in 1Ti 1:13. Treating someone else as though they were well beneath oneself; attempting to take the place of God.

arrogant: self-centered, attempting to impress others by status in life, etc.

boastful: arrogance particularly seen in one's speech

inventors of evil: mankind has the unique ability to take the God-given gift of creativity and turn it to find new ways to sin, particularly in hurting one's fellowman.

disobedient to parents: the breakdown of authority in the home is the first step to denying the authority of God.

without understanding: blinded to the truth; cp. the concept of "fool" in Proverbs

untrustworthy: someone who deals treacherously (cf. Lxx Jer 3:7, 8, 10, 11). The Greek term (ἀσύνθετος, *asunthetos,* literally means "covenant breaker").

unloving: the Greek word is ἀστόργη, *astorge,* alpha-privative with στόργη, *storge,* which means the love shown particularly between family members, thus KJV "without natural affection." Some point to the hideous practice in the Greco-Roman world of drowning unwanted babies and other forms of infanticide.

unmerciful: without the ability to show mercy, i.e., to grant kindness to someone who might otherwise deserve punishment.

If the chiastic arrangement was in Paul's mind as I have suggested, then we have a reason for his imbedding the triad in the heart of the chiasm, summed by "haters of God." In other words, if such an arrangement were in the mind of the Apostle, then he wanted us to know that hatred for God, displayed most aggregiously by slander and gossip against one's fellowman, is the fountainhead of all these sordid evils, or the final expression of them. Mankind's inability to bow before God and accept His rule issues in the growth of sin and the eventual demise of mankind's ability to portray the image of God in which he was created.

32 and although they know the ordinance of God, that those who practice such things are worthy of death, they not only do the same, but also give hearty approval to those who practice them.

As far as Paul is concerned, the "ordinance of God" which calls for capital punishment for those who fall to the depths of murder and sexual perversion, revealed specifically in the Torah, is likewise embedded in the creative order. Those who rebel against God in these ways know that the final punishment of such rebellion is their ultimate demise.

Thus, since Paul has already shown that the revelation of God is to be found in the creation itself, and even more surely in created man himself, those who rebel against God and make unrighteousness their lifestyle are fully aware that their actions will draw the death penalty. But what is fascinating about this verse is that those who give "hearty agreement" to such sinful activity are considered by Paul as perhaps more guilty even than those who commit the acts. Cranfield writes:

> But there is also the fact that those who condone and applaud the vicious actions of others are actually making a deliberate contribtuion to the setting up of a public opinion favorable to vice, and so to the corruption of an indefinite number of other people. So, for example, to excuse or gloss over the use of discrimination and oppression, while not being involved in them directly, is to help to cloak monstrous evil with an appearance of respectability and so to contribute most effectively to its firmer entrenchment. (*Romans*, 1.135)

Romans 2
Commentary

---

1 Therefore you have no excuse, everyone of you who passes judgment, for in that which you judge another, you condemn yourself; for you who judge practice the same things.

The opening word of the second chapter, "Therefore," has caused some difficulty in understanding how what Paul is now saying connects to what he has already said in chapter one. But to answer this question we must first ask ourselves to whom Paul addresses his remarks in the present text: to Gentiles who were a "cut above" in their moral outlook, or to Jews, or to a mixed group?

While each of these options have been held by scholars, I would think that several factors weight the case toward Paul addressing Jews beginning in 2:1. Here are the reasons:

1) the language of v. 4 fits the history of Israel but does not fit God's activity toward the nations. While it is true that He does show mercy to the Gentiles (such as at Ninevah), the strong language of mercy and patience in view of Israel's often rebellion seems to underly Paul's words here.

2) Since it seems clear that Paul has two groups in mind in 1:18-3:20, i.e., Jews and Gentiles, it seems most likely that he refers to Jews when he characterizes a group as morally superior, as he does in 2:1ff.

3) It is clear that he addresses the Jew at v. 17, but it does not seem that he begins to address someone different at this point than he has from the beginning of the chapter. Therefore, one would conclude that he addresses Jews from the beginning of the chapter.

4) It was characteristic, at least by the report of our extant literature, of some (perhaps a majority of) Pharisees that they had an attitude of superiority toward the Gentiles, so that the attitudes described in the opening verses of our chapter best describe the Jew rather than the Gentile.

In light of these things, I would think it best to interpret Paul's words in 2:1ff as addressed primarily to the Jewish congregant in the synagogue at Rome.

That being the case, how is one to understand the opening "Therefore?" How do the descriptions of wanton sin among the Gentiles have any connection to the Jew, so that Paul may begin with "therefore," as though he has already proven the Jew to be guilty as well?

Feeling these difficulties some have suggested amending the Greek διό, *dio*, "therefore," to δίς, *dis*, "twice," in the sense that "you are doubly guilty . . . ." Others have considered taking the entire verse as a later addition, and still others have suggested that the Greek διό looks forward in this instance rather than backward.

We may note, however, that the sins ennumerated in 1:18-32, while characteristic of the pagan Gentile in particular, describe in broad strokes the sin of idolatry, a sin with which Israel is constantly being charged by the Prophets. The sinful acts of the Gentiles deserve the death penalty, proving their utter lawlessness (1:32), and in general lawlessness may be described as failure to love God and to love one's neighbor (the two halves of the Ten Words). If one judges his brother, he has failed to love him as he ought, and in so doing has failed to love God as well, and has, just like the Gentile, broken the Torah and therefore stands guilty before God. This, in fact, is the conclusion of Paul in vv. 20-22 where the bottom line for the Jew he addresses is that he has broken the Torah and stands guilty before God. Idolatry is idolatry, whether it manifests itself in the gross immorality of the pagan ways, or in the sophisticated self-centeredness of "religion." Both manifestations are idolatry, and God hates them equally. Thus, proving that the Gentiles are guilty of idolatry is to prove the Jew apart from faith in Yeshua equally guilty of the same sin, the sin of lawlessness—of breaking God's righteous standard.

every man of you who passes judgment, for in that you judge another, you condemn yourself; for you who judge practice the same things – Here is Paul's argument in a nutshell. If a person condemns the actions of another while engaging in those selfsame actions, he equally condemns himself. Of course, no one in their right mind (spiritually speaking) would condemn someone for doing the same thing he or she was doing. We must presume, therefore, that the one doing the judging is blinded to the fact that he is sinning in the same way. Arrogance is blind by its very nature. Note the prayer in the Morning Daily Service:

> May it be your will, Adonai, my God and God of my fathers, to save me today and every day from arrogant men and from arrogance; from an evil man, from an evil companion, from an evil neighbor; from an evil mishap and from the destructive Satan; from a difficult judgment and a difficult opponent, whether he is a fellow Jew [בֶּן בְּרִית] or not a fellow Jew [לֹא בֶּן בְּרִית]. (*Metzudah Complete Siddur*, p. 20)

It is not as though Paul is here teaching that the judgmental Jew actually practices the debased sexual sins just previously described, but that he engages in a kind of idolatry, for in judging as he does he puts himself in the place of God, and in so doing commits idolatry.

But how should we define "judging" here? Certainly it is right to discern what is righteous and what is not! Are we to understand Paul as teaching that we should simply accept the sins of others when we see them? The obvious answer is that what Paul condemns here is hypocrisy in the sense of judging others when engaged in the same sin oneself. This accords with the words of Yeshua (Matt 7:3-5) that one ought to first remove the log from his own eye before attempting to take out the speck from someone else's eye. The issue of judging what is right and wrong is not before us here. It is rather the sin of hypocrisy that Paul addresses.

2 And we know that the judgment of God rightly falls upon those who practice such things.

Paul often introduces a statement with "we know" (οἴδαμεν, *oidamen*) when he is sure his readers will agree with him (cf. 3:19; 7;14; 8:22, 28; 1 Ti 1:8). Here, then, he affirms that God judges "according to truth" (κατὰ ἀλήθειαν, *kata aletheian*), i.e., fairly or righteously, those who commit sin. God is the only One able to judge perfectly, for He judges from the position of His infinite holiness. In His judgment He is never self-condemned, for He never has committed the sins He judges. (As an aside, it is this, among other factors, which render human judges fallible.)

Thus, Paul dispels any notion of pluralism where everyone is right in some measure and where judgment is, therefore, inappropriate.

3 And do you suppose this, O man, when you pass judgment upon those who practice such things and do the same yourself, that you will escape the judgment of God?

This may seem an obvious conclusion to us in our times, but it was not so obvious to at least some Jews in the time of Paul. Wisdom 15:1-2 records:

> But you, our God, are kind and true and patient, a merciful ruler of all that is. Even if we sin, we are yours, since we acknowledge your power. But because we know that we are accounted yours we shall not sin.

Wisdom was a well read work in the 1st Century CE, and this may capture the tone of at least some of the Judaisms. The idea that "every Jew has a place in the world to come" (b.*Sanhedrin* 105a, cf. m.*Sanhedrin* 10:1) may well have been accepted dogma among the Jewish communities of the 1st Century. If so, the viewpoint was that a person born a Jew, apart from being "cut off from his people" (punishment for a short list of gross sins), had a secure place in the world based not upon his personal piety, but upon his being part of the covenant nation. Thus, the scenario where one is able to "look" religious but in reality have nothing but self-centeredness in life, may have been encouraged or at least fostered by the idea that one's birthright secured the future.

Clearly the nation at the time of Jeremiah appears to have felt this way, for in the face of Jeremiah's warnings and prophecies, they listened to those who preached "peace, peace" when Jeremiah knew there was no peace (cf. Jer 14:13; 23:17) but the coming wrath of God. Why did they feel that there was peace? Because they believed that the covenant promises of God, which He had made to Israel, precluded any form of punishment. They were unaccountable for their sins because they felt they had been promised an unconditional blessing. What they failed to understand was simply that not all the descendants of Jacob were actually Israel (Rom 9:6). That the offspring of Abraham involved not only physical lineage, but also participation in the faith which he had, i.e., faith in God and His coming Messiah, a faith that is demonstrated in faithfulness to God and His righteous ways.

4 Or do you think lightly of the riches of His kindness and forbearance and patience, not knowing that the kindness of God leads you to repentance?

Paul, addressing the Jewish people at this point, asks them to consider the history of Israel and God's evident patience with them throughout their national existence. He asks them to consider whether or not they are taking for granted ("think lightly of"[28]) God's long suffering, for by the fact that the Jewish people rejected Yeshua as the Messiah, they test, as it were, the very patience of God. Thus, in this verse Paul does not describe yet another group of the Jewish community, but gives a further description of those described in v. 3, those characterized as passing judgment.

God's kindness, forbearance, and patience are abundant, for the word "riches" (πλοῦτος, *ploutos*) most likely applies to all three of the following terms. "Kindness" (χρηστότητος, *chrestotetos*) has its root in the word "goodness" (χρηστός, *chrestos*, used in the next phrase) which means "worthy," "suitable," "useful."

"Forbearance" (ἀνοχή, *anoche*) is used here and in 3:26 and means a "holding back," "cessation," "pause," being used in the classical Greek of a "halt" in a building project. Surely the wrath of God is "held back" for we all deserve to receive His righteous judgments. It is one thing to live as though one does not deserve God's judgment, and quite another to consider that judgment is actually being "held back." The former produces a smug arrogance, while the latter realization brings the soul to a constant state of thankfulness. Surely Israel, in the history of the nation, has more often than not taken the viewpoint that she is not deserving of God's punishments.

"Patience" (μακροθυμία, *makrothumia*) has the sense of "endurance," "steadfastness" and is linked to faith in Heb. 6:12. The piling up of synonyms and near-synonyms is reminiscent of the language of prayer in the Siddur.

not knowing that the kindness (grace) of God leads you to repentance – This ignorance is willful and therefore brings culpability. Israel was given example after example and revelation after revelation of the goodness of God that leads to repentance. Ignorance, in this case, then, is the fruit of a rebellious heart which refuses to acknowledge that it is God, not oneself, who is the author of repentance.

The term "repentance" (μετάνοια, *metanoia*) occurs only here and in 2Cor 7:9, 10; 2Ti 2:25 in the Pauline letters. The verb form (μετανοεῖν, *metanoein*) is found only in 2Cor 12:21. Some have wondered why Paul used such a strategic term so few times, and it may well be that the term itself had taken on such a legal definition among the rabbinic *halachah* of the day that he strove to avoid using it lest it be misunderstood. Additionally, it seems clear that for Paul repentance is an assumed part of "faith," for apart from repentance there is no real demonstration of faith in the first place.

The Hebrew term for "repentance" is the verb שׁוּב, *shuv* or the noun derived from it (תְּשׁוּבָה, *teshuvah*, note שׁוּבָה, *shuvah*, a *hapaxlegomenon* in Is 30:15). Repentance then, in its basic sense, is returning or coming back after straying away, coming back where one belongs. In the sense that we all, like sheep, have gone astray (Is 53:6), there is need for every person to repent, i.e., to return to his or her Creator. Since the very concept of "repentance" is rooted in the Hebrew verb שׁוּב, *shuv,* "to (re)turn," it is basic to the definition of repentance that it includes (1) turning from something, and (2) turning toward something. In the Scriptures this is described as turning away from evil and turning towards good. Obviously, since God is good and the source of all good, turning from evil to good is to turn to God and away from evil.

Interestingly, the term שׁוּב, "to return," is found often in covenant contexts describing the return of the nation of Israel after she has strayed from keeping the covenant. Her return to the covenant involved contrition, confession, and renewal of covenant vows. From a covenant perspective, "false repentance" is that condition in which one returns in taking up the form of the covenant, but not the heart of it. Thus, true repentance requires not only circumcision of the flesh but also of the heart (cf. Deut 10:16; 30:6; Jer 4:4).

The two sides of repentance are clearly indicated in the Scriptures, i.e., the sovereign act of God whereby He grants repentance (2Ti 2:25), and the responsibility of man to forsake his wicked way and turn to God in repentance (e.g., Ezek 18:32). This seeming antinomy is never considered such in the Scriptures, for we do not see the writers engaging in an attempt to resolve the tension. Yet the Bible is clear that apart from God's intervention, man will never seek to turn from his wicked ways, i.e., he will never repent. Paul has come to this conclusion in 3:10ff and teaches it without exception.

5 But because of your stubbornness and unrepentant heart you are storing up wrath for yourself in the day of wrath and revelation of the righteous judgment of God,

"Stubbornness" (σκληρότης, *sklerotes*) has the base meaning "hard," thus "hard-headed." This word is used in the Lxx of Israel, cf. Deut 9:27, "Remember Thy servants, Abraham, Isaac, and Jacob; do not look at the stubbornness of this people or at their wickedness or their sin."

The Greek σκληρότης translates Hebrew קָשֶׁה, *kasheh*, "hard," "difficult." Note the use of the same Greek term (verbal form) in Rom 9:18, "So then He has mercy on whom He desires, and He hardens (σκληρύνει, *sklerunei*) whom He desires."

"unrepentant heart" (ἀμετανόητον καρδίαν, *ametanoeton kardian*) characterizes the nation in her history as well. Turning to God when in trouble, she regularly turned away from Him once He had rescued her. Considered Hebraically, the heart is the seat of moral decision, the place where one makes the volitional choice between right and wrong. Unrepentant, then, as a description of the heart, means a heart unwilling to turn from its immoral decisions, and following after unrighteousness. While the Lxx does not use the exact Greek word (ἀμετανόητος), the description of Israel as having a "stubborn" or "rebellious" heart is found, cf. Jer. 5:23, "But this people has a stubborn and rebellious heart; They have turned aside and departed."

"Storing up" (θησαυρίζειν, *thesaurizein*) is usually used of storing up what is good and profitable, cf. Matt 6:20. Here, however, those who have a stubborn and rebellious heart are storing up that which is in their own heart. This is ironic, much like the wording of Prov 1:18, "But they lie in wait for their own blood; They ambush their own lives. "

Most have read this verse as indicating that the unrepentant person is storing up judgment against himself, a judgment which will be unleashed in the future. Some, on the other hand, noting the present tense of the verb "storing up" suggest that the action of storing up is being done during the present time, a time which is designated as "a day of wrath and revelation of righteousness of God." That is to say, like the present tense of the verb "being revealed" in 1:18, which describes the wrath of God against sinners, so Israel (as this interpretation goes), is storing up wrath now, in the time when God is revealing His wrath and thus the revelation of His righteousness. But in light of the following verses (6-10), it seems more natural to understand Paul's words here to mean that the individual who is stubbornly rebelling against God (in refusing to accept His Messiah, Yeshua), is storing up for himself wrath in the future day of God's judgment. In an attempt to be pious, the unbelieving Jew is ambushing himself.

We should thus understand the phrase "day of wrath" as indicative of the final day of judgment (cf. Prov 11:14; Zeph 1:15), a day in which the righteousness of God will be manifest (revealed) through His divine judgment.

6 who will render to every man according to his deeds:

At first glance this seems to be in conflict with the clear teaching of Paul elsewhere that God renders to His own, not according to their deeds, but on the basis of His forgiveness and grace. Yet that God will judge men according to their deeds is everywhere affirmed in Scripture: Ps 62:12 [Lxx 61:13]; Prov 24:12; Ecc 12:14; Is 3:10f; Jer 17:10; Hos 12:2; Matt 7:21; 16:27; 25:31-46; Jn 5:28f; 2Cor 5:10; 11:15b; Gal 6:7-9; Eph 6:8; Col 3:24f; 2Ti 4:14; 1Pt 1:17; Rev 2:23; 20:12f; 22:12.

What seems at odds is the simple fact that elsewhere Paul teaches clearly that God's gift of eternal life, i.e., being spared eternal judgment, is based, not upon one's works, but upon God's grace freely given. The two are reconciled, however, when one realizes that from the Bible's perspective, the renewed soul will inevitably bring forth good works. Good works can never bring right standing with God, but right standing with God (a matter of His pure and sovereign grace) always produces good works, cf. Eph 2:8-10. Thus, those who are redeemed by the gracious act of God are also recreated (Col 3:10) with a heart to do righteousness. Thus, God will render to the believer according to deeds. The believer's life has been transformed from a life of unrighteouness to one of righteousness.

7 to those who by perseverance in doing good seek for glory and honor and immortality, eternal life;

A literal translation of this sentence would be: "to those on the one hand according to perseverance in a good work glory and honor and immortality they are seeking life eternal." (I've left out all punctuation in order not to prejudice the translation). Note several things: first, the Greek sets up a "prodosis/apodosis" construction, where the opening "on the the one hand" will automatically look for a corresponding "on the other hand," which is to be found in v. 8. Secondly, the literal translation reveals the presence of the Greek κατά, "according to" which the English translation cannot render. The point is clear: doing good works is "according to perseverance," i.e., only as one perseveres in doing good works does one qualify for the reward, eternal life. Paul has much to say about perseverance, cf. 5:3, 4; 8:25; 15:4, 5. He makes it amply clear that apart from faith in Yeshua, and the subsequent indwelling of the Spirit, it would be impossible to persevere in doing good. Indeed, perseverance is the utlimate mark of possessing true, saving faith.

Thirdly, the Greek has the singular, "good work," which the translations all take as a characteristic singular, i.e., of the category of good works. But it is possible that the singular is to be understood not as good works in general, but as the specific "good work" of persevering under trial, which is itself a proving of genuine faith.

How should the phrase "good work" be defined? Some have suggested that it is faith, but Paul makes it clear in 4:4-5 that faith cannot be considered a "work." Others have suggested that it means generally living a "good" life, i.e., abiding by the Torah of God in all one does. Most, however, understand "good work" to refer to the inevitable fruit of faith and the sure guarantee of faith. We might consider "good work" to simply be a generalization of the "fruit of the Spirit."

This outworking of faith is generally characterized by Paul as "seeking after glory, honor, and immortality." All three of these terms may be identified as common terms in a 1st Century Jewish perspective of the resurrection and subsequent life in the world to come. In v. 10 Paul lists "glory, honor, and peace," and 1Pt 1:7 speaks of the "glory and honor in the revelation of Yeshua HaMashiach." We may say then that the reward promised those who persevere in good works is a place in the world to come.

While this may sound strange to the evangelical ear of our times, it was not strange to the Apostle, for he did not see faith as something which could exist apart from good works. On the contrary, he saw faith as the inevitable fountainhead of good works. Thus, those who were able to persevere in good works were those shown to possess true saving faith. To these and to these alone are given eternal life, i.e., a place in the world to come.

8 but to those who are selfishly ambitious and do not obey the truth, but obey unrighteousness, wrath and indignation.

In contrast to those who (v. 7) do good works, these are they who are "selfishly ambitious" (ἐξ ἐριθείας, *ex eritheias*), literally disobey "out of selfish ambition . . . ." Yet the exact meaning of the Greek ἐριθείας is disputed. The old RSV renders it "faction" — "unto them that are factious," based upon the use of the word in Classical Greek. But a related word ἔριθος, *erithos*, means "hireling," i.e., someone who does not care for the sheep but cares rather about himself. Thus, the sense of "selfish" enters into the meaning of the word, and may show how its sense of "factious" came to be as well—the selfish person is often a source of division, for he is unable to submit to the leadership of others, desiring only to have his own deeds recognized.

Two more characteristics are given of these who are self-centered: they "disobey the truth" and "obey unrighteousness." This answers directly to the statement of chapter one that those who oppose God "suppress the truth in unrighteousness." But Paul's words here are even more direct: "they obey unrighteousness." Instead of taking God and His standards as their rule for life, they seek that which is contrary to God, setting it forward as the "standard" of their "righteousness."

The rewards of obeying unrighteousness and disobeying the truth are "wrath and indignation" (ὀργὴ, *orge* και θυμός, *thumos*, cf. Col 3:8), a pair of words which no doubt describes the judgment of God against unrighteousness, ultimately in the final day or eschaton.

9-10 There will be tribulation and distress for every soul of man who does evil, of the Jew first and also of the Greek, but glory and honor and peace to every man who does good, to the Jew first and also to the Greek.

The rewards listed by Paul are now given in a chiastic arrangement, the first and last corresponding, and so forth. This chiastic arrangement is very common in ancient literature in general, and especially in biblical texts. Our present text may be graphically viewed in this way:

those who do good seeking glory, honor, immortality and receive eternal life	those who selfishly do not obey the truth but obey unrighteousness and receive wrath and indignation

there will be

tribulation and distress for every soul of man who does evil, to the Jew first and also to the Greek	glory and honor and peace to every man who does good, to the Jew first and also to the Greek

What is the emphasis upon "to the Jew first and also to the Greek?" The obvious answer is the biblical principle of the responsibility that accompanies revelation. God first revealed Himself and His salvation to Israel, so she stands first in His display of mercy and thus also first in punishment for rejecting it. Here Paul clearly teaches against what must have been the established teaching in some circles of his day, that every Jew, regardless of his life before God, has a place in the world to come. Paul, in concert with the Torah and Prophets, makes it crystal clear that only those whose lives evidence the righteousness of God will have a place in the world to come. Of course, he will go to great lengths in the coming chapters to show that only those who have right standing before God through faith in His Son have the ability to live a truly righteous life. In the final analysis, then, the whole issue revolves around or has its focus in Yeshua and one's relationship with Him.

The use of the word "soul" (ψυχή, *psuche*) answers to the Hebrew נֶפֶשׁ, *nephesh*, used as a synonym for אֲנָשִׁים, *'anashim*, "people" (cf. Num 31:35, 40, 46 and many places). Some cannot see the merciful God punishing people physically for all eternity and thus attempt to use Paul's use of "soul" here to support their view that the body ceases to exist in eternity. This overlooks the obvious Hebraic use of the word "soul." Moreover, Yeshua's comments about the "gnashing of teeth" (Matt 25:30) indicates a physical torment at the least, and the resurrection of the unbelieving dead in John's Revelation (Rev 20:11f), only that they might be punished, indicates a physical punishment as well.

11 For there is no partiality with God.

Here we have a second and perhaps most profound reason why there is an emphasis upon "to the Jew first and also to the Greek"—to show that though God, by His sovereign choice gave His glorious revelation to the Jewish nation first, He nonetheless gives that nation no "special treatment" when it comes to the requirement of righteousness. The reason for this is obvious: the righteousness which He requires for fellowship and communion with Him is not the product of man's efforts, but the free gift of His mercy. The Jew no less than the Gentile must admit his entire inability to obtain this righteousness on his own efforts and humbly accept the free gift of God's grace in the person of His Messiah, Yeshua. Attempting to find right standing before God on any other grounds will end in condemnation. On this whole theme, cp. Gal 2:6; Eph 6:9; Col 3:25, and Acts 10:34.

The term used for "partiality" (προσωπολημψία, *prosopolemspia*) derives its formation from the Tanach. The Greek word is made up of two Greek words, πρόσωπον, *prosopon,* "face" and λαμβάνειν, *lambanein,* "to take or lift," thus "to lift up the face." This is an exact representation of the Hebrew נָשָׂא פָּנִים, *nasa' panim,* as in Gen 32:21; Lev 19:15; Deut 10:17; 28:50; 2Sa 2:22; 2Ki 5:1; Is 3:3; 9:14; Mal 2:9; Jb 22:8; 32:21. This expression can have both positive and negative connotations in the Tanach: positive = "show consideration for," negative = "show partiality toward." The Lxx sometimes used the two Greek words πρόσωπον λαμβάνειν, *prosopon lambanein,* "to lift the face," to translate the Hebrew idiom, and it is doubtless from this that the Apostolic writings used the present compound word. However, in the Apostolic writings the word is always used negatively.

If we are to take the word at its root sense, then, we could say "God does not lift up His face toward a person based upon a prejudice or esteeming one better than the other." But then on what basis does God "lift His face" toward us (cf. Num 6:25, 26, the Aaronic Benediction)? God's favor upon any sinner is due entirely to the fact that He sees that sinner in His Son, Yeshua. Thus, one of Paul's favorite phrases, ἐν Χριστῷ, *en Christo,* "in Messiah," becomes the locus of blessing, for apart from Yeshua there is no pleasure which the Father sees. But when He sees Yeshua in us, or better, we in Yeshua, then there is heard "this is the son of My love—I am fully pleased with Him." The impartiality comes from the fact that being in Yeshua (as Paul puts it) or Yeshua in us is no work of our own—we've all come by this through God's grace and mercy.

12 For all who have sinned without the Torah will also perish without the Torah; and all who have sinned under the Torah will be judged by the Torah;

This is the first direct reference to the Torah in our epistle, and it seems beyond dispute that what Paul refers to here is the Mosaic revelation. Some have tried to argue that when the Greek word νόμος, *nomos,* "law" stands in the text without the article ("the"), it refers not to the Mosaic Torah directly but to the "principle of law."[29] But even a short testing of this thesis simply proves it wrong. In the following table I have listed the use of νόμος where it occurs in Romans, noting whether it is with or without the article. While there are obvious cases where the context would indicate to us that Paul is referring to the "principle of law," there are many times when the word "law" (Torah) without the article refers to the Mosaic Torah. The final criteria in determining the meaning must, of course, be the context.

ὁ νόμος (νόμος with the article)	νόμος (νόμος without the article)
2:14, 15, 18, 20, 23, 26, 27	2:12, 13, 14, 17, 23, 25, 27
3:19, 21	3:20, 21, 27, 28, 31
4:15, 16	4:13, 14, 15
7:1, 2, 3, 4, 5, 6, 7, 14, 16, 21, 22, 23	5:13, 20
8:2, 3, 4	6:14, 15
10:5	7:1, 2, 7, 8, 9, 12, 23, 25
	8:2, 7
	9:31
	10:4
	13:8, 10

One example will show that Paul's use of the article with νόμος does not differentiate its meaning. In 4:16, the article appears with νόμος, but in 4:13, 14, 15 νόμος is anarthrous (in 4:15 it is found once with and once without the article). Yet in the context, in each case Paul is surely speaking of the Torah. Moreover, the English translations (such as the NASB) that try to clarify the meaning by either capitalizing the word "Law" or leaving it lowercase seem to be less than consistent. In the final analysis, the use of the article with νόμος seems to have no clear affect on its meaning.

It appears that Paul is continuing his argument, begun in v. 6 by the quote from Ps. 62, that God deals with people fairly, justly, rendering to each according to his deeds. This naturally opens the discussion to the question of the position of those who have not known of God, i.e., have not received the revelation of Torah. Will they be condemned? Paul has already shown that the revelation of God is found in a broader sphere than the Torah, and that the very creation will render all without excuse before the Judge of all. Thus, those who have received the Torah, yet have rejected its message and call for faith, will be judged accordingly. Those who, on the other hand, have never received the Torah, will perish or be condemned by the very revelation which they did receive., i.e., the revelation of God via creation.

13 for not the hearers of the Torah are just before God, but the doers of the Torah will be justified.

Here then is the conclusion and the main point of this entire paragraph. "Hearing" שָׁמַע (shema) or ἀκούειν (akouein), from a Semitic viewpoint, may often mean much more than merely hearing in the phyiscal sense. Often, these terms have the fuller sense of "hear with intent to obey" (Gen 3:17; Ex 15:26; Deut 4:30; 6:4f; Josh 1:18; Is 1:19; Jer 11:3; 12:17; Mic 5:15[14]). In this case, however, the "hearing" is put in contrast to "doing," and thus means a deficient "hearing," a "hearing" which does not issue in "doing" (cf. Jms 2:22-25). Paul is constrasting the mere reception of the Torah with a full acceptance of it.

Such a deficient hearing has no salvific value. Merely hearing the Torah saves no one. The phrase "just before God" (δίκαιοι παρὰ τῷ θεῷ, "dikaioi para to theo) means "right standing before God," i.e., to actually be considered "not guilty" in God's court of Law, as the final clause makes clear by the use of δικαιωθήσονται, dikaiothesontai, "to be declared just."

This axiom, that only those who do the Torah will be justified in God's eyes, and the contrast of mere "hearing"with the essential aspect of "doing," is not a Pauline invention, or new revelation. Interestingly, in *Avot* 1.17, Rabban Simeon, the son of Gamaliel I (Paul's teacher) is quoted as saying, "All my days I grew up among the wise and have found nothing better for one than silence; not study is the chief thing but action and he who multiplies words brings on sin." That such a saying would be attached to a Sage of this stature indicates that there was a problem with merely "hearing" and not "doing" among the 1st Century Judaisms. Surely the Oral Torah, at times, afforded the opportunity to appear as though one was "doing" when in fact he was not. This is reflected in the arrogant (though I would expect sincere) response of the Rich Young Ruler when he answered Yeshua regarding the Torah, "Master, all these things have I observed from my youth" (Mk 10:20). Cranfield calls this man's perspective "an illusion supported by a constant tampering with the Torah. " He continues:

> Such a tampering with the Law of God the Jewish oral law largely was—Jesus bluntly called it 'the tradition of men' [Mk 7:8]; for, instead of recognizing in the demands of the Law the absolute demand of God, by which He claims us wholly for Himself and for our neighbor, and with which men cannot live on terms of merit but only on terms of divine forgiveness, it sought to turn them into something manageable and achievable.[30]

But though Paul agrees with at least some of the Rabbinic thought of his time (and of his teacher), he imbues it with a Messianic reality, for certainly he would never teach that someone could keep the Torah in such a way as to earn right standing before God. (In reality, neither did the rabbis.) Rather, Paul is speaking of obedience which flows out of faith, which though weak and imperfect and therefore without deserving of God's favor, is, as the expression of humble trust in God, well-pleasing in His sight.

Those who may interpret this verse as stating merely a hypothetical case are hard pressed to see how it fits in the overall structure of Paul's argument here. They would understand it's meaning to be that theoretically, or hypothetically, if someone could keep the Torah perfectly, that person would have right standing before God. But that no one can keep the Torah perfectly proves Paul's point, namely, that salvation is by faith alone apart from works.

But that is not Paul's point here. Paul's point is that God is not a respecter of persons, because He renders to every person according to his deeds, whether Jew or Gentile. The fact that He gave the Torah to Israel and did not give it to the nations (initially) does not mean that God is a respecter of persons either, because He judges actions, not mere "hearing," and as Paul will go on to show, some Gentiles do instinctively the very things the Torah requires even though they have not grown up learning the Torah. In the end, to take the point of view that our verse is speaking hypothetically as describing a theological impossibility cannot be sustained in terms of the overarching argument of Paul in this passage.

14-15   For when Gentiles who do not have the Torah do instinctively the things of the Torah, these, not having the Torah, are a Torah to themselves, in that they show the work of the Torah written in their hearts, their conscience bearing witness, and their thoughts alternately accusing or else defending them,

Our first task in this verse is to understand who Paul identifies here as "Gentiles … who do the things of the Torah." Several possibilities have been suggested:

1) some pagans, on the basis of natural moral law, fulfill God's Torah demands and so merit His favor.
2) understood hypothetically, i.e., if Gentiles could keep the Torah out of mere conscience sake, they would be regarded as righteous.
3) that some pagans have a hidden faith, known only to God, and in their paganism still manifest some regard for the Torah of God as far as they are able.
4) that "Gentile" here refers to Gentile believers (cp. the use of ἔθνος, *ethnos* in 11:13 and 15:9) who, though they have not been schooled in the Torah throughout their generations, still show a humble heart of willingness to obey God and to live according to His Torah, which in itself is an expression of their faith.

Of these possibilities, surely numbers 1 and 2 should be rejected for their inconsistency with Paul's teaching, indeed, with the teaching of the Scriptures in general. Number 3 is also to be rejected, for Paul's whole point is that there are not various ways of salvation for various groups of people, but that there is one way, a way of faith in Messiah, and all must come through this path to obtain salvation. Since Paul is here describing those who have right standing before God ("just before God," v. 13), it seems clear that these Gentiles who are not mere hearers but actually doers are therefore among the group that stand as just before God. As such, they are Gentiles who have faith in Yeshua.

There is, now, a second important consideration for us in this verse. This is whether to take the Greek φύσει, *phusei*, "naturally," with the clause that precedes it, or with that which follows. The two options would be:

[with what precedes]
> For when the Gentiles who do not have the Torah naturally, do the things of
> the Torah (meaning that even though the Gentiles do not have the Torah as
> part of their natural upbringing and culture, yet having come to faith in Ye-

shua they strive to do the Torah)

[with that which follows]
> For when the Gentiles who do not have the Torah, do naturally the things of
> the Torah (meaning that the Gentiles do the Torah naturally, i.e., through the
> possession of natural, moral Law, or as an outflow of their conscience)

If we look at how Paul has used the term φύσει (*phusei*) elsewhere, it appears very probable that we should translate the verse with "naturally" describing the manner in which the Gentiles have the Torah, not the manner in which they do the Torah. Note these other places where Paul uses the term φύσιε ("natural," naturally"):

> Rom 2:27 And will not he who is physically (out of nature = φυσει) uncircumcised, if
> he keeps the Torah, will he not judge you who though having the letter *of the Torah* and
> circumcision are a transgressor of the Torah?

> Gal 2:15 We *are* Jews by nature, and not sinners from among the Gentiles;

> Eph 2:3 Among them we too all formerly lived in the lusts of our flesh, indulging the
> desires of the flesh and of the mind, and were by nature children of wrath, even as the
> rest.

In each of these cases, though one cannot be dogmatic, it appears that Paul uses the term φύσει to designate one's ethnic or familial connections. It certainly is a valid option in our verse, and I think helps make sense of an otherwise very difficult passage. I would thus paraphrase the verse in this way:

> "For the Gentile believers, though they do not have the heritage of the Torah and were not
> taught to live life through the perspective of the Torah—these believers, when they do the
> things of the Torah even though it was not their natural possession or part of their cultural
> upbringing, show that they have acquired the Torah as their very own possession, and
> thus demonstrate their genuine faith."

Thus, verse 15 continues this train of thought: these Gentile believers prove their genuine faith because they "show the work of the Torah written on their hearts," the very goal of the New Covenant (Jer 31:31f). Here is not the mere letter of the Torah but the letter combined with the Spirit (cf. Rom 2:27, 29; 7:6; 2Cor 3:1ff), for the Spirit is the only One who can write the Torah upon the heart.

I therefore take exception with the popular way of interpreting this verse, as though the "law written upon the heart" expresses a natural morality with which mankind was created. I find no compelling reason to interpret "conscience" as connected with or equivalent to "the Torah written upon the heart." This phrase, straight out of the New Covenant which Jeremiah announced, was too well known and too theologically charged to be otherwise intepreted.

"Conscience" (συνείδησις, *suneidesis*) is literally "knowledge shared with oneself," i.e., either the knowledge of doing something wrong (a "guilty conscience") or of doing something right (a "clear conscience"). Now this is not the conscience of an unbeliever, but of a believer, for an unbeliever is not pricked in conscience as regards righteousness, but only as regards being found guilty. Yet here we have Gentiles who, with the Torah written on their hearts, actually do the things of the Torah.

How are we to understand the idea of the conscience "bearing witness" (συμμαρτυρούσης, *summarturoues*)? To whom does it bear witness? Some attempt to link it to verse 16 where the bearing witness is in the final day of judgment, but this hardly seems likely since Paul is describing current events as he understood them within the Roman synagaogue. Furthermore, the the role of the conscience in bearing witness is coupled with the "thoughts which alternately accuse or defend." It seems to me that what Paul is describing here is the inner workings of the heart or mind of the Gentile believer. On the one hand, having come to faith in Yeshua and seeing the Torah as the expression of God's holiness, he is dreadfully aware that for the majority of his life he lived in outward rebellion against the One true God. What is more, he is only now coming to learn how to please God in his life. Yet in spite of these thoughts which accuse him, he recognizes that he has truly believed and accepted the salvation procured for him by God. Furthermore, his conscience has changed, so that he longs to please God on the one hand, and grieves when he sins, on the other. Yet the very fact that his life is more and more conformed to a life of righteousness as prescribed in the Torah and demonstrated by Yeshua, gives him confidence that in the final day of judgment, when he stands before the Almighty, he will be judged righteous by the One who judges the secrets of men's heart.

Paul thus imagines within the Gentile believer the exact fighting which he experienced in his own soul when he became spiritually aware of the Torah as the Spirit revealed it to his regenerated heart. Surely he was learned in the Torah, being a student of Gamaliel. But what Paul came to understand was that if one studies the Torah yet misses Yeshua as the central issue of the Torah, his knowledge is greatly deficient. Only when the Spirit comes to open the eyes of the sinner will he see Yeshua as the goal to which the Torah points, and understand the Torah in light of the Messiah (2Cor 3). Paul underwent such an experience when the Holy Spirit regenerated him and gave him faith to see the Torah in its fulness.

He sees in the Gentile believers, then, this same inner struggle for righteousness, an inner struggle which bespeaks the reality of a changed heart and thus a *bona fide* expression of genuine faith. He sees the Gentile believer striving to know God in truth through a genuine acceptance of the Torah, an acceptance which is demonstrated through righteous living. In short, the Gentiles, though without the advantage of the Torah as part of their culture and upbringing, demonstrate their right standing before God gained by faith in Yeshua, because they are doers of the Torah, not merely hearers.

16 on the day when, according to my gospel, God will judge the secrets of men through Messiah Yeshua.

The faith of the believer, while active in the daily realm, nonetheless looks to the day of final judgment where his reward and rest will be realized. This final judgment day is, therefore, that ultimate issue around which one's thoughts both accuse and defend, and which the redeemed soul eventually rests in the knowledge that salvation is secure through genuine faith in Messiah.

The future judgment is often referred to as a "day," no doubt due to the use of the "day of the Lord" (Is 13:6, 9; Joel 1:15; 2:1, 11, 31; etc.) throughout the Tanach. The believer's conscience bears witness, not to the fact that he lived sinlessly, but that his true desires, i.e., to please the Lord, were generally borne out in the actions of his life. Such witness stands him in good stead as he approaches and comes to the day of judgment in which he will give account for the works of his life.

"according to my gospel" is an interesting insertion by Paul, and one that raises a few questions. He uses the phrase elsewhere (Rom 16:25; 2Ti 2:8; cf. 2Cor 4:3; 1Th 1:5; 2Th 2:14) but it is not clear in this context exactly what is "according to my gospel." Does he mean the judgment of the Gentiles? That the secrets of the heart will be revealed and judged? That the judgment is specifically carried out by Yeshua ("through Messiah Yeshua")? Some have argued that none of these are peculiar to Paul's teaching or preaching, and therefore wonder how these could be singled out as "according to *my* gospel." If there were any peculiar slant of Paul's teaching

which might bear upon the present context, it may well be a combination of these as it relates to the Gentile. In the same way that Paul teaches a singular salvation for both the Jew and Gentile (not two ways to God), so he teaches a unified standard of judgment for both, namely, the Torah of God. This is explicitly taught in v. 12: "For all who have sinned without the Torah will also perish without the Torah; and all who have sinned under the Torah will be judged by the Torah." It is the expression "perish without the Torah" that must be understood here. Those who have sinned without knowing of the Torah or having received the revelation of God's holiness and the method by which He declares sinners just, are judged as sinners precisely because they do not live according to the righteous standards of the Torah. While this may seem unfair or even arbitrary, it is nonetheless the heart of Paul's argument, namely, that the doers of the Torah stand as just before God. For Paul, righteous actions bespeak a regenerated heart, for apart from the inward work of righteousness, there is no true conformity to God's righteous standards.

Thus, "Paul's gospel" includes not only that Jews and Gentiles are saved in exactly the same way (by faith in Yeshua) but also that Jews and Gentiles will be judged on exactly the same basis, i.e., whether or not they lived righteously, the only absolute test of whether or not one possesses true faith. It is thus "according to my gospel," Paul can say, that the Gentiles along with all mankind will be judged in the final day, for they will be judged, not by One who is a respecter of persons, but by the infinitely just God who renders to every man according to his deeds.

The other emphasis which Paul makes in this regard is that the judgment which accompanies the Day of the Lord is administered through Yeshua. It is the Messiah Himself who will judge the secrets of man's heart, and reveal the inward realities of each one. For those who have genuinely submitted to the rule of Messiah through faith, there is no need for fear of that day, for the secrets of the heart have already been manifest. Confessing the need for Yeshua is to confess one's helplessness and inability to muster one's own salvation. The secret is out! "I'm a sinner unable to produce my own righteousness and in need of the righteousness of Messiah." But for those who have, on the one hand, deceived themselves into thinking that they could find righteousness in themselves, the secret pride and idolatry of their hearts will be revealed in that final day.

17-20 But if you bear the name "Jew," and rely upon the Torah, and boast in God, and know *His* will, and approve the things that are essential, being instructed out of the Torah, and are confident that you yourself are a guide to the blind, a light to those who are in darkness, a corrector of the foolish, a teacher of the immature, having in the Torah the embodiment of knowledge and of the truth,

Paul now specifically tells us who he addresses: the religious Jew. And in the list of actions which he describes, he mentions things which are, in and of themselves, honorable and even desirable. Yet we cannot overcome the feeling that Paul is using them, not as a description of what a Jew who is righteous should do, but what Jews often said of themselves but without the attended deeds of righteousness.

bear the name Jew – The term "Jew" (Ἰουδαῖος, *ioudaios*) is derived from the name Judah, and originally referred to those people living in the Judean region, who were characterized by their worship at the Temple of Israel's God in Jerusalem. Since the Judean region had become the primary place of those who remained from exiled Israel and Judah, the name *ioudaios* took on a national and religious meaning which it formerly did not have. In this sense, "Jew" became equivalent with "Israelite," meaning, "of Israel," or related to the sons of the Israel, primarily in terms of physical lineage, but also in terms of religious practice.

The morning prayers include: אָבִינוּ שֶׁבַּשָּׁמַיִם עֲשֵׂה עִמָּנוּ חֶסֶד בַּעֲבוּר שִׁמְךָ הַגָּדוֹל שֶׁנִּקְרָא עָלֵינוּ, "Our Father in Heaven, deal kindly with us, for the sake of Your great Name which is called upon us."

That the Jew carries the title "Israel," which contains the divine name אֵל, *El*, means that in bearing the name Israel, she also is to be known by that Name.

rely upon the Torah – The word "rely" translates the Greek ἐπαναπαύομαι, *epanapauomai*, which occurs only here and in Lk 10:6. Here the meaning is "rest upon," "rely upon," "rest one's hopes upon." There is nothing wrong with pursuing the Torah, and even seeing in it one's hopes, as it embodies the revelation of God Himself. At the end of the synagogue Torah service, the following is stated as the Torah scroll is raised for all to see: וְזֹאת הַתּוֹרָה אֲשֶׁר שָׂם מֹשֶׁה לִפְנֵי בְּנֵי יִשְׂרָאֵל עַל פִּי יהוה בְּיַד מֹשֶׁה עֵץ חַיִּים הִיא לַמַּחֲזִיקִים בָּהּ וְתוֹמְכֶיהָ מְאֻשָּׁר דְּרָכֶיהָ דַרְכֵי נֹעַם וְכָל נְתִיבוֹתֶיהָ שָׁלוֹם, "This is the Torah which Moses placed before the children of Israel, upon the command of Adonai, through the hand of Moses. It is a tree of life to those who grasp it , and those who support it are fortunate. Its ways are ways of pleasantness, and all its paths are peace."

It is not the pursuit of the Torah, nor even relying upon it as revealing the truth about God's heart that Paul casts in a negative light, but rather pursuing the Torah apart from faith (cf. 9:31).

boast in God – The concept of boasting in God is not a bad one, and Paul is very fond of claiming to "boast in God." He uses this word group a great deal (Rom 2:23; 3:27; 4:2; 5:2, 3, 11; 15:17) and especially of his desire to give all credit to Yeshua—to boast entirely in Him and in His work. Yet here, once again, there appears to be a pejorative use of the word "boast," for it appears to suggest a sense in which the Jew claimed to have "private rights" to God, that God was the "God of Abraham, Isaac and Jacob" and therefore not the God of the nations. Such a self-centered boasting produced a growing anti-Gentile bias among many of the Judaisms of the late 1st Century.

and know [His] will – The use of רָצוֹן, *ratzon* ("will") throughout the Siddur in the sense of עֲשֵׂה רְצוֹנוֹ "doing His will" or יְהִי רָצוֹן מִלְפָנֶיךָ, "may it be Your will" is well attested. Note *Perkei Avot* 2.4 (Gamaliel III),

> He used to say: Do His will as if it were your will, so that He may do your will as if it was His will. Nullify your will before His will, so that He may nullify the will of others before your will.

In and of itself this saying is good. But Paul's point is illucidated by the fact that it is assumed one is able to know the will of God, that is to say, at least some of the 1st Century Jews took as a beginning assumption that they, in fact, knew the will of God apart from a constant submission to it. This assumption could certainly lead to arrogance and pride.

and approve the things that are essential – The Greek words can be variously translated. τὰ διαφέροντα (*ta diapheronta*) translated in the NASB by "things that are essential" can also mean "things that differ," for the noun can mean either "differ" or (by extension) that which "stands out," i.e., that which is essential. Likewise the Greek δοκιμάζειν (*dokimazein*) can mean either "to judge" or "distinguish" as well as "approve." The Jewish communities of Paul's day prided themselves in distinguishing that which God approved from that which He disapproved. A great deal of time was taken up with separating that which was "holy" from that which was "unholy" or "profane." It seems to me that an alternate translation is therefore to be preferred: "distinguishing between the things that differ."

being instructed out of the Torah – This refers to the former characteristics, that they were able to distinguish between the things that differ precisely because they had been given the Torah so as to be able to know what pleased God and what did not, and thus through the Torah were able to discern the will of God. This, of course, is good! However, the tendency of the Sages was to interpret the text of the Torah in ways that supported their particular perspective. The hermeneutic of midrash had, in some cases, overshadowed the meaning of the text.

and are confident that you yourself are a guide to the blind, a light to those in darkness – It is the duty of Israel as a whole to be "light to the nations," so that those who walk in darkness and are blind may see the light of HaShem (cf. Is 42:7, 19f; Matt 7:3-5; 15:14; 23:16, 24). The problem arose when Israel, forsaking the Torah, made herself the goal rather than God and His Messiah. The irony is clear in the manner in which the phrase is cast: the confidence is not in Israel's God but in oneself. Here is the spirit of pride. Had Israel fulfilled this God-given role as she was supposed to, she would have been pointing the nations to Messiah, and thus to Yeshua. In her rejection of Yeshua, she proved that she had lost sight of the true light, and had manufactured her own.

a corrector of the foolish – Israel saw herself as the educator (NASB "corrector" παιδευτής (*paideutes* = educator) of the nations, which, if one were to consider the paganism and the immorality which the nations embodied, they would certainly be considered "foolish" or "ignorant." Moreover, the nations were surely ignorant of the Torah, not having been given the divine revelation of the Scriptures. Nonetheless, though surely Israel had the Torah, and was the possessor of the divine revelation, it had become easy for her to look at the nations with disdain, forgetting that her own beginnings were as a "wandering Aramean" (Deut 26:5).

a teacher of the immature – If the former phrase dealt primary with basic morality and life issues, this phrase perhaps deals with the deeper theological truths of the Torah. Once again, we may sense in Paul's choice of words the idea of Israel's arrogance. Instead of seeing herself as the recipient of God's mercy and grace, she considered her own advantaged place as somehow the result of her own efforts. Her maturity in the ways of God became a matter of pride as she compared herself with the pagan nations. She had forgotten the pit from which she was dug.

having in the Torah the embodiment of knowledge and of the truth – This explains the confidence which the Jew had in his role as the teacher and educator—he had the Torah of God which contained eternal knowledge and truth. Though Paul later teaches that Israel missed the treasure they had in the Torah through lack of faith, he never contradicts what he states here, that the Torah embodies real knowledge and truth. Thus, in each of these descriptions, Paul brings forward two sides of the same coin: the treasure which the Torah is in the hands of Israel, and (on the other side) the selfish attachment which Israel made to the Torah as being her own light rather than the light of God she was to shine to the world.

21 you, therefore, who teach another, do you not teach yourself? You who preach that one should not steal, do you steal?

Paul does not, here, raise an objection which is new or unfamiliar in the ears of the Jewish communities of his time—this is a theme woven throughout Rabbinic literature, and surely was extant in the years preceding the destruction of the Temple. Note, for example, Mid. Rab. *Deut* II.19–

> R. Simlai said: It is written, For their mother hath played the harlot, she that conceived them hath done shamefully (Hos 2:7). [The verse alludes to the leaders] who put their own words to shame before the ordinary people. How? The Sage expounds in public the prohibition against lending money on usury, and yet he himself lends his money on usury; he teaches, Thou shalt not rob, and yet he himself robs; Thou shalt not steal, and yet he himself steals. R. Berekiah said: Once it happened that a man had his cloak stolen and he went to complain to the judge and he found the cloak spread out on his bed. R. Berekiah further said: Once it happened that a man had his kettle stolen and he went to complain to the judge about it and he found it upon his oven. Hence [the force of] the words: 'Even as their teacher, so they sinned against Me.'
>
> Another explanation: The more they were increased, the more they sinned against Me. R. Tanhuma said: The more territory I gave them the more they sinned against me. Whence

this? For it is said, Yea, their altars are as heaps in the furrows of the field (Hos 12:12).

Another explanation: The more riches I gave them, the more they sinned against Me. Whence this? For it is said, Of their silver and their gold have they made them idols (Hos 8:4).

Another explanation: The more kings I gave them, the more they sinned against Me. Whence this? For it is said, All their kings are fallen, there is none among them that calleth unto Me. (Hos 7:7)

Another explanation: The more children I gave them, the more they sinned against Me, as it is said, WHEN THOU SHALT BEGET CHILDREN.

We find similar exhortations in Avot:

Shammai says: Make of your Torah a fixed practice, say little and do much, and receive all men with a cheerful countenance. (1.15)

Avot R. Natan (Chapter 13 [p. 72 in Goldin's translation]) adds:

say little and do much: what is that? This teaches that the righteous say little and do much, but the wicked say much and do not do even a little.

Mid. Rab. *Ecc* iv. §1, 1 says

"They had no comforter" (Ecc 4.1). R. Benjamin interpreted the verse to refer to the hypocrites in regard to the Law. People suppose that they can read the Scriptures and the Mishnah, but they cannot: they wrap their prayer shawls around them; they put their tefillin on their heads, and they oppress the poor. Of them it is written, 'Behold the tears of the oppressed, and they have no comforter; it is mine to punish,' says God, as it is said, 'Cursed be they who do the work of the Lord deceitfully' (Jer 48:10).

Indeed, one could list quote after quote of this kind of teaching from the Sages. So Paul is not alone in pointing out the dangers of hypocrisy among any group which professes to both know the true God, and know His will. Here, in turning to the Jewish congregants of the Roman synagogue, he reminds them that they (speaking in corporate solidarity) have not always been sincere in their handling of the truth, and therefore ought to be warned away from engaging in self-righteous judgment against those who did not have the Torah as a matter of their upbringing.

The language is pointed and terse: "you who teach, do you fail to teach yourself?" In *Avot R. Natan* (Chapter 29 [p. 29 in Goldin's translation]) we read:

Abba Saul ben Nannas says: There are four types of scholars: one studies himself but does not teach others; one teaches others but himself does not study; one teaches himself and others; and one teaches neither himself nor others.

The first priority is to study Torah in order to live a life pleasing to God through the power of the Spirit. But one must not stop there. He must also teach others what he has learned, both by deed and word. One who learns and fails to teach others gives the impression that what he has learned was of no lasting value.

22 You who say that one should not commit adultery, do you commit adultery? You who abhor idols, do you rob temples?

We thus have Paul listing three specific sins or categories of sin: stealing (κλέπτεις, *klepteis*), adultery (μοιχεύειν, *moicheuein*), and robbing temples (ἱερουσυλεῖς, *hierousuleis*), which he suggests have been committed by the Jewish community. Some commentators, feeling that Paul intends to indict all Jews under this challenge, sense the need to find definitions of these three categories which are wide enough to embrace the Jewish nation in the time of Paul.

But this is clearly not what Paul is driving at here. His point, that among those most favored by God's revelation of the Torah there is evidence of hypocrisy, is substantiated by even the few, notable cases with which everyone in his audience would have been familiar. Beyond that, what group of Jews, when put to such a challenge, would respond with a pious retort that "no hypocricy exists among us?" Such a response would likewise prove the Apostle's point! Paul therefore accomplishes his purpose as far as the Jews in the Roman *kehilah* are concerned, namely, that they have no basis to judge the non-Jews for their lack of Torah knowledge and therefore observance. Though, as I stated at the opening of this book, I am in substantial agreement with Nanos and his view that Paul in Romans attempts to counter the movement among the Gentiles to persuade their fellow, believing Jews to give up their observance of the Torah, it seems only fitting that Paul, having reminded the Gentiles of their pagan roots, would likewise turn to the Jew with a similar rebuke, so as to leave them both without grounds for becoming the judge of the other.

We have already looked at the manner in which "stealing" could be done by those in authority, but what are we to make of the "adultery" and "robbing temples" charge? It may be that "adultery" is to be explained along the lines of Matt 5:27-32 (cf. Matt 19:9f). In expanding the grounds for divorce for almost any reason, the Sages had actually caused the people to sin. For as Yeshua taught, marrying a woman who had received an invalid divorce was adultery.

As to "robbing temples," it may be confidently said that Paul's point of "abhoring idols" was well founded in the 1st Century. The Jewish community of Paul's day had surely (by all historical records) cleared out the idols from her midst. Yet Paul's point is that though they were free of idols *per se*, the taint of idolatry could still soil them. The desecration of idols was considered a holy duty among some of the Jews, and apparently this extended to desecration of the pagan temples and the ruining of the idols (cf. Ac 19:37). Yet though money tainted by idolatry was not to be used for the Temple (Deut 7:25f), the Sages found ways in their technical rulings to overcome the prohibitions, and to bring articles of value from the pagan temples into the coffers of the Temple. This was strictly forbidden in word (cf. Josephus, *Ant.* iv.8, 10) but carried out through remote hands and dealings. Thus, even in this act, though idols in outward symbol were abhorred, the wealth that one might gain through piously "destroying" idols was not. Here, then, is Paul's obvious point: the reality of our hearts makes each of us unable to be the final judge—this must be left to the One who alone judges what is righteous and what is not. We must submit to the revelation of God, and simply let His decrees be the decisive mark for judging what is right and wrong.

23-24 You who boast in the Torah, through your breaking the Torah, do you dishonor God? For "the name of God is blasphemed among the Gentiles because of you," just as it is written.

It seems most likely that this should be read as a statement rather than as a question as the NASB (along with NIV) has it. This is suggested not only by the grammar (ὅς, *hos*, followed by indicatives) but also because it is immediately substantiated by the following quote (Is 52:5). We might thus translate it "You who boast in the Torah, *and* through your breaking the Torah, you dishonor God. For …"

This is the only time in the Apostolic Scriptures (which I can find) where the noun παράβαισις, *parabaisis* (disobedience) is used with νόμος (Law/Torah). It is nonetheless a common term in the Tanach when used with the words בְּרִית ("covenant") or תּוֹרָה ("Torah"), (cf. Lev 26:5, 44; Deut 31:16, 20; etc.).

The concept of "boasting in the Torah" can be taken two ways: positively, in the sense that the Torah of God embodies the revelation of His will, and specifically the revelation of His Messiah (cf. Rom 10:4; Lk 24:27). Paul makes it clear that "boasting in the Lord" is the appropriate response of those who have come to faith in Yeshua (1Cor 1:31; 2Cor 10:17). Boasting in the revelation of the Lord is not far removed from this.

But there is obviously a second, negative, aspect to the phrase, for it is clear that "boasting in the flesh" was not uncommon for Paul's Jewish brethren (Gal 6:13), and that in some regards "boasting in the Torah" may envision a boasting in the flesh in regard to "keeping the Torah," especially since the keeping of the Torah (both written and oral) had become a matter (at least in some measure) of Jewish identity. Yet the very boasting in the Torah as a boast of the flesh (like the rich, young ruler—"all of these things I have kept since my youth") causes one to break the Torah, for it renders a person arrogant, and therefore unable to fulfill the Torah in loving God and loving one's neighbor.

It is to this point, that of arrogance and self-reliance, that Paul moves by quoting Is 52:5, a passage reminiscent in theme with Ezek 36:16ff. The quote is almost verbatum from the Lxx, though the Lxx is a loose translation of the Hebrew.

Isaiah 52:5

MT	Lxx	Paul
וְעַתָּה מִי־לִי [מַה־לִּי]־פֹה נְאֻם־יהוה כִּי לֻקַּח עַמִּי חִנָּם מֹשְׁלוֹ [מֹשְׁלָיו] יְהֵילִילוּ נְאֻם־יהוה וְתָמִיד כָּל־הַיּוֹם שְׁמִי מִנֹּאָץ Now therefore, what do I have here," declares Adonai, "seeing that My people have been taken away without cause?" Again Adonai declares, "Those who rule over them howl, and My name is continually blasphemed all day long. [Qere/Ketiv in backets]	καὶ νῦν τί ὧδέ ἐστε τάδε λέγει κύριος ὅτι ἐλήμφθη ὁ λαός μου δωρεάν θαυμάζετε καὶ ὀλολύζετε τάδε λέγει κύριος δι᾽ ὑμᾶς διὰ παντὸς τὸ ὄνομά μου βλασφημεῖται ἐν τοῖς ἔθνεσιν And now why are you here? Thus saith the Lord, Because my people was taken for nothing, you wonder and howl. Thus says the Lord, On account of you my name is continually blasphemed among the Gentiles.	τὸ γὰρ ὄνομα τοῦ θεοῦ δι᾽ ὑμᾶς βλασφημεῖται ἐν τοῖς ἔθνεσιν, καθὼς γέγραπται. For the name of God on account of you is blasphemed among the Gentiles, as it is written.

Interestingly, this Isaiah passage states that the exile of God's people was "without cause," while the corresponding Ezekiel passage makes it clear that the people were exiled because of their lawlessness:

> Then the word of the LORD came to me saying, "Son of man, when the house of Israel was living in their own land, they defiled it by their ways and their deeds; their way before Me was like the uncleanness of a woman in her impurity. "Therefore, I poured out My wrath on them for the blood which they had shed on the land, because they had defiled it with their idols. "Also I scattered them among the nations, and they were dispersed throughout the lands. According to their ways and their deeds I judged them. "When they came to the nations where they went, they profaned My holy name, because it was said of them, 'These are the people of the LORD; yet they have come out of His land.' "But I had concern for My holy name, which the house of Israel had profaned among the nations where they went. (Ezek 36:16-20)

It seems possible that Paul quotes the Isaiah passage but has the theology of Ezekiel in mind, namely, that they (Israel) gave the nations cause to blaspheme the Name by the fact that they, through their disobedience, provoked the Lord so that He exiled them from the Land. Such an exile allowed the nations to speculate that Israel's God was not able to keep them in the Land He had promised to give them. Thus, it is by the lawlessness of Israel that HaShem is blasphemed among the nations. For this reason, the expanded Lxx translation ("on account of you" added as the cause for the blasphemy, and "among the Gentiles" as the locus of the blasphemy) is allowed by Paul since it corresponds to the overall prophetic message.

It may be rightly said that while the Torah sanctifies God's people (אֲשֶׁר קִדְּשָׁנוּ בְּמִצְוֹתָו, *asher kid'shanu b'mitzvotav,* "Who sanctifies us with His commandments), it also gives guidelines for how God's people may sanctify His Name. Thus, the very reason for the existence of Israel (i.e., that the Name should be sanctified) is bound up with the ability to be sanctified by His holy commandments. This, Paul teaches, can only happen within the context of faith in Yeshua, and the power of the indwelling Spirit.

25 For indeed circumcision is of value, if you practice the Torah; but if you are a transgressor of the Torah, your circumcision has become uncircumcision.

The connective γαρ, "for" links this verse with what precedes as a proof or substantiation. Since boasting in the Torah is the subject, it is only reasonable that Paul should come to the issue of circumcision. This he does in these verses, tying it in with the major point of the paragraph, namely, that the doers of the Torah, not the hearers, stand just before God (v. 13).

"Circumcision" (περιτομή, *peritome*) is generally used in the Apostolic writings in one of three ways: 1) of the act of circumcising; 2) the state of being circumcised, and 3) the community of the circumcised, i.e., the Jews. It seems to be used here in the sense of number 2.

The phrase "practice the Torah" (νόμον πράσσῃς, *nomon prasses*) is used only here in the Apostolic writings, but parallel phrasiology is οἱ ποιηταὶ νόμου, *hoi poietai nomou,* "those who do the Torah" (Rom 2:13) and ὅλον τὸν νόμον ποιῆσαι, *holon ton nomon poiesai,* "all who do the Torah" (Gal 5:3). The corresponding Hebrew phrase (עֹשֶׂה אֶת הַתּוֹרָה, *'oseh et hatorah,* "do the Torah") is found in *Siphre* Deut 32:30, and is common in the Tanach (Num 6:21; Josh 1:7; Ps 119:126; Neh 9:34; 2Chr 14:3).

It seems that what is meant here is not a "perfect fulfillment of the radical demands of the Law, but a real faith in God and the serious engagement with obedience which springs therefrom." (Cranfield, 1.171, n. 3)

What then is Paul saying here? I would suggest at first what he is not saying, namely, that circumcision is wrong, or of no value (a conclusion only an anti-Semitic viewpoint could derive). No, circumcision (I would think he is directing his attention to Jewish people here) is valuable if in bearing of the mark of the covenant one is honestly striving to please God in all matters of life. That is to say, a Torah-pursuant Jewish person is doing what he ought to be doing, for he engages in the activities of the covenant of which He is a part. His circumcision is not an ethnic identity marker, but is a seal of the covenant in the flesh which is matched by the circumcision of the heart. Through his observance of the covenant sign he honors the God of the covenant.

Thus, in this case, circumcision is "valuable" (ὠφελεῖν, *ophelein,* found only here in Rom, but cf. 1Cor 13:3; 14:6; Gal 5:2; Heb 4:2; 13:9) because it functions as it is supposed to, to point to Messiah as the fulfillment of the covenant—as the promised Son.

We should carefully note how the verse continues: "but if you are a transgressor of the Torah, your circumcision has become uncircumcision." We might have expected "but if you are a transgressor of the Torah, your circumcision has become without value (οὐδέν ὠφελεῖ, *ouden ophelei*), but of course this is not what is said. Rather, "your circumcision has become uncircumcision." The church has often understood this to mean that the lawless Jew has annulled his circumcision in God's eyes, i.e., God has rejected him out of hand. If this clause were to stand by itself, one might be able to suggest such an interpretation, but of course it does not. In 3:3 Paul reminds us that the unfaithfulness (ἀπιστία, *apistia*) of the Jew in no way nullifies the faithfulness of God, and indeed, chapter 11 will show this plainly. We should therefore understand Paul's words here not to mean that a Jewish person's position as a member of the covenant people is discounted by God because of lawlessness, but that when, as a member of the covenant and therefore circumcised in the flesh, he breaks the Torah, he shows rather that his heart is uncircumcised. Cranfield has stated this well:

> It seems therefore better to understand v. 25b to mean, not that the Jew's circumcision has been annulled in God's sight, but that he has become uncircumcised in heart (i.e., one whose heart is far from God and whose life is a contradiction of his membership of the Covenant people), and now, though still a member of God's special people to whom God is still faithful, stands in his human existence in a negative, and no longer in a positive, relation to God's purpose in history, and is outside that Israel within Israel, to which Paul refers in 9:6ff. (*Romans*, 1.172)

26 If therefore the uncircumcised man keeps the requirements of the Torah, will not his uncircumcision be regarded as circumcision?

The term "uncircumcised" (ἀκροβυστία, *akrobustia*) can mean: 1) the foreskin; 2) the state of being uncircumcised, or 3) the community of the uncircumcised, i.e., the Gentile world or the individual Gentile. It seems clear that Paul uses the word first with the meaning of #3, and then with that of #2.

Once again, Paul, in the phrase "keeps the requirements of the Torah" is not referring either to a hypothetical case nor to a perfect maintenance of the Torah (something no one taught in his day), but to a grateful and humble faith in God and the resultant life turned in the direction of obedience which is its fruit, i.e., the "obedience of faith." It seems clear he has in mind the believing Gentiles who keep Torah though they have not been raised in its precepts. Thus, one interpretation would be to understand how the "outsider" viewed Torah observant Gentiles. Apparently, to the "outsider," a God-fearer may have looked like, and been treated as though he were Jewish. But perhaps the One doing the "regarding" is God (see below).

"Keeps the requirements of the Torah" (τὰ δικαιώματα τοῦ νόμου φυλάσσῃ, *ta dikaiomata tou nomou phulasse*) must be understood, once again, not as a keeping in perfection, but as a life characterized by maintaining the righteous requirements of the Torah

"will not his uncircumcision be regarded as circumcision?" This rhetorical question is a window into Paul's view of circumcision. Clearly, he does not judge this uncircumcised person to have neglected the Torah by not being circumcised. What the uncircumcised Gentile had not done was submit to the rabbinic ritual of the proselyte. The act of circumcision apart from the proselyte ceremony is not envisioned here.

Thus, Paul is not saying here that a Gentile believer becomes a Jew through his faith in Yeshua. What he is saying is simply that a doer of the Torah stands just before God, not the hearer (2:13). If circumcision is the sign of the covenant, then circumcision ought to always be accompanied by righteous living. In the same way, true righteous living (as defined by God, not man) assumes a status as true covenant member (cf. 9:6), for true covenant members are circumcised of heart.

An obvious question we must ask is who is doing the regarding (λογισθήσεται, *logisthe-setai*), "will not his uncircumcision be *regarded* as circumcision?" This is the same word translated "reckon, counted" (cf. Lxx of Gen 15:6; Rom 4:3-24) when referring to God reckoning faith as righteousness. It seems most likely, then, that Paul here specifically refers to God as the One who regards the uncircumcised as circumcised, that is, that He regards the Gentile who has by faith become circumcised in heart to be a *bona fide* covenant member and therefore a recipient of His eternal blessing.

27 And will not he who is physically uncircumcised, if he keeps the Torah, will he not judge you who though having the letter of the Torah and circumcision are a transgressor of the Torah?

"if he keeps the Torah" (τόν νόμον τελοῦσα, *ton nomon telousa*) translates a different term than found in v. 26. Here, τελεῖν, *telein,* is used in the sense of fulfilling the Torah, cf. Jms 2:8, "If, however, you are fulfilling the royal law, according to the Scripture, 'You shall love your neighbor as yourself,' you are doing well." There seems little reason for Paul to use a different word here, for he describes the same thing here as he did in the previous verse where he used φύλασσειν, *phulassein.* We should most likely, then, take the two words to be synonymns.

"will he not judge you," not in the sense of actually acting as the judge, but more as a witness for the prosecutor. The Torah pursuant Gentile will be "evidence of what the Jew ought to have been and could have been." (Cranfield, *Romans* 1.174).

"Letter" (γράμματος, *grammatos*) is sometimes used by Paul to refer to the attempt to keep the Torah apart from the Spirit (cf. v. 29; Rom 7:6; 2Cor 3:6). Here "letter" and "circumcision" are parallel in thought, so that we understand circumcision here to mean "circumcision of the flesh without the corresponding circumcision of the heart." The proof that the Spirit is not involved comes from the final phrase, "are a transgressor of the Torah."

Here then is a stunning picture: the covenant member, the Jew, is judged by the Gentile. In the final judgment the question will not be asked "are you Jewish?", but the question will be asked "are you righteous?" Only those who find their righteousness in Yeshua, and whose lives have the inevitable proof of that righteousness, will stand justified before God and will therefore have rest in the world to come.

28   For he is not a Jew who is one outwardly; neither is circumcision that which is outward in the flesh. But he is a Jew who is one inwardly; and circumcision is that which is of the heart, by the Spirit, not by the letter; and his praise is not from men, but from God.

These verses, taken by themselves, or even misinterpreted by neglecting to understand the wider context of the passage, have often been used to teach that the non-believing Jew has forfeited his status as covenant member, and that the community of believers, the Church, has replaced Israel as God's covenant people. If these verses stood alone, one might be able to interpret them in this way, but comparing Paul's teaching in 3:1-4 and especially 9:1-11:36, it is impossible to claim such a position for Paul. He fully recognizes the eternal promises which God has made to physical Israel, and that in fact the fulfillment of these promises yet in the future is the crowning jewel of God's omnipotence and grace.

What is Paul saying then? First, we should remember that he is addressing the Jewish constituents within the Roman synagoague at this point in the chapter. His reference to the Gentile who keeps the Torah is simply a way to rebuke and shame the Jews who were insincere in their pursuit of God. Secondly, he is speaking within the sphere of Jewishness, and asserts the same axiom which he speaks plainly in 9:6, namely, that not all physical (outward) descendants of Jacob are actually (inward) Israel. For Paul, it cannot merely be physical lineage which makes a person Jewish—there must be more. If "not every descendent from Israel is Israel" (9:6), who is a descendent of Israel? Paul's answer is that there must be circumcision of the heart to match the physical circumcision, or there is no value whatsoever in the physical circumcision. Physical lineage has value, even apart from faith, for the descendants of Jacob still comprise the chosen nation of God. What is more, the temporal blessings of the covenant (and these should not be minimized) remain the possession of the nation of Israel, even in their unbelief. But Paul is emphasizing the eternal promises of the covenant ("whose praise is not from men, but from God"), which are the possession only of those who believe and are therefore righteous. These are those who are circumcised both in flesh and in heart (cf. Ezek 44:7-9).

The circumcision of the heart is a Torah concept (cf. Lev 26:41; Deut 10:16; 30:6; Jer 4:4; 9:26), and apart from it the Jewish person fares no better than the pagan before the bar of God's justice. The circumcision of the flesh, which marks him as a covenant member and therefore the recipient of God's blessing, apart from the corresponding circumcision of the heart is considered as though he were no covenant member at all (his circumcision has become uncircumcision) in terms of the eternal promises of the covenant.

"By the letter" (in contrast to "by the Spirit") refers to mere external observance without genuine faith. Isaiah 1 indicates how God looks at such practices.

Romans 3
Commentary

1 Then what advantage has the Jew? Or what is the benefit of circumcision?

As is often the case throughout the book of Romans, Paul anticipates the objections of some of his readers. Having, it appears, leveled the playing field by making all things dependent upon faith, the question arises as to whether or not there is any advantage for the Jew. If both the Jew and the Gentile are covenant members by faith, what is the value of Jewishness? Surely the Tanach teaches that God chose Israel out of all the nations (cf. Gen 18:19; Ex 19:5, 6; Deut 4:32-37; 7:6; Amos 3:2) and promised His faithfulness to her. If God chose Israel out of all mankind to be His special people and gave them circumcision as a sign of the covenant which He made with them, then to indicate that the Jew has no special place in God's heart is either to disavow what the Tanach plainly teaches, or bring the faithfulness of God into question. This is the issue Paul anticipates in the minds of his readers.

It should be noted that the two sentences of this verse state the same thing but with different terms. Once again, the term "circumcision" is used as a metonym for someone accorded the status as a Jew.

2 Great in every respect. First of all, that they were entrusted with the oracles of God.

Some commentators are shocked at Paul's answer to his own question, feeling rather that he should have, on the basis of his foregoing exposition, answered "none whatever!" As an example, C.H. Dodd (*The Epistle of Paul to the Romans*, 1959) believes that Paul's prejudice simply could not be overcome, having been so much a Pharisee, and thus he answers, not from a grounded theology, but out of emotion and loyalty to his background:

> His Pharisaism—or shall we say, his patriotism?—was too deeply engrained for him to put right out of his mind the idea that somehow the divine covenant with mankind had a "most favoured nation clause." (p. 68)

Paul, however, is simply being consistent with what he knows to have been revealed in the Tanach.

We should first note that "great in every respect" (πολὺ κατὰ πάντα τρόπον, *polu kata panta tropon*) does not mean that the Jew outshines the Gentile in every aspect of life and being, but that the Jew has an advantage, a priority, a privilege, a preeminence, which in every respect is great and important. This advantage, priority, etc. is summed up in God's purpose, mission, and enabling for His chosen ones.

"First of all" (πρῶτον μὲν [γὰρ], *proton men gar*, the γάρ is not found in B or the first hand of D) would be most often followed by ἔπειτα δέ, *epeita de*, "and then," but we find nothing like this in the immediate context. Paul did the same thing in 1:8, so we might suggest this is simply a mark of his style.

"they were entrusted the oracles of God" – the word translated "entrust" is ἐπιστεύθησαν, *episteuthesan* (aorist passive indicative) from the root verb πιστεύω, *pisteuo* "to believe." God entrusted the oracles to Israel with the design that they should make them known to all of mankind. The oracles of God are therefore Israel's sacred trust.

"oracles of God" (τὰ λόγια τοῦ θεοῦ, *ta logia tou theou*) has been variously understood to be the Torah, promises made to Israel, Divine utterances in the Tanach, the Ten Words given on Sinai, or the promises relating to the coming of the Messiah. It would seem most natural to take the phrase to refer generally to the revelation of Scripture as a whole, entrusted to Israel throughout her history. Thus, the Torah, Prophets, and Writings comprise the "oracles of God." That Israel has guarded the sacred writings and preserved them for all mankind is a feat worthy of much gratitude, especially from the Christian Church who finds so much of her self-definition in these (so-called) "OT Scriptures." Barth has noted (quoted from Cranfield, *Romans*, 1.179, n. 5):

> The Gentiles, when they attain to faith, can in a way only be their [i.e., the Jews'] guests. It must remain at this: 'Salvation comes from the Jews' (Jn 4:22)

Surely all owe a debt of gratitude to Israel for preserving the oracles which were entrusted to her! What is more, since the text of the Tanach as we now have it is that which is based upon the faithful traditions of Masoretes, we are indebted to these traditions as the basis for the text we read and hold as the basis for our faith and *halachah*.

But if we take the broadest definition of "oracles of God," we still are struck with the fact that Paul takes a very high view of the Torah, for surely he would have viewed the books of Moses as foundational to both the Prophets and the Writings. Rather than viewing the Torah as some burden which Israel was destined to bear, he rather sees God's self-revelation in the Torah as one of Israel's greatest treasures. In like manner he lists "the giving of the Torah" as one of the Jewish privileges (9:4) and concludes that the Torah is "holy, and the commandment is holy and righteous and good" (7:12). Paul refers to the "Torah of faith" (3:27) and asserts that he is not teaching that faith nullifies the Torah: "on the contrary, we establish the Torah" (3:31). He even goes so far as to teach that Messiah is the goal to which the Torah points (10:4). Clearly, Paul is pro-Torah and not anti-Torah in the way he is often characterized!

3 What then? If some did not believe, their unbelief will not nullify the faithfulness of God, will it?

There is some discussion as to the correct punctuation for this sentence, but on the whole it appears that the manner in which the NASB has it, is correct. The NIV opts for a slightly different punctuation, but the resultant translation is not that different: "What if some did not have faith? Will their lack of faith nullify God's faithfulness?"

Perhaps the most important question to answer regarding the words used in this verse, however, is how "not believe" (ἠπίστησάν, *epistesan*) and "unbelief" (ἀπιστία, *apistia*) are to be defined. Technically, these words (having πιστευω/πιστις [*pisteuo/pistis*] as the root) could be understood as "be unfaithful" and "unfaithfulness" respectively, and this might seem the most natural rendering being combined with the phrase "faithfulness of God" (τὴν πίστιν τοῦ θεοῦ, *ten pistin tou theou*). But most often these words, when used elsewhere in the Apostolic Writings, convey the sense of "unbelief" or "failure to believe," and specifically "unbelief" (ἀπιστία, *apistia*) is used three times elsewhere by Paul in Romans (4:20; 11:20, 23) and the context here strongly suggests the meaning "unbelief," not "unfaithfulness." It seems best, then, to understand the terms as the English translations have rendered them, i.e., conveying a lack of faith or belief in what God has said, and specifically in God's Messiah, Yeshua.

With this in mind, and considering the context from the previous verse, Paul is teaching us not that the Jews proved unfaithful to the their trust in guarding and maintaining the oracles of God, but that they failed to believe them though they were entrusted to them. And how is their unbelief evident? For Paul this is bound up in the rejection of Yeshua as God's Messiah. He is the locus of the nation's unbelief.

Yet we must not so quickly decide between these alternative translations as though they are mutually exclusive. In a very real sense, "belief" and "faithfulness" go hand in hand in the Paul's mind, as do "unbelief" and "unfaithful." Israel was faithful to preserve the oracles, but her failure to entrust herself to what the *logia* of God commanded rendered the nation an unfaithful partner to the covenant.

The sense of the verse is clear, and will be taken up in greater depth in chapters 9-11. For the present context, however, Paul wants his readers to know that "it is unthinkable that God's faithfulness to His Covenant with Israel should be rendered ineffective even by the Jews' unbelief" (Cranfield, *Romans*, 1.181).

4 May it never be! Rather, let God be found true, though every man be found a liar, as it is written, "That You may be justified in Your words, And prevail when You are judged."

The phrase translated "May it never be" is μὴ γένοιτο, *me genoito,* in the Greek, and is found in the following places in the book of Romans: 3:6, 31; 6:2, 15; 7:7, 13; 9:14; 11:1, 11. Thus 10 times Paul uses this expression to emphasize the impossibility of a particular proposal.

There is an expression in Rabbinic literature to denote a line of reasoning which will never reach a valid conclusion. This expression combines the verb חזר, *chazar* "to move" and the word חֲלִילָה, *chalilah,* "to go in a circle." The expression is חָזַרְנוּ חָלִילָה, *chazarnu chalilah,* i.e., "we are moving in a circle," "this way of arguing will lead to no conclusion."[31]

It is true that in Epictetus the same expression is found following questions and so it may be that Paul is adopting a purely Greek expression at this point—an expression that negated any possibility proposed by the rhetorical question.

And what is the question that Paul first raises? It is the question of whether or not God's faithfulness is brought into question by the reality of Israel's unbelief. Paul's answer is simply that we must begin with the premise that God is true and that man is the liar. In other words, mankind's unbelief, and Israel's in particular, has nothing to do with God's faithfulness to His word, but rather to the inherent nature of fallen man.

Paul is emphatic about this. The Greek uses the imperative to enforce the idea that God is declared to be true. We might translate it "we confess rather that God is true." Calvin has described this single statement as "the primary axiom of all Christian philosophy."[32]

"and every man a liar" – this is in contrast to the perfect nature of God as true. In contrast to God, every person is a liar. Note Ps 116:11 [Lxx 115.2]: "I said in my alarm, "Everyone man is a liar." (ἐγὼ εἶπα ἐν τῇ ἐκστάσει μου Πᾶς ἄνθρωπος ψεύστης).

Paul quotes Psalm 51:4 to support his thesis, taking it almost directly from the Lxx (only the Lxx has the aorist of νικάω, *nikao,* "to conquer" while Paul puts it into the future.) The translation of זָכָה, *zachah,* ("be pure") by the Greek νικάω, *nikao,* "to conquer" is echoed in later usage (cf. Aramaic זְכֵי, *z'cheiy,* "to win, defeat," cf. Jastrow, p. 399; cf. b.*San* 39a, 107a, which actually alludes to Ps 51:4).

What is the context of the quote in Ps. 51? It is David's open, contrite confession of his sin before the Lord. When God states His judgment about David's sin, His judgment is true. Paul thus uses this quote, no doubt well known to his Jewish readers (since Ps 51 is used throughout the liturgy), to reinforce the axiom that God's judgments are always true, and that if His judgments are scrutinized, He will always be found blameless, righteous, and just.

5 But if our unrighteousness demonstrates the righteousness of God, what shall we say? The God who inflicts wrath is not unrighteous, is He? (I am speaking in human terms.)

In order to see Paul's full argument in this chapter, we may summarize as follows:

Is there an advantage in being a Jew?	Yes, the godly heritage attached to the Scriptures which Israel were given first.
But the Jewish nation has rejected Yeshua as Messiah. Has this brought God's faithfulness to His word into question?	No, not at all. The rejection of Yeshua by the Jewish nation is a reflection of mankind's basic, sinful nature. God is always true and man a liar.
Then what you're saying, Paul, is that Israel's unbelief is actually a good thing because it hightlights God's righteousness and justice. And if so, why would God punish Israel for something that actually works in His favor? Isn't it wrong for God to punish Israel when her unbelief actually demonstrates His righteousness?	No. If God is unjust, everything is lost and the very judgment day that will wrap up history cannot happen.
But if my rejection of Yeshua gives an opportunity for God to be seen as all that much more glorious, why should I get punished for something that makes God look good? Maybe my evil actually brings about good!	People who think this way deserve the condemnation they will receive.
So if there's an advantage in being Jewish, are Jews better (or worse) than Gentiles?	No. The greatest proof of the equality of Jew and Gentile is that both are naturally sinners—both are equally guilty before God, and unable to achieve their own righteousness before Him.

Thus, we see that Paul finds the equality of Jew and Gentile, first and foremost, in the common sinful or depraved nature each has from birth. Rather than beginning with Abraham, he goes back to Adam. His teaching about God's grace was, in some measure, so radical to the rabbinic rule of the day, that he had been slandered as though he taught an Epicurean philosophy of overcoming evil by overindulging it. He was accused of antinomianism because he was preaching a soteriology entirely based upon God's grace, a grace that produced a law-abiding heart and not *vice versa*.

Therefore, to substantiate his point about the depravity of mankind (both Jew and Gentile), he quotes from a number of texts: Ps 14:1-3 (cf. Ps 53); Ps 5:10; Ps 140:3; Ps 9:28 [Lxx, English 10:7]; Is 59:7-8a; Ps 35:2b [Lxx, English 36:1b]. Such a stringing together of texts is common in Rabbinic writings and may employ the principle of גְּזֵירָה שָׁוָה, *gezeirah shavah,* meaning that texts which have a word or phrase in common are speaking to the same issue.

We may rightly ask ourselves what is meant by the theological term "total depravity." First, it does not mean that all people are as bad as they could be. Surely we know that even the laws of society keep, to one extent or another, the depravity of mankind in check. Nor does the term mean that all are equally "bad" in the sense of "evil." Once again, human history has given us ample evidence of those who are remembered in infamy for their heinous acts. What the term does mean, however, is that all people, regardless of race, gender, or station in life, are entirely unable to come to God on their own. In reality, what Paul teaches here is "total inability." Apart from the work of God upon the sinner, that person has absolutely no innate ability to know God or to come into relationship with Him. His very nature will, apart from God's work, do all it can to resist God and exalt self.

6 May it never be! For otherwise how will God judge the world?

The very thought of God being anything but entirely righteous is simply impossible for Paul. God is righteous in all His ways, and kind in all His deeds (Ps 145:17). At the heart of all true worship is the foundational belief that God is good. Consider the 18th benediction of the *Shemonei Esrei* and the line הַטּוֹב כִּי לֹא כָלוּ רַחֲמֶיךָ, *hatov ki lo chalu rachamecha*, "You are the Good One, for Your mercies never fail." Here, the term "Good" is used as a name for God, describing it as an essential attribute of His character.

But Paul's argumentation takes a slightly different turn here. Rather than arguing from the essential nature of God's revealed character, Paul argues from what he must believe is axiomatic in the minds of his readers, namely, that God is the eschatological Judge of the world. As Cranfield notes (1.185),

> That God who shall judge the world is just is a fundamental certainty of all theological thinking (cf., e.g., Gen 18:25; Deut 32:4; Jb 8:3; 34:10ff). God would in fact not be God at all, if He were unjust.

The theme of final judgment is expressed sharply in the apocryphal book of 1 Enoch (90:15, 18-26; 91:14f) where the godless are threatened in constantly repeated woes with death at the sword of the faithful in the eschatological Holy War, with condemnation in the final judgment, eternal torment in the underworld and annihilation by the fire of judgment.[33] Though apocryphal, 1 Enoch was very popular in the 1st Century and no doubt gives a sense of general beliefs of that time. We may discern from it and other similar works that there was a widespread belief in the final judgment of all the wicked.

7 But if through my lie the truth of God abounded to His glory, why am I also still being judged as a sinner?

Paul now brings up again the objection he raised in v.5b, though there he discounts it by adding "I speak as a man," indicating that to consider God to be unrighteous is to think as a mortal apart from divine revelation.

The logic seems inescapable: if the truth of God has been more abundantly manifested through my lie, then why should God judge me as having done something wrong? Or, to put it another way, "How can it be fair for a man to be blamed for his falsehood, when it has actually rebounded to God's glory?

8 And why not say (as we are slanderously reported and as some affirm that we say), "Let us do evil that good may come"? Their condemnation is just.

We may first ask in what situation Paul would be thus slandered. The Acts 21 text, in which James describes Jewish believers as zealous for the Torah and under the false impression that Paul was teaching the abolishment of the Torah (21:20-21), comes immediately to mind. Under what circumstances would Paul have been slandered in this way? It seems to me that the debates over the oral *halachah* might best fit this scenario. If Paul, for instance, was teaching that strict adherence to all of the Rabbinic laws was really not required, some would, no doubt, have construed this to be the same as teaching that one was not required to keep the Torah (since the written and oral Torahs were considered as equally necessary by some).

If this were the case, than "doing evil that good may come" might have come about by teaching that a disregarding of certain rabbinic *halachaot* was actually necessary in order to fulfill the Torah. (We may also be mindful of Yeshua's teaching that "by the traditions you have set aside the Torah of Moses.")

Paul in 3:8 denied the "slanderous report (βλασφημούμεθα, *blasphemoumetha*, "blasphemous charge"") that he was teaching the righteousness of the Torah should be disregarded (and instead we should do unrighteousness to provoke God's mercy). In Paul's view, no one was able to be righteous by keeping the Torah perfectly, because no one was completely faithful to the righteousness set out in the Torah (3:1-7). Paul taught instead that God was faithful to manifest in the gospel the "power of God for salvation for every one who believes, to the Jew first and also to the Greek" (1:16). God was also faithful to reveal his "wrath" "from heaven against all ungodliness and unrighteousness of men, who suppress the truth in unrighteousness" (1:18). Thus the righteousness of the Torah still miraculously manifests God's faithfulness even when some have been unfaithful to its precepts and demands (3:1-7).[34]

9 What then? Are we better than they? Not at all; for we have already charged that both Jews and Greeks are all under sin;

Paul now brings us back to the original question of this section, and appends a fitting conclusion. The original question asks whether or not the Jew has an advantage over the non-Jew, and the answer is a resounding "Yes." This advantage is the possession of the written revelation of God, the "oracles." But the further question is whether or not this advantage which the Jew has also secures for him a privileged place in terms of righteousness. Does the fact that the Jew has the written revelation of God secure for him a more favorable judgment from the Almighty? No! Here again Paul returns to the premise of the previous chapter, that not the hearers of the Torah will be justified, but the doers. And Paul has charged both Jew and Gentile as existing under the penalty and control of sin. Thus, while the Jew may have an advantage in one respect, there is at least one area where there is no advantage, i.e., in respect to sin. The Jew, in respect of sinfulness, has no claim on God in virtue of his merit. Jew and Gentile alike suffer under the same penalty for sin, and the controlling force of its presence within the human soul and body.

10 as it is written, "There is none righteous, not even one;

This is a quote from Ps 14:1 (cf. 53:2).

MT	Lxx	Paul
אֵין עֹשֵׂה־טּוֹב no one does good (Ps 14:2)	οὐκ ἔστιν ποιῶν χρηστότητα οὐκ ἔστιν ἕως ἑνός no one is doing what is upright, there is not even one (Ps 13:3)	καθὼς γέγραπται ὅτι οὐκ ἔστιν δίκαιος οὐδὲ εἷς as it is written, there is no one who is righteous, not one

Paul adapts the opening sentence for his purposes, substituting δίκαιος, *dikaios*, "righteous" for χρηστότητα, *chrestoteta*, "upright." Δικαιος, *dikaios*, "righteous" is a very important word in this epistle. For Paul, the status of being righteous is an imputed status that issues in true faithfulness (righteousness) in the life of the believer.

We may presume that what Paul intends to convey by quoting this verse is to prove that no person is able to achieve, on his own merits, the status of "righteous" in God's eyes. Moreover, it is clear that Paul does not consider association within the chosen people of Israel to award the individual person the status of righteous. For Paul, it is not association within Israel that produces the status of righteous, but association in the person of Messiah. Thus, Paul's theology of righteousness is not one of "in Israel" but of "in Messiah." While association within the people group of Israel could be achieved via natural birth (the flesh) or through rabbinic conversion (works of the Torah), association "in Messiah" is available only through faith.

11-12 There is none who understands, There is none who seeks for God; All have turned aside, together they have become useless; There is none who does good, There is not even one.

Psalm 14:2-3

MT	Lxx	Paul
יהוה מִשָּׁמַיִם הִשְׁקִיף עַל־בְּנֵי־אָדָם לִרְאוֹת הֲיֵשׁ מַשְׂכִּיל דֹּרֵשׁ אֶת־אֱלֹהִים הַכֹּל סָר יַחְדָּו נֶאֱלָחוּ אֵין עֹשֵׂה־טוֹב אֵין גַּם־אֶחָד Adonai from heaven looked upon the sons of man to see if there is anyone who understands, who seeks after God. All of them have turned aside, together they become worthless. There is no one who does good, not even one. (Ps 14:2-3)	κύριος ἐκ τοῦ οὐρανοῦ διέκυψεν ἐπὶ τοὺς υἱοὺς τῶν ἀνθρώπων τοῦ ἰδεῖν εἰ ἔστιν συνίων ἢ ἐκζητῶν τὸν θεόν πάντες ἐξέκλιναν ἅμα ἠχρεώθησαν οὐκ ἔστιν ποιῶν χρηστότητα οὐκ ἔστιν ἕως ἑνός The Lord out of heaven looked down upon the sons of the men in order to see if there were those who understand or who seek after God. All have turned aside, together they have become corrupt; there is no one who does uprightness, there is not even one. (Ps 13:2-3)	οὐκ ἔστιν ὁ συνίων, οὐκ ἔστιν ὁ ἐκζητῶν τὸν θεόν. πάντες ἐξέκλιναν ἅμα ἠχρεώθησαν· οὐκ ἔστιν ὁ ποιῶν χρηστότητα, [οὐκ ἔστιν] ἕως ἑνός. no one understands, no one seeks after God. All have turned aside, together they have become useless. There is no one who does what is upright, [there is not] even one. (Rom 3:11-12)

13 Their throat is an open grave, With their tongues they keep deceiving, The poison of asps is under their lips;

Psalm 5:10

MT	Lxx	Paul
קֶבֶר־פָּתוּחַ גְּרוֹנָם לְשׁוֹנָם יַחֲלִיקוּן an open grave is their throat, with their tongue they flatter	τάφος ἀνεῳγμένος ὁ λάρυγξ αὐτῶν ταῖς γλώσσαις αὐτῶν ἐδολιοῦσαν an open grave is their throat, with their tongue they flatter	τάφος ἀνεῳγμένος ὁ λάρυγξ αὐτῶν ταῖς γλώσσαις αὐτῶν ἐδολιοῦσαν an open grave is their throat, with their tongues they flatter

Psalm 140:3[4]

MT	Lxx	Paul
חֲמַת עַכְשׁוּב תַּחַת שְׂפָתֵימוֹ סֶלָה the burning [fury=poison] of a viper is under his lips. Selah (Ps 140:4)	ἰὸς ἀσπίδων ὑπὸ τὰ χείλη αὐτῶν διάψαλμα the poison of a viper is under their lips. Selah (Ps 139:4)	ἰὸς ἀσπίδων ὑπὸ τὰ χείλη αὐτῶν the poison of a viper is under their lips (Rom 3:13)

14-18 Whose mouth is full of cursing and bitterness; Their feet are swift to shed blood, Destruction and misery are in their paths, And the path of peace have they not known. There is no fear of God before their eyes.

Psalm 10:7

MT	Lxx	Paul
אָלָה פִּיהוּ מָלֵא וּמִרְמוֹת וָתֹךְ his mouth is full of cursing and bitterness and oppression	οὗ ἀρᾶς τὸ στόμα αὐτοῦ γέμει καὶ πικρία καὶ δόλου whose mouth is full of cursing and bitterness and deceit (Ps 9:28)	ὧν τὸ στόμα ἀρᾶς καὶ πικρίας γέμει whose mouth is full of cursing and bitterness (Rom 3:14)

Isaiah 59:7-8a

MT	Lxx	Paul
רַגְלֵיהֶם לָרַע יָרֻצוּ וִימַהֲרוּ לִשְׁפֹּךְ דָּם נָקִי מַחְשְׁבוֹתֵיהֶם מַחְשְׁבוֹת אָוֶן שֹׁד וָשֶׁבֶר בִּמְסִלּוֹתָם דֶּרֶךְ שָׁלוֹם לֹא יָדָעוּ וְאֵין מִשְׁפָּט בְּמַעְגְּלוֹתָם נְתִיבוֹתֵיהֶם עִקְּשׁוּ לָהֶם כֹּל דֹּרֵךְ בָּהּ לֹא יָדַע שָׁלוֹם Their feet run to evil, and they hasten to shed innocent blood; their thoughts are thoughts of iniquity; devastation and destruction are in their highways. They do not know the way of peace.	οἱ δὲ πόδες αὐτῶν ἐπὶ πονηρίαν τρέχουσιν ταχινοὶ ἐκχέαι αἷμα καὶ οἱ διαλογισμοὶ αὐτῶν διαλογισμοὶ ἀφρόνων σύντριμμα καὶ ταλαιπωρία ἐν ταῖς ὁδοῖς αὐτῶν καὶ ὁδὸν εἰρήνης οὐκ οἴδασιν Their feet run to evil, and they hurry to shed innocent blood and their thoughts are thoughts of iniquity; devastation and destruction are in their ways and the way of peace they have not known.	ὀξεῖς οἱ πόδες αὐτῶν ἐκχέαι αἷμα, σύντριμμα καὶ ταλαιπωρία ἐν ταῖς ὁδοῖς αὐτῶν, καὶ ὁδὸν εἰρήνης οὐκ ἔγνωσαν. Their feet are swift to shed blood, destruction and misery are in their paths, and the path of peace have they not known. (Rom 3:15-17

Psalm 36:2

MT	Lxx	Paul
אֵין פַּחַד אֱלֹהִים לְנֶגֶד עֵינָיו there is no fear of God before his eyes	οὐκ ἔστιν φόβος θεοῦ ἀπέναντι τῶν ὀφθαλμῶν αὐτοῦ there is no fear of God before his eyes	οὐκ ἔστιν φόβος θεοῦ ἀπέναντι τῶν ὀφθαλμῶν αὐτῶν there is no fear of God before their eyes

We may now begin to analyze the quotes in vv. 10-18.

In v. 10, Paul once again gives us an understanding of his theological thinking process when he, through his own quote, interprets the MT and the Lxx, both of which have verbs of "doing": עָשָׂה, *'oseh* and ποιέω, *poieo,*—"no one does good." Paul, however, quotes it with a stative verb: "no one is righteous," interpreting both the action verb "to do" with the stative verb "to be," and the noun "good" with the corresponding noun "righteous." Once again, Paul demonstrates for us what is his normative theology, namely, that one who does good is good. To say "no one does good" and "no one is righteous" is, for Paul, to say the same thing. Yet surely Paul's use of δίκαιος, *dikaios* (righteous) emphasizes one's righteous standing before God as well as moral (what the reformed theologians called "practical") righteousness.

The additional phrase "not even one" is found at the end of v. 3 in the Hebrew, but not in the opening verse. The Lxx, however, includes it both in the opening phrase as well as in the concluding verse. Obviously Paul follows the Lxx. The phrase itself is emphatic in the Hebrew, and is well represented in the Lxx by ἕως ἑνός ("not even one"), though Paul's οὐδὲ εἶς ("not one") in the opening phrase represents the Hebrew a bit closer. Surely this emphatic and inclusive statement of the Psalmist was what attracted Paul to this passage initially. Since he is proving that everyone (particularly both Jew and Gentile) is guilty before God, to find the Psalmist saying that not even one person is righteous certainly fits his current emphasis.

It is interesting to note that R. Eliezer ben Hyrcanus (late 1st Century CE) was very fond of Ecc 7:20 (which Paul may also have in mind in this section of quotes): "Indeed, there is not a righteous man on earth who continually does good and who never sins." In b.*Sanhedrin* 101a an interesting interchange is recorded between R. Akiva (the disciple of R. Eliezer ben Hyrcanus) and Hyrcanus. Hyrcanus is ill and his disciples are discussing why. Some say there must be great anger in the world, and they mourn for their master. But Akiva laughs. When asked why he laughed, he responded that he often saw how well life went for Hyrcanus, and so he feared he might be receiving his reward in this world, and therefore receive nothing in the world to come. But now that he saw his master sick, he knew that his reward was still awaiting him in the world to come. Hyrcanus responded to this by asking "have I left out anything at all from the whole of the Torah?," which is a way of saying "have I done anything wrong to deserve this sickness?" Akiva's response is insightful, for it indicates that Ecc 7:20 was apparently one of Hyrcanus' favorite verses, or at least one often spoken of with his disciples. Akiva responded: "Indeed so [surely you have neglected something in the Torah] for you have taught us, our master, 'for there is not a just man upon the earth, who does good and does not sin.'" Thus Hyrcanus, like Paul (and contrary to the majority of the Rabbis of that time) taught the basic sinfulness of mankind as over against the typical Rabbinic view that everyone is born "neutral" and makes the choice to become sinful.

In vv. 11-12, Paul skips past the phrase which says "God looked down from heaven upon the sons of man to see if there was anyone who understands...." He instead takes the phrase "anyone who understands and seeks after God" and casts it in the negative: "no one understands, no one seeks after God."

"Understands" translates the Greek συνίων, *sunion*, from the root συνίειν, *suniein*, which is used both in the Psalm and by Paul as a reference to religious or moral understanding. The Hebrew word is שָׂכַל, *sachal*, which in the hifil often refers to "understanding" (Deut 32:29; Neh 8:13; Dan 9:13; Is 41:20) but can also mean "to have success" (1Sa 18:5; 2Ki 18:7) or "to act with insight, devotion, piety" (Is 52:13; 2Chr 30:22). That Paul seems to have all of these in mind appears very possible, for the concepts of moral understanding, success and piety all coalesce in the life of true faith.

who seeks after God – the concept of seeking after God is quite common in the Tanach, but only for those who have covenant relationship with Him (Ex 33:7; 2Chr 15:12, 13, 15; Ezra 8:22; Ps 9:10; 24:6; 27:8; Prov 28:5; Is 9:13; 31:1; 51:1; 55:6; Jer 29:13; Zeph 1:6). As far as the pagan, Paul's point is that there are none who seek after God, but rather all have turned aside (סוּר, *sur*). "To turn aside" means to cease to follow directly after God, and therefore to walk in one's own ways, to go after one's own heart.

together they have become worthless – the Hebrew word translated "worthless" is אָלַח, (in the nifil), used only here, in the parallel Psalm (53:4) and in Jb 15:16, "How much less one who is detestable and corrupt, Man, who drinks iniquity like water!" Here, as in the Psalms, the word is used of moral corruption. Job's picturesque "drinks iniquity like water" gives the poet's description of "corrupt."

there is no one who does what is upright – the Lxx uses the word χρηστότητα, *chrestoteta*, to translate the Hebrew טוֹב, *tov*, though in the corresponding Psalm (53) the Lxx uses the more common ἀγαθός, *agathos*, in both cases. The Hebrew uses the simple טוֹב in both instances. Paul quotes the Lxx here, and no doubt wants to emphasize that the "good" he is speaking of is in the realm of morality, i.e., in right standing before God.

In v. 13 Paul quotes Ps 5:10 and strings it together with Ps 140:3, describing the throat/tongue/lips of the wicked by the analogy of an open grave (entirely unclean and full of stench) and a venomous snake (something that kills with its mouth).

Paul quotes Ps 5:10 directly from the Lxx, which is a literal translation of the Hebrew. יַחֲלִיקוּן, *yachalikun*, "flatter" in the Psalm is translated in the Lxx with ἐδολιοῦσαν, *edoliousan*, from the root δολιόω, *dolioo*, which means "to deal treacherously." חָלַק, *chalak*, the Hebrew word translated "flatter" by the NASB has its root meaning in the concept of "smooth, slippery." The concept of "deception" then is within the semantic range of both words, and the Lxx has translated the Hebrew with a term that conveys its intended meaning here.

Here, then, is the life of the unrighteous, characterized by their inability to control the tongue. This theme is also taken up by James (1:26).

The quote from Ps 140:3 is likewise verbatim from the Lxx which is, at this point, a literal translation of the MT.

In vv. 14-18 Paul strings together phrases from Ps 10:7, Is 59:7-8a, and Ps 36:2. The common theme, of course, is the continuation of the mouth as the instrument of wickedness, and then other parts of the body, namely feet and eyes.

In quoting Ps 10:7, Paul includes the first two of three descriptors, but leaves off the final "oppression" (תֹּךְ, *toch*) or "deceit" (δόλου, *dolou*). What he does quote is very close to verbatim of the Lxx.

Not only is mankind not righteous, but he is actively engaged in obvious unrighteousness. He is full of cursing and bitterness, two elements which inevitably accompany the self-centered heart, especially in times of calamity. It is the trial which purges the dross, and in the believer results in greater likeness to the Messiah. But in the heart of an unbeliever, trials will inevitably bring cursing and bitterness. In other words, trials often offer a true window into the soul.

In the next quote Paul actually makes a kind of abridgement of Is 59:7-8a, but essentially quotes the Lxx. He uses this quote to show the total sinfulness of mankind. Wherever he goes he leaves destruction and misery in his path. Feet that are swift to shed blood were often interpreted by the ancient sages not only of physical violence, but even more of the "killing" that goes on when someone is slandered. Thus "feet swift to shed blood" may continue the theme of the throat/mouth/tongue of the previous verse. In this case "feet swift to shed blood" would also include those who hurry to gossip or engage in לָשׁוֹן הָרַע, *lashon hara*, "evil speech."

Rather than building up, they tear down; rather than edifying, they destroy. Everywhere mankind sets his foot, he establishes yet another center of idolatry with himself as the one to be worshipped. Instead of *shalom*, "peace," the unrighteous man attempts to find contentment in his unrighteouness—attempts to build himself up by tearing others down. The "peace" he thinks he is attaining is actually an unending war with God—"the path of peace they have not known." Surely for Paul this path of peace is the path upon which the believer walks in the footsteps of Messiah.

Paul closes the string of quotes with Ps 36:2, which, except for the change of a singular (αὐτοῦ, *autou*, "his") to a plural (αὐτῶν, *auton*, "theirs"), he quotes directly from the Lxx which also, at this place, is a literal translation of the MT. "There is no fear of God before their eyes"— a fitting conclusion to all that Paul has indicated by stringing these quotes together in the first place. Consider the following:

> Job 4:6 Is not your fear of God your confidence, And the integrity of your ways your hope?
> Job 28:28 And to man He said, 'Behold, the fear of the Lord, that is wisdom; And to depart from evil is understanding.'"
> Ps. 19:9 The fear of the LORD is clean, enduring forever; The judgments of the LORD are true; they are righteous altogether.
> Ps 111:10 The fear of the LORD is the beginning of wisdom; A good understanding have all

those who do His commandments; His praise endures forever.

Prov 1:7 The fear of the LORD is the beginning of knowledge; Fools despise wisdom and instruction.

Prov 8:13 The fear of the LORD is to hate evil; Pride and arrogance and the evil way, And the perverted mouth, I hate.

Prov 10:27 The fear of the LORD prolongs life, But the years of the wicked will be shortened.

Prov 14:26 In the fear of the LORD there is strong confidence, And his children will have refuge.

Prov 14:27 The fear of the LORD is a fountain of life, That one may avoid the snares of death.

Prov 15:16 Better is a little with the fear of the LORD, Than great treasure and turmoil with it.

Prov 16:6 By lovingkindness and truth iniquity is atoned for, And by the fear of the LORD one keeps away from evil.

19 Now we know that whatever the Torah says, it speaks to those who are under the Torah, that every mouth may be closed, and all the world may become accountable to God;

The NASB begins the verse with "Now . . .," a translation of δέ, *de*, a conjunctive particle that often anticipates a corresponding μεν, *men*, giving the sense of "on the one hand … on the other hand." Or, the word can be nearly equivalent to the conjunction "and" or mildly disjunctive, like one use of the English "but." The NASB translates it in a conjunctive sense, tying this verse to the previous context, and most agree with this perspective. As such, the Torah referred to here must be the Scriptures in general, for being tied to the previous context means Paul is considering the quotes as Torah, even though they are from the Prophets and the Writings. This is not uncommon for Paul's day, for the Sages regularly use the term "Torah" to refer to the whole of the Tanach. Paul uses Torah in this way in 1Cor 14:21 as does John in his gospel (10:34; 15:25).

"Under the Torah" is a bad translation of τοῖς ἐν τῷ νόμῳ, which literally would be "those in the Torah." "Under the Torah" would be ὑπὸ νόμον, *hupo nomon*, which is found in 6:14, 15. Our expression, "those in the Torah" is found in 2:12 and is contrasted in 2:14 by the negative expression (τὰ μὴ νόμον ἔχοντα) "those not having the Torah." Thus the expression here, "those who are in the Torah" should be understood to mean "those who possess the Torah" or "those who know the Torah." Thus, the phrase repeats the premise already given by Paul that the Jews were the first to possess the Torah (Scriptures) and thus those parts which clearly denote the universal sinfulness of man most surely apply to the nation to which God first revealed this truth. Since they were privileged to have the Scriptures first, "so far from imagining themselves excepted from its condemnations of human sinfulness, they ought to accept them as applying first and foremost to themselves." (Cranfield, *Romans*, 1.196)

that every mouth may be closed – Paul's logic is clear at this point, based upon *kal v'chomer*, (light and heavy): if the nation of God's choosing stands condemned by the very Scriptures He gave first to them, then it is certain that all the nations are likewise condemned. Or to say it another way, if the nation who first received the Torah stands guilty before God, certainly those nations to which she must teach the Torah would also be rendered guilty.

The expression of a closed mouth simply means that no valid excuse will be forthcoming when the guilty verdict is rendered. As Calvin puts it, "without saying a word [he] awaits his condemnation."

The word translated "become accountable" is ὑπόδικος, *hupodikos*, and is found only here in the Apostolic Scriptures. The word in its non-biblical usage denotes one who has offended the law and therefore is liable to prosecution and punishment. Associated with this meaning is that of the injured party having his "day in court" and receiving recompense from the offending party. NASB "become accountable" probably says too little, as does the NIV and NRSV, "held accountable." NKJV has "become guilty" which is far closer to the mark.

κόσμος, *kosmos*, ("world") here means "mankind," no doubt, and in the context is an inclusive term. Elsewhere, Paul uses this same word to denote Gentiles (11:12, 15).

20 because by the works of the Torah no flesh will be justified in His sight; for through the Torah *comes* the knowledge of sin.

The word "because" should most likely be taken to mean "for" (like ὅτι, *hoti*), as indicating that this supports what has just been said. Paul echoes as his support Ps 143:2b, though he does not introduce it with the customary "it is written" or equivalent.

Psalm 143:2 states: "And do not enter into judgment with Your servant, For in Your sight no man living is righteous."

Obviously Paul adds "by the works of the Torah" to the quote. We have had the phrase "work of the Torah" (in the singular) at 2:15, and the plural (as here) will be found again in 3:28, as well as in Gal 2:16 (3 times); 3:2, 5, 10. All of the occurrences of the phrase in Galatians, like here, have the preposition: ἐξ ἔργων νόμου, *ex ergon nomou*, "out from the works of the Torah."

Some have wanted to interpret "works of the Torah" or "work of the Torah" to mean only those deeds done with a view to making oneself righteous, as over against the "works of the Torah" done out of a heart of obedience. But it is never clear that Paul has anything in mind about the motivation for doing what the Torah commands when he uses the phrase "works of the Torah." What is clear, however, is that Paul can never imagine any instance, even with the most righteous motivations, when obedience to the Torah could bring a sinner to right standing before God.

It stands to reason that if the Scriptures teach that "no flesh will be justified in His sight," that this must also include those who, though not perfect, are nonetheless striving to obey the Torah and actually do so, at least a good deal of the time. Thus even those whose lives conform to the Torah cannot, in that obedience, manufacture the righteousness needed to measure up to God's holy standards and be declared without guilt (justified).

Until recently the phrase "works of the Torah" had no extra-biblical counterpart, not being found in the extant rabbinic literature. However, recent publications of the Qumran materials have revealed a similar phrase used by the sect who produced Dead Sea Scrolls. In 4QMMT, section C 25-32 we read:

> Remember David, he was a pious man, and indeed he was delivered from many troubles and forgiven.
>
> Now, we have written to you some of the works of the Torah (מִקְצָת מַעֲשֵׂי הַתּוֹרָה, *miktzat ma'asei hatorah*) those which we determined would be beneficial for you and your people, because we have seen [that] you possess insight and knowledge of the Torah. Understand all these things and beseech Him to set your counsel straight and so keep you away from evil thoughts and the counsel of Belial. Then you shall rejoice at the end time when you find the essence of our words to be true. And it will be reckoned to you as righteousness (ונחשבה לך לצדקה), in that you have done what is right and good before Him, to your own benefit and to that of Israel.[35]

Regardless of what the interpretation might be of this quote (and of similar language in 4Q174), it seems significant that "works of the Torah" and "reckoned as righteousness" are found in close proximity, language which heretofore has been thought to be exclusively Pauline. We may now speculate that the debate of how one gained righteousness did indeed exist in the 1st Century[36] and that there were those, who though recognizing the need for God's mercy, nonetheless felt that their association within the people-group of Israel *as they defined Israel* was the all-important factor in having a righteous status before God. For the Qumran sect, their entrance requirements (their particular *halachah* which distinguished them from other sects) were the "works of the Torah" necessary to become part of the "*yachad*" (unity, society, or the true expression of Israel) and thus to be reckoned as righteous.

However, for Paul, people-group status was not the basis for right standing before God, but rather Messiah-status, being "in Messiah" was the requirement. This position, of course, struck at the very heart of what the Sages had defined as "righteous."

for through the Torah [comes] the knowledge of sin – For the person who has not yet come to faith and therefore stands guilty before God, the Torah, rather than being a means of growing in righteousness, points out sin and reveals (if the Spirit is willing to open the eyes) the utter sinfulness of the soul. Apart from faith the Torah is not the remedy to the sin problem but merely the magnifying glass by which the malady is known.

We now come to 3:21-26, a paragraph which is not only the heart of this particular section of Romans (1:18-4:25) but is perhaps also the heart of the entire teaching section of the epistle (1:16b-15:13). Having noted how 3:21-26 has a distinct literary style and unity, Cranfield remarks that its content is what sets it apart as central:

> It stands out much more of course by virtue of its content; for it proclaims the fact that the one decisive, once for all, redemptive act of God, the revelation both of the righteousness which is from God and also of the wrath of God against human sin, the once for all revelation which is the basis of the continuing revelation of the righteousness (1:17) and of the wrath (1:18) of God in the preaching of the gospel, has now taken place. It shows that the heart of the gospel preached by Paul is a series of events in the past (not just the crucifixion of Christ—for the Cross by itself would have been no saving act of God—but the crucifixion together with the resurrection and exaltation of the Crucified) a series of events which is the Event of history, an act which as the decisive act of God is altogether effective and irreversible.[37]

21 But now apart from the Torah *the* righteousness of God has been manifested, being witnessed by the Torah and the Prophets,

"But now" (νυνὶ δέ, *nuni de*) can be understood temporally, as indicating the present as opposed to the past, or logically, as indicating a conclusion to a given line of argumentation. It seems most likely that here the temporal sense must be in view, in that Paul intends to mark the appearance of the Messiah as the decisive and (relatively speaking) present-day event which in every way is the means by which God intends to declare sinners righteous.

This method of declaring sinners righteous (for so we should understand the phrase "righteousness of God," as in 1:18) is now fully revealed, a salvation which was witnessed by the Torah and the Prophets. Thus, faith in the Messiah has always been the means by which God declares a sinner just, but it is in the present day (from Paul's perspective) that the Messiah Himself has been fully revealed.

This method of salvation has always been God's method of righteousness, having been spoken of before the Messianic event by the Torah and Prophets, and now being realized in the appearance of Yeshua and the teaching of His apostles. This method of declaring a person righteous has always been "apart from the Torah" (χωρὶς νόμου, *choris nomou*), but the very focal point of it, i.e., Yeshua, was only prophesied before—now He has come and in His coming has revealed the fulness of God's way of salvation.

Those who might want to understand this verse as teaching that Paul regarded the Torah as no longer valuable or necessary since the Gospel has come, must surely twist the words as we find them, for Paul himself recognizes that the Tanach (Torah and Prophets) taught the same message of salvation by faith—not a message which was contrary to Messiah and thus needed to be abandoned at His arrival. As Cranfield so aptly puts it:

> To appeal to these words as evidence that Paul regarded the law as superseded and set aside by the gospel as something now out of date and irrelevant is surely perverse.[38]

The addition of the phrase "being witnessed by the Torah and the Prophets" is significant, for it substantiates not only the teaching that the gospel is contiguous with the Tanach, but also that the Tanach is properly understood as witness to this righteousness which is by faith alone, that is, to the gospel which is centered in the person and work of Yeshua. Had Paul believed that the Tanach was contrary to the gospel as it is in Yeshua, he most certainly could not have appealed to it as he does time and time again to substantiate the gospel message, nor would he have, in this verse, named it as corroborating witness to the righteousness of God which is apart from the Torah, that is, apart from the "works of the Torah."

22 even *the* righteousness of God through faith in Yeshua Messiah for all those who believe; for there is no distinction;[39]

Here, the opening of the verse with δέ, *de* ("but, and") indicates a closer definition of what has just been discussed. Paul uses the term in the same way in 9:39; 1Cor 2:6; Gal 2:2; Phil 2:8. The righteousness of God of which Paul is speaking is through faith in the Messiah and is available to all who believe.

faith in Yeshua Messiah – διὰ πίστεως Ιησοῦ Χριστοῦ, *dia pisteos Iesou Christou,* the genitive indicating the object of the faith (thus the English "in" is added to give the proper sense but is not represented by an equivalent Greek ἐν, *en*). This is the first time in the epistle that Paul explicitly names Yeshua as the object of saving faith, but he does so while having just, in the same breath, argued that the Torah and the Prophets witnessed this means of salvation which is apart from the works of the Torah. Thus, the Tanach witnesses to Yeshua, and we know that this was the unified teaching of the Apostles and of Yeshua Himself (cf. Lk 24:27).

for there is no distinction – in the same way that all are guilty before God, so there is no distinction in the method of salvation God applies to sinners. There is only one way of salvation, and this is through faith in Yeshua. 10:12, "for there is no distinction between Jew and Greek" makes the same claim. But it is going too far to say that this abolition of distinction between Jew and Greek must necessarily mean that the privileges of national Israel have also been abolished. The utter lack of distinction in this sense is in the means by which God declares a sinner righteous (=the righteousness of God). God does not have one plan of salvation for the Jew and a different one for the non-Jew. As far as right standing before God, it makes absolutely no difference what race or gender a person is, nor their station in life. This, of course, does not negate real distinctions between race, gender, or station in life as to particular issues of life and the attended responsibilities.

23 for all have sinned and fall short of the glory of God,

Perhaps the most important question to be asked initially is how these verses are structured, particularly how v. 24 fits together with vv. 22-23. Specifically we must ask how δικαιού-μενοι, *dikaioumenoi* ("being justified") attaches to what comes before, and who the subject of that participle is. The following options seem apparent:

1) that those being justified are the "all" of v. 23, so that the sense is that all are sinners (v. 23) but all are being justified.

2) that those being justified are the "all" of v. 22, i.e., "all who believe," and that
v. 23 is a parenthetical statement to explain or give explanation why there is
no distinction (because all have equally sinned and are therefore sinners).

3) that v. 24 begins a new and independent sentence.

I am inclined to go with option #1, though with a further explanation, that the "all who
believe" of v. 22 is the governing idea, and that therefore the "all have sinned" of v. 23 refers
specifically (in this case) to those who have believed, proving that among these there is no
distinction of race. Thus, v. 24 goes on to show yet another reason why there is no distinction,
namely, that all who have commonality in their sinful status, and who share in the singularity of
their faith, also share equally the eternal gift of God's righteousness (i.e., the method which God
employs in order to declare sinners righteous) .

If this interpretation is correct, then v. 23, one of the most often memorized verses of
Romans, is generally misunderstood. For it is usually taught as giving substantiation for the
universal sinfulness of mankind, but in the context would (in this interpretation) only be speaking of the sinfulness of all who believe.

V. 23, then, emphasizes that all those who have believed and have therefore been given
right standing before God, find a commonality in being sinners and having fallen short of
God's glory. The past tense (aorist) in the word "have sinned" should not be forced as teaching
that those who have come to faith in the Messiah no longer sin. Rather, the aorist is most likely
"collective," being viewed as it were from the vantage point of the final judgment day. That the
judgment day may well be in Paul's mind is hinted at by "every mouth may be stopped" of v.
19. Thus, the final judgment will reveal that all have sinned.

Secondly, the commonality among all who believe is that they fall short of the glory of
God. The word translated "fall short" is from the Greek ὑστερεῖν, *husterein*, which means "be
behind," "come too late," "fail to obtain," "lack," "be inferior to," and "fail" or "be wanting."
Paul uses the word elsewhere in 1Cor 1:7; 8:8; 12:24; 2Cor 11:5, 9; 12:11; Phil 4:12.

This verse thus teaches that not only all other men, but also all believers still lack this
"glory of God" in the sense that the transcendent majesty that we will receive when we see Him
(for we will become like Him, cf. 1Jn 3:2) is not yet ours. This is not to deny that there is a radi-
ant glory (in one sense of the word) that eminates from believers through the indwelling Spirit.
But it does emphasize that we have not yet received all that we have been promised, and, to use
Paul's words, we will be transformed "from glory to glory" (2Cor 3:18) when we are ushered
into the world to come. This future glory may be conceived of as a status in which the full glory
of God can shine upon us without any diminished effect, so that we may reflect, as it were, the
glory of God in all His perfections. It is, therefore, our constant goal to reflect more and more
this glory of God without diminishing it in the least.

24 being justified as a gift by His grace through the redemption which is in Messiah Yeshua;

If the interpretation above is correct, and v. 23 is a kind of parenthesis, then the basic sentence with which we are dealing is: "But now apart from the Torah the righteousness of God has
been manifested, the righteousness of God through faith in Yeshua Messiah for all who believe,
being justified as a gift by His grace through the redemption which is in Messiah Yeshua."

We have encountered the term "justified" several times already in Romans (2:13; 3:4, 20),
though here it is used for the first time "directly and positively in reference to what is the leading theme of this epistle."[40] The word itself is cognate with the noun for "righteous" (δίκαιος,
dikaios) and "righteousness" (δικαιοσύνη, *dikaiosune*) and means "to show justice," "vindicate,"
"be treated justly" and in the passive "to be acquitted," "be pronounced and treated as righteous." At the heart of the gospel is the fact that God pronounces sinners to be righteous and

treats them accordingly. The difficulty this represents, of course, is that it brings God's justice into question, a difficulty dealt with in v. 26. For the "righteousness of God" (=the method by which God declares a sinner righteous) involves the due payment of sin by the death of His Messiah.

as a gift of His grace (δωρεὰν τῇ αὐτοῦ χάριτι, *dorean te autou chariti*) – The Greek word which lies behind the translation "as a gift" is δωρεά, *dorea* which often in the Lxx translates חִנָּם, *chinam,* "without compensation (=free)," "without cause, undeservedly." Its appearance in the Lxx no doubt influenced its use in the Apostolic writings. Note the following where the Hebrew term חִנָּם, *chinam* is translated by our Greek word δωρεά, *dorea*:

> Ex 21:2 If you buy a Hebrew slave, he shall serve for six years; but on the seventh he shall go out as a <u>free</u> man without payment.

> 2Sam 24:24 However, the king said to Araunah, "No, but I will surely buy it from you for a price, for I will not offer burnt offerings to the LORD my God which <u>cost me nothing</u>." So David bought the threshing floor and the oxen for fifty shekels of silver.

> Is 52:3 For thus says the LORD, "You were sold <u>for nothing</u> and you will be redeemed without money."

The idea, then, of a "gift" has to do with the picture of being set free without payment— the sabbatical year (שְׁמִיטָּה, *sh'mittah*) and the Jubilee (יוֹבֵל, *yovel*) thus set up the framework for God's revelation of His method for declaring a sinner righteous, not on the basis of their own efforts or payment, but entirely as a free gift.

This concept, then, of the free gift is substantiated by the added phrase "of His grace"—it is a gift of His grace. The Greek actually has the dative where we might expect the genitive, so that literally we might translate "gift by His grace," which is not substantially different in meaning. The dative of means, however, indicates the avenue through which we did receive the gift, i.e., through the means of His grace. The genitive (of His grace) would emphasize the source of the gift more than the means by which it was given. Of course, both are true, for God's grace is both the source and the means of giving the divine gift of the Messiah.

through the redemption which is in Messiah Yeshua – two questions confront us at the outset of this phrase: 1) to what does the phrase attach, and 2) what is the meaning of "redemption" (λύτρον, *lutron*)?

As to the first question it is clear that the phrase attaches to the opening participle (being justified), so that it describes the exact means by which, in God's method of salvation, a sinner is declared righteous. This means is one of redemption, a redemption accomplished through the work of Messiah.

The second question is exactly what Paul meant by using the word "redemption." The Greek word is λύτρον, *lutron,* but the argument rages among scholars as to whether the word simply describes "deliverance," "emancipation" without any sense of "payment," or whether the word always entails the idea of a ransom paid. While it appears that one cannot be dogmatic on this issue, the evidence in my opinion is weighted toward the idea that the word and its cognates (as ἀπολύτρωσις, *apolutrosis,* used here) always carries with it some sense of paying the price necessary for deliverance. The evidence to support this is:

1) the word group in the non-biblical Greek literature seems to always retain the idea of "payment of price" in the process of deliverance;
2) the Lxx's use of the word group, while not consistent, seems often to attach the meaning of payment of price to the word.
3) Paul's use of the word elsewhere in 1Cor 6:20; 7:23 where those who are be-

lievers have been "bought with a price," as well as his use of the term in Gal 3:13 and 4:5 would favor the idea of a price paid for redemption.

4) The use of the term elsewhere in the Apostolic Scriptures often incorporates the idea of payment of price (Mk 10:45; Acts 20:28; 1Ti 2:6; 1Pet 1:18f; Rev 5:9)

Thus, our right standing before God has come about by a decisive and historical act of God, brought about by His own, sovereign initiative and carried out by His own strength through payment of a price. This redemption which He wrought is a redemption from the slavery of sin and the inevitable condemnation and wrath of God which it brings upon the sinner. Through the payment of the price, His justice is satisfied, and He is therefore able to redeem the guilty sinner from the bonds of slavery and to bring him into freedom. In this way God is both "just and the justifier" (v. 26).

which is in Messiah Yeshua – that is, in the work which He has accomplished. It is interesting that Paul reverses the ordering of the names. In v. 22 it is Yeshua Messiah—is this significant? It may well be that by putting Messiah first, Paul focuses our attention upon the finished work of redemption (that for which Messiah came) rather than upon our present union with Him. While it certainly is true that union with the Messiah through faith in Him is the only channel through which an individual personally receives the benefits of salvation, the redemption upon which Paul here focuses is the redemption gained by Yeshua at the cross.

in Messiah Yeshua – the redemption which Paul here delineates is "in Messiah Yeshua." This is the first time in the book that Paul utilizes this, one of his favorite phrases (he uses it approximately 75 times in the entirety of his epistles) and it is important for us to ask what he means by "in Messiah Yeshua."

The Greek preposition "in" (ἐν, *en*) can be used to indicate "means," i.e., the means by which something is done or accomplished. Thus, one might suggest that the meaning here is that the redemption is carried out by Yeshua—"by the redemption which Yeshua accomplished." The difficulty with this explanation, however, is that elsewhere Paul speaks of the believer being "in Messiah Yeshua," using the same language as he uses here. Note, for instance:

> 2Cor 5:17 Therefore if any man is in Messiah, he is a new creature; the old things passed away; behold, new things have come.
> Gal 3:28 There is neither Jew nor Greek, there is neither slave nor free man, there is neither male nor female; for you are all one in Messiah Yeshua.
> 1Th 4:16 For the Lord Himself will descend from heaven with a shout, with the voice of the archangel, and with the trumpet of God; and the dead in Messiah shall rise first.

So while it is possible at times that the phrase "in Messiah" may mean "by means of Messiah," there is clear evidence that Paul often had a different sense in mind.

Apparently he actually saw all who had true faith as being so much in union with the Messiah that he could describe them as "in Messiah." That is to say, like the sacrifice of old, upon which the worshiper placed his hands, stood in every way as a substitute for the sinner, so Yeshua is that sacrifice taking the place of the one who believes in Him by faith. Thus, to be "in Messiah Yeshua" is to have all of His work accredited to oneself, and to be viewed by the Father in precisely the same way as He views His own Son. To be "in Messiah" is to be entirely encompassed by His majesty and therefore safe from all and every harm which might otherwise destroy. For Paul, there is only one locus of salvation—"in Messiah." Even as the Temple and the priesthood which served within it constituted the only God-ordained place of atonement under the Aaronic priesthood as the foreshadowing of Messiah, so Yeshua is the only place of eternal forgiveness. The only hope the sinner has is to be "in Messiah Yeshua."

We should also reckon with the fact that in the 1st Century, rabbinic theology accorded high significance to being "in Israel," that is, having the status of being an Israelite. However,

Yeshua as the Messiah is the zenith of Israel, the full expression of the Servant of the Lord. Thus, while the Sages may have considered "being in Israel" the means of righteousness in God's eyes, Paul saw being "in Messiah" as the true way of being "in Israel," and thus the true way of being reckoned righteous in God's eyes.

25–26 whom God displayed publicly as a propitiation in His blood through faith. This was to demonstrate His righteousness, because in the forbearance of God He passed over the sins previously committed; for the demonstration, I say, of His righteousness at the present time, so that He would be just and the justifier of the one who has faith in Yeshua.

The opening word "whom" (Greek ὅν, *hon*) can be understood either as "whom" or "which," allowing the following description to apply either to Yeshua Himself, or to the redemption which He brought about.

The verb translated "displayed" is προτιθέναι, *protithenai,* and is used only three times in the Apostolic Scriptures (Rom 1:13; 3:25; Eph 1:9). Its main meanings are (1) "to purpose," "propose to oneself," and (2) "set forth publicly," "display."

Many have found the second definition most appealing (NASB, NIV, RSV, KJV, NKJV, and many commentators). But Cranfield shows compelling reasons to understand the word's use here as meaning "purpose": (1) it is used this way in 1:13 and Eph 1:9, (2) the related (and cognate) verb πρόθεσις, *prothesis,* in eight of its twelve occurrences in the Apostolic Writings, means "purpose" (the other four describe the bread of the Presence). Furthermore, it seems most likely that Paul's overriding concern here is to show the eternal attribute of God's righteousness (justice) in light of the cross and the justification of sinners. Thus it fits that he would highlight the eternal purpose in the cross more than its public display. God is righteous because He had always determined or purposed that Yeshua would be the sacrifice for sinners. Thus, His willingness to overlook (as it seemed) the sins "previously committed" was with a view to the payment Messiah would make, thus establishing His righteousness.

With this in mind, we might therefore translate the verse "which (i.e., the redemption) God purposed as a propitiation in His blood through faith."

"Propitiation" is the Greek word ἱλαστήριον, *hilasterion,* a word found 27 times in the Lxx, 21 of which refer to the כַּפֹּרֶת, "mercy seat."[41] In fact, the only other time that the word is found in the Apostolic Writings (Heb 9:5) it refers to the mercy seat of the Ark of the Covenant. It is clear, then, that this meaning (i.e., "mercy seat") must have been attached to the word in its 1st Century usage. In fact, it is from this association with the mercy seat of the Ark that the term gained its general meaning of "propitiation," for the mercy seat is that place where the wrath of God is conciliated. Thus, to be propitiated to God is to be in that place where His wrath, rightly deserved by sinners, is quenched and He rather extends a call for friendship and peace. This place of propitiation is perfectly symbolized by the mercy seat, being as it was the place where the blood was applied, interposed between the watchful eye of the Cherubim and the symbols of God's kingship against which Israel rebelled (the 10 Words, jar of manna, Aaron's rod).

The word "propitiation" is now followed by five descriptive phrases, all explaining some particular aspect of it:

(1) "through faith," that is, this propitiation to God is available to the one who believes. It follows, then, that apart from faith it is impossible to escape the wrath of God, for propitiation is available only by faith. This, once again, excludes any possibility that one could gain propitiation through physical lineage (=the flesh, i.e., being Jewish) or through obtaining the status of "Jewish" through becoming a proselyte (the works of the Torah).

(2) "in His blood" (ἐν τῷ αὐτοῦ αἵματι, *en to autou haimati*) – This phrase is the second to describe the "propitiation" and should not be connected to "faith," as though Paul is teaching about faith in Messiah's blood instead of faith in the Messiah Himself. Rather, the propitiation

is "in His blood." This is to teach us, rather, that the only means by which Yeshua could be the propitiation the Father had purposed Him to be was through the shedding of His blood, connecting the ultimate sacrifice of Yeshua to all of the sacrifices prescribed in the Torah which were nothing more nor less than signposts pointing to Calvary. Yeshua is the ultimate sacrifice to which all other sacrifices point.

Consider Lev 17:11 in the Lxx and the parallel Greek terms (especially when one considers that ἐξιλάσκεσθαι (*exilaskesthai*) is cognate to ἱλαστήριον (*hilasterion*): ἡ γὰρ ψυχὴ πάσης σαρκὸς αἷμα αὐτοῦ ἐστιν καὶ ἐγὼ δέδωκα αὐτὸ ὑμῖν ἐπὶ τοῦ θυσιαστηρίου ἐξιλάσκεσθαι περὶ τῶν ψυχῶν ὑμῶν τὸ γὰρ αἷμα αὐτοῦ ἀντὶ τῆς ψυχῆς ἐξιλάσεται. ("For the life of every flesh is its blood and I have given it to you upon the altar to make propitiation for your souls. For it is its blood in exchange for the soul that makes propitiation.")

(3) The third descriptive phrase considers the seeming contradiction of God overlooking sin and describes yet another aspect of the propitiation, namely, that by it God answers the objection of justice which demands that sinners be punished. He would not be the good and merciful God, had He been content to pass over sins indefinitely; for this would have been to condone evil—a denial of His own nature and a cruel betrayal of sinners. Cranfield explains:

> God has in fact been able to hold His hand and pass over sins, without compromising His goodness and mercy, because His intention has all along been to deal with them once and for all, decisively and finally, through the Cross. Paul is saying in these two verses that God purposed (from eternity) that Christ should be ἱλαστήριον, in order that the reality of God's righteousness, that is, of His goodness and mercy, which would be called in question by His passing over sins committed up to the time of that decisive act, might be established. (*Romans*, 1.121)

(4) The fourth phrase describing the propitiation is "to demonstrate at the present time His righteousness ...." This is almost identical with the previous phrase (at least in theme) with the addition of "at the present time." Here Paul seems to lump together the actual event of the Cross as well as the proclamation of the gospel during his time. Thus, for Paul, the propitiation that God made for sinners is attached to an historical event, and is proclaimed by the preaching of that event. In one sense, then, both the historical event as well as proclamation of it are part of God's determined plan to accomplish His salvation.

(5) The fifth phrase describing the propitiation is "that He might be just and the justifier of the one who has faith in Yeshua." The emphasis in this phrase is not that God purposed to show His righteousness by the propitiation in Yeshua, but that He actually is righteous. For to forgive without repayment of the damages is hardly to be righteous. God could only, therefore, have predetermined the propitiation through Yeshua as a public event for His very righteous nature required it so. He is therefore "just, even the justifier" of the ungodly. The word "and" in this phrase can surely be taken adverbially, and the sense then would be "that God might be righteous even in justifying."

27 Where then is boasting? It is excluded. By what kind of Torah? Of works? No, but by a Torah of faith.

Paul now comes to the conclusion of this most important section in which he has proved the utter guilty condition of all mankind, and thus that the only means of right standing with God is through the propitiation which He accomplished in the sacrifice of His Son.

The overall argument of these last five verses is quite obvious: no one can boast as though he has gained right standing with God through his own merits. What is difficult to ascertain, at least at first reading, is the manner in which Paul supports this summary statement through the argument that God is the God of both the Gentile and the Jew, and that the Torah itself confirms the exclusion of boasting.

Consider the following as a possible explanation:

Premise: Boasting about right standing with God is excluded
Proofs:

1) God has justified both Jew and Gentile
2) Since the Gentile obviously is justified without becoming a Jew (Abraham will be the obvious test case), his justification could never be argued as gained through his own merits or the merits of his people-group identification
3) Since God is one, and since He is the God of both Jew and Gentile, it is clear that He has only one method of declaring a sinner righteous, and this one method applies equally to Jew and Gentile.
4) Once the Torah is understood through the "eyes of faith," it will be seen that the Torah has always taught that right standing with God can be achieved only through faith in the Messiah
5) Thus, justification by faith does not negate the Torah but actually confirms it.

Where then is boasting? It is excluded – It seems certain that for Paul, the thinking that one could have God in his debt by doing good works is entirely excluded first and foremost by the very coming of Yeshua and the redemptive work that He accomplished. If there were any other way to gain right standing with God than through the death of His Son, He surely would have spared Yeshua the agony. Thus, the fact of the incarnation itself excludes anyone from boasting about a self-made propitiation.

But Paul's immediate argument rests upon the fact that the Torah itself, when rightly understood, excludes any boasting: "by what Torah? of works? No, but by the Torah of faith." How are we to understand the two designations "Torah of works" and "Torah of faith?" First, it seems clear that the two are put as opposites, at least in this case, the Torah of works teaching one thing, the Torah of faith, the opposite. In fact, it would appear that the "Torah of works" would include boasting, while the Torah of faith excludes it.

The following are suggestions which have been generally offered for a definition of the "Torah (Law) of faith":

1) That Paul uses the terminology "Torah of faith" simply because he wants to parallel the former "Torah of works"
2) The "Law of faith" is a special law under which the Christians stand. This explanation would find corroboration in Rom 8:2, "the Law of the Spirit of life;" Gal 6:2, "the law of Messiah;" 1Cor 9:21, the "commandment of Messiah." Most would consider this the Law of love: to love one's neighbor in particular.
3) The word "law" in this case is to be understood as "principle," "ethical norm," "divine institution," "system," or "way of salvation;" that "principle of works" verses "principle of faith" is the issue.
4) That by "Torah of faith" is meant the Torah of Moses understood through faith in the Messiah.

The fourth suggestion above best fits the context, as Cranfield notes:

We may then understand Paul's meaning to be that the correct answer to the question 'By what kind of law (has such glorying been excluded)?' is 'By God's law (i.e., the law of the OT)—that is, by God's law, not misunderstood as a law which directs men to seek justification as a reward for their works, but properly understood as summoning men to faith.

(*Romans*, 1.220)

The Torah of faith is the Torah understood through faith, that is, the Torah unveiled to reveal the Messiah Yeshua (cf. 2Cor 3). Conversely, the Torah of works is the Torah viewed as the means of either maintaining (for Jews) or attaining (for Gentiles) the status of "Israelite," and the belief that God automatically reckons Israel to be righteous (based upon Is 60:21 and m.*Sanhedrin* 10:1).

For Paul, then, the Torah has always taught a righteousness by faith, but for those who lack true, saving faith, this is missed, for the Messiah is veiled. In fact, apart from the possession of true, saving faith, one will inevitably misinterpret the Torah as teaching a righteousness based upon ethnic status and the maintenance of the covenant through obedience (which he labels "works-righteousness"), a viewpoint Paul attributes to present Israel (9:31f; 10:16ff).

28 For we maintain that a man is justified by faith apart from works of the Torah.

This is simply a restatement of the conclusion and further substantiation of the fact that no one can boast. The plural "we" may either be a rhetorical "authorial" plural or (more likely) an indication that Paul sees the whole community of believers agreeing with his statement.

On the phrase "works of the Torah" as defining covenant member status, cf. the comments on v. 20 above.

29 Or is God *the God* of Jews only? Is He not *the God* of Gentiles also? Yes, of Gentiles also,

This verse appears to be given in support of the summary statement in the previous verse. It is universally accepted (among those who have placed their faith in Yeshua) that a person is justified by faith and not by the works of the Torah, and the most fundamental proof of this is the Oneness of God, as confessed in the *Shema* (Deut 6:4f; 11:13f). Since the God of Abraham, Isaac, and Jacob is the only God (in reality no others exist but in the imaginations of fallen man), and since God foretold that all the nations would worship Him and be blessed in Abraham and his seed, it follows that this One God must be the God of the Gentiles as well as the Jews. As such, relationship with Him must be on the basis of His mercy, not on the merits of those He draws close. If, for the sake of the argument, it is allowed that Israel, in her privileged position of election, might have found right standing with God on the basis that she is the only chosen nation, it is obvious that the same could not be said for the Gentile nations. Yet if it is true that God is the God of the Gentile nations, being the only true God (and no Jew would have denied this at the time of Paul), then it is likewise logical that He would employ the same method of declaring a sinner righteous regardless of that person's ethnicity or people-group status.

30 since indeed God who will justify the circumcised by faith and the uncircumcised through faith is one.

The Oneness (uniqueness) of God is such that there can be none to compare with Him—there is none like Him. He alone is able to justify the sinner, and He alone has the rightfully sovereignty to determine the method by which He will declare a sinner just. This method of declaring a sinner righteous centers upon His Son, Yeshua, whom the sinner lays hold of by faith.

Some have attempted to draw a clear distinction between "by faith" (ἐκ πίστεως, *ek pisteos*, literally "out from faith") and "through faith" (διὰ τῆς πίστεως, *dia tes pisteos*, literally "through the faith") but the data simply cannot support such a view. For Paul, the variation in preposition is most likely a simple matter of rhetorical style. Note 4:11, (ἐν τῇ ἀκροβυστίᾳ, *en te akrobustia* "in uncircumcision" [="while uncircumcised"] and δι᾽ ἀκροβυστίας, *di akrobustias,* "through uncircumcision" [="while uncircumcised"]); 5:10, (διὰ τοῦ θανάτου τοῦ υἱοῦ αυτοῦ, "through the death of His Son and ἐν τῇ ζωῇ αὐτοῦ, "in His life") ; and 2Cor 3:11 (διὰ δόξης, *dia dokses,* "through glory" and ἐν δόξη, *en dokse,* "in glory").

31 Do we then nullify the Torah through faith? May it never be! On the contrary, we establish the Torah.

Why would anyone have questioned whether or not the preaching of Paul "nullified" the Torah? Most likely the answer to this question is simply that Paul's teachings of grace fostered in the hearts of some the notion that forgiveness on the basis of pure grace would surely lead to unrighteous living ("let us sin that grace may abound"). But Paul's obvious conclusion is that justification on the basis of faith alone, far from nullifying the Torah, establishes it. For the Torah has always had faith at its core, and was given to point to the Messiah. The Torah, then, pointed all who would have eyes to see and ears to hear, to the Messiah. Having come to faith in the Messiah is then to confirm the message of the Torah, not to nullify it.

What is more, Paul's premise is that the doers of the Torah, not merely the hearers of the Torah, are justified before God (2:13). Thus, the Torah, leading the sinner to Messiah, is established in that the believer walks, not according to the deeds of the flesh, but through the Spirit Who fulfills the requirements of the Torah within him (this will be the theme of chapter 8). In this way, faith in the Messiah establishes the Torah as it recreates within the believer a heart upon which the Torah is written, and therefore lived out in humble obedience. Here is a strong corrective to those who teach that the Torah is abolished ("nullified," translating καταργέω, *katargeo,* a word which means to "nullify," "render of no consequence," "render ineffective") through faith in the Messiah. Paul speaks in direct opposition to such teaching.

Chapter 4
Commentary

Chapter four moves Paul's argument along by presenting primary proof to substantiate 3:27, that all boasting is excluded. In a kind of *kal v'komer* argument, Paul goes to the man who, in Jewish history, should be the one most apt to boast, Abraham himself. If it can be shown that Abraham had no grounds for boasting, then all other boasting is likewise excluded.

After presenting Abraham as the argument *par excellence* in vv. 1-8, Paul continues in five more sections to expound the nature of Abraham's faith. The chapter as a whole may be broken down as follows:

1-8	Abraham had no grounds for boasting since his right standing with God was also on the basis of faith
9-12	Abraham gained right standing with God before he was circumcised. Therefore, faith precedes covenant membership, and circumcision is a sign of this covenant membership already possessed.
13-17a	Abraham's right standing with God was not something merited through fulfillment of the Torah, but simply on the basis of the righteousness which is by faith.
17b-22	Expounds the text found in Gen 15:6 and draws out the meaning of "Abraham believed God"
23-25	shows the relevance of Abraham's faith to all believers, and puts him forward as the paradigm for saving faith.

1 What then shall we say that Abraham, our forefather according to the flesh, has found?

Abraham is now brought forward as the example of someone who, if there were a basis for boasting, certainly it would be him. He is referred to as "our forefather (προπάτορα, *propatora*, though a variant exists as πατέρα, *patera*) according to the flesh," an indication that Paul plans to show how Abraham is a "forefather" on an other than fleshly basis as well, cf. v. 16.

The use of the expression "has found" is interesting. While from an English standpoint we might most naturally understand this to mean "what has Abraham found from his investigations into the matter" but in fact the word "found" (εὑρηκέναι, *eurekenai*) is most reminiscent of the common "find grace" or "find mercy" in the eyes of someone (cf. Lxx Gen 6:8; 18:3; 19:19; 30:27; 32:5[6]; 33:8, 10; 34:11. We might paraphrase it this way: "What shall we conclude then, about how Abraham found grace in the eyes of God?"

2 For if Abraham was justified by works, he has something to boast about; but not before God.

It seems very probable that by the time of the 1st Century the Rabbinic idea that Abraham had won favor with God through his willingness to sacrifice Isaac was gaining favor. The later writings reflect this. For instance, m.*Kiddushin* 4.14 indicates that Abraham had performed the whole Torah before it was even given, on the basis of Gen 26:5. So righteous were Abraham, Isaac, and Jacob in the eyes of the Sages that their deeds secured God's favor upon subsequent generations. It was noted, for instance, that Elijah's prayer on Mt. Carmel was not answered until he evoked the "God of Abraham, Isaac, and Jacob" (cf. Mid. Rab. *Exodus*. xliv, §1). In Mid. Rab. *Canticles* 1, §14 we read, "A bundle of myrrh (kofer) is my well-beloved" (Cant. 1.14). This refers to Isaac, who was tied up like a bundle upon the altar. Kofer, because he atones for the sins of Israel." Yet the Sages knew that even Abraham needed God's grace: "R. Haggai said in the name of R. Isaac: All need grace, for even Abraham, for whose sake grace came plenteously into the world, himself needed grace" (Mid. Rab. *Genesis* lx.2). Even the phrase "who remembers the pious deeds of the Patriarchs" in the opening prayer of the Amidah could be interpreted to indicate some kind of attributed righteousness.

But Paul simply cannot allow such a thing, for though the covenant with Abraham is surely, in one sense, the reward of his obedience, its blessing comes only to the individual who, like Abraham, places faith in God and thus gains the righteousness which comes via faith. For Paul, Gen 15:6 could only be understood in this sense, namely, that Abraham had savingly believed upon God, and this act of faith in God was the means by which God declared him righteous.

But not before God — Does Paul here actually indicate that Abraham has a valid grounds of boasting before men? Not likely, especially since the subsequent verses indicate that none of Abraham's righteousness was the result of his good deeds. What is more, the conclusion (that he has the right to boast but not before God) is based upon the premise that he was actually justified by works. Since this is false, the conclusion does not stand.

More than likely the meaning is simply that in the eyes of men there may be many who feel that Abraham actually has a proper basis for boasting, but what really counts is God's opinion, and before God none can boast, not even Abraham. The reason is given in the following quote.

3 For what does the Scripture say? "And Abraham believed God, and it was reckoned to him as righteousness."

This quote from Gen 15:6 is essentially in line with the Lxx, which faithfully renders the Hebrew. This is a crux text both for Paul's argument here, and for his exposition of God's method for making a sinner righteous.

MT	Lxx	Paul
וְהֶאֱמִן בַּיהוה וַיַּחְשְׁבֶהָ לּוֹ צְדָקָה And he believed in Adonai and He reckoned it to him righteousness	καὶ ἐπίστευσεν Αβραμ τῷ θεῷ καὶ ἐλογίσθη αὐτῷ εἰς δικαιοσύνην And Abram believed in God and it was reckoned to him for righteousness.	ἐπίστευσεν δὲ ᾿Αβραὰμ τῷ θεῷ καὶ ἐλογίσθη αὐτῷ εἰς δικαιοσύνην. And Abraham believed in God and it was reckoned to him for righteousness.

It is easy to see that Paul quotes the Lxx almost exactly, only substituting δε for και and using "Abraham" rather than the Lxx "Abram." The Lxx differs from the MT in translating ויחשבה with the passive ἐλογίσθη. Other than these minor differences the Lxx and Paul's quote substantially represent the original Hebrew text.

In the Mekilta, an early midrash on Exodus, R. Shemaiah (who lived around 50 BCE) on Exodus 14:15 enters the discussion on whose merits God divided the Red Sea. He suggests "the faith with which their father Abraham believed in Me is deserving that I should divide the sea for them. For it is said: And he believed in the Lord." (Gen 15:6)[42]

Further on in the same midrash (on 14:31) we read:

> "And so also you find that our father Abraham inherited both this world and the world
> beyond only as a reward for the faith with which he believed, as it is said: 'And he believed
> in the Lord, etc.'"[43]

A similar use of our text is to be found in Mid. Rab. *Exodus* 33.5:

> "in the time to come the Israelites will sing a fresh song, as it is said, 'Sing unto the Lord
> a new song' (Ps 98:1). By whose merit (זכות) will they do so? By the merit of Abraham, be-
> cause he trusted in God, as it is said, 'And Abraham trusted in God' (Gen xv. 6)."

The crux question is whether the Rabbis saw faith as meriting something, that is, whether or not faith is a work deserving a reward. Did the contemporaries of Paul see Abraham's faith in God as a good work deserving a reward? Cranfield categorically answers this question "yes" after surveying a few rabbinic quotes:

> Thus it is apparent that, in appealing to Gen 15:6 in support of his contention that Abraham
> was not justified on the ground of works and has no right to glory before God, Paul was
> deliberately appealing to a verse of Scripture which his fellow Jews generally assumed to
> be clear support for the diametrically opposite view. That he did so is highly significant,
> but in no way surprising.[44]

But I'm not sure Cranfield has correctly interpreted the few rabbinic texts he lists. In the first place, he follows Strack and Billerback in saying that the rabbinic phrase used to describe the "merit of faith" is זְכוּת אֱמֻנָה, *zachut 'emunah,* but in the texts he quotes from Mekilta, this is not the phrase used, but rather שְׂכַר אֱמֻנָה, *sachar 'emunah,* "reward of faith." Secondly, that faith is rewarded (a scriptural concept for certain) does not necessarily lead, in the rabbinic writings, to the notion that faith is therefore a "work." No one will argue with the fact that, at least in some measure, the Jewish communities of faith in the 1st Century and even up until the present hold to some form of works-righteousness. But to say that the rabbis universally held that faith was something that each individual accomplished on his own is perhaps to say too much.

What did the early interpreters of the Torah, the Sages, understand Gen 15:6 to mean? Two possibilities present themselves for the interpretation of this text in all ages: (1) faith is a right-eous act, and the attended action of God in relationship to one's faith is a reward for it, or (2) faith is a gift from God, the means by which the sinner comes to know and enjoy the infinite goodness and mercy of God in the forgiveness of his sins and a "not guilty" verdict.

It is difficult, if not impossible, to categorically state that the rabbis had one or the other view of faith, for the rabbis themselves are multifaceted in their understanding of Scripture and of specific texts. But the strong teaching on the rewards of faith found in the rabbinic literature does not necessarily mean that they saw faith as a righteous deed. In fact, one of the issues which arises in such a discussion as this is whether one should translate the verb הֶאֱמִין *ha'amin* "to exercise faith" or "to be faithful." God rewards the faithful (Ps 31:23; 101:6) and often faith-fulness and obedience are considered synonymous (Ps 119:30). In fact, the Scriptures seem clear on the fact that one who has faith acts faithfully, and this acting faithfully is the only sure guar-antee the one possesses faith.

Thus, to see that God rewards the exercise of faith does not mean that the existence of faith in our souls is first and foremost a result of our own efforts. What it does mean is that the re-newed soul, now in possession of faith, is enabled to say "yes" to the Lord and His commands, and is therefore in a place to receive the accompanying blessings of obedience. The unregenerate soul is unable to please the Lord, for apart from faith it is impossible to please Him (Heb 11:6).

We must now turn our attention to the next important term in our verse, namely, the word translated "reckoned": "And Abraham believed God, and it was reckoned to him as righteousness." "Reckoned" translates the Greek term λογιζομαι, *logizomai* which means "to think, consider, reckon." The corresponding Hebrew term in Gen 15:6 is חשב, *chashav* "to think, consider." Actually, as we attempt to understand Paul's use of this term, it will be helpful for us to consider verses 4 and 5, for here he uses the term again with further explanation.

4-5   Now to the one who works, his wage is not reckoned as a favor, but as what is due. But to the one who does not work, but believes in Him who justifies the ungodly, his faith is reckoned as righteousness,

Here we have a clear antithesis set up by Paul: one who works for a wage has his wages counted out to him as what is owed because of the work, while in contrast one who believes does not work, and therefore whatever is counted out to him must be the result of grace, not works.

We see from this verse that the concept of "reckon" (λογιζομαι, *logizomai*) is used by Paul as something entirely appropriate for faith as well as for good works that accompany faith, for the one who works has wages reckoned to him as what is owed him. Thus, λογιζομαι must simply mean to accredit to someone what is rightfully his.

It is understandable how one's wages are owed on the basis of contracted work, but how are we to understand that righteousness is the rightful possession of each one who believes? Here is the wonderful reality of true, saving faith—faith appropriates to the believer the very righteousness of Messiah, so that by faith one may honestly claim that he possesses it. It is not as though God all along knows that the child of faith is really evil but "doctors" the account so that he appears righteous. No, when God ascribes His verdict of "not guilty," He does so on the basis of reality, not as a "let-us-pretend" scenario. The work of Messiah has made our practical righteousness inevitable, a truth which allows the just and timeless God to treat us on the basis of that inevitability.

Thus, the accusation of some, that God does what is forbidden to human judges ("Who justifies the ungodly"), entirely misses the mark. For human judges are forbidden from declaring the guilty just or taking bribes from the guilty in order to change the verdict (Ex 23:7; Prov 17;15; 24:24). When God declares the guilty just, He does so on the basis that the debt owed by the guilty has been fully paid by them through their substitute, Yeshua, and that He intends, through the act of recreating them, to actually make them live in righteousness.

So, if by faith we lay hold, as it were, of the righteousness of Yeshua, then God, Who is just, must certainly reckon it to us as our rightful possession. But it is rightfully ours because, through faith in Yeshua, we receive from Him the fruit of His labors in His death, resurrection, session and intercession. Righteousness is not ours because we earned it, but because Yeshua has "earned it" on our behalf. Faith is the God-given ability to receive what Yeshua has prepared, to stand before Him clothed in the righteousness of the Messiah.

For other places in the Apostolic scriptures where the term λογιζομαι is used, cf. Lk 22:37; Acts 19:27; Rom 2:26; 8:36; 9:8; 2Co 5:19; 2Co 12:6; 2Ti 4:16.

6-8   just as David also speaks of the blessing upon the man to whom God reckons righteousness apart from works: Blessed are those whose lawless deeds have been forgiven, And whose sins have been covered. Blessed is the man whose sin the Lord will not take into account.

Let us first take into account the quote. It is from Psalm 32:1-2

MT	Lxx	Paul
אַשְׁרֵי אָדָם לֹא יַחְשֹׁב יהוה לוֹ עָוֺן וְאֵין בְּרוּחוֹ רְמִיָּה כִּי־הֶחֱרַשְׁתִּי בָּלוּ עֲצָמָי בְּשַׁאֲגָתִי כָּל־הַיּוֹם Happy the one whose transgression is carried away, whose sin is covered, Happy is the man to whom Adonai does not reckon iniquity, and in his spirit there is no deceit.	μακάριοι ὧν ἀφέθησαν αἱ ἀνομίαι καὶ ὧν ἐπεκαλύφθησαν αἱ ἁμαρτίαι μακάριος ἀνήρ οὗ οὐ μὴ λογίσηται κύριος ἁμαρτίαν οὐδὲ ἔστιν ἐν τῷ στόματι αὐτοῦ δόλος Happy is the one whose lawless deeds are forgiven and whose sins are covered, Happy is the man to whom the Lord does not reckon sin neither is there in his mouth deceit.	μακάριοι ὧν ἀφέθησαν αἱ ἀνομίαι καὶ ὧν ἐπεκαλύφθησαν αἱ ἁμαρτίαι· μακάριος ἀνὴρ οὗ οὐ μὴ λογίσηται κύριος ἁμαρτίαν Happy is the one whose lawless deeds are forgiven and whose sins are covered, Happy is the man to whom the Lord does not reckon sin.

It is clear that Paul employs the rabbinic גְּזֵרָה שָׁוָה (*geserah shavah*) whereby two passages both sharing a common term may be linked together. The shared term in this case is "to reckon" (חָשַׁב, λογίζομαι). It is likewise clear that Paul quotes our present recension of the Lxx without changes, and that the Lxx accurately represents the MT. The Hebrew text is very poetic, and the assonance of the terms נְשׂוּי, n'sui ("carried away, forgiven") and כָּסוּי, k'sui ("covered") most probably entered into the psalmists choice of words.

What is of initial interest to us as we attempt to understand Paul's words here is the commentary Paul gives by way of introduction to the quote from Psalm 32. Paul writes "just as David also speaks of the blessing upon the man to whom God reckons righteousness apart from works." Yet David says nothing about reckoning righteousness, only about sins being forgiven and transgressions covered. The point is obvious: for Paul the one inevitably secures the other. To have one's sins forgiven means that one has the righteousness of Messiah accredited to his account—there simply is no neutral ground where one is forgiven but not declared righteous! Thus, it is entirely wrong-headed to interpret, as some do, a verse like 2Co 5:19 as though it teaches that God forgave everyone of their sins and now He awaits their choice to live righteously. For when Paul teaches that "God was in Messiah reconciling the world to Himself, not counting their transgressions against them . . . . .," we must understand that "reconciling the world" and "not counting their transgressions" means that God was likewise imputing righteousness to each one as well. With this in mind, the term "world" simply cannot mean all people everywhere, unless one holds to a theology which has no room for the biblical teaching that some will reject God's offer and therefore be punished eternally.

Cranfield agrees:

> The validity of his appeal to Ps. 32:1f as helping to interpret Gen 15:6 is not just a matter of the presence of a common term (λογίζομαι / חשב) in both places: his appeal to the psalm-passage has an inward and substantial validity, for God's reckoning righteousness to a man χωρὶς ἔργων [apart from works] is, in fact, equivalent to His forgiving of sin. [45]

Psalm 32:1-2 is commented on several times in the Bavli, at b.*Berchot* 34b:

> R. Kahana said: I consider a man impertinent who prays in a valley. R. Kahana also said: I consider a man impertinent who openly recounts his sins, since it is said, Happy is he

whose transgression is forgiven, whose sin is covered.

And in b. *Yoma* 86b:

> It was taught: R Meir used to say, Great is repentance. For on account of an individual who repents, the sins of all the world are forgiven, as it is said: I will heal their backsliding. I will love them freely, for mine anger is turned away from him. 'From them' it is not said, but 'from him,.' How is one proved a repentant sinner? — Rab Judah said: If the object which caused his original transgression comes before him on two occasions, and he keeps away from it. Rab Judah indicated: With the same woman, at the same time, in the same place. Rab Judah said: Rab pointed out the following contradictions. It is written: Happy is he whose transgression is covered, whose sin is pardoned; and it is also written: He that covereth his 'transgression shall not prosper? This is no difficulty, one speaks of sins that have become known [to the public], the other of such as did not become known. R. Zutra b. Tobiah in the name of R. Nahman said: Here we speak of sins committed by a man against his fellow, there of sins committed by man against the Omnipresent.

What is interesting in the second of the two quotes is that the Sages considered it a problem to be resolved, that the Scriptures should speak of sins covered on the one hand, and yet reprove one who covers his sins. While this might simply be explained as the result of a "wooden" hermeneutic, it also may emphasize that there was some debate over the matter of how a person's sins were forgiven.

The words used in the Psalm quote are also worthy of our investigation. In the first verse of Psalm 32, the term translated "transgressions" (פֶּשַׁע, *pesha'*) has its root meaning in "rebellion," and the Lxx translation ἀνομίαι, *anomiai*, "lawless deeds" is right on the mark. Rebellion against God is seen first and foremost in a disregard for and breaking of God's Torah. Also, as mentioned above, two of the Hebrew terms of Ps 32:1 have similar sound, namely, נְשׂוּי, *nasui* and כְּסוּי, *k'sui*, both qal passive participles. נָשָׂא *nasa'* is the common verb "to lift" or "to carry," but is used of "lifting away a debt" and thus came to be used for the concept of "forgive." The second verb, "to cover," is the Hebrew root כָּסָה, *kasah*, and is used in a negative sense (of someone covering one's sins, i.e., trying to hide them) in Jb 31:33 and Prov. 28:13, but in a good sense in Prov 10:12 and 17:9. The same verb is used of God covering sin in Ps 85:2.

The term אַשְׁרֵי, *'ashrei*, is usually translated "blessed," though its primary meaning is "to be happy" or "to make one happy." Obviously, to be "blessed" is, in fact, to "be happy." There is a very real sense, then, that our happiness, our joy, ought to be based upon the pronouncement of our sins being covered and our transgressions removed rather than upon the circumstances of our lives. Can we honestly say that our souls are happy with the position we have in Yeshua? If so, then there ought to be a sort of "continual happiness" (or perhaps more rightly "joy") that pervades our thinking and acting, for nothing in all of the universe can ever reverse the "not-guilty" pronouncement made over us by the Father on the basis of our faith in Yeshua, the chosen Messiah. I do not, of course, intend this to mean that those forgiven walk about with a plastic, forced smile, all the while failing to acknowledge the sorrow and pain which is an inevitability in this world. What I do mean is that the knowledge of our forgiveness in Yeshua ought always and finally to set us upon a course of "happiness" or "blessedness," even in the midst of sorrow.

In these three verses (vs. 6-8) we have a number of terms and phrases used to denote "sin" and "forgiveness."

lawless deeds (ἀνομίαι)	—	forgiven (ἀφίημι)
sin (ἁμαρτία)	—	covered (ἐπικαλύπτω)
sin (ἁμαρτία)	—	not taken into account (οὐ λογίζομαι)

As noted above, "lawless deeds" translates פֶּשַׁע, pesha' of the original Psalm quote, and stresses the idea of "rebellion." "Forgiven" (ἀφίημι, aphiemi) means literally "to send away" and answers well to the underlying Hebrew of the Psalm which uses the verb נָשָׂא, nasa', "to bear up" or "carry away." Here is a wonderful reality, a reality which the Psalmist rejoices in, namely, that God has carried away the rebellious sin of those He has forgiven.

"Sin" (ἁμαρτία, hamartia) denotes any departure from the straight path of righteousness, and its remedy is to be "covered," once again the Greek term fitting the Hebrew verb of the quote. The idea of "covered" reminds of Yom Kippur and the place where the blood was poured, "covering," as it were, the transgressions of the people from the sight of the cherubim who guard the sanctity of God's holiness from the intrusion of any uncleanness.

The significant word, however, by which Paul links Gen 15:6 with Psalm 32:1-2 is the word "reckon" or "take into account" (λογίζομαι, logizomai) as noted above. Here the legal sense is in view, as a judge or king officially noting the crime or trespass, marking it, as it were, upon the ledger of the offender. This word indicates the results of the "covering," for if the sin is covered or out of the sight of the Almighty, then He does not consider it in a legal sense, and does not charge it against the individual. As such, the individual stands innocent before Him.

One additional point can be made from the tenses of the verbs found in our text: each of the verbs ("forgiven," "covered," "not taken into account") is in the aorist tense, indicating a finality to the action. A sinner who has been forgiven, and whose sins are covered, and whose sins the Lord does not take into account never stands the risk of losing this "forgiven status" before the Lord. The incisive, once-for-all action of God in His atoning work renders the sinner eternally forgiven. It is for this reason the forgiven sinner is labelled "blessed" (אַשְׁרֵי, 'ashrei).

9-10 Is this blessing then upon the circumcised, or upon the uncircumcised also? For we say, "Faith was reckoned to Abraham as righteousness." How then was it reckoned? While he was circumcised, or uncircumcised? Not while circumcised, but while uncircumcised;

Some of the Rabbinic literature suggests that the opinion among leading teachers was that God's forgiveness extended only to the nation of Israel and no further. Consider, for instance, the statement in *Pesikta Rabba* 45 (185b):

> On the Day of Atonement God cleanses Israel and atones for its guilt, as it is written, 'For on this day shall atonement be made for you, to cleanse you,' Lev 16:30. And, if you would say, 'Another nation too [he cleanses,' know that] it is not so, but it is only Israel; for so spake the prophet Micah (7:18): 'Who is a God like unto You, that pardons iniquity, and passes by the transgression of the remnant of His heritage?' It is only Israel that He forgives. When David saw how God forgives the sins of the Israelites and has mercy upon them, he began to pronounce them blessed and to glorify them: 'Blessed is he whose transgression is forgiven, etc., Ps. 32:1[46]

Yet there are indications in the later rabbinic writings (Mishnah, Talmud) that the Sages did acknowledge the fact that God provided atonement for the nations as well as for Israel. For instance, the question of the seventy bullocks sacrificed at Sukkot and their meaning yields this:

> R. Eleazar stated, To what do those seventy bullocks [that were offered during the seven days of the Festival] correspond? To the seventy nations. To what does the single bullock [of the Eighth Day] correspond? To the unique nation. This may be compared to a mortal king who said to his servants, 'Prepare for me a great banquet'; but on the last day he said to his beloved friend, 'Prepare for me a simple meal that I may derive benefit from you'.

> R. Johanan observed, Woe to the idolaters, for they had a loss and do not know what they have lost. When the Temple was in existence the altar atoned for them, but now who shall

atone for them?[47]

If this later Talmudic text gives an accurate description of R. Eleazar's and R. Yohanan's positions (though it is not absolutely clear which Sages these names denote), then it seems clear that they believed the Gentile nations would receive forgiveness from HaShem in the eschaton, and that this forgiveness would be the result of sacrifice. Even more telling is the addition of R. Johanan, that the altar of the temple atoned for the sins of the nations as well.

Yet it may well be that while some of the Sages taught that God would make atonement for the Gentile nations, they believed that this would occur only when the Gentiles became proselytes. In fact, we perhaps should understand R. Yohanan's remarks regarding the fact that the altar of the Temple atoned for the Gentiles to refer to those Gentiles who came to the Temple as observing the Torah with a view to eventually becoming proselytes.

Whatever the case, Paul is clear about this fact, that Gentiles have no need to become Jews in order to receive forgiveness of sins. This he intends to prove by showing that Abraham was forgiven of his sins before he bore the sign of the covenant, i.e., circumcision. In this regard we should remember that Paul sometimes uses the term "circumcision" to mean "Jewish" and "uncircumcision" to mean "Gentile" (cf. 2:25, 26 and the comments on these verses above, pgs. 76-77).

According to *Seder Olam* 48, Abraham's circumcision was twenty-nine years after the promise of Gen. 15:6. Some of the Sages put the day of Abraham's circumcision as Tishri 10 (Yom Kippur) while others put it on Nissan 13 (day to search for *chametz* at Pesach). The exact day is obviously speculative, but the important thing to see is that there was a significant span between the time that Abraham was accorded righteousness on the basis of his faith (Gen 15:6) and the time that he was circumcised (Gen 17). Paul's point is obvious: if circumcision actually secured a place in the covenant, then one would expect Abraham to have been circumcised in advance of or at least at the time of his stated faith. To have been declared righteous on the basis of his faith well in advance of being circumcised shows conclusively that circumcision has nothing to do with obtaining right standing before God. And the next logical statement is that the blessing pronounced by David in Psalm 32 cannot be limited to those who are circumcised.

11   and he received the sign of circumcision, a seal of the righteousness of the faith which he had while uncircumcised, that he might be the father of all who believe without being circumcised, that righteousness might be reckoned to them,

Here circumcision (περιτομῆς, *peritomes*) is called a "sign" (σημεῖον, *semeion*) and a "seal" (σφραγίς, *sphragis*), unfolding for us in these two descriptive terms the divine purpose of the ceremony itself. As a "sign," circumcision pointed to the essence of the covenant, for circumcision itself is said to be the covenant "in your flesh." To refer to circumcision as "the covenant in your flesh" (וְהָיְתָה בְרִיתִי בִּבְשַׂרְכֶם לִבְרִית עוֹלָם, Gen 17:13) shows that it bears in its significance the essence of the covenant.

What then is the essence of the covenant to which circumcision pointed as a sign? Since circumcision is performed upon the organ of procreation, it can only relate to that element of the covenant reiterated a number of times: "in your seed all the nations (families) of the earth shall be blessed" (cf. 12:3; 18:18; 22:18; 26:4; 28:14), for this relates to the promised Son, and is the zenith of the covenant itself. Thus, circumcision first and foremost is a sign pointing to the promised Son, first in Isaac, and then in the Messiah. The cutting of the flesh, though a ceremony known in the ancient world as a rite of passage to marriage, was to be done on an infant male to stress the impossibility of bringing the promised Son by human efforts. No eight-day old son could ever father offspring. The act of circumcision on the infant reinforced the picture that the promised One would have to come by above-human means.

As a "seal," circumcision was to teach that the benefits of the covenant were guaranteed only to those who trusted in the promised Son. Though the covenant made with Abraham and his offspring is ostensibly unilateral, depending upon God entirely, it requires reciprocity on the individual level. As far as the covenant as a whole is concerned and the promises envisioned on a national level, these are only dependent upon God's faithfulness. But to the extent that the individual wishes to participate in the blessings of the covenant, it was necessary to obey God and to trust in His promise regarding the long-awaited Son. Carrying out the ceremony of circumcision was an outward act which was intended to demonstrate an inward faith. As such, circumcision was a seal of the covenant promises, always reminding the faithful indiviudal that the covenant itself rested entirely upon divine fiat. The very act of circumcision showed forth a possessed faith in the God who had made promises and would keep them.

For Paul, the story of Abraham is very simple and clear on this matter: surely Abraham had faith well before Gen 17, when he is instructed by God to circumcise all males in his household on the eighth day. Thus to obey God and circumcise himself as well as his household as God had commanded him to do, showed an incredible faith in God and an adherence to His ways. This is Paul's obvious and brilliant argument: Abraham surely had a genuine saving faith in God before he obeyed the command to be circumcised. Conclusion: obedience flows from faith in God, not visa versa.

Circumcision is described by Paul as "a seal of the righteousness of faith," meaning a seal of the reality that God declares a person righteous on the basis of faith. Of course! If circumcision itself was chosen as a perfect sign that one would have to rely, not on one's own powers to bring the promised Son, but leave entirely in the hands of God, this is the demonstration of faith. Abraham was relying upon the flesh when he took Hagar as Sarah suggested, and thus the ritual of circumcision, coming immediately after the Hagar event, emphasized the need for Abraham and Sarah to rely entirely upon God for the completion of the covenant. In this way, obedience in the act of circumcision showed forth the underlying faith in God and a clear disdain for trusting one's own abilities.

that he might be the father of all who believe without being circumcised – Here Paul ties together the promises of God made to Abraham and to his seed with the issue of faith. The promises of the covenant come only to those who may rightly call Abraham their father. But since Abraham believed before he was circumcised, he stands as the Father of faith both to those who, like him, believe and are circumcised as well as those who believe without undergoing the rabbinic ritual of the proselyte (=circumcision). Cranfield articulates this point well when he writes:

> . . . it was God's intention in causing Abraham to be circumcised that he should be the point of union between all who believe, whether circumcised or uncircumcised, being, on the one hand, by virtue of his having been justified while still uncircumcised, the father of all those who as uncircumcised believe, and, on the other hand, by virtue of the fact that he subsequently received circumcision, the father of all those who, being circumcised, are not only circumcised but are also believers.[49]

that righteousness might be reckoned to them – To the non-Jew who is uncircumcised of flesh (i.e., not relying upon his status as a proselyte) yet circumcised of heart (i.e., part of the people of God through faith in the Messiah), this one stands as righteous before God having been accredited the righteousness of Yeshua appropriated by faith.

12 and the father of circumcision to those who not only are of the circumcision, but who also follow in the steps of the faith of our father Abraham which he had while uncircumcised.

The NASB has "father of circumcision" while the NIV has "father of the circumcision." Though the Greek lacks the article "the" in this instance, the sense is surely equivalent to the next phrase used by Paul as well as in Tit. 1:10, and the NIV has it right: "father of the circumcision," meaning, "father of those who have physical Jewish lineage."

It is clear by any reading of the extant rabbinic literature that Abraham was viewed as the father of the nation of Israel. In fact, the term "father Abraham" is found repeatedly in the Mishnah and Talmud. This fact is also well attested in Torah, for it is first with Abram/Abraham that God promises to establish a nation with whom He will have covenant relationship. But the idea of Abraham being the father of more than just those who physically descend from him was also known in the Sages' writings. Consider the following from the Talmud:

> Abram is the same as Abraham. At first he became a father to Aram [Ab-Aram] only, but in the end he became a father to the whole world. (b.*Berchot* 13a)

> R. Nathan b. Abba further said in the name of Rab: The rich men of Babylon will go down to Gehenna; for once Shabthai b. Marinus came to Babylon and entreated them to provide him with facilities for trading and they refused this to him; neither did they give him any food. He said: These are the descendants of the 'mixed multitude', for it is written, And [He will] show thee mercy and have compassion upon thee, [teaching that] whoever is merciful to his fellow-men is certainly of the children of our father Abraham, and whosoever is not merciful to his fellow-men is certainly not of the children of our father Abraham. (b.*Beitzah* 32b)

But the Sages also taught that Abraham was the father of all proselytes,

> The father of all proselytes was Abraham. Therefore when a proselyte is named, he is called N., son of our father Abraham. (*Tanchuma, Lek leka*, 32a)

as well as a type of proselyte himself:

> After the return of the spies, there arose contention between Israel and the gerim. God said to Moses, 'Wherefore do the Israelites contend with the proselytes?' Moses said to God, 'Lord, thou alone knowest.' God replied, 'Did I not say one statute, one Torah, for Israel and the gerim alike? Hence they say: There are three types of proselytes, some are like Abraham, some like Homer, son of Shechem, some like a pagan in every respect. How is this? The last named is the man in whose house is flesh of animals found dead, or killed by wild beasts, or creeping things, or other abominations, and he thinks, 'If I become a proselyte, I should eat good food as the Jews do, and the nasty food would cease in my house; and the Jews, moreover, have Sabbaths and festivals. I will prevail upon myself, and become a proselyte.' But then he relapses to his original leaven, yet in the end sufferings come upon him for his good, and to deliver him from the evil he has wrought. And God says, 'Just as he loved you, so do you love him.' Then there is the proselyte like Hamor, who wants to marry a Jewess, and they say to him, 'You cannot marry her unless you become a proselyte.' Then he prevails upon himself, and becomes a proselyte. He too relapses, and he too is delivered by suffering. God says of him, 'My sons, just as he sought for rest among you, so do you grant him rest, for the proselyte shall you not oppress' (Ex 22:20). Finally, there is the proselyte like Abraham, who says, 'When can I become a proselyte, and dwell beneath the wings of the Shechinah,' as it is said, 'Let not the son of the foreigner say, I am separated from God's people' (Is 56:4). (*Tanna DeBe Eliyyahu*, p. 146)

Thus, the rabbinic view of Abraham as father of both his descendents as well as the proselytes fits very well into Paul's understanding of Abraham as father of all who have faith.

But Paul is not content to simply say that Abraham is the father of those who have physical lineage alone. The sentence is structured in a "not only . . . but also" form, meaning that there are two essential qualities attached to this group, namely, (1) physical lineage, and (2) genuine faith. Yet it is clear, both by the grammar as well as by the logic of this passage, the faith, not circumcision, is the decisive factor. The Gentile gains the same righteousness as the Jew and does so without physical circumcision, i.e., apart from the works of the Torah. And in the same way, Abraham, though eventually circumcised, was declared righteous by God before he was circumcised, proving again that circumcision is not the means upon which a person stands righteous before God.

13 For the promise to Abraham or to his descendants that he would be heir of the world was not through the Torah, but through the righteousness of faith.

The Rabbinic approach to Abraham and the Torah was that he kept the entire Torah (including the Rabbinic additions such as *eruv*). In a discussion of what produces wealth, the Mishnah contends that wealth and poverty are entirely the result of one's keeping Torah, and thus comes to a conclusion regarding Abraham:

> But they that wait upon the Lord shall renew their strength; of his old age what is said? They shall still bring forth fruit in old age. And thus it is said of our father Abraham, and Abraham was old . . . and the Lord blessed Abraham with everything. We find that our father Abraham observed the whole Torah before it was given, for it is said, Because that Abraham obeyed my voice, and kept my charge, my commandments, my statutes, and my laws. (b.*Kiddushin* 82a)

Again, the question of Abraham's Torah observance is noted as including the Oral Torah:

> Rab said: Our father Abraham kept the whole Torah, as it is said: Because that Abraham hearkened to My voice [kept My charge, My commandments, My statutes, and My laws]. R. Shimi b. Hiyya said to Rab: Say, perhaps, that this refers to the seven laws?— Surely there was also that of circumcision! Then say that it refers to the seven laws and circumcision [and not to the whole Torah]? — If that were so, why does Scripture say: 'My commandments and My laws'? Raba or R. Ashi said: Abraham, our father, kept even the law concerning the 'erub of the dishes,' as it is said: 'My Torahs': one being the written Torah, the other the oral Torah. (b.*Yoma* 28b)

Yet Paul's point is that the promise was not given through the Torah[50], for the promise (i.e., the promise of the coming Messiah) was the very heart of the Abrahamic covenant given well before the revelation of the Torah at Sinai. So while the Sages intend to teach that the Torah as precept is eternal, its revelation as covenant at Sinai is well fixed within the historical consciousness of the nation, as is the Abrahamic promise.

That Paul should use the term "promise' (ἐπαγγελία, *epangelia*) here is significant, for Paul has coined the term to refer to the Messianic promise contained in the covenants given to the patriarchs (cf. Eph 2:12). The promise began with the word of the Messiah to Eve (Gen 3:15) and continued to unfold as it was specifically attached to the Abrahamic covenant in the repeated phrase "in your seed all the nations of the earth shall be blessed." But the choice of the term "promise" to define the central issue of the Abrahamic covenant emphasizes the unilateral nature of that covenant. It is "promise" because it depends in every way upon God Himself and nothing else. It is "promise" because in God's eternal plan of salvation nothing could ever stand in the way of its fulfillment. It is "promise" because the revelation of God's means of saving sinners is attached historically to the words He spoke to a man, to Abraham, words which He must keep as the faithful God of Israel.

We should understand the repeated use of the word "through" (διά) in connection with the promise, not so much as identifying chronology (though this is possible), but as showing instrumentality. That is to say, Paul's point goes well beyond the obvious fact that the promise given to Abraham was given well before the Sinai event. His point (if we take the context seriously) is that the promise, i.e., the object of true saving faith, was not something apprehended and made one's own through adherence to a set of commandments given by God, but rather the promise was laid hold of by faith. The righteousness which Abraham enjoyed was in every way attached to his faith in the promised One, the seed which God had promised within the covenant. As such, the promise becomes active in the life of Abraham by means of faith, not by means of obedience. Obedience inevitably follows the act of faith, for faith and faithfulness are two sides of a single coin.

Thus, the "promise" is summed up in our verse this way: "that he (Abraham) would be heir of the world." This particular language is not found in the Tanach (*per se*) but was extant in the Rabbinic discussions of the early centuries. Note, for instance, Ecclus 44:21 (and cf. the quote of Berechot 13a above):

> Therefore he assured him by an oath, . . . that he would . . . exalt his seed as the stars, and cause them to inherit from sea to sea, and from the River unto the utmost part of the earth.

Paul gives his understanding of this in 1 Co 3:21b-23

> For all things belong to you, whether Paul or Apollos or Cephas or the world or life or death or things present or things to come; all things belong to you, and you belong to Messiah; and Messiah belongs to God.

Here the restoration of all things to those who have faith is the final outcome of the salvation promised through Abraham. If those who believe are heirs of Abraham, and if he was promised to inherit the whole world, then "all things belong" to the heirs.

14 For if those who are of the Torah are heirs, faith is made void and the promise is nullified;

While there are a number of possible ways to understand this verse, if we are to interpret it within its context, surely the meaning is straightforward, and it is this: if the promise that Abraham would inherit the world (i.e., that in him all the nations would be blessed) was based upon his attaining the status of a proselyte, then there would have been no need for the covenant to have been couched in terms of a promise, and there would have been no need for Abraham to exercise faith. What is more, the promise that was made, had it been contingent upon the performance of the ritual of proselytism (=circumcision), then surely the promise would be null and void, and the whole discussion would be moot.

In point of fact, the narrative structure of Genesis constantly reminds the reader that God's covenant to Abraham is not based upon his ethnic status, nor even upon his obedience, but upon God's faithfulness. Consider the episodes: Abram is given the covenant (Gen 12), a drought comes so Abram descends to Egypt for food and lies about Sarai to protect himself (Gen 13). God preserves Abram in spite of himself and he returns to the Land (Gen 14). After success in battle and gifts to Melchizedek, Abram still has no son (Gen 15) so God confirms the covenant by ceremony. Impatient, Abraham attempts to bring the promise through Hagar (Gen 16), an act which failed to demonstrate true faith. So we can see that throughout the Abrahamic narrative, Moses is intent on showing us that in spite of Abraham's failings, the promise remains in place. He no doubt does this in order to reinforce a central truth of the Abrahamic covenant, namely, that its success depends entirely upon God and not upon Abraham.

What is meant by the phrase "of the Torah" (ὁι ἐκ νόμου) in "if those who are of the Torah are heirs . . .?" Paul uses similar language in three other texts:

Gal. 3:18 For if the inheritance is based on Torah (ἐκ νόμου, *ek nomou*), it is no longer based on a promise; but God has granted it to Abraham by means of a promise.

Gal. 3:21 Is the Torah then contrary to the promises of God? May it never be! For if a law had been given which was able to impart life, then righteousness would indeed have been based on law (ἐκ νόμου, *ek nomou*).

Phil. 3:9 and may be found in Him, not having a righteousness of my own derived from the Torah (ἐκ νόμου), but that which is through faith in Messiah, the righteousness which comes from God on the basis of faith...

It seems obvious that the phrase "of the Torah," in this context, speaks of those who would naturally claim that their status granted through observance of Torah apart from faith in Yeshua was what guaranteed their reception of the covenant blessings. In v. 16 below, the similar language (only in the singular) speaks of those Jews who, with faith in the Messiah, keep the Torah.

Next we must ask what Paul intends to convey by the word "heirs" (κληρονόμοι, *kleronomoi*). The manner in which the word is used in the previous verse gives us the grounds for its meaning here. It was promised to Abraham that he would be "heir of the world," i.e., that in him all the world would be blessed, and that therefore a host that no man could number would be attached to him via covenant and benefit from the promised blessings. Thus, those who are the offspring of Abraham are his heirs and participate in the covenant God made with him.

"Heirs," then, speaks of those who share the promise with Abraham, and Paul is clear that entrance into Abraham's family and thus into his covenant cannot be achieved through the works of the Torah (i.e., Jewish status or gaining Jewish status through becoming a proselyte) . Entrance into the covenant made with Abraham is by faith alone—faith in the Messiah.

Furthermore, if it were possible to enter Abraham's covenant and enjoy the eternal blessings promised therein through the works of the Torah, this would make faith "void" (κεκένωται, perf. pass. of κενόω, *kenoo*, "to be empty" cf. 1Co 1:17) and "nullify" (κατήργηται, perf. pass of καταργέω, *katargeo*, "to destroy, render ineffective," cf. Rom 3:3, 31) the promise. How so? Because it is clear that the covenant given to Abraham is dependent upon God, not Abraham. In Abraham's attempts to bring the promised son who would be the heir of the covenant, it is clear that Abraham failed. If it were up to Abraham to bring the fulfillment of the covenant, all is lost. But the Genesis narrative makes it clear that the covenant depended upon God, not Abraham. As such, participation in the covenant is based upon faith in God and what He can do, not in one's own ability to attain a status of righteousness. What is more, had the covenant depended upon Abraham's faithfulness, and through his own faithlessness (the Hagar event) the covenant had failed, then God would have been seen as unable to secure the very promises He had made, and He would have been revealed as an impotent god who was unable to bring about what he had promised. Abraham, left to himself, would have never been able to bring in the covenant blessings. Abraham's only hope (and the hope of all who call Abraham "father") was to rely upon God's faithfulness to bring about the promise He had made.

15 for the Torah brings about wrath, but where there is no Torah, neither is there violation.

The *sitz im leben* (circumstances) of the giving of the Torah demonstrates Paul's point here. Hardly had the tablets of the Ten Words been given to Moses when the people lost hope and resorted to idolatry. The Torah, God's gracious teaching in righteousness, established not only the clear standard of God with regard to Israel's sanctified status, it also established punishment for those who acted unfaithfully. In other words, the Torah in and of itself could never establish the covenant made with Abraham, but rather set forth to identify those who were genuine covenant members, and those who were not. Cranfield notes:

. . . so far from the law's being something which a man might hope so adequately to fulfil
as thereby to establish a claim on God, its actual effect, men being what they are, is to bring
God's wrath upon them by turning their sin into conscious transgression and so rendering
it more exceeding sinful.[51]

We should not fall into the trap of thinking that the Torah was given as a means of covenant entrance, nor that it was given with the premise that if one kept it perfectly, one would be
accorded the status of righteous. Clearly, obedience to the Torah included adherance to the pro-
visions it granted for one who transgressed (i.e., establishing appropriate restitution, or bringing of a sacrifice by the repentent sinner). But the point is that the Torah, in clearly establishing
God's standards of righteousness, likewise manifested Israel's inability and therefore made sin
all that more evident. Where there may have been debate over what exactly constituted sin from
man's point of view, the Torah made clear what constituted sin from God's viewpoint. Moreover, it also established punishment for sin. The point is obvious: where there is no Torah, there
can be no proper punishment because, technically, there is no violation. Thus, the existence of
Torah in clear, written form raises the possibility of violation of that Torah, and thus of punishment for its violation.

Furthermore, the Torah, while setting forth God's revelation of what constituted holiness
and therefore what constituted sin, never offered Israel the means by which she could overcome
the wayward bent of the sinful nature, and therefore, apart from an attended work of the Spirit
in relationship to the Torah, inevitably established the basis for punishment of the transgressor.
In short, for the person who attempted obedience without first having the heart circumcised in
the realm of faith, the Torah functioned primarily in terms of condemnation rather than in the
establishment of true holiness.

**16 For this reason it is by faith, that it might be in accordance with grace, in order that the
promise may be certain to all the descendants, not only to those who are of the Torah, but
also to those who are of the faith of Abraham, who is the father of us all,**

The opening "for this reason" may at first appear to connect the thought back to v. 14 or 15
as a supporting statement. But the structure of the sentence itself would lend support to reading
the opening "for this reason" as looking forward in the sentence, not back, so that the meaning
is: The reason it (i.e., the covenant made to Abraham) is by faith is so that God's grace might be
the means by which the promise is established, in order that all may benefit, both Jew and Gentile (i.e., to the Jew, who has the Torah before coming to faith, and to the Gentile, who comes to
faith and then comes to espouse the Torah.) "God has made His plan of salvation to depend, on
man's side, not on fulfillment of the Law but solely on faith, in order that, on His side, it might
be a matter of grace."[52]

The reason the Abrahamic covenant could only be a unilateral type of covenant is because
God's means of salvation, i.e., the Messiah, is the zenith of the covenant. If the covenant were
dependent upon man's obedience it surely would have failed and God's plan of salvation with
it. Thus, the only way that the promise could be certain to all of the elect would be if the outcome of the covenant was entirely in God's care, as a matter of His infinite grace. Thus, those
who are "of the Torah" in this verse are those who have combined their possession of the Torah
with a genuine faith in the Messiah, while "those who are the faith of Abraham" are those who
have come to faith in the Messiah before receiving the Torah (just as Abraham did).

who is the father of us all – Abraham is not only the father of those who have physical lineage to him (cf. v. 1), but he is likewise a father in a different, but no less real, sense of all believers without exception. To call Abraham one's father is to be counted as an heir and thus as

member of the covenant, since the covenant is made with Abraham and his descendants.

17 (as it is written, "A father of many nations have I made you") in the sight of Him whom he believed, even God, who gives life to the dead and calls into being that which does not exist.

In typical fashion Paul supports his claim that Abraham is the father of all who believe, whether Jew or Gentile, from the Tanach, quoting Gen 17:5 directly from the Lxx.

MT	Lxx	Paul
וְלֹא־יִקָּרֵא עוֹד אֶת־שִׁמְךָ אַבְרָם וְהָיָה שִׁמְךָ אַבְרָהָם כִּי אַב־הֲמוֹן גּוֹיִם נְתַתִּיךָ No longer shall your name be called Abram, but your name shall be Abraham; For I will make you the father of a multitude of nations.	καὶ οὐ κληθήσεται ἔτι τὸ ὄνομά σου Αβραμ ἀλλ᾽ ἔσται τὸ ὄνομά σου Αβρααμ ὅτι πατέρα πολλῶν ἐθνῶν τέθεικά σε And your name shall no more be called Abram, but your name shall be Abram, for I have made you a father of many nations.	καθὼς γέγραπται ὅτι πατέρα πολλῶν ἐθνῶν τέθεικά σε as it is written, "A FATHER OF MANY NATIONS HAVE I MADE YOU"

The Lxx is a good representation of the Hebrew, and Paul quotes the Lxx verbatim. The promise to Abraham that he would be a father of a multitude[53] of nations was tied in, no doubt, with the promise that all the nations would be blessed in him, for they would be blessed by being able to call him "father," i.e., become his rightful descendants and thus inherit the blessings of the covenant.

The fatherhood of Abraham, then, reminds us of the words of Yeshua to the unbelieving Pharisees (Jn 8:39ff) that, though they claimed to have Abraham as their father, Yeshua proclaims Satan to be their father. Are we to understand this to mean that those who reject Yeshua cannot call Abraham their father? The church has often opted for this interpretation, but the context tells us this is not the case, for Yeshua twice refers to Abraham as their father even though they had rejected Him (8:53, 56). Yeshua is rather calling them to live in accordance with who they claim to be. If Abraham is their father, then they should do the works of Abraham, i.e., works which flowed from genuine faith.

The sentence, begun in v. 16, is actually interrupted by the quote as a parenthetical proof. Thus, Abraham is the father of all who believe in the sight of the One on whom Abraham believed, that is to say, while certain Jewish communities may not have considered Abraham to be the father of Gentile believers, Paul asserts that God does.

The controversy over the status of proselytes within the Jewish community no doubt raged during the 1st Century and slightly afterward. Some, like the 3rd Century Rabbi Simeon ben Lakish[54], write that the "proselyte is dearer to God than the born Jew because the latter would not have accepted the Torah if he had not witnessed the miracles at Sinai (according to tradition, those present at Sinai included all those Jews yet to be born), whereas the proselyte saw none of these things."[55] According to b.*Yevamot* 22a, the proselyte has the status of a newborn babe. Yet others argued that one could not trust a proselyte because they often relapse to their paganism[56] and that they were not to be fully received until the 24th generation.[57]

Interesting in connection with our text is m.*Bikkurim* 1:4 —

These may bring but do not make the declaration: the proselyte may bring but does not make the declaration because he can not say Which the Eternal swore to our fathers to give

95

unto us. But if his mother were an Israelite, he may bring and make the declaration. And when he prays privately, he says, O God of the ancestors of Israel; and when he is in the Synagogue, he says, O God of your ancestors; and if his mother were an Israelite, he may say, O God of our ancestors. [58]

Paul thus takes his stand on the issue by speaking in the most powerful of terms, that the believing Jew as well as the believing Gentile, has every right to address Abraham as his father, and therefore he is a legitimate heir of the covenant promise which God made to Abraham.

Paul lists four attributes of the relationship which God had with Abraham. First, God was the object of Abraham's faith: "the One on whom he believed." Abraham's faith was not in a set of truths but in the very eternal person of God from whom he had received the truth. Secondly, this one in whom Abraham had placed his faith is referenced as "God," θέος, *Theos*, אֱלֹהִים, *Elohim*. Abraham's faith was well defined by the object of his faith, for the object was the unique and only eternal God. Thirdly, God is referred to as "the One who gives life to the dead." This reiterates the main theme of the 2nd of the *Shemonei Esrei,* (18 Benedictions) which ends, "Blessed are You, O Lord, Who makes the dead alive" (בָּרוּךְ אַתָּה יהוה מְחַיֵּה הַמֵּתִים).

Paul, like his contemporaries, viewed "live from the dead" in a broader sphere, to include spiritual awakening, the ability to conceive after being barren, or even an escape from near-death situations. That all of these involve Abraham, Sarah, and Isaac fit perfectly into the plans of the Apostle as he unfolds his thesis of how God declares a sinner righteous.

The fourth character of God which Paul emphasizes is "who . . . calls into being that which does not exist." I think there can be little doubt that the point is God's creative ability, i.e., creation *ex nihilo,* creation from nothing (or into nothing).[59] But as in the statement of God's ability to raise the dead, so here the emphasis is not only the physical creation, but God's ability to affect a spiritual creation, to bless the nations through Abraham—to secure the promise that Abraham would be the father of many nations, and this would both require and exemplify the creative ability of HaShem. Faith in God, at its very heart, is the belief that God can overcome death and give life, and that He can create what does not exist in order to bring about His designed plan.

18 In hope against hope he believed, in order that he might become a father of many nations, according to that which had been spoken, "So shall your descendants be."

The Greek which underlies the translation "in hope against hope he believed" is: παρ᾽ ἐλπίδα ἐπ᾽ ἐλπίδι ἐπίστευσεν. The NASB "in hope against hope" is rendered by the NIV as "Against all hope, Abraham in hope believed. . .," which is essentially the same. The phrase itself (παρ᾽ ἐλπίδα, *par elpida*) can be understood generally in two ways: (1) against hope, or (2) beyond hope. "Beyond hope" would envision the scenario where Abraham, after anticipating the promise of a son through the normal means of procreation, came to the limit of human hope after so much time elapsed without the appearance of the child. Thus, having exhausted all hope in human ability, he rested in God's promise.

"Against hope" would emphasize Abraham's realization that the child would never come through human efforts, and that he therefore despised reliance upon human strength and leaned entirely upon God's promise.

The Vulgate (Latin version) took it as "against" and a good number of expositors, both modern and ancient agree. Both options are viable and lead essentially to the same end. The point is that, whether Abraham despised hope in human effort ("against") or whether he exhausted it ("beyond"), he ultimately rested upon the promise which God had made, and found his hope in Him. The lesson for us is obvious: too often we admit defeat when we have exhausted human resources, or we continue to attempt to accomplish through human effort what can only be obtained through the power of the Almighty. We are called to follow the example of Abraham, who "hoped against or beyond human hope."

But note well that the act of casting oneself upon God for hope is the act of faith: "he believed." It is by faith that we lay hold of God's promise and power to live in the reality of that promise. And this faith, at its foundation, is taking God at His word regardless (or even especially) if it goes contrary to human ability and efforts.

in order that he might become a father of many nations – Some suggest that this phrase actually comprises the content or primary focus of Abraham's faith, while others prefer to put a comma between the two phrases and see this final phrase as indicating the resultant end of his faith, namely, that on the basis of his faith he became the father of many nations. Here we have, once again, a perfect picture of the human/divine cooperative. For God promises to Abraham, in a unilateral covenant, that he would indeed be the father of many nations, yet Paul appears to teach us that he obtained this blessing through the exercise of his faith. Here we see the manner in which God's determined providence works together with the faith of His chosen one to accomplish the eternal purpose. Thus, Paul, having spoken of Abraham's personal faith, connects it with "as it was spoken, 'so shall your seed be'," a quote from Gen 15:5 pointing out to Abraham that his seed would be as numerous as the stars. This human impossibility is received as viable by Abraham because he has believed in God who is able to do all of His holy will.

And so, as Abraham demonstrates the manner in which we are to hope in God—as the father of many nations he "sets the pace," as it were, of what faith should be. He is "father" not only in the sense of passing to his offspring the blessings promised, but as demonstrating as well the way we are to walk in faith. As we participate in the same faith that Abraham had, we show ourselves to be his children, and he, our father.

19 And without becoming weak in faith he contemplated his own body, now as good as dead since he was about a hundred years old, and the deadness of Sarah's womb;

And without becoming weak in faith – What are the means by which one "grows weak in faith?" The only other time that Paul employs the phrase "weak in faith" in Romans is at 14:1-2, admonishing the congregation to receive those "weak in the faith," but not to pass judgment on their opinions. 14:2 uses the same Greek word for "weak" (ἀσθενέω, *astheneo*) but does not specifically add "in faith." However, those "weak" are those who feel they must only eat vegetables and is put in contrast to the one who has faith that he can "eat all things." "Weak in faith" here seems to imply that the person restricts himself unduly, unaware of the broader horizon. The same could apply to Abraham's example, that he did not limit himself to the human horizons set before him, but, laying hold by faith upon what God had said, he was able to do what otherwise would have been (and always is) humanly impossible.

What then are the steps which lead to a weak faith (and which are therefore to be avoided in order that one might grow strong in faith)? The first step to weak faith is the willingness to shut oneself up to the limits of human power and ability. This may be fear of failure, or a spiritual timidity. How often we look at the available human resources and plan our spiritual journey accordingly. God rather intends that we listen to Him and move at His bidding, anticipating that He will supply what the human capacity lacks. This dynamic faith is the result of trusting God's word, for the word informs us of the truth of who God is, who we are, and what He has accomplished and will accomplish. Yet the tendency of the flesh is to rely upon one's own strength and to disregard the revelation of God (Prov. 3:5-6).

Another way in which the child of God grows weak rather than strong in faith is by failing to make a distinction between the ways of the world and the way of God. As an overall characteristic, Abraham walked with God and lived life from the perspective of faith. Yet even Abraham became persuaded that the cultural norms and answers to life's dilemmas were, in some measure, acceptable. Taking Hagar as a means of securing the promised son was culturally acceptable—indeed, it was the method of choice in Abraham's day for a man who lacked a legal heir. What is more, Sarah, his own wife, was in favor of the plan and encouraged Abraham in it.

Yet Abraham did not act in faith at this point. Faith would have sought the Lord for council, yet in the text of Genesis 16:3-4 we find Abraham moving headlong into his own plans. Note how quickly the verbs come in the narrative:

> And after Abram had lived ten years in the land of Canaan, Abram's wife Sarai took Hagar the Egyptian, her maid, and gave her to her husband Abram as his wife. And he went in to Hagar, and she conceived; and when she saw that she had conceived, her mistress was despised in her sight.

Abraham had grown weary of waiting and his weariness allowed him to be weak in faith. Though this did not characterize his life (for as our text indicates, Abraham did not grow weak in faith in terms of ultimately trusting God for the outcome of the covenant), his lapse of faith at this crucial moment would effect his family forever. What Paul focuses on in this text, however, is Abraham's response to God when he is told that Ishmael will not be the counted as the promised seed. Confronted with the fact that the Hagar event was not God's intended means of realizing the covenant promises, Abraham willingly submits and believes God's promise.

We may derive yet another principle from the Genesis narrative as we contemplate the mechanics of faith. Genesis 17 opens with these words:

> Now when Abram was ninety-nine years old, Adonai appeared to Abram and said to him, "I am El Shaddai; Walk before Me, and be blameless."

Here we have, in this one verse, a summary of the points made thus far. "I am El Shaddai" identifies God as the One able to bring children.[60] First, then, growing strong in faith involves believing that God is who He says He is. Secondly, "walk before me" means to walk or live in such a way that one is constantly aware of God's watchful eye. As R. Yehuda ha-Nasi is recorded as saying:

> . . . Reflect on three things and you will not come into the clutches of sin; know what is above you, a seeing eye, a hearing ear, and all your deeds are written in the book." (*Pirke Avot* 2:1).

This means living life God's way, not man's way. The Hebrew text of Gen 17:1 has הִתְהַלֵּךְ לְפָנַי, (*hithalach liphnei*) using the hitpael of הלך (*halach*, "walk") rather than the common qal. Other uses of הלך in the hitpael (Gen 3:8; 5:22, 24; 6:9; 13:17; 24:40; 48:15; Ex 21:19; Lev 26:12; Deut 23:14) would indicate that the emphasis is upon a pattern or characteristic of life. Thus, in Gen 17:1 we might more accurately translate the phrase "keep on walking before me and be blameless."

Thirdly, "be blameless" (וְהְיֵה תָמִים, *v'hayah tamim*) means to live in a way that is righteous before HaShem. The word translated "blameless" is the same word used for sacrificial animals which are ritually pure ("without blemish" cf. Ex 12:6). Here we learn that obedience itself is a way to strengthen faith. As Solomon admonishes in Prov 3:5-6, "in all your ways acknowledge Him," which can meaning nothing less than acting in a way that recognizes the righteous demands of God upon one's life. When we live constantly recognizing God's rightful place as Lord, we live in obedience, and this obedience is itself a means by which our faith is strengthened. Conversely, a life incorporating patterns of disobedience will be constantly dragging faith down and weakening it.

he contemplated his own body, now as good as dead since he was about a hundred years old, and the deadness of Sarah's womb; – The first thing we encounter in the study of this text is an interesting textual variant. In some of the Greek manuscripts (D G K P Ψ 33, etc.) the word "not" is inserted: "he did not contemplate his own body . . ." If we accept the reading without the inserted "not," then the meaning is that even though he gave full consideration to the fact that physically fathering children was something his old age prohibited, yet he believed in God. If, on the other hand, we receive the texts which insert the word "not," then Abraham's faith is extolled as so strong as not even bothering to consider the seeming impossible barrier of old age. Textually, the reading as taken by the NASB (which does not include the word "not") is to be preferred (it is read by א A B C).

It seems most probable that Paul has Genesis 17:17 in mind as he speaks of the deadness of both Abraham and Sarah when it came to childbearing:

> Then Abraham fell on his face and laughed, and said in his heart, "Will a child be born to a man one hundred years old? And will Sarah, who is ninety years old, bear a child?"

The emphasis upon the ages of each seems to indicate that Abraham considered this to be a major obstacle (from the human standpoint) to the realization of the promise. Genesis 18:11 is even more specific:

> Now Abraham and Sarah were old, advanced in age; Sarah was past childbearing.

The Hebrew text is more pointed than the English translation: וְאַבְרָהָם וְשָׂרָה זְקֵנִים בָּאִים בַּיָּמִים חָדַל לִהְיוֹת לְשָׂרָה אֹרַח כַּנָּשִׁים, "Now Abraham and Sarah were old, advancing in days, it ceased to be for Sarah, the manner of women." This phrase "manner of women" is euphemistic for the menstrual cycle. Sarah had stopped having a monthly period. This is precisely what Paul indicates when he writes καὶ τὴν νέκρωσιν τῆς μήτρας Σάρρας, "and the deadness of Sarah's womb."

Granted, Abraham had fathered Ishmael only 14 years earlier (Gen 16:16 indicates Abraham was 86 years old when Ishmael was born), but in that 14 years he must have considered that, like Sarah, he had grown past the age when he would be able, naturally, to father children. Yet the fact that after the death of Sarah, Abraham fathered six sons by his second wife, Keturah (Gen 25:1f), would indicate that he actually was able to father children, and that he only thought he was too old.

This difficulty, i.e., that Abraham at one point considers himself too old to father children, but then later fathers sons through Keturah, has been solved a number of ways by various scholars. Some have simply considered the possibility that the narrative is not in chronological order, having been rearranged by later editors. Others simply say that while Abraham thought himself unable to father children, in reality he was able to. Still others consider the possibility that when the promised son (Isaac) came, Abraham was so revived in body and spirit that he was able once again to produce offspring.[61] Whatever the explanation, Paul's point is simply that at the time when God appeared to Abraham (Gen 17), he thought of himself as unable to produce the promised offspring, and thus entrusted himself wholly to the God who does the impossible.

20 yet, with respect to the promise of God, he did not waver in unbelief, but grew strong in faith, giving glory to God,

Once again we see the Pauline emphasis upon "the promise," for "the promise" is the focal point of Abraham's faith, being the promise of the son to whom the covenant would pass, a foreshadowing of the ultimate Son, Messiah. Abraham's faith is squarely cast by Paul as centered in the promise of God, a promise which ultimately included blessing for all the nations through the Seed (cf. Gal 3:16). This fits the primary emphasis of Paul's teaching here, that Abraham's faith encompassed the divine promise of blessing not only in his own son to whom the covenant would be confirmed, but ultimately in the Promised Son, the Messiah.

Abraham's faith is characterized by two opposing verbs: "waver" on the one hand, paralleled by its opposite, "grow strong." The word translated "waver" is the common Greek verb διακρίνω, *diakrino*, "to consider, judge" or, in a negative sense, "to doubt." The sphere of such activity is stated by Paul to be "in unbelief" (τῇ ἀπιστίᾳ, *tes apistia*). "To doubt in unbelief" is described by the NASB as "waver in unbelief," by the NIV as "waver through unbelief" and by the NRSV as "no distrust made him waver." The picture of doubting in unbelief is that of questioning what one knows to be true. When, having understood the truth, we doubt it, that is when we "waver in unbelief." For other instances in the Apostolic writings where διακρίνω is used in this sense of "divided within oneself, doubting," cf. Mt 21:21; Mk 11:23; Acts 10:20; Jms 1:6, 2:4; Jude 22.

The opposite is stated by Paul to be that Abraham "grew strong in faith" (ἀλλὰ ἐνεδυναμώθη τῇ πίστει). The verb translated "grew strong" is ἐνδυναμόω, *endunamoo*, a word made up of the preposition "in" and the verb "to be strong." The preposition may be perfective in this case, indicating a heightened sense of strength, though five of the six times the verb is used in the Apostolic Scriptures it speaks of spiritual strength (inner strength, cf. Eph 6:10; Phil 4:13; 1Ti 1:12; 2Ti 2:1; 4:17). Thus, in this context "growing strong" in faith is put over against "doubting." When one comes to know the truth, it becomes his or her obligation to grow strong in that truth—to receive it fully. "Doubting" is not to be confused with "testing." Our faith is tested constantly as we strive to walk as God intends. "Doubting" is a conscious negation of what one knows to be true. "Growing strong in faith," on the other hand, is a willingness to take God at His simple word, apart from external signs or manifestations.

giving glory to God – Calvin comments on this phrase:

> . . . no greater honor can be given to God than by sealing His truth by our faith; as, on the other hand, no greater dishonor can be done to him, than to refuse his offered favor, or to discredit his word. It is hence the chief thing in honoring God, obediently to embrace his promises: and true religion begins with faith.[62]

A more contemporary author and teacher has stated "God is most glorified in us when we are most satisfied with Him."[63] The life of faith is the life that is overwhelmed by the satisfaction which is to be found in God alone. Reliance upon the flesh or upon man's strength pales in the light of God's all-encompassing power, enjoyed through the grip of faith. Here, then, is the Apostle's direct statement to the means of obtaining man's chief end, i.e., to glorify God. The means that he here identifies is nothing more nor less than a life of obedience lived through the means of faith.

Now such a life of obedience which Paul here attributes to Abraham, and which he declares "gives glory to God," is not evident when life moves along without a contest. But it is in the moment of conflict, when what our limited eyes see does not match what God instructs us to do. It is in that time of conflict that our faith is tested, and so it is in that time of conflict that we are afforded the opportunity to give glory to God as never before. One might surmise, therefore, that at least one reason why God brings trials into our lives is to afford the greater opportunity for giving Him glory through the exercise and demonstration of our faith. But only if our life's goal is the glory of HaShem will we receive the trial as an opportunity rather than a dismay. This is what faith accomplishes, for faith willingly affirms what the natural eyes do not see.

21 and being fully assured that what He had promised, He was able also to perform.

This phrase now completes the description of Abraham's faith, and stresses yet again that Abraham's faith was in the person of God and His word, not merely in what had been promised. Abraham believed the promise because He knew and believed in the One who had spoken it. He refused to believe what would be common for mankind to believe, that God speaks more than He can do.

"fully assured" translates the Greek πληροφορηθείς, *plerophoretheis,* an aorist passive participle from πληροφορέω, *plerophoreo,* which means to be "completely persuaded," cf. 14:5. It is used in a different sense ("fulfilled") in Lk 1:1; Col 4:12; 1 Ti 4:5, 17. The word itself is made up of two words, one meaning "full" and the other "to wear" or "to hold." The obvious sense is to hold something in its fullness, or to be fully "clothed" with a given garment. Thus, "to be fully assured" is to carry the full conviction that what God has said is true indeed.

Calvin's comments are valuable:

> . . . we do not sufficiently exalt the power of God, unless we think it to be greater than our weakness. Faith then ought not to regard our weakness, misery, and defects, but to fix wholly its attention on the power of God alone; for if it depends on our righteousness or worthiness, it can never ascend to the consideration of God's power. And it is a proof of the unbelief, of which he had before spoken, when we mete the Lord's power with our own measure. For faith does not think that God can do all things, while it leaves him sitting still, but when, on the contrary, it regards his power in continual exercise, and applies it, especially, to the accomplishment of his word: for the hand of God is ever ready to execute whatever he has declared by his mouth.[64]

22 Therefore also "it was reckoned to him as righteousness."

Paul now draws his conclusion for this section, bringing back to the reader's attention the quote (from Gen 15:6) which he began with in v. 3. The statement of Gen 15:6 was simply that "Abraham believed God and it was counted to him for righteousness." What Paul has done, then, in this section, is to show us clearly what is meant by "believed God"—what this kind of saving faith looks like. It is a faith in the person of God, first and foremost, and a faith therefore in the Savior He promises. It is a faith that issues in obedience and can be seen in the way one lives. It is a faith that disregards the human incapabilities and trusts God for the impossible. It is a faith which glorifies God by laying hold of Him as the eternal promise-keeping God, who not only speaks, but is able to carry out all that He has declared.

23-24 Now not for his sake only was it written, that it was reckoned to him, but for our sake also, to whom it will be reckoned, as those who believe in Him who raised Yeshua our Lord from the dead,

Paul wants us to understand that the declaration made by God regarding the righteous standing of Abraham was not recorded simply so that Abraham could occupy an exalted status in history, but because Abraham's faith and the righteousness which God afforded him on the basis of his faith has direct bearing upon us. For Abraham stands as the representative *par excellance* of saving faith. As such, he stands as the prime example for all people of all ages for what faith accomplishes and what it "looks like." Thus all who have faith ("those who believe") like that of Abraham may likewise be assured of right standing before the Lord.

Paul notes, as does the writer to the Messianic Jews (Hebrews), that the faith of Abraham was nothing less than resurrection-type faith. V. 17 speaks of God as the One "who gives life to the dead and calls into being that which does not exist." Here the faith is in Him "who raised Yeshua our Master from the dead." The inward connection is much more than the similarity of the two events, both of which display God as the "life-giving" One. The even more vital connection is simply that the Messiah would, in the course of God's providence, come from the very line of the promised son, Isaac, and would, in one manner of speaking, be the prime example of God's power to "give life to the dead" as the ultimate descendent of Abraham.

The Apostolic scriptures regularly attribute the resurrection of Messiah to the direct working of the Father (Rom 8:11; 10:9; Ac 3:15; 4:10; 1Co 6:14; 15:15; 2Co 4:14; 1Pt 1:12), though there are a number of times in the gospel of John where the resurrection is attributed to Yeshua Himself (Jn 2:19, 21; 10:17, 18).

The designation "Yeshua our Master" (Ἰησοῦν τὸν κύριον ἡμῶν) should not be passed over as ordinary. To designate Yeshua as "our Master (Lord)" in light of the fact that in the Lxx the Tetragrammaton (יהוה) is translated by κύριος (*kurios*) more than 6000 times must be considered significant. Add to this the fact that Lxx passages which clearly refer to God Himself in the use of κύριος are applied by Paul to Messiah (e.g., Rom 10:13; 1Th 5:2; 2Th 2:2) and that in Phil 2:10 κύριος is designated as the "the name which is above every name" (τὸ ὄνομα τὸ ὑπὲρ πᾶν ὄνομα), and one cannot help but admit that Paul's use of κύριος as a title for Yeshua is intended to convey his belief in the Messiah's divine nature. The confession of Yeshua as κύριος (cf. Rom 10:9) is surely to be understood in this vein.

25 *He* **who was delivered up because of our transgressions, and was raised because of our justification.**

This clause sounds like a well known formula or confession and, if so, was no doubt constructed on the basis of Isaiah 52:13-53:12, in which the "delivering up" is represented by the Greek παραδιδόναι, *paradidonai*, found in 53:6 and twice in 53:12. Further, the Isaiah passage speaks of being "delivered up on account of our sins" (καὶ κύριος παρέδωκεν αὐτὸν ταῖς ἁμαρτίαις ἡμῶν, 53:6) and "on account of our sins He was delivered up" (καὶ διὰ τὰς ἁμαρτίας αὐτῶν παρεδόθη).

It should also be noted that the Lxx of Isaiah 53 (which varies widely from the MT in vv. 11 and 12) has what most consider to be a reference to the resurrection of the suffering servant in its insertion of the word "light" in v. 11, a reading which is also supported by the Dead Sea Scrolls (1QIs). The Lxx reads: "by the suffering of his soul he will see light and be satisfied . . ." (ἀπο τοῦ πόνου τῆς ψυχῆς αὐτοῦ, δεῖξαι αὐτῷ φῶς καὶ πλάσαι τῇ συνέσει. . . 1QIs has: מעמל נפשׁוה יראה אור). The reference to "light" is very likely an allusion to resurrection (cf. Ps 13:3; 36:9; 56:13 and the comments in *The Letter Writer*, p. 202).

The justification, then, which Paul here attaches specifically to the resurrection of the Messiah, is that which Isaiah 53 concludes with, namely, (v. 11) "As a result of the anguish of His soul, He shall see light and be satisfied; By His knowledge the Righteous One, My servant, will justify (בְּדַעְתּוֹ יַצְדִּיק צַדִּיק עַבְדִּי לָרַבִּים). The use of "knowledge" (דַּעַת, *da'at*) here may well have covenant overtones, for the concept of "knowing" is found in covenant context throughout the Tanach, and emphasizes a relationship of loyalty within the covenant. When the text of Isaiah 53 indicates that it is "by His knowledge" that He succeeds in His vicarious sacrificial work, we should understand this to mean "by having fulfilled completely the covenant requirements." For "know" in covenant contexts, cf. Gen 18:19; 2Sa 7:21; Amos 3:2; Hos 13:4; Jer 24:7; 31:34.

Paul does not envision the death of Yeshua and His resurrection as two distinct events, but as two aspects of the one all-important event of the Messiah's work of salvation. Obviously, both were important, for the death pays the penalty for our sin and the resurrection declares the worth and acceptance of the sacrifice before the throne of the Almighty.

The word translated "because" (NASB) or "for" (NIV) is the Greek preposition δία, *dia* which can have either a causal or final sense, and it is used in both ways here. To paraphrase for clarification: "He was delivered as a result of our transgressions and the conclusion of His having been raised is our justification." The two aspects of Messiah's work, i.e., His death and resurrection, answer to the two primary needs we have as sinners, namely, that our sin requires death, and that being separated from God through our sins and thus dead in that sense, we are in need of life. The negative (death) and positive (life) aspects of Yeshua's redemptive work for us will thus become Paul's platform for declaring that those who have died with Yeshua do not stay dead, but rather raise in "newness of life," thus doing those things which please the Lord.

Chapter 5
Commentary

---

1 Therefore having been justified by faith, we have peace with God through our Master Yeshua Messiah

We come, now, to a new section in the epistle based upon the teaching Paul has given in the first four chapters. If we were to sum up the first section (Chapters 1-4) it seems obvious that Paul's main concern is the method or manner by which God brings a sinner into right standing before Him. That is to say, having shown conclusively that all, both Jew and Gentile, are at enmity with God because of their sin, and that no one is capable in and of himself to overcome this enmity, Paul goes on to outline the manner by which God, of His own mercy, reconciles the sinner to Himself, overcoming the utter inability of the sinner.

The opening verse of the new section (cf also v. 11) thus summarizes this "right standing before God" as "peace with God," the concept of *shalom* being grounded in the sense of that which is "complete" or "whole." *Shalom* in the Hebrew envisions things as they ought to be; life as God intends it.

We thus should understand the opening "Therefore having been justified by faith" (Δικαιωθέντες οὖν ἐκ πίστεως) as gathering together the essential truth of 1:18-4:25, bridging the former section with what follows. And yet even in this summary statement there is an advancement, for Paul has naturally linked "righteousness" with "peace" which has thus further defined "righteousness."

The key thought of the former section has surely been summed up in the single word "justified" (δικαιόω, *dikaioo*, on which see comments on 3:24 above), that declaration of the Almighty that an individual is righteous in His eyes. That He could make such a declaration and remain righteous Himself is possible only because of the vicarious sacrifice of the Messiah on behalf of His people. Combining then the substitutionary sacrifice of Yeshua with the declaration of righteousness as regards the sinner, Paul has summarized for us the divine method of bringing sinners into right standing with God.

To add the phrase "by faith" emphasizes the means by which personal right standing before God is obtained, namely, through acceptance of what God has said and commitment to life accordingly. Yet deeds of righteousness come as the fruit of faith, not as the means of it. One therefore obtains right standing before God through faith, not through the works of the Torah.

we have peace with God – The Greek text contains a variant at this point, some manuscripts having ἔχομεν, *echomen* (with *omicron*), the present indicative ("we have peace") while other manuscripts have ἔχωμεν, *echomen* (with *omega*), the present subjunctive ("let us have peace"). Interestingly, the weight of manuscripts falls to side of the subjunctive reading (ℵ* A B* C D K 33, 81, 181 etc.), but most translators and compilers opt for the indicative (found in ℵª B³ Gᵍʳ P Ψ, etc.). Cranfield explains why:

Though the indicative ἔχομεν is a good deal less strongly attested than the subjunctive ἔχωμεν, it is almost certainly to be preferred on the ground of intrinsic probability. It is clear from v. 10f that Paul regards the believers' peace with God as a fact. It would therefore be inconsistent for him to say here "let us have peace," meaning thereby "let us obtain peace" (Paul would anyway hardly think of peace with God as something to be obtained by human endeavor). If the subjunctive is read, we must understand it in some such sense as "let us enjoy the peace we have" or "let us guard the peace we have" (cf. e.g., Origen, Chrysostom). But this is not free from objection; for it would surely be strange for Paul, in such a carefully argued writing as this, to exhort his readers to enjoy or to guard a peace which he has not yet explicitly shown to be possessed by them.[65]

Thus, it seems warranted to take the minority reading at this point and understand Paul to be making a statement of fact that, we have peace with God on the basis of having been declared righteous by Him.

The peace which is the possession of all who have been declared righteous on the basis of faith is not a subjective inner feeling, but an objective state of being at peace instead of being enemies. This is made clear by v. 10 (a summary of the section 5:1-9) in which our status as "enemies" has been done away with through the work of Messiah's "reconciliation." Here this is a most important fact, that God in His declaring the sinner righteous on the basis of his faith also extends Himself in friendship.

> Whereas between a human judge and the person who appears before him there may be no really personal meeting at all, no personal hostility if the accused be found guilty, no establishment of friendship if the accused is acquitted, between God and the sinner there is a personal relationship, and God's justification involves a real self-engagement to the sinner on His part.[66]

Thus, for Paul to combine the two concepts of "justified" and "peace" is not merely to employ theological synonyms but to show the logical extension of justification from God's vantage point based upon what He is. Since He is infinite in love, He will always extend Himself in relationship to the one He declares righteous.

through Adonai Yeshua HaMashiach – In the same way that justification is through the Messiah (3:24), so reconciliation is through the Messiah—the two are, in God's plan of redemption, bound together inseparably.

The combination of the names Lord, Yeshua, and Messiah (in one combination or another) is found also in v. 21 and in 7:25, as well as in 6:23 and 8:39. It seems as though Paul begins and ends major sections in this part of the epistle with this three-name formula.

What are we to make of the use of κύριος, *kurios* (Lord) in combination with Yeshua the Messiah? One cannot escape the emphasis that this combination of words places upon the sovereign, divine nature of the Messiah. To call Him "Lord," a term repeatedly used by the Lxx to identify יהוה (YHVH) is surely to credit Yeshua as being Immanuel.

2 through whom also we have obtained our introduction by faith into this grace in which we stand; and we exult in hope of the glory of God.

"Through whom," i.e., through Yeshua the Messiah—that we are participants in God's grace is the direct result of Yeshua and His work. Yeshua Himself taught that friendship with the Father was possible only through Him: "I am the way, the truth, and the life. No one comes to the Father but through me." (Jn 14:6)

we have obtained our introduction by faith into this grace in which we stand – The verb ἐσχήκαμεν (*eschekamen*, "we have obtained") is in the perfect tense and may therefore express the idea that having gained access through initial faith/confession of Yeshua, this access remains the possession of all true believers. The concept of "introduction" (προσαγωγή, *prosagoge*) is most likely that of "the privilege of being introduced into the presence of someone in high station."[67]

Some of the major manuscripts (B D G it Or[lat]) omit the phrase "by faith" in the verse, though most consider the phrase original. Why it would be omitted in some of the major manuscripts remains a mystery, though its omission would not alter the meaning of the text, for Paul surely teaches that our entrance into God's favor is gained via the avenue of faith.

into this grace – Paul uses the demonstrative "this" (ταύτην, *tauten*) in connection with the word "grace" to indicate a reference to what he has just written. We should most likely, then, consider the term "grace" (χάρις, *charis*) here to have direct reference to the "peace" just spoken of. We find ourselves at peace with God because by faith we have obtained forgiveness and right standing with Him.

in which we stand – The verb ἵστημι, *histemi*, "to stand" (it is in the perfect tense in our verse, ἑστήκαμεν, *estekamen*) can at times be synonymous with the simple verb "to be" (εἰμί, *eimi*) and in this text could thus mean ". . . into the grace in which we are." But Paul's use of the verb in Romans (3:31; 10:3; 11:20; 14:4) seems rather to be used in the sense of "stand firm" or "abide."[68] Thus Paul's emphasis here is, once again, of the abiding position the believer has in his righteous standing before HaShem.

and we rejoice in hope of the glory of God – Our right standing with God considered here as "peace with God" is cause for rejoicing, but so is the prospect of God's glory being revealed in us at the coming of Messiah. Paul's use of the phrase "glory of God"[69] indicates that he sees the revelation of God's glory in connection with the victorious return of Yeshua and the glorification of the believer at that time. The ability mankind was given to radiate the glory of HaShem was marred by the fall but is restored through the redemptive work of Yeshua and will be fully manifest in those who are His at His return. It is thus the hope of His return and the ultimate completion of our sanctification that is the focal point of our hope. "Hope" here is the confident anticipation of that which we do not yet see (cf. Heb 11:1).

The status of "peace with God" which the believer now enjoys also guarantees his inevitable growth in holiness to the point where he will be perfectly restored as one who bears the very glory of God. This hope of seeing God's creative act come to its ultimate end is all the more wonderful in light of the fact that Yeshua Himself became man—entered into the realm of humaness—thus showing that mankind, when he realizes his creative purpose, will indeed reflect the very glory of God.

3 And not only this, but we also exult in our tribulations, knowing that tribulation brings about perseverance;

While we rejoice in the hope of what is yet future, by faith we must also rejoice in our sufferings. Note well that Paul does not set this forth as an exhortation but as a mere statement of fact. This is so because of who we are—we are those who rejoice in tribulation because of the faith we have.

Rejoicing in suffering is not a foreign concept in the Rabbinic writings.

> Our Rabbis taught: Those who are insulted but do not insult, hear themselves reviled without answering, act through love and rejoice in suffering, of them the Writ saith, But they who love Him are as the sun when he goeth forth in his might.[70]

> To him who gives thanks for his afflictions and rejoices over them, God grants life in this world and, in the world to come, life without end, "for a lamp are the commandments and the Torah is light" (Prov. 6;23). Why, then, did Moses merit that his countenance should shine, even in this world, with a light destined for the righteous in the next world? Because

> . . . he was ever striving, yearning, watching to establish peace between Israel and their Father in Heaven.[71]

> Truly, God is good to Israel, even to the pure in heart. That is, the sufferings which He has brought upon them are good. For whom are they good? For the pure in heart, to purify the heart of the righteous (Ps 73:1).[72]

Indeed, the Rabbinic teachings are replete with admonitions about receiving suffering as from HaShem and for the good of the one who suffers.

knowing that tribulation brings about perseverance – Several words exist in the Greek to bring forward the idea of "knowing." The word used here (which is a common word, εἰδότες, *eidotes*, is from the root οἶδα, *oida*, which means "to perceive," "to see" (in the sense "understand").[73] Here Paul refers to the knowledge which faith brings, a knowledge which claims absolute validity. This knowledge allows the believer to know that the tribulation he may be enduring at any given time is suffering which HaShem has allowed for the believer's good and His glory. It is not that the believer rejoices in tribulation because he believes that if he does so he will merit God's favor, but because the believer has come to know that God subjects those He loves to periods of tribulation in order to teach them how to wait patiently for His deliverance.

Now this is true for the believer, but it is not generally true for mankind. As Calvin remarks, tribulation causes "a great part of mankind . . . to murmur against God, and even to curse his name."[74]

In contrast to the unbeliever, then, when the child of God receives suffering within the context of sustained faith, he receives it as God's fatherly discipline and rather than producing bitterness or anger it produces patience or perseverance (ὑπομονή, *hupomone*). This Greek word is made up of two words, ὑπο, *hupo*, "under" and μένω, *meno*, "to remain." It may come from the idea of carrying a load which one is required to remain under it even though it is heavy. As with the athlete who is willing to endure some measure of pain during training in order to condition himself for the competition, so the child of faith can recognize that tribulation trains for the struggle to be righteous.

4 and perseverance, proven character; and proven character, hope;

The patience or perseverance which tribulation brings yields yet another godly attribute, "proven character" (δοκιμή, *dokime*). This word (and cognates) is grounded in metallurgy in which a metal is heated until molten and the impurities separated in order to refine the metal to its purest state.[75] Thus the translation "proven character" used in the NASB, which speaks of character which has been refined through suffering.

Furthermore, this proven character is able to produce "hope." Cranfield writes:

> To have one's faith proved by God in the fires of tribulation and sustained by Him so as to stand the test is to have one's hope in Him and in the fulfillment of His promises, one's hope of His glory (v. 2), strengthened and confirmed.[76]

Once again, "hope" is used in the sense of that which is expected by reason of that which is certain. It is therefore "the looking forward to something with some reason for confidence respecting fulfillment; hope, expectation" (*BDAG*, "ἐλπίς").

5 and hope does not disappoint, because the love of God has been poured out within our hearts through the Holy Spirit who was given to us.

The hope that is the result of persevering via faith is a hope that does not put those who cherish it to shame by proving illusory. Paul seems clearly to be relying upon numerous texts in the Psalms which teach that faith in God does not disappoint or cause those who call upon him to be ashamed.[77] When by faith the child of God hopes in Him, this hope will always be shown to be well-founded.

because the love of God has been poured out within our hearts – This is the first occurrence of ἀγάπη (*agape*, "love") in Romans (a cognate form was used in 1:7). We may question whether the genitive construction ("love <u>of</u> God") is objective or subjective. Objective genitive would yield the meaning "love to God" (where God is the object of the love) while a subjective genitive would yield "God's love to us," i.e., God is the subject Who acts in love. Is the hope we have of an enduring nature because we love God or because He loves us? It seems to me that a statement of God's love for us is a much greater proof of why our hope does not disappoint than an argument based upon our love for Him. Furthermore, our ability to persevere in tribulation is better formulated on the basis of God's love for us than upon our love for Him, because in the midst of suffering when we find our strength gone, and thus our ability to love diminished, God's love for us remains as firm as always and thus forms a foundation upon which we may rest in hope.

Thus, the fact of God's love for us has been "poured out within our hearts." Paul uses the metaphor of "pouring" (ἐκχεῖν, *ekchein*) as fitting when speaking of the giving of the Holy Spirit. In Acts 2:17ff and the report by Peter in Acts 10:45, the Spirit is spoken of as "poured out," no doubt based upon the metaphor of water in the act of cleansing such as that given by Ezekiel in his prophecy (cf. 36:25ff; Joel 2:28 [Heb. 3:1]). The metaphor of "pouring" is also used of God's wrath, mercy, and blessing. That Paul should thus combine the love of God with the giving of the Spirit in the metaphor of "pouring" is very natural.

The meaning, then, is that God has lavished upon us His love (spelled out more specifically in the following verses) and made us to know it absolutely and actually by giving us the Spirit Who dwells within us, and Who, therefore, communicates to our very souls this love that otherwise we would not comprehend. The ultimate proof that our hope in God will not disappoint us is in the manner in which we have come to know God's actions toward us in redemption and salvation. The fact that God has graciously given us the Spirit to dwell within us is a guarantee (עֵרָבוֹן, *'erabon*, ἀρραβών, *arrabon*, "pledge, down payment" cf. Eph 1:14) that He will maintain His faithfulness in every way, even to bringing us to be with Him, face-to-face, as it were. It is thus by the very work of the Spirit in illuminating our minds that we are able to comprehend the love of God which has been poured out in our hearts.

6 For while we were still helpless, at the right time Messiah died for the ungodly.

The verse begins ἔτι γὰρ (*eti, gar,* "For still") and is then followed by a second ἔτι at the beginning of the second clause.[78] This construction is a little unusual, though it is possible that ἔτι was placed at the beginning of the sentence for emphasis, and then repeated after the genitive absolute for the sake of clarity. We might thus translate, "For still, while ourselves being dead, still at that very time Messiah died on behalf of the ungodly."

Surely this verse dispels the notion of Poor Richard that "God helps them that helps themselves"! Paul has already shown that Scripture teaches the utter helplessness of the sinner when confronted with the need to atone for one's sin. Since mankind is incapable of beginning the process, the only hope he has is that God Himself might step in and accomplish what would otherwise be impossible. The metaphors of "death," "birth," and "creation," used of the event of regeneration, all speak to this issue of inability. For the one who is dead is unable to bring himself to life; the one who is unborn is unable to affect his birth; and the one who is uncreated is unable to bring about his own creation.

The word translated "helpless" (NASB), "powerless" (NIV) is ἀσθενής, *asthe-es*, meaning "weak," "powerless," "feeble," "sick." This word is used of "weak faith" (1Co 9:22), of those who were sick (Ac 4:9), as well as those who were physically weak (1Co 11:30). Here it speaks about the inability to gain right standing before God on one's own efforts.

at the right time – The death of Messiah was not determined by man, but by God. The Scriptures are clear on this matter: Mk 1:15; Lk 22:22; Ac 2:23; Gal 4:4. While the events leading up to the crucifixion may have appeared to some as though they were random and the result of unforeseen calamity, the truth of the matter is that God determined from all eternity (Rev 13:8) that His own Son should take upon Himself the sins of all His chosen ones.

Messiah died for the ungodly – Messiah's death on behalf of sinners is spoken of throughout the epistle (3:25; 4:25; 6:10; 7:4; 8:32; 14:15) and surely is one of the primary refrains of the Apostle. Here, in our text, as well as 8:32 and 14:15, the preposition ὑπέρ, *huper,* is used, translated "for," or better "on behalf of." The emphasis is upon substitution of a vicarious nature, one on the behalf of another, but especially one who is innocent on the behalf of one who is ungodly. The Greek ἀσεβής ("helpless") describes the impious person, the one who is without any connection to God, who is rightly condemned by his deeds. This forms one of the truly amazing aspects of God's grace, as Paul now goes on to show.

7-8 For one will hardly die for a righteous man; though perhaps for the good man someone would dare even to die. But God demonstrates His own love toward us, in that while we were yet sinners, Messiah died for us.

The amazing aspect that Paul here highlights is that the righteous God should ever want anything to do with unrighteous sinners, not to mention laying down the life of His beloved Son for them!

While it is clear that these verses are given to clarify and amplify the meaning of the former "Messiah died for the ungodly," it has not always been agreed upon as to how this verse should be understood. Is the "righteous man" of the first clause simply clarified by the "good man" of the next clause, or is the "good man" a better prospect for self-sacrificing love than the "righteous man?" Still others have suggested that we're not talking here about laying down one's life for a person, but for a cause (taking the word "righteous" and "good" as neuter). Another option is that "righteous" refers to any person of upstanding character, while "good" refers to one's own benefactor (since the term was used in this way and the presence of the article before ἀγαθοῦ, *agathou,* might suggest this usage).

Whatever the exact meaning of the terms, the general meaning is clear: we might be able to understand why a person would give up his life for the sake of a righteous or good man, but, in fact, the Messiah gave up His life for neither—not a righteous nor a good person, but instead He gave up His life for the ungodly. This truly is the mystery of God's love!

But God demonstrates His own love toward us – This contrast of God loving the ungodly is surely a demonstration of the greatest of love! The verb συνιστάναι (*sunistanai,* from συνίστημι, *sunistemi*), "to demonstrate," "to prove," was used in 3:5 but most likely should be understood here in the sense of "prove." Most interesting in this regard is that Paul uses the present tense, "God demonstrates," even though the cross is past. The very fact that the death of Messiah occurred remains a proof in the present of God's love; so does the fact that the historical event of the cross continues to bear present reality in redeeming sinners and reconciling them to God. Though Messiah died nearly 2000 years ago, the reality is that this event continues to be the greatest demonstration of God's love for the ungodly.

Note that God's love is contrasted with that of man's by the emphatic "His own love" (τὴν ἑαυτοῦ ἀγάπην). God is able to love in an infinite way, with an infinite capacity. As such, His love forms the model for all genuine love.

We may rightly ask how God's love is demonstrated by giving Messiah to die for the ungodly. Would it not be more natural to say that Messiah's love was demonstrated? But here we have, as often, the accepted theological axiom of the Apostle, that the Father and the Messiah are one, so that what the Messiah does can be rightly accredited to the Father, and *vice versa*. It is for this very reason that the Apostle can say, without hesitation or explanation, that God purchased the church "with His own blood" (Acts 20:28).[79] Thus, as far as the Apostle is concerned, the pain and suffering which the Messiah underwent on behalf of those for whom He died was no less the pain and suffering of the Father, and that in the death of the Messiah the Father's love is surely demonstrated as is the love of Yeshua for His own.

while we were yet sinners, Messiah died for us – This is parallel to the former "while we were still helpless." Thus, our helplessness is the result of our sin. Yet God did not wait for us to respond to Him, for we were unable. He forgave us while we still clung to our sin—while our lives were characterized by it. Here, the designation "sinners" refers to the primary characteristic of the unregenerate life. We may rightly extrapolate from this that once a person is born from above, this prime characteristic of being "sinner" changes. Even though we all sin and continue to battle against the flesh, the primary or most obvious attribute of a child of God is not that of "sinner" but of "holy one" (ἅγιος, *hagios*, often in the plural and translated "saints," meaning "holy ones"). Passing from darkness to light is an actual passage that results in a changed life and an ongoing process of being conformed to the image of Yeshua.

9-10 Much more then, having now been justified by His blood, we shall be saved from the wrath of God through Him. For if while we were enemies, we were reconciled to God through the death of His Son, much more, having been reconciled, we shall be saved by His life.

This *kal v'chomer* (light and heavy) argument is a favorite one of the Sages. If something is true for the greater, then it surely is true for the lessor. Thus, in this case, if the act of reconciliation of sinners to God required the very death of the Son (the greater case), surely it is true that maintaining our lives through His living must be true. Or to say it another way, if the greater task is loving the ungodly, then surely we can expect God to love those who are holy.

The participle "having been justified" (δικαιωθέντες, *dikaiothentes*) picks up the theme of v. 1, which is itself a concluding summary of 1:18-4:25. Paul is linking together "how one gets in" with "how one stays in." In both cases, coming into the family of God and staying in the family of God are the result of God's omnipotent and eternal love and grace whereby He reconciles the sinner to Himself and provides for his eternal salvation. If our "getting in" was the result of God reconciling us to Himself through the death of His Messiah, then we may well reason that He will also "keep us in" through His life. The object reconciled is far too valuable to ever be lost.

We are justified "by His blood" (ἐν αἵματι αὐτοῦ[80], *en haimati autou*), that is, by His death (v. 10). The shedding of blood, so well portrayed in the sacrifices of the Tabernacle and Temple, depicts a violent death—a death of a victim, not death by natural means. Whenever we encounter this sacrificial language applied to the work of Messiah we must gather together all we know of the sacrificial ritual as foreshadowing His ultimate sacrifice.

we shall be saved – The future tense emphasizes a very real aspect of salvation, namely, that ultimately we are saved from the fury of God's wrath in the final day of judgment. Thus, at times the words "saved" or "salvation" refer to our final rescue from the sentence of "guilty" to be uttered by the Judge of all the earth. Yet this salvation is not only future, but has present realities (note the use of "now" [νῦν, *nun*] in v. 11). Indeed, the Apostle has already told us that

God's wrath "is being revealed against all ungodliness" (1:18). So while there is a clear future reality to our salvation, there is, nonetheless, a present and real salvation for all who believe.

We should be careful to gather all of Paul's words together and not try, based upon this verse, to make a rigid distinction between the efficacy of Yeshua's death (blood) and His resurrection (life). Granted, Paul says we have been justified by His blood and that we are saved by His life, but in 4:25 he teaches that we were justified as a result of His resurrection. The point is that Paul does not envision a separation between the death and resurrection of the Messiah, for surely one without the other is either impossible or worthless. Rather, the work of the Messiah in all aspects is the fountain from which our salvation flows.

For if while we were enemies, we were reconciled to God – Here we have, for the first time in this epistle, the use of the word "reconcile" (καταλλάσσειν, *katallassein*). The verb is found only in Pauline epistles (1Co 7:11; 2Co 5:18, 19, 20) and the same is true of the noun (καταλλάγη, *katallage*). The definition of this word has already been described in the opening phrase "we have peace with God" (5:1).

When definitions are sought in the Greek of the 1st Century for this word group, it is hardly surprising that one finds no use of it in a religious sense. In Hellenistic religion the relation between deity and man was not conceived of as the deeply personal thing that it is in the Bible. In the salvation described by God in the Scriptures, reconciliation to Him is the essential element. Sin has brought enmity between the Creator and His creation, but in the outworking of salvation this enmity is removed. This enmity involves both God's hostility toward the sinner (His wrath) and the sinner's hostility toward God (enemies). But there is a great difference in how this hostility is done away with, for with man the removal of hostility is tied to a dramatic change within him, while the removal of God's hostility involves no change in His character at all. Rather, God's hostility toward the sinner is the direct outworking of His righteous character which demands that justice be served and therefore that sin be punished.

But reconciliation is the direct outflowing of God's character as well, for it comes from His infinite love. It is interesting to note that in all of the uses of the verb καταλλάσσειν, every time God is the subject the verb is in the active voice, while those occurrences which have man as subject are in the passive. Thus "God reconciles" but "man is reconciled." God is therefore always the initiator—never man. This hearkens back to the quote from Psalm 14 or Psalm 53 (Rom 3:10-11) in which Paul emphasizes "there is none who seek for God." Thus, if reconciliation is to occur, it must be as the result of God's initiative toward the sinner.

Yet though the active voice is always used of God when the verb καταλλάσσειν comes into play, 2Co 5:20 shows us that from Paul's perspective there was still the necessity of man to respond to God's call for reconciliation: "Therefore, we are ambassadors for Messiah, as though God were entreating through us; we beg you on behalf of Messiah, be reconciled to God." Surely, while God must be the initiator in the whole reconciliation process, the very fact that a term like "reconciliation" is used indicates strongly that man does not play a purely passive role. Quickened by the inner work of the Spirit, the soul pressed upon by God responds from the gift of faith which he has been given. And in that response of faith, the sinner lays hold of the eternal reconciliation which has been purchased for him by the blood of the Messiah.

much more, having been reconciled, we shall be saved by His life. – This parallels the *kal v'chomer* argument already given in v. 9. If the love of God demonstrated in the death of the Messiah is able to overcome the enmity which existed between Himself and those who were ungodly, then surely this same love will extend itself to maintain and guard those who are now reconciled.

11 And not only this, but we also exult in God through our Lord Yeshua Messiah, through whom we have now received the reconciliation.

What does the opening "not only this" refer to? Most commentators supply the idea of reconciliation, so that they take the meaning to be, "And not only are we reconciled to God. . . ." However, it may well be that the primary theme in mind in this paragraph is that of "salvation" in general, and specifically being saved from the wrath of God, a theme which has been picked up again in the previous clause ("we shall be saved through His life"). The point, then, is to stress the tense of the verb (future) and contrast it with the present: not only shall we be saved in the world to come, but we already exult now. The *eschaton* has broken into the present by the coming of Messiah.

we exult in God (καυχώμενοι ἐν τῷ θεῷ) – "we exult" is a present participle which may well indicate continuous action: "we keep on exulting." This is a bit of a paradox, for Paul himself informs us that we also "groan within ourselves" (8:23) as we await our final redemption. How is it, then, that we continually rejoice while at the same time we groan? The answer comes enwrapped in the element of faith, for faith brings into the present what, in reality, awaits the future. The very knowing that God will maintain His promise to bring us to Himself does, even in the midst of our groaning, cause us to exult. Thus, our exultation is "through Adoneinu Yeshua HaMashiach," for it is in His finished work that we are able to possess this abiding faith. It is through the finished work of Yeshua on our behalf (death, resurrection, ascension, intercession) that we are able to look beyond the groaning of this sphere to the joy of the עוֹלָם הַבָּא, *'olam haba'*, the world to come.

12 Therefore, just as through one man sin entered into the world, and death through sin, and so death spread to all men, because all sinned—

Paul begins this section with "Therefore" (Διὰ τοῦτο, *dia touto*) and it seems most likely, both on the basis of the Greek grammar as well as the context, that he intends his readers to understand that what follows is the inevitable result of the truth stated in the previous section (vv. 1-11). The fact that reconciliation exists between sinners and a just God is the result of the application of Messiah's work to the sinner via faith. Thus, those who have right standing with God do so as a matter of God's undeserved love by which they have been transformed from enemies of the Most High into His dearest friends. But what Paul now goes on to teach us is that this undeserved love of God whereby He brings into right standing those who otherwise would be condemned, goes well beyond the individual—it has an effect as wide as the effect of Adam's sin. For if the sin of Adam cast its effect upon all mankind, then in like manner the existence and work of Yeshua HaMashiach affects all. Adam condemned all who would come through him—Yeshua redeems all who would come to Him. The parallels between Adam and Messiah are thus close and direct.

just as through one man sin entered into the world – Paul uses "just as" (ὥσπερ, *osper,* the protasis) but does not follow it with the expected "so also" (the apodasis). In fact, he enters into an explanation (vv. 13-15) and a kind of long parentheses (vv. 16-17), and only in v. 18 comes back to the original theme. Apparently the parenthesis became so long that he is compelled, in v. 18, to repeat his "just as" and follow it immediately with the expected "so also."

With this in mind, we must understand that throughout this section it is Paul's intention to show the parallels (some in similarity, others in contrast) between Adam and Yeshua. Though he does not state it explicitly until v. 18, it is clear from the structure of the section as well as the content that this is the Apostle's intention.

through one man – Sin is almost personified or at least quantified, for it comes "through one man," i.e., as the result of one man. It is surely to be noted that the avenue for sin into the world is considered as Adam, not Eve, even though she was the first to disobey. The *Apocolypse of Moses* 32 has Eve declaring " . . . all sin is come into the creation through me."[81] b. *Yevamot* 103b shows that at least some of the rabbinic authorities of the Talmudic period believed that sin was passed on to Eve's children:

When the serpent copulated with Eve, he infused her with lust. The lust of the Israelites who stood at Mount Sinai, came to an end. The lust of the idolaters who did not stand at Mount Sinai did not come to an end.

Indeed, Ben Sira states this exactly:

From a woman did sin originate, and because of her we all must die.[82]

Yet the rabbinic material also contains hints that some held to the belief that Adam's sin caused death and decay to be imputed to all of mankind's generations.[83]

Consider the work of God: for who can make that straight which He hath made crooked (vii. 13)? When the Holy One, blessed by He, created the first man, He took him and led him round all the trees of the Garden of Eden, and said to him, "Behold My works, how beautiful and commendable they are! All that I have created, for your sake I created it. Pay heed that you do not corrupt and destroy My universe; for if you corrupt it there is no one to repair it after you. Not only that, but you will cause death to befall that righteous man [Moses].[84]

[Then the Lord God formed] the man: for the sake of Abraham. R. Levi said: It is written, The greatest man among the Anakim (Josh 14:15): "man" means Abraham, and why is he called the greatest man? Because he was worthy of being created before Adam, but the Holy One, blessed be He, reasoned: "He may sin and there will be none to set it right. Hence I will create Adam first, so that if he sins, Abraham may come and set things right."[85]

In one sense, the Golden Calf of Exodus played a similar role in Judaism as Adam does in Pauline theology, for every generation carries a bit of the Golden Calf (i.e., the sin and consequences of Israel's rebellion at Sinai):

R. Oshaia said: Until Jeroboam, Israel imbibed [a sinful disposition] from one calf; but from him onwards, from two or three calves. R. Isaac said: No retribution whatsoever comes upon the world which does not contain a slight fraction of the first calf [i.e.. the molten calf in the wilderness], as it is written, nevertheless in the day when I visit, I will visit their sin upon them. R. Hanina said: After twenty-four generations [the doom foretold in] this verse was exacted, as it is written, He cried also in mine ears with a loud voice, saying, cause the visitations of the city to draw near, even every man with his destroying weapon in his hand.[86]

Yet though it is clear that the Sages taught the passing of death from one generation to another as a result of Adam and Eve's sin, the passing of a "sin nature," something Christian theology insisted upon from the earliest years, is not a general tenet of rabbinic theology. Man is endowed with freedom of will and thus becomes a sinner entirely on the basis of each person's choice, not because of a predispositon inherited from one's forefathers. Though death is passed on from Adam and to each generation, the presence of sin is the result of individual choice. And, it is not universally agreed upon that death and sin are always linked. Death is a matter of God's providence for each person, according to Akiva, but one's evil deeds can shorten one's life. However, one's good deeds cannot lengthen it because the length of days has been determined.[87] Death is thus the result of providential decree, not necessarily the reward for evil deeds.[88]

Since many of the Sages denied the passing of the sinful inclination from one generation to another, they also denied the Pauline (and later Christian) insistence upon the need for redemption from the "sin nature." In general, rabbinic teaching of the Talmudic period was that each person is created with both the ability to do good and to do evil, and that the freedom of choice in the individual is the deciding factor. In this way, the keeping of the Torah is the antidote against the sinful inclination,[89] and therefore the constant emphasis upon Torah study and doing of the *mitzvot* is better appreciated.

Futhermore, since God is the One who created both the evil and good inclinations within mankind, one need not be "redeemed" from the evil inclination—one needs rather to control it—to subdue it through the doing of the *mitzvot*.

The contrary inclinations in mankind were described in rabbinic literature as *yezter ra'* (יֵצֶר רַע, also with the article, יֵצֶר הָרַע) or "evil inclination" and *yezter tov* (יֵצֶר טוֹב, also with the article, יֵצֶר הַטּוֹב) or "good inclination." The following gives a general picture of the Sages teaching on this duality within mankind:

1) The *yetzer ra'* was created in man by God:

Raba said: Though God created the *Yetzer ha-Ra*, He created the Torah as an antidote [lit. spice] against it.[90]

2) God created within man the ability to overcome the *yetzer ra'*

Thus the Holy One, blessed by He, said to Israel: My children, I have created for you the Evil Inclination, (but I have at the same time) created for you the Torah as an antidote. As long as you occupy yourselves with the Torah, he shall not have dominion over you.[91]

3) Though the Torah could enable one to overcome the *yetzer ra'*, it could never eradicate it altogether:

When Israel heard the words Thou shalt have no other gods, the Evil Inclination was eradicated from their hearts. Then they came to Moses and said to him: Moses, our teacher, be an emissary between us, as it is said: Speak thou with us, and we will hear. Now therefore, why should we die? What benefit will there be if we perish? Forthwith the Evil Inclination returned to his place. Thereupon they went back to Moses and said to him: Moses, our teacher, would that He revealed Himself to us a second time, would that He would kiss me with the kisses of His mouth. He answered them: This will not happen now, but in the time to come, as it is written: And I will take away the stony heart out of your flesh (Ezek 36:26).[92]

4) One must overcome the *yetzer ra'* or it will gain more and more control over one's entire being:

And the evil inclination is like a king over two hundred and forty-eight parts of the body. When a person goes to perform a precept, all his bodily parts become indolent, because the evil inclination in his bowels is king over the two hundred and forty-eight parts of a man's body; but the good inclination is only like one confined in prison, as it is said: For out of prison he came forth to be king (Ecc. 4:14)—this refers to the good inclination.[93]

5) The righteous and wicked can be determined on the basis of how each control the *yetzer ra'*:

The righteous are ruled by the good inclination . . . the wicked are ruled by the evil inclination . . . average people are ruled by both.[94]

While there are many parallels and similarities which we may draw between the later rabbinic view of sin and Paul's teachings, the differences are clear. First, the Apostolic Scriptures nowhere ascribe the presence of the sinful nature to the creating hand of God. Herein lies a very important difference between the later rabbinical viewpoint and that of the Scriptures, for the Scriptures ascribe (as we shall see below) the presence of evil in the world and within man as the result of man's own sin, not as part of God's creation. Since God declared that all He had created was good, the Apostles could not envision that an inclination toward rebellion and sin could have been part of the original work of creation. It could not have been labeled "good." For Paul, the sinful nature was inherited from Adam as a result of his sin and rebellion, and that it was, in some measure, contrary to the original purpose of God's creation, and must therefore be eradicated and ultimately put to death if mankind is ever to regain his ability to accomplish the end for which he was created.

Secondly, Paul is clear that the Torah, in and of itself, has no ability to overcome the sinful nature. This is a major difference between Apostolic teaching and the later rabbinical dicta found in the Mishnah and Talmuds. The inability of mankind to "pull himself up by the bootstraps" is a clear teaching of Yeshua, Paul, and the other Apostles, yet it is a standard teaching of so-called "rabbincal judaism" that man, endowed with a free will, is able to pit the good inclination against the evil inclination and win the battle if one but tries hard enough and if one gains strength from the Torah. In contrast, Paul teaches that such strength can come only from the indwelling Spirit, an indwelling which is the direct result of the redemption won for believers by Yeshua. As far as Paul is concerned, apart from the power of Spirit, one is unable to subdue the deeds of the flesh.

Surely the Holy Spirit utilizes the Torah, that is to say, empowers and encourages (even convicts) the child of God to walk in righteousness according to the commands of God's gracious teaching (Torah). But the Torah, in and of itself, is unable to overcome sin in the life of any individual—it simply has no reforming power with in it. The power of the Torah is that which the Spirit supplies as He writes it upon the heart.

Thirdly, a primary difference between Paul and the rabbinic teaching is that the final victory over the sinful nature has been won by Yeshua, and only by appropriating His redemption via faith is there hope of overcoming one's sinful nature. For Paul, the sanctifying work of the Spirit in connection with the Torah is directly tied to the priestly work of Yeshua in His sacrifice, resurrection, ascension and intercession. While it therefore is necessary for the child of God to appropriate by faith the means of sanctification which God provides, his sanctification is, in the final analysis, the purchased reward of Yeshua's death and life.

Is Paul's view of the sinful nature new, or is it substantiated by the Tanach?

Having given a very brief survey of the rabbinic view of the *yetzer ra'* and the *yetzer tov* (evil and good inclinations) and how this informs their view of the "sinful nature," it is worthy of our time to investigate what the Tanach says in regard to this issue. If the rabbis of the Talmud differ so radically with the views of Paul on "original sin" (and the passage we are presently studying is the primary text in which Paul deals with this issue), a fundamental question must be raised, namely, is Paul's teaching something new or is he simply restating an accepted interpretation of the Tanach? What does the Tanach have to say about the sinful condition of mankind?

The Tanach teaches that the heart of man is inherently evil:

Gen 6:5

MT	NASB
וַיַּרְא יְהוָה כִּי רַבָּה רָעַת הָאָדָם בָּאָרֶץ וְכָל־יֵצֶר מַחְשְׁבֹת לִבּוֹ רַק רַע כָּל־הַיּוֹם	Then the LORD saw that the wickedness of man was great on the earth, and that every intent of the thoughts of his heart was only evil continually.

Note that the word translated "intent" is יֵצֶר, *yetzer,* the very term adopted by the Talmudic sages to describe the "evil and good inclination." Yet here the statement of HaShem Himself is that the *yetzer* of man is only evil all day long. In fact, in the Tanach the noun יֵצֶר, "intent" (built upon the verb which means "to fashion," "to shape," "to create") is never followed by the adjective טוֹב, "good" when referring to mankind. As Gen 6:5 states, fallen mankind had come to be characterized only as evil in terms of his heart's intent.

Gen 8:21

MT	NASB
וַיָּרַח יְהוָה אֶת־רֵיחַ הַנִּיחֹחַ וַיֹּאמֶר יְהוָה אֶל־לִבּוֹ לֹא־אֹסִף לְקַלֵּל עוֹד אֶת־הָאֲדָמָה בַּעֲבוּר הָאָדָם כִּי יֵצֶר לֵב הָאָדָם רַע מִנְּעֻרָיו וְלֹא־אֹסִף עוֹד לְהַכּוֹת אֶת־כָּל־חַי כַּאֲשֶׁר עָשִׂיתִי	The LORD smelled the soothing aroma; and the LORD said to Himself, "I will never again curse the ground on account of man, for the intent of man's heart is evil from his youth; and I will never again destroy every living thing, as I have done.

Once again the term יֵצֶר, *yetzer,* is used, this time with לֵב, *leiv,* "heart." Speaking of mankind in general, HaShem states that the "intentions of the heart are evil from his youth." The parallel to 6:5 is obvious. The addition of "from his youth," however, takes 6:5 a step further. Investigating the 19 occurrences of "from youth" (נעור + מן) in the Tanach (Gen 8:21; 46:34; 1Sa 12:2; 1Sa 17:33; 2Sa 19:8; 1Ki 18:12; Is 47:12, 15; Jer 3:24; 22:21; 48:11; Ezek 4:14; Zech 13:5; Ps 71:5; 71:17; 129:1; Jb 31:18) it becomes clear that the expression defines a general starting point when describing one's life, so that "from my youth" generally means "all of my life." What it surely emphasizes, however, is that the ability to sin is not something one must learn or which requires practice, but is something which naturally occurs in all of mankind.

Jeremiah 17:9

MT	NASB
עָקֹב הַלֵּב מִכֹּל וְאָנֻשׁ הוּא מִי יֵדָעֶנּוּ	"The heart is more deceitful than all else and is desperately sick; Who can understand it?

The context of this Jeremiah text speaks of the difference between those who trust in the Lord, and those who trust in man (17:5-8). Why does Jeremiah insert this "wisdom" saying here? Apparently he does so to explain why, if righteousness brings blessing and wickedness yields the curse, anyone would choose wickedness. The point is that man, if he follows his own heart, will inevitably stray from what is right, for his heart is deceitful and sick. עָקֹב, *'akov,* rendered "deceitful," has its root in the word for "heel" (note the name יַעֲקֹב, *Ya'acov*), which also means "cunning" or "deceitful." אָנֻשׁ, *'anush,* is the Hebrew term translated "desperately sick" and usually carries the sense of "incurable" (cf. Is 17:11, Jer 17:16). Once again the Scriptures make a very broad statement regarding mankind's sinfulness. The prophet describes the "heart" because by doing so he describes basic intent of mankind's volition.

Psalm 51:5 [Hebrew 51:7]

MT	NASB
הֵן בְּעָווֹן חוֹלָלְתִּי וּבְחֵטְא יֶחֱמַתְנִי אִמִּי	Behold, I was brought forth in iniquity, And in sin my mother conceived me.

This remarkable statement by the Psalmist puts the issue of sin (עָווֹן/חָטָא, *chata'/'avon*) at the point of conception. What does the Psalmist imply by this? Kraus writes:

> The basic declaration of the judgment doxology in v. 4 is further expanded by means of profound insight into man's fateful deterioration into guilt as it is expressed in vv. 5-6. עָווֹן and חָטָא have from the hour of birth been the determining forces under whose signature life began. The petitioner wants to say that the primordial cause, the root cause of my existence is interwoven with corruption.[95]

Surely in the context of confession, David recognizes that the bent of his heart was naturally inclined to sin against the Almighty, and that this condition was one of his basic nature—that which proceeds from his very conception within his mother's womb.

Psalm 58:3 [Hebrew 58:4]

MT	NASB
רְשָׁעִים מֵרָחֶם תָּעוּ מִבֶּטֶן דֹּבְרֵי כָזָב	The wicked are estranged from the womb; These who speak lies go astray from birth.

Again, the Psalmist puts the bent to sin as co-terminus with birth itself. The word translated "estranged" is תָּעָה, "to be confused," "wander," "stagger." It is used of erring in spirit in Is 29:24 and describes sheep who "go astray" (Is 53:6), causing iniquity to be placed upon the sacrificial animal. The word's parallel here with "speak lies" surely denotes sin. And if this is the case from birth, then it is certain that the nature which produces such activity is a sinful one.

Job likewise speaks of the inevitability that those who enter this life do so as sinners (14: 4; 15:14f; 25:4). Other writers in the Tanach agree: Ecc 7:20, 29; 9:3; 2Chron 6:36 (cf. 1Ki 8:46); Ps. 130:3; 143:2; Jer 13:23.

Thus, it seems quite clear that from the perspective of the Tanach, mankind is, by nature, sinful—that it is an inevitability that everyone who is born into this world will be reckoned as a sinner by God. What is more, the Tanach is equally clear on the fact that no one is able, in and of himself, to reverse this tendency to sin. As Job says, "Who can bring a clean thing out of an unclean? There is no one" (14:4) and Jeremiah agrees: "Can the Ethiopian change his skin or the leopard his spots? Then also you can do good who are accustomed to do evil" (13:23).

If we collate the words of Yeshua on this subject, we find Him in concert with the Tanach. His insistence upon the necessity for a new birth must be understood against the backdrop of teaching which saw all who were born into this life as sinners. If the bent to sin is a generational issue, then the only way out of this is a new birth, and it is to this that Yeshua gives His attention when conversing with Nicodemus (Jn 3). The answer for the inevitable sin which comes through generational ties is nothing less than a new birth. Yeshua also teaches that the heart of mankind is wicked and sinful (Mk 7:21-23) and that mankind has a natural tendency to love darkness rather than light (Jn 3:19). Furthermore, Yeshua clearly taught that left to himself man will not come to righteousness. Only when drawn by the Father will one respond in faith and follow righteousness (Jn 6:44, 65).

We see, then, that the rabbinic perspective of offsetting *yetzer hara* and *yetzer hatov* (evil and good inclinations) simply lacks Scriptural foundation. Nowhere in the Tanach can one find Moses and the prophets declaring the existence of the *yetzer hatov*, "the good inclination" in mankind in general. In every case when fallen mankind's intentions are referenced, it characterizes them as evil and contrary to God's ways and character. Only through the divine impartation of a "new heart" can righteousness become the norm (cf. Jer 31:31ff; Ezek. 11:19; 18:31; 36:26). The fact that the metaphor of a new heart is used once again emphasizes that the sinful bent is part and parcel of the fallen human nature.

Let us now turn back to Romans and the parashah in which Paul most clearly defines this issue of sin which is inherited from Adam.

12 Therefore, just as through one man sin entered into the world, and death through sin, and so death spread to all men, because all sinned

As noted above, Paul clearly states that sin "entered the world" (by which we should most likely understand the "world" in the sense of "mankind") through the sin of one man, i.e., Adam. Adam is held responsible in the primary sense for the presence of sin in the world, not Eve, though she was the first one to take the forbidden fruit for food. By this we must understand that Adam stands in some kind of representative relationship to his progeny. If the doorway for sin was simply the first to sin, then Eve would have filled that position but she does not—Adam does. This gives insight into the frame-of-reference from which Paul is writing.

and death through sin – Death follows sin like a shadow—wherever you find sin, there you likewise find death. God, from the beginning, linked death (both spiritual and physical) with sin (Ezek 18:4).

and so (καὶ οὕτως, *kai houtos*) – "as a natural consequence." In the same way that children are born and carry the characteristic of the parents, so it was the expected phenomenon that sin, and death intertwined with it, would be passed on to each successive generation.

death spread to all men – The use of the word "spread" (διῆλθεν, *dielthen* aor. act. ind. from διέρχομαι, *dierxomai*) gives sin the perspective of a communicable disease. As the Tanach portrayed a concept of sin through the laws of purity in which uncleanness could be transmitted through contact, so the bent to sin, in reality, is inherited. It spreads from one generation to another.

because all sinned – This phrase is not as easy to interpret as it may first appear. The Greek (ἐφ' ᾧ πάντες ἥμαρτον) could literally be translated "upon which all sinned." There are a number of ways this phrase has been understood:

1) because of the death which passed to all, all sin
   (taking ᾧ, "which," to refer to ὁ θάνατος, *ho thanatos*, "death" as its antecedent;
   note: the article is often used with abstract nouns)
2) because everyone sinned in Adam

(taking ᾧ, "which," to refer to ἑνος ἀνθρώπου, "one man," and ἐπί, *epi,* "upon"
as equivalent to ἐν, *en,* "in")

3) because everyone sinned because of Adam
(same as #2 but understanding ἐπί to mean "because of")

4) because everyone sins personally
(taking ἐφ᾽ ᾧ as meaning "because" and disavowing any direct connection to
Adam other than that he is followed as a bad example).

5) because everyone sins personally
(taking ἐφ᾽ ᾧ as meaning "because" and understanding the connection to
Adam as real, i.e, everyone sins on their own because they participated in sinning in Adam).

6) because everyone sins personally
(same as #4 but everyone sins because they have received a corrupt nature
from Adam. In other words, it is inevitable that death will pass to all because,
having received a corrupt nature from Adam, all will inevitably sin).

7) and the proof is everyone sins
(taking ἐφ᾽ ᾧ to mean "and the proof is." Thus, death passes upon all men,
the proof being that all sin, something which inevitably results in death.)

#1 is difficult and somewhat forced, because the clause seems to function for the purpose
of explaining how sin came to all men, not merely restating the obvious fact that it did.

#2 was championed by Augustine and later Latin writers, but seems to stretch the syntax a
bit, for ἑνος ἀνθρώπου, "one man" is too far away grammatically to be a natural antecedent.

#3 was held by Chrysostom and a number of other ancient writers but is unlikely for the
same reasons as #2.

#4 was held by Pelagias because he could never accept anything charged to a person's ac-
count for which they were not personally involved in the act.

#5 was and still is held widely, on the basis that ἐφ᾽ ᾧ grammatically must mean "be-
cause." This view differs from #4 in that there is a real connection to Adam in that everyone in
a real sense sinned in Adam. Thus, the bent to sin comes from having a real corporate solidarity
with Adam, the first sinner.

#6 is also popular and very probably the most natural way to understand the phrase. It
understands ἐφ᾽ ᾧ to be similar in usage as 3:23.

#7 possible but the burden of proof is on finding ἐφ᾽ ᾧ to mean "and the proof is," some-
thing which is difficult since the exact construction (ἐφ᾽ ᾧ, prep. ἐπί followed by relative neuter
pronoun ὅς in the dative) is found only 3 other times in the Apostolic scriptures, 2Co 5:4; Phil. 3:
12; 4:10. Though Phil 4:10 may approach the sense of "the proof is" (in the sense of "indeed"), it
does not provide enough evidence to support this view.

If we consider the wider context of vv. 12-21, it is clear that Paul's primary purpose in this
section is to show both the similarities as well as the dissimilarities between Adam and the sin
which entered into the world through him, and Messiah with the righteousness which He gives
to those who believe in Him.

In this regard we may rightly ask why Paul feels compelled to find a parallel between
Adam and Messiah at all. The first and most apparent reason to find a parallel between Adam
and Yeshua is the place Adam played as the first man, i.e., as the *editio princepts,* "first edition"
(as it were) of mankind. In a sense Adam should have stood as the model *par excellence* of what
a human should be, he being formed by the very hands of the Creator. Yet in his disobedience
he casts forever a mold in which mankind would be seen, a mold tainted and marred by sin.
The glory of man, then, is forever tarnished by the first man. In this regard, one of the purposes
of Messiah's redemption was to restore to mankind the glory with which he was created. As

such, the Messiah would come as the last Adam, the Man who would not fall to temptation and would, in His righteous triumph, be the model which God has always intended for mankind.

But there is a second aspect of the parallel between Adam and Messiah which Paul no doubt wishes to emphasize, an aspect which is connected to the whole concept of imputation (λογίζομαι, see comments above on 5:4-5). As noted above, the concept of imputation or reckoning is simply to accredit to someone what is rightfully his. Thus debt is reckoned to the one who has incurred debt, just as, in the same way, credit is applied or reckoned to the account of one who has made payment. In this way, the righteousness of Yeshua is accredited to the account of the one who believes, for in believing the sinner lays hold of the righteousness of Messiah as his own possession through God's grace. The means, then, by which righteousness is reckoned to a sinner is faith. By faith, the sinner is able to acquire the righteousness (obtain right standing before God) of Yeshua, his savior, precisely because the redeemed sinner is viewed as ἐν χριστῷ, *en xristo*, "in Messiah." To whatever extent Yeshua is seen as righteous in the sight of God, so is the one who is "in Messiah." Our union, then, with the Messiah, is obtained through the avenue of faith.

The parallel to Adam is clear: we find ourselves "in Adam," not through the avenue of faith (the new birth), but through physical birth. Even as those who are in Yeshua are seen by the Father as righteous, so all who are in Adam are seen as transgressors. The corruption which entered the world through Adam attaches itself to all who are "in him."

Now we may take this second parallel a step further, for even as those who are "in Messiah" by faith are reckoned or considered as righteous by God, so are they made righteous through the indwelling Spirit who leads them to live righteously. In the same way, those who are "in Adam" by birth are not only viewed or reckoned by God as unrighteous, but also are lead by the corruption of their nature to engage in sin. Thus, the character of the life of any individual is in concert with his standing before God: those who are reckoned as righteous before Him pursue righteousness, and those who are considered as unrighteous walk in the ways of unrighteousness.

It would seem, then, that taking the wider context would lead to the conclusion that #6 above is the most probable interpretation of the phrase "because all sinned," i.e., the phrase emphasizes that solidarity with Adam through birth connects each person to the sin of Adam which in turn is worked out through one's own sinful actions.

13 for until the Torah sin was in the world; but sin is not imputed when there is no Torah.

The opening "for" (γάρ, *gar*) indicates that Paul is here supporting something in the previous verse, and the most natural connection would be the last phrase "because all sinned." Paul explains how it was possible to say "all sinned" even though generations existed before the giving of the Torah. His explanation is straightforward: even though the Torah had not yet been given, sin still existed in the world, and people still sinned.

but sin is not imputed when there is no law – Most commentators understand this phrase to mean that somehow, before the giving of the Torah, while sin existed and the sinner was held responsible for his sin, it was not until the giving of the Torah that sin was seen for what it truly was. Cranfield is representative of this view:

> οὐκ ἐλλογεῖται [not reckoned] must be understood in a relative sense: only in comparison with what takes place when the law is present can it be said that, in the law's absence, sin is not reckoned. Those who lived without the law were certainly not 'innocent sinners'—they were to blame for what they were and what they did. But in comparison with the state of affairs which has obtained since the advent of the law sin may be said to have been, in the law's absence, 'not registered', since it was not the fully apparent, sharply defined thing, which it became in its presence.[96]

However, it seems likely that Paul held that the Torah, as the revelation of God's immutable character and holiness, existed before its giving at Sinai. Therefore, the same standard of righteousness existed before Sinai, and the imputation of sin was likewise extant even before the written Torah was revealed.

The agrument would follow this pattern: 1) there is no imputation of sin apart from Torah; 2) the penalty for imputed sin is death; 3) all men who existed between Adam and the giving of the Torah died; 4) therefore, sin must have been imputed even though the written Torah had not yet been given.

The eternality of the Torah is well established in the Rabbinic literature:

> R. Yudan said: The world was created for the sake [lit. because of the merit] of the Torah. R. Joshua b. Nehemiah said: For the sake of the tribes of Israel.[97]

> When the Torah was about to be given to the Israelites, a loud noise went forth from one end of the earth to the other; terror seized the peoples in their palaces, and they sang, as it is said, 'in their palaces all say Glory' (Ps 29:9). They gathered together to Balaam and said, 'What is this tremendous noise which we have heard? Is a new flood coming upon the earth? He replied, 'God has sworn that He will never bring another flood.' They said, 'But perhaps He is going to bring a flood, not of water, but of fire?' He replied, 'He has sworn that He will never again destroy all flesh.' Then they said, 'What then was the noise?' He replied, 'God has a precious treasure in His storehouse which has been stored up there for 974 generations before the creation of the world, and now He proposes to give it to His children.' . . . . Then they said, 'May God bless His people with peace.' (Ps xxix. 11).[98]

> . . . The beautiful Torah, which You have hidden away since the creation and for 974 generations before creation, do You purpose to give it to one of flesh and blood? (i.e., Moses)[99]

Some Sages taught that Adam and the Patriarchs kept the Torah, while others suggest that they kept only Noahic laws:

> R. Judah said: it was fitting that the Torah should have been given through Adam. Whence does this follow?—This is the book of the generations of Adam. The Holy One, blessed be He, said: 'I gave him six commandments, and he did not remain loyal to them; how then shall I give him six hundred and thirteen precepts, viz., two hundred and forty-eight positive precepts and three hundred and sixty-five negative precepts?' Hence it is written, And He said la-adam—I will not give it to Adam. But to whom will I give it? To his descendants: hence, This is the book of the generations of Adam.[100]

Paul has already shown that all mankind (both Jew and Gentile) are guilty before God because all are sinners. Here he stresses that the universal guilt of mankind is legally connected to the universal application of the Torah. Even before its actual giving at Sinai, the Torah functioned to condemn sinners. In the same manner that Adam was condemned for disobeying God's commandments, so all mankind stands condemned before the bar of God's justice, because all mankind are transgressors of the Torah. The irrefutable proof of this is that death became the norm for all who came from Adam, proving that the penalty given to Adam (the penalty for transgressing God's commandment is death) is passed on to all of mankind even though each new generation is not given a similar test for obedience as was given to Adam.

14 Nevertheless death reigned from Adam until Moses, even over those who had not sinned in the likeness of the offense of Adam, who is a type of Him who was to come.

The connection of death with sin continues as Paul unfolds his teaching on mankind's plight. Death is said to "reign," ἐβασίλευσεν, *ebasileusen*, aor. act. ind. of βασιλεύω, *basileuo*, "to reign as king," "to have royal power." Paul's metaphorical sense of sin as "king" sets the stage for his description of sinners as "slaves to sin." This metaphor gives power to sin and inability to mankind to overcome the rule of sin.

Since it is without dispute that people experienced death during the generations from Adam to Moses (just read the generational accounts in Genesis), it must likewise be true that they were reckoned as sinners by the One Who holds in His hand both life and death. But Paul's specific point here is that each generation was counted as sinful and awarded the penalty for sin, i.e., death, even though they had not sinned in exactly the same way as Adam had sinned. That is to say, they were not given a specific test or prohibition as was Adam—yet they sinned in such a way as to be deserving of death. This proves, then, beyond dispute, that Adam's sin (the corrupt sinful nature) as well as the penalty for sin, was passed on to all his offspring. Adam as the representative of mankind is therefore shown, and this sets up the comparison with Yeshua as the representative of His people. The actions and attended pentaly/reward of each representative are imputed to those they represent. It is in this way that Adam stands as a "type" of the Messiah who was to come.

A "type" (used also of Adam in 1Co 10:6ff, Greek τύπος, *tupos*) denotes a mark made by striking, an impression made by something, such as an impression used as a mold to shape something else (e.g., 6:17), hence a form, figure, pattern, example. The word gains a specialized use in bibilcal interpretation: a "type" is a person or thing prefiguring (according to God's design) a person or thing pertaining to the time of eschatological fulfilment. Thus,

> Adam in his universal effectiveness for ruin is the type which—in God's design—prefigures Christ in His universal effectiveness for salvation.[101]

In this way, in vv. 15-21 Paul shows the parallels between Adam and Messiah, first (vv. 15-17) the manner in which the parallel demonstrates the contrast between the two, and secondly (vv. 18-21) the similarities.

Paul refers to Yeshua as "the coming one" (τοῦ μέλλοντος, *tou mellontos*) which reminds one of Mt 11:3 (=Lk 7:20):

> "Are you the Coming One, or shall we look for someone else?"

Some have suggested that the term "affikomen," the matzah hidden away at the Pesach seder, derives from the Greek ἀφικόκομενος, *aphikokomenos,* aor. participle of ἀφικνέομαι, *aphikneomai,* which would be translated "the coming One." Since in the seder the broken matzah, wrapped and hidden away, and then brought back to the table, symbolizes the Pesach sacrifice according to the Sages, this "coming one" as a Messianic symbol makes good sense. We are not certain, however, how early this tradition of the affikomen existed in the Pesach seder. The term אֲפִיקוֹמָן, *'aphikoman,* is found in the Mishnah at m.*Pesachim* 10:8, but Jastrow (p. 104) considers the meaning "dessert," relating it to a Greek form ἐπικῶμον, *epikomon,* but normally the Greek for "dessert" would be ἐπιφόρημα, *epiphorema.* The form ἐπικῶμον is uncertain. Blackman translates אֲפִיקוֹמָן as "Passover offering" (*Mishnayoth,* 2.221), but notes that traditionally the word has been taken to mean "sweetmeat or dessert."

Note also that Paul specifically states that those who came in the generations following Adam, died even though they had not sinned in the same manner as Adam (καί ἐπὶ τοὺς μὴ ἁμαρτήσαντας ἐπὶ τῷ ὁμοιώματι τῆς παραβάσεως Ἀδάμ). What we should most likely understand this to mean is that though the people following Adam had indeed sinned, they had not broken a specific command of God as Adam had, for they were not given a similar test of obedience as God had given Adam ("in the day that you eat you will surely die"), or as God would give to Israel after receiving the Torah at Sinai. Here, once again, Paul links sin and death, and shows that even though the specific sin may have been different in kind and even quantity, sin, regardless of its "shape or size" was still worthy of death. "The soul who sins shall die" (Ezek 18:4).

15 But the free gift is not like the transgression. For if by the transgression of the one the many died, much more did the grace of God and the gift by the grace of the one Man, Yeshua Messiah, abound to the many.

The comparison of Adam with Yeshua as the "last Adam" continues now as Paul unfolds the parallels. It might be helpful to lay out these comparisons in a table:

Adam	Yeshua
Sin entered into the world through one man, and death came from sin (v. 12)	The gift of righteousness will reign in life through One, Yeshua the Messiah (v. 17)
By the transgression of one the man died (v. 15)	The grace of God and the gift of grace of the One Man, Yeshua the Messiah, abound to the many (v. 15)
Judgment arose from one transgression resulting in condemnation (v. 16)	The free gift arose from many transgressions resulting in justification (v. 16)
Through one transgression there resulted condemnation to all men (v. 18)	Through one act of righteousness there resulted justification of life to all men (v. 18)
Through one man's disobedience many were made sinners (v. 19)	Through the obedience of the One the many will be made righteous (v. 19)

Verse 15 begins Paul's detailed comparison of Adam and Yeshua as the representatives of their respective peoples. The opening statement is straightforward: "But the free gift is not like the transgression." How is it different? What is the negative comparison Paul wishes to point out?

A number of suggestions have been given. Calvin[102] believes that the difference pointed to by Paul is this, that "there is a greater measure of grace procured by Christ, than of condemnation introduced by the first man." In other words, the free-gift is unlike the transgression because it comes with exceedingly more power than the transgression. Cranfield[103] simply thinks Paul wants to point out the obvious, namely that the transgression brings condemnation while the obedience and righteousness of Yeshua yields justification. In addition to these two suggestions I would also add that there may be an emphasis upon the words "free gift" (τὸ χάρισμα, *to charisma*), for the transgression differs from the free gift in this important way, that the death which came as a result of Adam's sin was a penalty well deserved, but the life which becomes the possession of the believer is his entirely by grace—he deserves none of it.

These contrasts, then, set up the reverse *kal v'chomer* argument, that if the act of a mortal man (Adam) could so affect mankind and bring all under the domain of sin, then how much more could the work of the Messiah accomplish God's purpose for redemption. And, the purpose of God is realized through the outworking of His grace, for even the coming of the Messiah is stated here to be the result of God's grace.

the grace of God and the gift by the grace of the one Man, Yeshua the Messiah – Why does Paul mention both of these (the grace of God and the gift of Messiah), since surely the grace of God encompasses the work of Yeshua? Most likely the grace of God (the Father) is seen in sending the Messiah, while the gift by the grace of the one Man is most likely the justification we receive as the result of His death and life for us (note "gift of righteousness," v. 17). Once again, the inclusion of the word "gift" emphasizes the difference between the transgression of Adam and the grace of God—the former attracts a punishment well deserved, but the grace comes entirely by grace, not as a reward for good deeds done.

It should also be noted how clearly Paul intends his readers to see the humanity of Yeshua—"the one Man, Yeshua." Whether or not Paul was facing an increased number of pre-gnostics in the congregation at Rome as well as in other cities, it seems clear that he intends his readers to affirm the truth that Yeshua, though eternally with the Father, became incarnate as a man—truly man and that without reservation. Errors of Christology either deny Yeshua's manhood or His divine nature. While explaining the manner in which these co-exist within the Messiah is impossible, we nonetheless affirm both to be true, that He is fully man and fully divine and that as such He is Immanuel ("God with us").

The characteristic of God's grace as a gift, i.e., that which is given and not earned, is emphasized by the word "abound," ". . . did the grace of the one Man, Yeshua Messiah, abound to the many." The word is ἐπερίσσευσεν, *eperisseusen*, aor. act. ind. from περισσεύω, "to abound," "be extremely rich or abundant," "overflow." The word is often used by Paul to describe the riches of salvation (2Co 3:9), of love among believers (2Co 8:2), or of thanksgiving that the redeemed soul offers (2Co 4:15). The word was used in the classics to describe those who were superior in rank or in acumen, as well as those who were wealthy. Paul thus expresses the grace that has been given as that which was lavished, not in small measure, but in abundance, making sinners rich. "For you know the grace of our Lord Yeshua HaMashiach, that though He was rich, yet for your sake He became poor, that you through His poverty you might become rich." 2Co 8:9.

16 And the gift is not like that which came through the one who sinned; for on the one hand the judgment arose from one transgression resulting in condemnation, but on the other hand the free gift arose from many transgressions resulting in justification.

Here we have a second difference between the condemnation which came as a result of the sin of Adam, and the righteousness which comes through Yeshua. The contrast is obvious: Adam's transgression was singular, resulting in death to all, but the work of Yeshua dealt with many transgressions, resulting in justification to those who believe. Thus, the gift is far more powerful (for it overcomes many transgressions) than the disobedience which was only one sinful act.

Furthermore, as noted earlier, the one act of Adam is contrasted to the obedience of Yeshua in that Adam's sin secured condemnation while Yeshua's obedience won salvation for the elect. So while Paul wants to eventually note a similarity between the work of Adam and that of Yeshua, he wants, first and foremost, to show the real dissimilarities.

Note also that justification is linked to the free gift. Justification cannot be earned, it must be awarded.

17 For if by the transgression of the one, death reigned through the one, much more those who receive the abundance of grace and of the gift of righteousness will reign in life through the One, Yeshua Messiah.

Paul continues, now, to substantiate what he has just said. It seems, on the basis of the similar structures, that this verse is given to support the claims of 16a (that a difference between Adam's sin and Messiah's obedience is the difference between one sin and many transgressions) rather than 16b (that Adam's sin yields condemnation while Yeshua's obedience brings justification). And the point Paul here emphasizes is that the life that Yeshua's work brings is not simply a replacement of the death which came as a result of Adam's sin, but it is a life which in every way surpasses and overcomes the death of sin.

It should be noted that Paul makes a clear yet subtle statement about the superiority of the life we have as believers in Yeshua. For one would expect that he would balance the opening statement (protasis) by the concluding one (apodosis), so that "death reigned" would be matched by "life reigned." But rather than talking about life reigning, he rather substitutes the believers themselves as reigning in life. Here the abstract concept of death is replaced with the reality of reigning forever with Yeshua our Messiah.

> The effectiveness and the unspeakable generosity of the divine grace are such that it will not merely bring about the replacement of the reign of death by the reign of life, but it will actually make those who receive its riches to become kings themselves, that is, to live 'the true kingly life' purposed by God for man.[104]

gift of righteousness – This expression should also add support to the intepretation given early for the phrase "righteousness of God" as being "the means or method by which He declares a sinner righteous." Here, the manner of becoming righteous is to receive the gift of righteousness, namely, the declaration of our right standing before Him, and the gift of His Spirit poured out in our hearts as the divine Agent directing and enabling our own sanctification.

18 So then as through one transgression there resulted condemnation to all men, even so through one act of righteousness there resulted justification of life to all men.

Having shown clearly the dissimlarities between Adam and Yeshua, both acting as the "first man," Paul goes on now to show the important similarity, namely, that God considered each as representing his offspring, and thus as acting on their behalf. What each did had an inevitable affect upon all those being represented.

The obvious question which first arises in the mind of any attentive reader is the inclusive language found both in the protasis as well as in the apodosis. How can Paul speak both of condemnation and justification attaching to all men? Does he here teach a universalism which elsewhere in Scripture is clearly denied (e.g., Mt 7:22f)? Surely Paul is not teaching that all people of all ages will inevitably be justified—he recognizes that there are those who will be lost eternally and who, as a result of their own rebellion and sin, will be punished (cf. 2:2, 18ff). What then does he mean?

Some[105] consider the possibility that what Paul means is this: condemnation came upon all men as a result of Adam's sin, and the opportunity for justification came to all men as a result of Yeshua's obedience.

> How can Paul speak of both κατακρίμα (*katakrima*, condemnation) and δικαίωσις (*dikaiosis*, righteousness) as resulting for all men? and 'Does he really mean "all?"' The important thing here is to remember that vv. 15-17 have specially stressed the vast, superiority of Christ to Adam, and made it abundantly clear that Adam's sin and Christ's obedience are not on an equal footing and that there is no equilibrium between their respective consequences. Condemnation does indeed result for all men from Adam's sin, but this condemnation is no absolutely irreversible, eternal fact: on the contrary, Christ has in fact already begun the process of its reversal, and therefore the πάντες (all) of the protasis,

while it really does mean 'all', is no eternally unalterable quantity. What then of the 'all' of the apodosis? It will be wise to take it thoroughly seriously as really meaning 'all', to understand the implication to be that what Christ has done He has really done for all men, that righteousness of life is truly offered to all, and all are to be summoned urgently to accept the proffered gift, but at the same time to allow that this clause does not foreclose the question whether in the end all will actually come to share it.[106]

But I cannot agree with this interpretation, as appealing as it is for solving the "problem" of the 'alls', for one, quite simple reason. It seems to me that the very point of comparison between Adam and Messiah which Paul wishes to make here is the inevitability of each one's actions as causing a sure effect upon their progeny. That is to say, in the same way that Adam's disobedience plunged mankind into condemnation, without respect to anyone's choice, so the effectual work of Yeshua, in His obedience to the cross (to use the language of Hebrews, cf. 5:8; 12:1-2), secured and ultimately affected all those for whom He died as a vicarious, substitutionary sacrifice. To say that the phrase "there resulted justification of life to all men" means "there was offered the way of justification to all men" causes the parallel between Adam and Yeshua to fail at the crucial point in which Paul juxtaposes them. It seems patently clear that if Yeshua actually died as a substitute for sinners, then they must necessarily be declared righteous on the basis of His sacrifice (this presumes, as do the Scriptures, that Yeshua's sacrifice was fully accepted by the Father as payment for sin, e.g., Col 2:13, 14; Rom 5:9, etc.). Likewise, it seems just as clear that if in Yeshua's death He simply made justification possible but not inevitable, then we cannot speak of His death as efficacious, and we cannot hold it to be substitutionary, for surely in this case there are many for whom He died who will still spend eternity in Hell, for they have rejected the offer of the gospel even to their death. In this scenario the salvific work of Yeshua (His death, resurrection, ascension, and intercession) can in no wise be considered efficatious, but only potential.

Yet the Scriptures, and particularly Paul, do not speak this way. In our own context, Rom 5:9, Paul speaks directly as justification being procured (not made possible) by the blood of Yeshua. That he could likewise speak of condemnation being "nailed to the cross" (Col 2:13-14) shows quite surely that he considered the work of Yeshua upon the cross as having actually affected justification, not merely making it possible.

This being the case, it seems highly unlikely to me that Paul here intends for us to understand him to be teaching that while, on the one hand, Adam's disobedience had the inevitable affect of making all who are related to him sinners, on the other hand Yeshua's work on the cross only gave the potential for sinners to be justified. The emphasis of vv. 15-17 in which Yeshua's work is seen in every way to be more powerful than Adam's disobedience, and to outshine Adam's affect upon mankind, would thus be entirely set aside, for the disobedience of Adam surely would (in this scenario) have a greater affect than that of Yeshua's obedience. This is surely contrary to the whole thrust of Paul's point here.

19 For as through the one man's disobedience the many were made sinners, even so through the obedience of the One the many will be made righteous.

Note that the verse begins with "For" (γάρ, *gar*), showing us that Paul is not merely repeating the former thought for emphasis or some such thing, but that the verse before us functions as further commentary on the essential aspects of v. 18. These essential aspects may, in my view, be summed up in the use of the Greek particles ὡς, *hos* and οὕτως, *houtos* in v. 18, namely the "as . . . so" construction. The point may be understood by paraphrasing this way: "in the same way as the disobedience of one resulted in making all sinners, so, in this same way, the obedience of One will make all righteous." That is to say, the inevitability of Adam's actions in rendering all to be sinners foreshadows and prefigures the same inevitability in regard to Yeshua's work as sacrifice—all who are His can never run the risk of being lost, for surely they will be made to have right standing before HaShem.

In stark contrast to those who apparently were teaching that one could find right standing with HaShem through works of righteousness (i.e., works of the Torah in the sense of the Torah marking Jewish status, either through lineage or proselytism), Paul puts the status of us all in the hands of Adam and Messiah. The one made us sinners, the One makes us righteous.

What should we understand by the word "righteous" (δίκαιος, *dikaios*)? I have regularly used the phrase "right standing" in order to draw the mental picture of audience before a King in which one must be properly attired to make one's approach. Consider the custom in the court of Ahasueras—only the one to whom he pointed his golden scepter was allowed to approach him. With this metaphor in mind, I would ask "to whom does HaShem point His scepter, He Who cannot even look upon sin?" Surely He accepts only those who come before Him entirely clothed in righteousness. But how is it possible to "wash away" the filth of sin—the unclean state in which we find ourselves? Here Paul gives us only one answer—by the obedience of Yeshua—by His work and His work alone are we able to be cleansed and made righteous. Only by His work are we able to be made righteous in the sight of the Almighty. In the same way that Adam's sin made our status as "sinner" inevitable, so the obedience to the cross which Yeshua undertook makes our status as "righteous" a surety. He cleansed us—made us clean by His sacrifice so that we might stand before HaShem, the Holy One of Israel.

Note that in this explanatory verse, the "all" (πάντας, *pantas*) of v. 18 is replaced with the word "many" (οἱ πολλοί, *hoi polloi*). What are we to make of this change? First, this helps us understand why Paul used "all" in the previous verse. There he wishes to stress the one-for-one aspect of the cause/effect—Adam's disobedience and Yeshua's obedience respectively. Each one represented by Adam receives the effect of Adam's sin, and each one related to Yeshua receives the effect of His obedience. The change to "many" in our verse emphasizes the one-to-many aspect, i.e., that each (Adam and Yeshua) in turn occupied the position of representative, Adam for his race, and Yeshua for His. Their respective acts affected the many they represent.

Excursus on Yeshua's Death as a Substitutionary Sacrifice

Modern Christian theology has, by and large, adopted the view that in the death of Yeshua He offered to each and every person the opportunity for salvation. The metaphors are plentiful, but one will demonstrate this line of thinking. It is suggested that Yeshua's death may be compared to a wealthy man who, on behalf of a poor village, deposits a large sum of money into the local bank with these instructions: anyone who wishes to have some of the money for himself must simply come to the bank and withdraw the funds. So, it is said, the salvation won by Yeshua is deposited, as it were, for all into the "bank." Now all anyone must do is come and claim it. By this illustration the heart of the theology is seen, namely, that the salvation-work of Yeshua makes salvation possible but it by no means makes it inevitable. Since each must make his or her own decision to withdraw the deposited goods, it is conceivable that all will decide not to, and all will perish without anyone ever enjoying the benefits of eternal life for which Yeshua gave His life.

But when we look at the Scriptures, both the Tanach and Apostolic, it is clear that the writers of these sacred texts believed that the salvation-work of Yeshua actually saved sinners. The picture of making salvation possible simply is not there. Rather, in every case, the work of Yeshua is described as that which gains an inevitable result, the salvation of His people.

By His own words He declared "the Son of Man has come to seek and to save those who are lost" (Lk 19:10, cf. Mt 1:21), not make salvation possible but to actually seek and save. Paul claims that the goal of Yeshua's coming to earth was "that we might become the righteousness of God in Him" (2Co 5:21). Furthermore, Yeshua "gave Himself for our sins to deliver us from the present evil age" (Ga 1:3, 4), not to make a way possible for our deliverance. Peter concurs when he writes (1Pt 3:18) "For Messiah also died for sins once for all, the righteous for the unrighteous, that he might bring us to God." In each of these the question that must be asked is, "did Yeshua reach the goal for which He went to the cross?" If the answer is "yes," then His death makes the salvation of those for whom He died an inevitability. Since He paid for their sins as an actual substitute, God would be unjust to require payment ever again on their behalf.

The language and metaphor of the Scriptures shows as well that the writers took this view of the atonement, i.e., that it actually accomplished the salvation of sinners. Colossians 1:13-14 uses the metaphor of war:

> For He delivered us from the domain of darkness, and transferred us to the kingdom of His beloved Son, in whom we have redemption, the forgiveness of sins.

Even as a conquering warrior actually conquers and redistributes the conquered peoples to lands under his control, so HaShem actually rescued us from the domain of darkness and actually transferred us to the kingdom of His Son. There is nothing potential in this language—it is all actual.

Or consider Colossians 2:14 in which Paul describes our transgressions as being

> cancelled out, the certificate of debt consisting of decrees against us and which was hostile to us: and He has taken it out of the way, having nailed it to the cross.

Paul speaks here in terms that cannot be denied, namely, that the death of Messiah had an inevitable cause/effect relationship for all of those whom the Father had given Him (cf. Jn 6:46ff; Jn 10:9ff; Jn 17:1-11). Never once in all of Scripture do the Prophets or the Apostles cast the saving work of Yeshua in potential terms, as though He does some of the work and the sinner must add to it his acceptance. As the author to the Hebrews says (9:12),

> He entered once for all time into the Holy Place, taking not the blood of goats and calves but his own blood, there securing eternal redemption.

When Yeshua cried "it is finished," He had accomplished all of the payment for sin necessary to secure to Himself the people He had purchased. Even as HaShem would never have allowed the plagues against Egypt to have any other result than the full extraction of Israel out from the land of their slavery, so the suffering and death of Yeshua must inevitably secure the eternal freedom of all those for whom He died. To have anything less is to mark His death as less than efficacious.

We may also consider the classic text of the Tanach on this subject, Isaiah 53. Here the Messiah is lead to slaughter as a sheep. Within this sacrificial language, He dies for the sinners as a vicarious sacrifice, the innocent one sacrificed on behalf of the guilty (v. 5):

> But He was pierced through for our transgressions, He was crushed for our iniquities; the chastening for our well-being fell upon Him, and by His scourging we are healed.

This is a one-for-one correspondence, and therefore bespeaks actual substitution. But the prophet goes on to say (v. 10):

> If He would render Himself as a guilt offering He will see His offspring.

Here the result of His sacrifice is clearly described— "He will see His offspring," that is to say, He will see those who live because of His death—who reap the benefits of His sacrifice. He does not see the potential but He sees the direct result of His having died for sinners, i.e., they live. In the next verse (v. 11) this is stated directly:

> "As a result of the anguish of His soul He will see light and be satisfied; By His knowledge the Righteous One, My servant, will justify the many, As He will bear their iniquities."

Once again, the inevitable result of His salvation-work is the salvation of sinners.
For other passages, cf. 1Ti 1:15; Tit 2:14; Rom 5:8-9; Gal 3:13; Phil 1:29; Jn 6:35ff; Jn 10:11ff.

---

20 And the Torah came in that the transgression might increase; but where sin increased, grace abounded all the more,

Many modern commentators take the idea that the Torah "came in" (παρεισῆλθεν, *pareiselthen*) as pejorative, or at least containing a negative perspective of Torah.

> Then Law came in, as a sort of "afterthought," a secondary and subordinate state, in the Divine plan.[107]

> The Law took its subordinate place.[108]

> Παρεισῆλθεν is somewhat pejorative: the law was not foreseen in the original plan of God; it was the disobedience of Adam which rendered its promulgation necessary.[109]

But it is one's own perspective which interprets the phrase this way, not the words or syntax itself. Παρεισέρχομαι (*pareiserxomai*, the word translated here "came in") occurs only one other time in the Apostolic Scriptures, at Gal 2:4. There the meaning is most likely something like "intrude." But the context of Gal 2 is what determines this, not the word itself. A quick look at the word's use in non-biblical writers shows that it can mean "to insert," and "to occur" (as an idea coming into one's mind). The most natural way of understanding the word in our context

> is surely to take it as a simple reference to the undisputed fact that the law was given at a later date than that of Adam's fall, namely in the time of Moses. To refer to this fact is not, in itself, to say anything about the worth of the law depreciatory or otherwise.[110]

Paul here gives one purpose of the Torah, namely, "that the transgression might increase." What does he mean by "increase" (πλεονάσῃ, *pleonase* from the verb πλεονάζω, *pleonazo*)? Several suggestions present themselves: 1) that the very presence of the Torah causes people to sin in a way they otherwise would not, as Paul says in 7:8, "But sin, taking opportunity through the commandment, produced in me coveting of every kind; for apart from the Torah sin is dead." Paul goes on to explain that it is not as though the Torah is faulty, but that the sinful heart of man, rebellious as it is, increases rebellion when required to conform to God's righteousness; 2) what was before not considered sin would, in light of the revealed standards of God's Torah, now be classed as sin. Thus, sin increases; 3) that fallen mankind in his attempts to be independent from the Creator would, when confronted with the Torah, attempt to keep it as a means of gaining right standing with God, and that this in itself is a sin.

It furthermore seems clear that from Paul's perspective, the Torah was given for this reason (among others), that sin might be fully manifested for what it really is—a rejection of God and His righteousness. Thus, as the Torah points out the reality of sin, it also points to the inability of man to overcome sin on his own. In this way the Torah pointed to Yeshua, for it constantly directed mankind to the only remedy for his sin, namely, the salvation procured by the Messiah. This was revealed to one people, Israel, as God graciously gave the Torah. It became Israel's mission, then, to make this known to all the peoples of the earth. And, in fact, wherever the Torah has gone, it has effectively shown sin to be sin, and thus to be instrumental in forging civilizations which recognized the ethical standards of the God of Israel.

There is an added measure to the meaning to this "increase of transgressions" as well.

> But πλεαυάση (*pleanase*, "might increase") covers more than this; for, when the advent of the law makes sin increase in the sense of becoming manifest as sin, it also makes it increase in the sense of being made more sinful, since the law by showing men that what they are doing is contrary to God's will gives to their continuing to do it the character of conscious and wilful disobedience.[111]

This purpose of God in the Torah which Paul emphasizes here is, however, surely an intermediate purpose, not the ultimate or final one. For we will understand Paul's view of the Torah best if we understand that for him Messiah is, in every way, the goal (τέλος, *telos*, cf. 10:4) to which the Torah proceeds. In as much, then, as the Torah increases transgressions, it does so ultimately that man might be driven to seek refuge from his sinfulness in the only place where solace can be found, namely, in the person and work of Yeshua the Messiah.

but where sin increased, grace abounded all the more – If the Torah was given to Israel, and the giving of it did, on the one hand, cause the increase of transgression, then it was also in Israel that grace abounded all the more to overcome the sin and transgression. It seems most likely that for Paul, the locus of this increase of transgression equalled and overcome by the abundance of grace is none other than the person of Yeshua Himself. Yeshua, who was born "under the Torah" (Gal 4:4), bore the transgressions of His people and in accepting the death which the Torah itself prescribed for sin (prefigured in the sin offering and other sacrifices, and cf. Ezek 18:4), He, the sinless One, purchased as it were the grace which all the more abounded to sinners. The very event of the cross, then, tells both the story of the increased transgression and the abounding grace of HaShem toward sinners.

This is, once again, the *kal v'chomer* argument where the lesser being true guarantees the greater. If the Torah causes sin to abound (as noted above), and if the goal to which the Torah proceeds is the Messiah, than surely the Torah anticipates the grace of God which abounds.

21 that, as sin reigned in death, even so grace might reign through righteousness to eternal life through Yeshua Messiah our Lord.

Paul began this section by noting that "sin reigned" (v. 14). By this Paul emphasizes that every person must come under the reign of death because every person is a sinner. The universality of death is for Paul the proof-positive that sin has passed on from Adam to all of his offspring.

But in what way may it be said that "sin reigned in death?" On one hand we may say that death is the result of sin, but we would be more accurate to say that death is the result of God's justice in the face of sin. That is to say, God is the Just One who prescribed death as the penalty for sin (cf. Gen 2:17), and therefore death, which comes as the result of sin, comes actually from the hand of God. Death's ability to "reign," and sin to reign in death, is because God's justice is eternal and His judgment everlasting. Thus, sin could count on reigning in death because God had promised that death would be the penalty for sin: "the soul that sins shall die."

Yet in the eternal providence of God not only was His justice and righteousness to be demonstrated in the history of sinful man, but also His grace and mercy. In the very One who would suffer the justice of the Father, bearing the just reward of sin (i.e., death), so it would be that through His death He would gain eternal life for all who would come to faith in Him. In this way, the very triumph of sin, that God would necessarily prescribe death as its penalty, became the very means (through His sacrifice) by which grace would abound all the more.

The obvious parallel (in dissimilarity) makes the opposing concepts all the more stark:

sin reigns in death	grace reigns in eternal life
sin reigns in unrighteousness	grace reigns through righteousness
sin reigns in the death of Yeshua	grace reigns from the death of Yeshua
sin reigns in death	grace reigns through resurrection

Thus, grace reigns "through righteousness." Here again it seems to me that we should understand "righteousness" not only as the attribute of God or of Yeshua, but rather the whole process by which a sinner is declared righteous. Grace abounds and reigns through God's plan of having Yeshua suffer as the vicarious substitute for the sinner. This means of "declaring a sinner just on the basis of his faith" is the "righteousness" through which grace reigns. When God declares a sinner righteous on the basis of Yeshua's death, He has demonstrated that "where sin increased, grace abounded all the more."

Chapter 6
Commentary

Having developed his teaching on God's means of declaring a sinner righteous, Paul now goes on to show that such a declaration, while made in the court of HaShem, has, nonetheless, real and moral implications for the believer. This is so because God's declaration of righteousness upon the redeemed sinner is always accompanied by the inner work of the Spirit, a work which inevitably results in love for God and obedience to His will. Far from some theoretical theology, Paul's view of justification is that sanctification is always the practical and inevitable result.

He proves this in the passage before us by 1) showing that the redeemed sinner shared a union with Messiah in His death and resurrection, so that the redeemed sinner may rightly claim to have died and risen again; 2) showing what the implications are of having died and risen, and 3) showing that our union with the Messiah is a present reality, and that therefore our life in Him must be one of sanctification.

It is not Paul's intent to give us the complete teaching on the life of sanctification in this chapter, for the work of the Holy Spirit is not metioned. We should therefore be reminded that the whole section of 6:1-8:39 is centered on this issue of sanctification, and interpret the sections in light of the whole. But here, in the immediate passage, Paul is intent upon showing his readers that sanctification is not optional, but is the necessary event which follows justification. He teaches that ". . . the life promised for the man who is righteous by faith is a life characterized by sanctification. . . ."[112]

This section of the epistle may be outlined as follows:

The life of faith is not a life of sin but rather a life of righteousness
  A.   The believer died to sin
      1.   union with Messiah in His death
          a.   old man was crucified
          b.   body of sin will be done away with
          c.   freed from sin
      2.   union with Messiah in His resurrection
          a.   raised to a new life
          b.   walking (*halachah*) in that new life
  B.   The believer is alive to God
      1.   sin therefore should no longer reign
      2.   slaves to righteousness, not sin

1 What shall we say then? Are we to continue in sin that grace might increase?

Paul uses the opening phrase "what shall we say" to introduce a false premise which he recognizes could be drawn from what he has said, but which he wants to repudiate before explaining his view (cf. 3:5; 7:7; 9:14).

The idea that some might draw from his strong assertions in 5:20f is that God, in the Messiah, has so paid for sins, that additional sins in the life of the believer are actually of no consequence, since they have already been paid for through the eternal sacrifice. This is far from the truth, as Paul will show, not because the death of Yeshua is somehow less than infinite in terms of covering the sins of all those for whom He died, but because the union of the believer with the Messiah assures an actual transformation within the being of the sinner, a transformation which results in a new way of living.

But before we discount this inference as impossible in the minds of true believers, we should take stock of what, in practice, has been the witness of the church in general. The disparagement of the Torah as something unnecessary in the life of the believer comes from the mistaken notion that the life of faith is not a life concerned with actually living righteously. "I'm not perfect, just forgiven" [bumper sticker] may be true in theory, but it has no place in Pauline theology, for someone thoroughly involved in the scriptural revelation of how God declares a sinner righteous would never be satisfied to say "I'm not perfect." Rather, biblical sanctification, while recognizing that perfection is not the possession of any mortal, still holds "perfect" as the goal to which one strives. Pauline theology would cast the bumper sticker this way: "I'm not perfect now, but because I've been forgiven I'm striving to become perfect." In other words, Paul sees that the desire to live righteously comes from the fact that the redeemed sinner has actually been changed by his or her death and life in the Messiah. Likewise, for Paul, to deny one's inevitable growth in holiness (=sanctification) is to deny the reality of Yeshua's work in His death and resurrection.

continue in sin (ἐπιμένωμεν τῇ ἁμαρτία) – "to continue living the life of sin I once lived." Paul is not saying by the use of this phrase that one ceases to sin (the following contexts show this clearly). What he is saying, however, is that one's life, characterized by sin, is changed through faith in the Messiah so that one no longer lives the life of sin one once did.

so that grace might increase – "so that God's grace might be seen to be bigger than it otherwise might look."

2 May it never be! How shall we who died to sin still live in it?

"May it never be" (μὴ γένοιτο, *me genoito*) – a formula of strong denial and is found in classical Greek as well (in Epictetus) which Paul always uses only after asking a question (cf. 3:4, 6, 31; 6:2, 15; 7:7, 13; 9:14; 11:1, 11).

A great deal of misunderstanding has surrounded this verse and the section which follows, and the errors seem to have been on one of two sides of the issues. Some have, based upon this verse, taught that once a person genuinely comes to faith in Messiah, he or she ceases to sin. Yet Paul's own confession in chapter 7 (which I'm convinced is to be understood as the confession of the redeemed Paul) speaks contrary, for he admits to sinning even though he confesses to have believed in the Messiah for his salvation.

Others, seeing that perfectionism (no longer sinning) is both unscriptural and unreal (in that such a view would seem to say no one has ever genuinely believed), have tried to diminish the sense of "sin" in the verse, making it to stand for the sin of denying Messiah or some such sin which would otherwise condemn the soul.

The proper interepretation, however, understands the phrase "died to sin" as having various aspects. Cranfield lists four which he charges must be kept distinct while at the same time understood to be in closest relationship to each other. I have summarized his points here:

> 1)   died to sin *in God's sight* — (juridical sense), that is, as God looked upon His Son who died, He reckoned all those who would believe in Him as actually dying and likewise, as actually rising with Him. In that sense, in God's sight all of their sins have been paid for and they stand before Him as though sinless. In the same way that He reckons the death of Messiah on their behalf,

so He reckons the perfect life of Messiah to be theirs as well.

2)   died to sin *as the confession of their faith, symbolized in the mikvah* — (*mikvah* sense), that is, as Jew and non-Jew acknowledged the change of status through the waters of the *mikvah*, so each one acknowledged their acceptance of God's decision on their behalf (to regard Yeshua's death and resurrection as their own death and resurrection) and His giving of His seal and pledge (the Spirit) that His decision really concerned them individually, personally.

3)   died to sin *on a daily basis* — (moral sense), that is, through God's having given them the Spirit and made known His decision to accept Yeshua's death and resurrection as their own, they have the ability and freedom to die daily (or hourly) to sin by putting to death the desires of the sinful nature and to raise daily (or hourly) to newness of life, i.e., obedience to God.

> The man who has learned through the gospel message the truth of God's gracious decision on his behalf is now to strive with all his heart to approximate more and more in his actual concrete daily living to that which in God's decision of justification he already is.[113]

4)   died to sin *when mortal puts on immortality* — (eschatological sense), that is, when the believer dies he or she will finally and irreversibly be done with sin forever and will, being raised in the final resurrection, live forever a life which is entirely without sin.

Paul seems to include, to one extent or another, all four of the above nuances of the phrase "died to sin," and he likewise appears to move freely between them as he describes the life of faith and exhorts his readers to live as having "died to sin."

Which of the above does Paul have in mind in this opening verse? It seems clear that he has either 1 or 2, since the next verse continues the theme of the *mikvah*. If we take the meaning of number 1 and apply it, the sense would be, "how could we continue to sin having come to understand and appreciate that HaShem decided to consider Yeshua's death and resurrection as though it were each of our own?" Having considered the supreme gift of God's grace in such a reckoning, our hearts would surely be changed to do His will and to fight our own sinful desires. "We love Him because He first loved us" (1Jn 4:19).

3 Or do you not know that all of us who have been baptized into Messiah Yeshua have been baptized into His death?

Paul points his readers now to the reality behind the ceremony of ritual immersion (βαπ-τίζω, *baptizo*, "to immerse," "undergo a *mikvah*"). It will serve our purpose well to take a brief survey of the *mikvah* (ritual immersion) of the 1st Century CE in order to understand the wider scope of "baptism" as found in the Apostolic Scriptures.

Excursus on Baptism

We may begin our inquiry into "baptism" by looking at the use of the *mikvah* in the ceremony of conversion, when a proselyte was admitted into the people of Israel.[114] The *mikvah* was a gathering or pool of running water most often used for ritual cleansing after becoming unclean. This was the case for those who are defiled by contact with the dead[115], or any other defiling object, or through an unclean flux from the body[116] and especially for a menstruant.[117] Vessels which had become ritually unclean or were suspect of uncleanness were likewise immersed in the water of the *mikvah*. Beyond these regular uses for the *mikvah*, it was also customary for a convert (proselyte) to undergo a *mikvah* as part of his or her conversion.

During the time of the second Temple, a proselyte was required, according to Rabbinic ruling, to make a sacrifice, be circumcised, and undergo immersion in a *mikvah*. After the destruction of the Temple, the sacrifice was no longer required, nor the giving of money equivalent to the sacrifice.[118] R. Eliezer argues that one is a proselyte even if he performs only one of the two required rituals (circumcision or *mikvah*) but R. Joshua disagreed and the *halachic* decision went in favor of R. Joshua.[119] Therefore, the proselyte of the 1st Century and later was required both to be circumcised and immersed. Furthermore, the Sages concluded that both the circumcision and the immersion must be witnessed by a *bet din*, a court of three witnesses. An individual which claimed he had immersed himself but could not produce witnesses was not accepted as a legitimate proselyte.

The parallels to the apostolic *halachah* are evident. Agreeing with R. Eliezer in the final analysis, the council of Acts 15 decided that the Gentile believer did not have to be circumcised, leaving baptism as the single ritual of conversion. One cannot help but imagine that the words of Yeshua in the Great Commission figured into this debate, for He specifically names the ritual of the *mikvah*, but did not mention circumcision.

What, then, did the ritual immersion signify for the proselyte to Judaism during the 1st Century CE? Traditionally, scholars have held that the *mikvah* performed a cleansing of one's life from the pagan uncleanness in which the proselyte had lived. Like vessels purchased from Gentile craftsmen which needed to be purified in the waters of the *mikvah*, so the proselyte himself must pass through the waters before he is accepted into the believing congregation. Maimonides expresses this interpretation of proselyte baptism in the *mikvah*:

> It is plain that the laws about immersion as a means of freeing oneself from uncleanness are decrees laid down by Scripture and not matters about which human understanding is capable of forming a judgment; for behold, they are included among the divine statutes. Now 'uncleanness' is not mud or filth which water can remove, but is a matter of scriptural decree and dependent on the intention of the heart. Therefore the Sages have said, 'If a man immerse himself, but without special intention, it is as though he has not immersed himself at all.'
> Nevertheless we may find some indication [for the moral basis] of this: Just as one who sets his heart on becoming clean becomes clean as soon as he has immersed himself, although nothing new has befallen his body, so, too, one who sets his heart on cleansing himself from the uncleannesses that beset men's souls—namely, wrongful thoughts and false convictions—becomes clean as soon as he consents in his heart to hear those counsels and brings his soul into the waters of pure reason. Behold, Scriptures say, 'And I will sprinkle clean water upon you and ye shall be clean; from all your uncleannesses and from all your idols will I cleanse you [Ezek. 36:25]'. [120]

Jewish Proselyte Baptism

Not all scholars are in agreement, however, about the practice and significance of proselyte baptism in the 1st Century CE. Some are not even sure it was a prevalent practice. For example, proselyte baptism is not mentioned in either Josephus or Philo, though both speak of converts. The first unambiguous references to proselyte baptism belong to the later 1st Century, most importantly the debates recorded in the Mishnah.[121] Still, the references in the Mishnah deal with an apparent standard practice, meaning it must have been in place for a sufficient amount of time prior to the codification of the Mishnah in the 2nd Century CE.

There are further debates about how a Gentile was viewed as unclean by the Jewish community of the 1st Century CE. Zeitlin argues that Gentiles were not regarded as unclean until the year 65 CE, when Jews were forbidden to associate with them, as a measure intended to promote Jewish nationalism in the face of the threat from the Romans, and it was only after this declaration that the necessity for proselyte baptism arose.[122] Some scholars discount the year 65 as significant, claiming that the laws requiring separation from Jews were, in reality, nothing new. Furthermore, Zeitlin's argument rests upon his assumption that the NT is generally much later than traditionally held, and that the various references to proselyte baptism are therefore also late.[123] Others note that Rabbinic language would confirm the belief that Gentiles were unclean. Jeremias states that

> . . . in the time of Herod the uncleanness of the Niddah (a menstrual woman) was ascribed to the Gentiles; in the first decades of our era the uncleanness of a corpse; in the last time before the destruction of the temple the uncleanness of the Zab (=a man with a seminal issue). [124]

Josephus says that when one of the lower order of the Essenes touched a member of the highest grade, the latter washed himself "as though he had associated himself with a foreigner." [125]

Yet, the Rabbinic discussion on this point is itself not unified. In b.*Pesachim* 91a, the school of Hillel lays down a particular ruling about a proselyte on the ground that, "he (the proselyte) will not understand that the previous year he was a heathen and not susceptible to uncleanness, whereas he is now an Israelite and susceptible to uncleanness." On the basis of this datum, Daube is convinced that proselyte baptism was outside the levitical sphere, i.e., was not considered to wash away the unclean status of a non-Jew.[126] It functioned purely as an initiation rite into the Jewish community. [127]

I would like to offer a suggestion at this point. Is it possible that proselyte baptism was envisioned as mystically connecting the convert to the nation at the time of the exodus? Paul's comment that all were "baptized into Moses" (1 Corinthians 10:2) may have arisen from a common understanding regarding the non-Jews who left with Israel on that historic day. They ate the Passover (which required circumcision, Exodus 12:48) and then walked through the Sea (*mikvah*). Furthermore, the Passover seder puts much emphasis upon the fact that it was not merely the Israelites of old who passed through the Sea, but every generation of Israel was to view themselves as personally being redeemed from Egypt.[128] Perhaps, then, the proselyte was acting out the crossing of the Red Sea in the *mikvah*, and identifying with Israel as the "sojourner" did at the time of the exodus. If this thought has merit, it might find a parallel to the "ingrafting" motif used by Paul in Romans 9-11. Baptism would, under this rubric, identify the believer with the redeemed Israel of the exodus, and with Abraham, the father of all those who have righteousness by faith.

Another interesting debate in the Mishnah deserves our attention. In the Hillel/Shammai debate over proselyte baptism (b.*Pesachim* 91b), the question is raised whether or not a proselyte can eat the passover the evening on which he is baptized. Shammai ruled that the proselyte could eat the Passover the same day he had undergone baptism, but Hillel ruled he must wait seven days. Why? "He who separates himself from his uncircumcision is as one who separates himself from a grave." That is, the proselyte is considered to have died and raised again, and therefore must undergo the common seven day ritual of purification for corpse defilement.[129] Beasley-Murray points out, however, that this dying and coming to life is attached to circumcision and not baptism.[130] However, it seems highly significant that proselytizing in the 1st Century was apparently viewed as moving from death to life. Further corroboration of this is found in b.*Yebamoth* 22a: "One who has become a proselyte is like a child newly born." Thus, proselytism in the 1st Century enjoyed two symbols common with the Apostolic gospel: resurrection from the dead and new birth.

At what point the immersion ceremony in the Christian community was understood to picture death and resurrection with Messiah is not certain. Perhaps this was emphasized at the outset, though this is not explicit by any means. Commentators debate whether or not the language of Romans 6 refers to water or Spirit baptism.[131] Certainly for the proselyte, immersion signified an identification with the Jewish nation and faith. In the same manner that Israel was willing to follow Moses through the sea,[132] the proselyte was willing to follow the laws of Judaism. Thus, for the convert to be baptized "in the name of the Father and the Son and the Holy Spirit" was to identify with the true God of Israel as represented in His Messiah, Yeshua, and to take upon himself the obligations of obedience and loyalty to Him. Paul refused to allow people to be baptized in his name,[133] for the disciples were to be of the Messiah, not Paul. It may well be for this reason that Paul refrained from baptizing very many people. His position as apostle may have made it unwise to baptize converts, for the simple reason that some would have inevitably put more emphasis upon being baptized by Paul than being baptized into the Messiah!

John's Baptism

Having looked briefly at proselyte baptism in the Jewish sources, I turn to the question of John's baptism.[134] It evidently was not proselyte baptism, for both Pharisees and Sadducees were coming to him.

At the outset it appears that John's baptism had two primary foci: one eschatological and the other repentance. John as an eschatological figure is easy to prove. The opening citation of Malachai 3:1 and Isaiah 40:3-4 in Mark's gospel account clearly announces John as the eschatological prophet who would prepare the way for Messiah and the time when "all flesh" would "see it together," i.e., the salvation of the Lord.

John's preaching was centered on repentance and his baptism is defined as "a baptism of repentance for the forgiveness of sins" (Βάπτισμα μετανοίας εἰς ἄφεσιν ἁμαρτιῶν, Mk 1:4). The most natural way to interpret this phrase is "a baptism which marked repentance." Clearly, John did not believe that physical lineage constituted a guarantee of "blanket" forgiveness by God, and therefore he adds his voice to the general tone of Rabbinic writings.[135] It is not clear in the gospels exactly how John viewed the Gentiles in his ministry. It should most probably be assumed that, like Yeshua, John concentrated his efforts on the Jewish community and ministered little, if at all, to non-Jews.

The baptism John administered signalled repentance, a "turning" from sin to righteousness. It seems clear that the many people who came to John (including religious leaders) were seeking to make their lives right before God in view of the approaching, Messianic Age. For John's baptism was also given as a precursor to the "One who would come after." Thus, it was a call to the nation of Israel to make herself right with her God, and to prepare for the rule of Messiah in their midst. And, as Beasley-Murray has shown, the anticipation of the Messiah so evident in John's baptism also predicts the baptism He would bring, i.e., of the Spirit. John's baptism symbolized repentance and forgiveness of sins, but the baptism which Messiah would bring would actually affect this forgiveness and cleansing through the work of the Spirit.[136]

The discussion may be advanced by remembering that Yeshua was not known to perform many baptisms during His earthly ministry (if any at all).[137] It seems very likely to me that the reason lies in the essential message of John the Baptist, that he baptized in water, but the One following him would baptize in the Holy Spirit. Thus, for Yeshua to baptize as John did would cloud the significance of John's baptism as preparation for the Messianic Age.

Thus, John's baptism had its parallels to both the proselyte baptism and the *mikvah* for ceremonial cleansing. With the former, John's baptism emphasized a newness, and moving from sin to righteousness, and turning from the old to the new. After all, the *mikvah* of 1st Century Judaisms primarily marked a change in status. Insofar as it paralleled this "repentance," it envisioned the baptized as beginning a new life. With the latter, John's baptism emphasized preparation for the approaching, Messianic rule. If ceremonial cleansing were necessary for worship in the temple, how much more would one need to be clean in heart and body for the rule of Messiah.

Perhaps most puzzling in this discussion of John's baptism, however, is the fact that Yeshua Himself is baptized by John. While this short excursus cannot deal with the issue of Yeshua's baptism, it seems important to ask how it informs the meaning of baptism as a whole, and especially how it relates to the command to baptize disciples.

The gospels differ in their retelling of the event, particularly in the wording of the declaration of the Father upon Yeshua as He came up out of the water. Matthew puts it in third person: "This is My beloved Son, in whom I am well pleased."[138] Mark and Luke adopt second person: "You are My beloved Son, in You I am well pleased." Matthew and Mark clearly have John baptizing Yeshua, but Luke does not mention John's part, noting Yeshua's baptism after remarking that John was put in prison by Herod.[139] The gospel of John never mentions the baptism of Yeshua.

What significance are we to derive from these data? Clearly, it must have been an issue not easily resolved why the lesser (John) should baptize the greater (Yeshua), especially when John's baptism was defined as a "baptism of repentence for the forgiveness of sins." John's protest as recorded in Matthew ("But John tried to prevent Him, saying, 'I have need to be baptized by You, and do You come to me'?"[140]) surely echoed the sentiments of many when confronted with this event. What then was the purpose from the standpoint of Yeshua?

His response is the answer: "But Yeshua answering said to him, 'Permit it at this time; for in this way it is fitting for us to fulfill all righteousness.'"[141] From the vantage point of those who looked on, Yeshua must be known as fully righteous—He must be recognized as ceremonially clean. His resurrection would substantiate His diety. For now it was necessary for Him to conform to the established criteria of holiness.

If this interpretation is correct, we must assume that John's baptism was a kind of personal, religious cleansing—perhaps an extreme manifestation of one's longing for purity and holiness, of a confession of inward cleansing as well as outward conformity. For John rebukes the leaders who come to him, calling upon them first to bring forth works which manifested true inward repentance. If this understanding of John's baptism is correct, we may rightly say that it in some measure combines the aspects of proselyte baptism with those of the *mikvah*. For repentance or turning from sin is represented, as is purity and cleanness.

The Baptism of the Great Commission

It is possible now to see the evolution of baptism, beginning with proselyte baptism, progressing to John's baptism and culminating in the baptism prescribed by Yeshua in Matthew 28: 18f. John's baptism prepared the Jew for the rule of Messiah, a rule marked by His crucifixion and resurrection. If the proselyte baptism marked the beginning of life as a follower of God, then Messiah's question to the disciples is decisive for determining the import of baptism as He commanded in the Great Commission:

> But Yeshua said to them, "You do not know what you are asking for. Are you able to drink the cup that I drink, or to be baptized with the baptism with which I am baptized?" And they said to Him, "We are able." And Yeshua said to them, "The cup that I drink you shall drink; and you shall be baptized with the baptism with which I am baptized."[142]

To be identified with Yeshua, even to the extent of dying for His teachings, was, in every way, to identify with His death. The forensic reality of union with Messiah in His death and resurrection (which Paul develops and teaches) was impossible apart from the foundational confession that one was actually willing to physically die for Him. To become a disciple of this Yeshua meant that one was to follow Him, even to the point of death. It seems to me highly probable that the disciples collated this saying of their Lord with His final instructions to disciple the nations.

And, it seems equally sure that Paul's union-with-the-Messiah theology was based upon this saying of Yeshua, for to be baptized with His baptism was also to participate in His resurrection. Thus, baptism took on the full scope of the confession as the gospel spread: it was symbolic of conversion (change of status), of life from death, of resurrection from the grave, of new birth, of repentance and forgiveness of sins, and of union with the Messiah in His baptism, including the baptism of the Holy Spirit. This highly symbolical act thus took on supreme importance in the early church, and, when divorced from biblical theology, offered a ceremony easily misused.

One final word on the significance of baptism as a conversion ritual: it envisions a community. If the parallels to Jewish baptisms are true as I have suggested, then it is clear that baptism marks the entrance into the congregation of God. Baptism, therefore, assumes a believing community into which the baptized person enters and within which he or she enjoys the benefits and responsibilities of the community. Thus, baptism assumes the congregation (synagogue) and cannot rightly exist without it. It may be for this reason, more than any other, that the Great Commission must be viewed as primarily our Master's methodology for fulfilling His promise that He would build His congregation (*ekklesia*).

Back, then, to verse 3 and the immediate question before us: to what does Paul refer when he uses the term "baptized?" Is he speaking of the *mikvah*, common in the Judaisms of the 1st Century, and commanded by Yeshua as a symbol of one's change of status, or is he referring to the baptism of the Spirit?

In 1Co 12:12-13 Paul uses baptism language in regard to the work of the Spirit in the life of the believer:

> For even as the body is one and yet has many members, and all the members of the body, though they are many, are one body, so also is Messiah. For by one Spirit we were all baptized into one body, whether Jews or Greeks, whether slaves or free, and we were all made to drink of one Spirit.

Yet it seems most likely that Paul has in mind the *mikvah* which most (if not all) of the congregants had undergone in their confession of Yeshua as Messiah. This baptism was understood, among other things, as a confession of union with the death of Yeshua, for Paul begins this verse with the question ἤ ἀγνοεῖτε, *he agnoeite*, "or are you ignorant . . .," implying that he expected his readers to both be aware of the teaching, and to have accepted it, namely, that one's baptism manifested a belief in one's union with the Messiah in His death. Since Paul had not founded the congregation at Rome, this teaching of union with the Messiah in His death and resurrection must have been something very much a part of the early Messianic confession, not something which Paul himself had taught them.

The terminology baptized εἰς Χριστὸν, *eis Christon*, "into Messiah" is slightly different in other instances. In Mt 28:19, Acts 8:16 and 19:5, the formula is baptized εἰς τὸ ὀνόματι Χριστοῦ Ἰησοῦ, "baptized *into* the name of Messiah Yeshua," while in Acts 10:48 it is baptized ἐν τῷὀνόματι Χριστοῦ Ἰησοῦ, "baptized *in* the name of Messiah Yeshua." Again, Acts 2:38 has ἐπὶ τῷ ὀνόματι Χριστοῦ Ἰησοῦ, "baptized *upon* the name of Messiah Yeshua" (though a textual variant has ἐν, "in"). What are we to make of these differences?

Some have tried to make a significance to these differences, implying that to be "baptized into" is different than to be "baptized in or by" (for ἐν is sometimes used to imply means, thus "by"), but it appears when these phrases are studied in context that they all refer to the same activity and that they are therefore generally equivalent. I would suggest that the terminology or formula for baptism was in the process of being set during the early days of the Messianic congregations, and that only later did it gain the status of liturgy in which the exact phrasiology was used each time. Thus, to be baptized in the Messiah and to be baptized into the name of Messiah Yeshua is equivalent.

But Paul's main point in our text is that one's confession of faith in the Messiah Yeshua as demonstrated by the *mikvah* is a confession of having died with Him. Now this union with the Messiah in His death (and resurrection) is not a theory for Paul, but a reality with clear ramifications for the life of the believer. For it was not the act of baptism which brought the believer into union with Messiah in His death and resurrection, since this relationship was already an objective reality before baptism takes place, having been brought into being by God's gracious decision (cf. 5:8, 2Co 5:14). But rather baptism points to, and is a pledge of, that death which the person concerned has already died—in the sight of God.

It appears that the Qumran society considered baptism, in some measure, to act as a purification for those who entered the community (*yachad*). Note this passage from the Rule of the Community (1QS):

> Anyone who refuses to enter [the society of G]od, preferring to continue in his willful heart, shall not [be initiated into the Ya]chad of His truth, inasmuch as his soul has rejected the disciplines foundational to knowledge: the laws of righteousness. He lacks the strength to repent. He is not to be reckoned among the upright. His knowledge, strength , and wealth are not to enter the society of the Yachad. Surely, he plows in the muck of wickedness, so defiling stains would mar his repentance. Yet he cannot be justified by what his willful heart declares lawful, preferring to gaze on darkness rather than the ways of light. With such an eye he cannot be reckoned faultless. Ceremonies of atonement cannot restore his innocence, neither cultic waters his purity. He cannot be sanctified by baptism in oceans and rivers, nor purified by mere ritual bathing. Unclean, unclean shall he be all the days that he rejects the laws of God, refusing to be disciplined in the Yachad of His society.[143]

The text goes on to show that once the sinner repents, his uncleanness may be washed away through the purifying *mikvah*. What may be of interest to us, however, is that even the Qumran society appears to understand ritual immersion as a sign of one's repentence, not the cause of it.

4 Therefore we have been buried with Him through baptism into death, in order that as Messiah was raised from the dead through the glory of the Father, so we too might walk in newness of life.

Burial is the final seal and verification that a death has taken place. This is why it is both important and difficult for those who remain to shovel the sod and dirt upon the casket, for it seals the reality of death. For Paul to rephrase v. 3 by saying that we have been buried with Yeshua, makes the death with Him described in the former verse all the more certain and unambiguous.

The issue to which Paul obviously points is that the death and burial of the Messiah gave way to His resurrection—He did not remain dead. In like manner, therefore, our union with Him in death and burial must also result in our own resurrection, which further results in walking in a new way—a new life.

Yeshua was raised from the dead through the glory of the Father, (διὰ τῆς δόξης τοῦ πατρός), which most likely means through the power of the Father shown especially to be glorious through overcoming death. So entwined are the concepts of "glory" and "power" that in the Lxx δόξα, *doxa*, "glory" is sometimes used to translate Hebrew words denoting power (e.g., 2Chron 30:8 translates ‏יד‎, *yad*, "hand, power" with δόξα). Surely God's glory is shown when by His power He overcomes death through resurrection. In this He is seen clearly to be the God of the living. (In the Scriptures glory and power are often associated, e.g., Ex 15:6; 1Chr 16:28; Ps 145:11; Col 1:11; 1Pt 4:11; Rev 1:6; 4:11; 5:12f; 7:12; 19:1). Surely the glory and power of God are likewise displayed in the new life lived out by the believer.

so also we walk in newness of life – The connection to the resurrection of Messiah is clear: even as He arose, so we likewise (in the same way) arose to newness of life. The use of "walk" περιπατεῖν, *peripatein*, to denote one's moral life is frequent in Paul (e.g., Rom 8:4; 13:13; 14:15; 1Co 3:3) as well as in other Apostolic texts (e.g., Mk 7:5, et al). This reflects the common use of הָלַךְ, *halach*, "to walk, go" in the Tanach (e.g., Ex 16:4; Dt 8:6; Ps 101:6; Prov 6:12; Dan 9:10) to speak of the proper moral life. The rabbinic term *halachah* derives from this word, meaning "how one was to walk."

The "newness" is represented by the Greek καινός, *kainos* which at times (not always) may be distinguished from νέος, *neos*. Καινός often denotes what is "new" meaning "different, unusual, impressive, better than the old, superior in value" while νέος usually denotes that which "was not there before," or "what has just arisen or appeared." If this distinction were to be applied in the present text, the emphasis would be upon the value of the new life in comparison to the old and that it was transcendent in comparison.

Cranfield also notes that the term καινός is particularly associated with the eschatological (end-time) hope (cf. Mk 14:25; 2Pt 3:13; Rev 2:17; 3:12; 5:9; 21:1, 5), and thus he infers that "The newness of life, of which Paul speaks here, is a foretaste of the final renewal."[144]

This newness of life is characterized, then, by moral decision-making within the life of the believer, decision-making which aligns itself with the ways and commands of HaShem. This means (in broadest strokes) that the new life is characterized by love for God and for one's neighbor. Though there may be (and most assuredly will be) a struggle between the flesh and spirit within the sphere of this new life, there is no question as to whose *halachah* one should follow. Through the death and resurrection of the Messiah, and the believer's union with Him, God has become the Master, the One under Whose rule the believer gladly dwells. The question of "should I obey or not" has been settled—obedience is the inevitable mark of genuine faith. While the believer at any given time within his or her life may be ignorant of God's will, the committed direction of the heart is for obedience.

This "newness of life" was just as real for the Jew as for the non-Jew, for in either case, the depraved will was seeking self, not God (3:10ff) and even when actions may have appeared pious, they came from an essentially self-centered heart.

5 For if we have become united *with Him* in the likeness of His death, certainly we shall be also in the likeness of His resurrection,

Beginning with "for" (γάρ, *gar*) we understand this verse to be in support of what Paul has previously stated, namely, that we have risen with the Messiah so that we walk in newness of life.

The Greek word translated "become united" is σύμφυτος (*sumphutos*) from the root συμφύω (*sumphuo*) meaning "to make to grow together," "unite," and in the passive, "to grow together," "unite," "become assimilated," "become natural." In the classical Greek, examples of its use and meaning are "born with one," "congenital," "innate," "natural," "cognate," "grown together," and "united." Some have suggested (on the basis of this word) that Paul has grafting in mind, and that he sees the redeemed sinner has having been "grafted into Messiah" much like a branch is grafted into the trunk of a tree. In this way, the branch gains its life from the trunk and the two are intimately united. But the Greek word itself does not necessarily suggest this meaning, and the basic idea of "united" or "assimilated" is most likely Paul's intent.

The Greek does not include the words "with Him" (αὐτῷ, *auto*), so that the actual, literal translation should be "For if we have become united in (or by) the likeness of His death . . . ." That is to say, our union is such that we actually take on the likeness—we become one with the likeness of His death. The inclusion, then, by the translators of the words "in Him" certainly convey the sense of the verse, for our union with the Messiah in His death is that which inevitably secures the conforming process.

What exactly is our union with the Messiah in His death? We may consider this on two levels: justification and sanctification. On the one hand, then, we are united with the Messiah in His death for the very reason that HaShem views His death as though it were ours. The vicarious substitution—the one-for-the-other aspect of sacrifice, means that the death of Yeshua is accredited to the sinner as though he or she had actually died. Since the penalty for sin is death, the death which Yeshua died on our behalf is accredited to our account as payment in full. In this way, from a legal standpoint, each one who has put his or her faith in Yeshua as the Messiah has become united in His death.

On the other hand, the union each believer has with Yeshua is a matter of one's sanctification or the process by which each one is more and more set apart wholly unto HaShem. For in the death and life of the Messiah there is illustrated, in an eternal or infinite way, the manner in which one could love HaShem with the whole heart, soul, and might. In the manner of the עוֹלָה, *'olah*, the whole-burnt offering, in which the entire sacrifice is burnt and rises in its entirety to HaShem, so the ultimate and final dedication to HaShem is seen in Messiah's death. For it was in His death that He demonstrated to the extreme the reality of the words "not My will but Yours be done." Thus, to have been united in the likeness of His death is to have likewise confessed that HaShem's will is supreme over all others, and that one's life is willingly given to Him.

But Paul's central point here is simply that Messiah could not have remained dead and in the tomb. It was impossible that death should hold Him, for He through death had conquered death. Therefore, all who have been united with Him in the likeness of His death will surely be united with Him in the likeness of His resurrection. If conformity to His death means being set apart from sin (I turn from my sin), then conformity in the likeness of His resurrection means being set apart unto (i.e., dedicated to) the righteousness which characterizes the Messiah Himself (I engage in righteous living). Death is leaving behind the old life; resurrection is walking in a new life.

Here, then, we have a most important truth taught: if one has died with Messiah, one will surely live with Him. Or to state it differently: the inevitable consequence of turning from sin is walking in righteousness. There is no neutral ground!

This truth is emphasized by the word ἐσόμεθα, *esometha*, "we shall be" — "we shall be united in the likeness of His resurrection." For Paul this is the inevitable result of union with the Messiah in His death. We may therefore critique the teaching of some regarding what has been called the "carnal Christian" doctrine, namely, that true salvation does not necessarily result in changed living. Those who teach such doctrine believe that one may truly have their sins forgiven by believing in Yeshua as their savior, but may never "go the next step" and "grow in holiness." But such a false teaching would have Yeshua remaining in the grave! For to have one's sins paid for by His death, but not to "walk in newness of life" is to teach that one has died with the Messiah but has not risen with Him. For Paul this is simply an impossibility.

6 knowing this, that our old self was crucified with Him, that our body of sin might be done away with, that we should no longer be slaves to sin;

Paul now gives further substantiation for his teaching that those whose sins have been covered by the death of Messiah will inevitably walk in newness of life.

that our old self (man) was crucified with Him – What exactly does Paul mean by the label "our old man" (ὁ παλαιὸς ἡμῶν ἄνθρωπος)? Some take it to mean "the whole of our fallen human nature, the whole self in its fallenness."[145] Others simply see it as one's entire life before faith in the Messiah, before one's new birth.[146] Still others take the expression to mean "human nature such as it has been made by the sin of him in whom originally it was wholly concentrated, fallen Adam reappearing in every human ego that comes into the world . . .," i.e., the fallen nature of man.[147]

The same expression ("old man") is found in Eph 4:22 and Col 3:9. In Eph 4:22 Paul is exhorting his readers to "put away the old self," while in Col 3:9 he states the fact that "you laid aside the old self with its evil practices." How can Paul speak of the "old self (man)" as having been crucified (Rom 6:6) while in another place admonishing his readers to "put away the old self?" Cranfield gives this explanation:

> Our fallen human nature was crucified with Christ in our baptism in the sense that in baptism we received the divinely-appointed sign and seal of the fact that by God's gracious decision it was, in His sight, crucified with Christ on Golgotha. It is not implied that the old man no longer exists. [On the contrary], the old fallen nature lingers on in the believer. That is why in Col 3:9 believers have to be exhorted to put off the old man. The Christian has still to fulfil on the moral level, by daily dying to sin, the death which in God's merciful decision and in the sacrament of baptism he has already died.[148]

But I find this explanation of Cranfield to hardly fit the text, for Paul surely indicates that just as Messiah underwent an actual death, so our old self (man) died. And just as Yeshua's death was a once-for-all-time event, never again to be repeated, so the death of the old man was a final and forever-finalized event. There is no need to put the old man to death time and time again (as Eph 4:22 is interpreted by some) since the old man has been crucified. The Greek tense (συνεσταυρώθη, *sunestaurothe*, aorist passive indic. from συσταυρόω, *sustauroo*) indicates that this crucifixion, like that of Yeshua's, is viewed as a one-time, past event. To build upon the union of the believer with Messiah in His death and resurrection, and then to explain it as "daily dying to sin" seems to miss the point.

Yet the "old self" cannot mean the sinful nature, for surely those who believe continue to sin (Rom 7; 1Jn 2:1ff; etc.), and do so as a result of the active sin nature. If the sinful nature is crucified, then one would expect sin to stop altogether.

I would like to suggest that by the phrase "new self" Paul wishes to indicate what the Tanach referenced as a "new heart," and that therefore what he means by the "old man" is what we might term the "old heart." In Hebrew thinking, the heart is the place of moral decision-making:

> Gen. 6:5–6 Then the LORD saw that the wickedness of man was great on the earth, and that every intent of the thoughts of his heart was only evil continually. And the LORD was sorry that He had made man on the earth, and He was grieved in His heart.

> Isa. 59:12–13 For our transgressions are multiplied before Thee, And our sins testify against us; For our transgressions are with us, And we know our iniquities: Transgressing and denying the LORD, And turning away from our God, Speaking oppression and revolt, Conceiving in and uttering from the heart lying words.

> Prov. 4:23 Watch over your heart with all diligence, For from it flow the springs of life.

Furthermore, the prophets spoke of the time when the hard heart of Israel would be removed and a "new heart" of flesh put in its place. This "hard heart" (=old heart) and "new heart" symbology seems to me to fit well the sense of "old man"/"new man," for the old heart is bent away from God, while the new heart is inclined toward him. Consider the following:

> Ezek. 11:19 And I shall give them one heart, and shall put a new spirit within them. And I shall take the heart of stone out of their flesh and give them a heart of flesh,

Ezek. 36:26 Moreover, I will give you a new heart and put a new spirit within you; and I will remove the heart of stone from your flesh and give you a heart of flesh.

I would suggest, then, that the "old man" (=old heart) is that bent to sin under the control of the volition of the unregenerate soul. This "old man" is crucified, by which is meant "put to death" so that it is taken out and replaced by the "new man" (=new heart). As Murray states:

> The "old man" can no more be regarded as in the process of being crucified than Christ in his sphere could be thus regarded. Furthermore, as was noted already, Paul is insisting in this context upon the definitive breach with sin which occurs through union with Christ in his death, and the appeal to the crucifixion of the old man is coordinate with this insistence and particularly illustrative or probative of it.[149]

Thus, what is put to death in the union with the death of the Messiah is that heart which is slave to sin, and must therefore, in each and every instance, move in accordance with sin. In its place is put a new heart, one which "concurs with the Torah of God" (Rom 7:22) and which therefore longs to please the One who has made redemption a reality.

If, however, the "old self" is that heart of stone which could not and would not respond to the call of God, how is Eph 4:22 to be explained, which, at the outset, appears to admonish the readers to "put off the old self?"

> Eph 4:20–24 But you did not learn Messiah in this way, if indeed you have heard Him and have been taught in Him, just as truth is in Yeshua, that, in reference to your former manner of life, you lay aside the old self, which is being corrupted in accordance with the lusts of deceit, and that you be renewed in the spirit of your mind, and put on the new self, which in the likeness of God has been created in righteousness and holiness of the truth.

Here, the phrase "lay aside the old self" is not in the imperative (command) mood, but is an aorist mid. infinitive (ἀποθέσθαι, *apothesthai*) indicating what should be the characteristic of one's life if indeed one has properly understood what a new creature he or she is in the Messiah.[150] The verb rendered "lay aside" has its root meaning in "removing a garment," and thus the picture is not that one should ever "put it back on," but that there is a definitive change of "dress," from the rags of unrighteousness to the glory of Yeshua's holiness. This aorist infinitive ("lay aside") is matched by a parallel aorist infinitive in v. 24, "put on" with regard to the "new self." In each case, the aorist infinitive points back to what the Apostle had apparently taught them to be the reality of their new birth in the Messiah (note how the paragraph begins, "But you did not learn Messiah in this way"). Thus, what the Apostle admonishes his readers to do in this context is to live in accordance with what they know to be true, namely, that the old man has been put off (as an old, tattered garment) and the new man has been put on, a new man which involves the "renewal of the spirit of your mind."

If it is correct to interpret the Ephesians passage in this way, then Paul is consistently using the term "old self" to refer to that heart of sin which was crucified with the Messiah and therefore is no more. In its place has been put a new heart which, though still within the "flesh," and battling with the sinful nature, longs to please God in every way. It is, in fact, the presence of this "new man" (=new heart) which creates the conflict between the renewed desire and the sinful bent of the flesh.

that our body of sin might be done away with – The old self was crucified with this purpose in mind, that the "body of sin" (τὸ σῶμα τῆς ἁμαρτίας) might be "done away with" (καταργηθῇ, *katargethe*). Some commentators have suggested that the "old self" and "body of sin" denote the same thing, i.e., the corrupt nature. But in the scenario suggested above, the "old self" is the old heart, the volition, the "decision-maker" within us, while here the "body of sin" would be the remaining bent to sin which is inherent in the fallen human nature. It is inevitable that if there has been a change of "commanders" (=volition), the bent to sin within the fallen human nature will be more and more subdued and mortified, and thus done away with. In its place will reside those "members of the body" that willingly submit as "slaves to righteousness." Thus, the very purpose of the implantation of the new heart, the heart of flesh rather than stone, is that the actions of the redeemed individual might conform to righteousness—that God's commands might be both guarded/remembered and done—that they might be written on the heart. We must be careful to understand "body" (σῶμα, *soma*) here as referring, not to one's physical body, but to the sinful nature which is being subdued and put to death.

The result of the new heart (new self) is that as the sinful nature is subdued and mortified, the believer in Yeshua is enabled (through the power of the Spirit) to live in liberty unto HaShem—he or she is no longer a slave to sin. The new heart has been given the renewed ability to actually make a valid decision—a choice between right and wrong. Before this salvific renewal, however, the old man was a slave to sin, meaning that the old man was bound to sin's whims and fancies, and could never help himself from following the sinful bent and passions of the corrupt nature.

In this we must define freedom as the ability to do or perform God's will, not as the ability to do what one's sinful nature wants. For a slave to sin is one who, try as he will, is unable to become free from the chains with which sin binds. But it is God's intention for all of His own that they be His servants, not slaves to sin. Thus, the goal to which sanctification always proceeds is that of true liberty, that is, the ability to do all of God's holy will—to conform to His standards—to be keepers of His Torah, not breakers of it.

Excursus on Paul's use of the term "flesh" (σάρξ, sarkz)

The Greek term usually translated "flesh" by our English Bibles is σάρξ, *sarkz*. It is found 91 times in the Pauline epistles. Cognate terms include σαρκικός, *sarkikos*, "belonging to this world," "not under the control of God's Spirit" (found 6 times in Pauline literature, Rom 15:27; 1Co 3:3; 9:11; 2Co 1:12; 10:4) and σάρκινος, *sarkinos*, which has similar meanings as σαρκικος with the additonal meaning "human" (found 3 times in Pauline literature, Rom 7:14; 1Co 3:1; 2Co 3: 3).

The Greek word σάρξ can have several meanings. First, it can have a physical reference and refer to the flesh of a man as distinct from his bones, sinews, etc. 1Co 15:39 is an example, as may be 2Co 12:7 ("thorn in the flesh" = sickness?), Gal 4:13 ("infirmity of the flesh"), Gal 4:14 ("my flesh" = Paul's sick body?).

Secondly, it can denote man in general, and particularly man as mortal and therefore weak. According to 2Co 7:5, "our flesh" "(=we) had no rest because there were fightings without and fears within." Paul comments that before he began to preach he did not confer with "flesh and blood," by which he means other people (Gal 1:16).

Thirdly, and closely aligned with second meaning above, σάρξ may denote relationships which have a physical bond as its basis. Thus, Yeshua is a son of David according to the flesh (Rom 1:3) and Paul speaks of his fellow Israelites as "kinsmen according to the flesh" (Rom 9:3). In the same way Yeshua was "revealed in the flesh" (apparently an early credal formulary, 1Ti 3:16). Thus, "flesh" can mean mankind or a person in his entirety, for "no flesh can boast before God" (Rom 3:20) and "the wise according to the flesh" are those wise according to human standards (1Co 1:16).

Fourthly, Paul uses the phrase "according to the flesh" (κατὰ σάρκα, 21 times in the Pauline literature) to mean life lived apart from the power of the Spirit, or life within the realm of sinful depravity. Looking at life from a strictly human point of view was no longer possible for Paul who had been redeemed and given a new life in the Messiah. "From now on, therefore, we regard no one from a human point of view (*kata sarka*); even though we regarded the Messiah from a human point of view (*kata sarka*), we regard Him thus no longer" (2Co 5:16). Likewise, one who has been born again by the Spirit no longer walks (=lives) "according to the flesh" (=from the perspective of a depraved mind) but "according to the Spirit" (Rom 8:4). In this way, "works of the flesh" or "desires of the flesh" are those deeds or desires which stem from the soul which is in battle against the sinful depravity of the fallen nature (Gal 5:16, 19; cf. Rom 13:14). The opposite of the "flesh" as depraved thinking is the Spirit: "The desires of the flesh are against the Spirit and the desires of the Spirit are against the flesh, for these are opposed to each other to prevent you from doing what you would" (Gal 5:17).

Finally, there may an overlapping meaning of the term "flesh" with the sense of "life apart from the Spirit," for it appears that at times Paul uses the term to denote reliance upon one's ethnic status for righteous standing before God. For instance, in Gal 3:3 Paul queries whether those who had begun "in the Spirit" thought they could be perfected "in the flesh." By this he may well mean that Gentile believers were being persuaded into thinking that becoming proselytes (gaining the status of "Jew") would advance their standing before God. Likewise, in 6:12 he speaks of those who strive to make a "good showing in the flesh," which most likely means "wish to show their Jewish status as significant for covenant membership."

One must carefully study the context to determine exactly how Paul is utilizing the term. For instance, Paul says that the believer no longer lives in the flesh (Rom 7:5; 8:8f; Gal 5:24), yet on the other hand Paul still lives in the flesh (2Co 10:3; Gal 2:20; Phil 1:22f), by which we understand him to mean that though we still live within the physical realm of mankind, we no longer live our lives with the perspective of the depraved nature.

The phrase "body of flesh" (σῶμα τῆς σάρκος) found in Colossians (1:22; 2:11) combines the sense of mortality and depravity so that the "body of flesh" is put off through union with the Messiah in faith even as the flesh is "put off" in the ritual of circumcision. While this may appear to have strong Hellenistic overtones, it is interesting to find similar verbiage in the Qumran literature. In 1QpHab (on 2:8, column 9.2) we read "being distressed by the punishments of sin; the horrors of terrifying maladies acted upon him, as well as vengeful acts on his fleshly body" (ונקמות בגוים בשרו). "Fleshly body" here means "physical body."

"Flesh" in the Tanach

The concept of "flesh" in the Tanach can be seen to underly the use of σαρξ by Paul, though it is common for modern theologians to charge Paul with Hellenized thinking in his use of the term. In the Tanach בָּשָׂר, *basar*, "flesh" can refer to the flesh of animals and therefore as food for mankind (Gen 41:2; Dt 14:8; 1Sa 2:13, 15). It can also be used to denote human flesh as distinguished from bone and sinew (Gen 2:21). "Flesh" can also stand for the whole person: "O God, You are my God, I seek You, my soul thirsts for You, my flesh longs for You" (Ps 63:2; cf. 54:3). Likewise, "all flesh" can mean "all mankind," (cf. Is 66:23). While there is no clear evidence that "flesh" is used in the sense of "depravity," there are times when the term denotes mortality and weakness. Note, for instance, Is 40:6f, "All flesh is grass, and all its beauty is like the flower of the field. The grass withers, the flower fades." Furthermore, the flesh is puny when compared to God: "Sennacherib's Assyrian horde is called the "arm of the flesh" (2Chr 32:8), and God considers Israel's weakness (Ps 78:39), for He "remembered that they were but flesh—a wind that does not return." From this sense of "weakness" comes also the idea of self-centeredness, or independence from God: "Cursed is the man who trusts in man and makes flesh his arm, whose heart turns away from Adonai" (Jer 17:5).

"Flesh" in the Rabbinic Literature

The use of "flesh" (בָּשָׂר) in the Tanach is replaced (by and large) by Rabbinic גוף, *guf*, "body" (perhaps from an original root which meant "cavity," cf. Arabic *gauf*). The Sages looked at the body as a vessel to be filled and therefore as neutral in the good vs. evil scheme of things. It may be that this viewpoint was strengthened in an effort to combat Hellenism and particularly Platonic idealism which put the material and non-material at such odds. Furthermore, the Sages no longer look at the body (*guf* as substitute for *basar*, "flesh") as a way of speaking of the whole man. While the spirit is derived from heaven, the body is of the earth. Only through acceptance, study, and implementation of Torah is man enabled to rise above the level of mere animal existence and attain the level of the higher creatures (*Siphre* Deut. 305, 233, 2).

---

7 for he who has died is freed from sin.

It was understood by the later rabbis that death in every way severed one from responsibility to the Torah and the *mitzvot*.[151] A midrash on Jb 3:19 and Ps 88:6 also teaches that one is freed from the "mastery" of sin when one dies.[152] Whether or not these kinds of discussions/rabbinic dicta were in the mind of Paul as he wrote this pithy yet profound line no one can be sure, but it seems possible. Yet, in the context, it is clear that Paul refers to the one who has placed his faith in the Messiah, and having thus died and risen with Him, is now freed from the whole "body" (=sin as a whole) of sin which would otherwise stand to condemn him. Nothing is more settling of heart and soul than to know that one stands forever free from the condemnation of sin.

The word translated "freed" by the NASB and NIV is δεδικαίωται, *dedikaiotai* from δικαιόω, *dikaioo* "to justify," "declare righteous." Thus, more literally the phrase would be "for he who has died has been declared righteous from sin." This helps us understand the fuller picture of "justification," for justification produces the state of "freedom" or "liberty" from the condemnation of sin as well as from the slave master of sin.

8–9 Now if we have died with Messiah, we believe that we shall also live with Him, knowing that Messiah, having been raised from the dead, is never to die again; death no longer is master over Him.

The grammatical construction employed in the opening of this verse (εἰ δέ followed by indicative) functions as a true condition: "It is really true" or "Now if we have died (and we have) . . . . "

The actual phrase "with Messiah" (σὺν Χριστῷ, *sun Christo*) is found only here in Romans, though the concept is prominent, especially in this chapter.[153]

we believe we shall also live with Him – "We believe" is inserted to underscore once again the absolute necessity of personal faith if one is to enjoy life in the Messiah. We do not "live with Him" through ritual or lineage, but through personal faith in Him.

The future "we shall live" is understood to include the present life as the larger context clearly shows (cp. v. 11), yet has its ultimate goal in the world to come in which our living with Him will be unhampered by our present mortality and sin.

knowing that Messiah – The confidence we have, that we have died with the Messiah and that we also live and will live with Him, is based upon knowing what God has said, and then believing it. Here Paul sets forth two crucial truths: 1) Messiah has been raised from the dead, and 2) He never will die again. Yeshua was not raised, like Lazarus, to a mere extension of natural life, only to succumb once more to death, for His resurrection was final, a foretaste of the final resurrection in the eschaton. Thus, He is the "first-fruits from the dead" (1Co 15:20), being the first of mankind to have died and risen, never to die again.

In the same way, His resurrection has no parallel to the mythic nature-god in which his death and resurrection is a part of the endlessly recurring cycle of death and renewal. Yeshua's resurrection is the beginning of the eschaton, so to speak, in that it ushers in for us all the reality of man living eternally with his God.

death no longer is master over Him – The fact that οὐκέτι, *ouketi* ("no longer") is used indicates that there was a time when death did exercise lordship over Yeshua. How is this possible, that death should be the master of the Creator? How can one explain such a thing? The only viable explanation is that He willingly bore our sins upon Himself and as such submitted Himself to the unyielding lordship of death. He was willing to recognize death as having mastery over Him because He was willing to take our sins upon Himself as our sacrifice.

But that He died for our sins, He died once, for His death was an infinite death. He therefore does not need to die again and again because the debt of our sins has been fully paid—the death which HaShem requires of us has been given once for all. Therefore, His eternal life goes on now uninterrupted by any need to deal with sin, for He has already and eternally accomplished this work. Any part of worship, then, which pretends to inflict upon the Messiah a re-crucifixion (such as the Roman Catholic mass) is not only in error, but is blasphemy, for it would subject Yeshua to that which He no longer could ever be subjected, and calls into question both the value and finality of His death on our behalf.

10 For the death that He died, He died to sin, once for all; but the life that He lives, He lives to God.

This profound truth, that Yeshua's death on behalf of sinners was a completed and eternal work, is the keystone of Paul's message.

The Greek construction is abbreviated, ὃ γὰρ, *ho gar* standing for τὸν γὰρ θάνατον ὃν, "the death which" and ὃ δέ, *ho de* for τὴν δὲ ζωήν ἥν, "the life which." For similar construction cf. Gal 2:20b.

The symbolism of Yom HaKippurim (Day of Atonement) is thus worked out in the reality of the "one-for-all-time"[154] (ἐφάπαξ, *ephapaks*) aspect of Yeshua's death. Even as the Torah is specific that the Cohen HaGadol could only go into the Most Holy Place one time each year,[155] on Yom HaKippurim, so the reality of Yeshua's once-for-all-time death was foreshadowed. As the year may be considered a complete unit in that the cycle of *mo'edim* (festivals) is completed, so the fact that the Cohen HaGadol enters only once in this complete cycle surely taught beforehand that Messiah's death would be a once-for-all-time event.

But if death touched Yeshua only once, in contrast He lives forever because He lives "to God." That is, death had mastery over Him once because He willingly took upon Himself the sins of those who were His. He willingly dealt in the realm of sin in order to redeem those who were dead in that realm. But having dealt with that realm, He now deals only in the realm in which HaShem dwells, i.e., in that place of life and holiness. Thus He lives forever "to God."

Here we find, once again, the inner workings of the godhead, for Yeshua lives "to God" (τῷ θεῷ, *to theo*), that is, He lives to accomplish the will of the Father and to carry out His eternal plan. This willingness to serve the Father in no way diminishes His equality with the Father, for varying roles within any relationship do not necessarily bespeak inequalities in that relationship. Yeshua Himself taught that greatness may be seen through the instrumentality of servanthood. We see, then, that in eternity past as well as present and future, the role of the Son has always been to do what the Father wills yet He is equal in time, power, and holiness with the Father, for they are one.

11 Even so consider yourselves to be dead to sin, but alive to God in Messiah Yeshua.

Here, then, is the conclusion to which Paul wished to arrive in this part of his polemic. He wants his readers to understand that if they are one with the Messiah in His death and resurrection, and if the Messiah died only once, never to die again, and now lives forever unto God, then the same must be true of each one who has believed.

Even so you (οὕτως καὶ ὑμεῖς) – indicates that in Paul's thinking what is true of the Messiah is equally true of all who are "in Him" by faith.

consider yourselves (λογίζεσθε, *logizesthe*) – is most likely to be taken as an imperative (command) and not indicative (statement of fact). As such it represents not a pretending ("convince yourself that . . .") nor a mere ideal ("best case scenario is . . .") but a

> "deliberate and sober judgment on the basis of the gospel, a reasoning which is subject to the discipline of the gospel in that it accepts as its norm what God has done in Christ"[156]

Thus, "consider yourselves to be dead" means "recognize that the truth of the gospel means that you are dead." This is to see oneself, not as one feels or one surmises, but as God Himself has seen and declared me to be. This "self image" is revealed in the gospel, and understanding this and confessing it to be true on an individual basis is an important and decisive step on the way of obedience. We may assert from this that one's primary duty in the way of maturity is not to discover what one thinks of oneself, but rather to discover what God thinks, for what God thinks is the reality!

dead to sin – The Greek has "dead to the sin" (the article being included), and we should rightly ask what its presence here indicates. In Greek, the article is often used with abstract nouns, and particularly when the idea of the noun is the primary point of discussion. Thus, the presence of the article here would indicate that the believer has died "to all that sin is and all of its effects." In the same way that Yeshua died "to sin" once for all time, so we have had just such a decisive break with sin—it no longer is a master over us, and we are never to be condemned by it. The penalty prescribed by God for sin has therefore passed us by forever, and we never need fear that we should one day have to undergo the penalty of sin (=death). So in the same way that Yeshua is done with sin, so we also have died to it.

but alive to God – Even as Yeshua lives now to do HaShem's will, so we also live with a newness of life to do what pleases Him. Our focus and attention in life is toward Him. This is true in all aspects of life, so that all of life may be considered to be sacred, for it is lived out "to Him." This agrees with the emphasis of Paul in 1Co 10:31 when he writes, "Whether, then, you eat or drink or whatever you do, do all to the glory of God." The fact that in Judaism we find a blessing for every aspect of life, regardless of how mundane it may be, also emphasizes that our lives are to be entirely lived "to God." All that we have, all that we are, all that we hope to be—all of it is from the hand of God, and thus we live entirely to Him. The idea of segments within our lives that are secular on the one hand and sacred on the other is entirely contradictory to the new creatures we are in Yeshua. If we should live out the reality of who we are, we would live a life that is dead to sin and alive to God.

in Messiah Yeshua – What exactly does Paul mean by this phrase (which many have said is the locus of his theology)? A great deal of effort and writing has gone into answering this question among Pauline scholars, but it seems to me that the answer is quite obvious, at least in the broad stroke of things. For Paul the sacrificial system of worship in the Temple was in every way the foreshadowing of Messiah and His redemptive work. The one-for-one correspondence between the worshiper and the sacrificial animal he brought; the placing of hands upon the head of the innocent animal as a symbolic way of indicating the transfer of sin; the slaying of the animal for the sins of the worshiper—all of this speaks of being, as it were, one with the sacrifice as it was slaughtered and rendered up to HaShem. This union with the sacrifice—this vicarious oneness—is what Paul speaks of when he uses the phrase "in Messiah" or "in Yeshua the Messiah" (and variations of these). By this he wishes to draw attention to the manner in which HaShem sees us, which is "in Messiah." That is to say, He sees a one-for-one substitution, that Yeshua both died and lives for all those who are in Him. As such He stands as an absolute vicarious substitute for each one who, through faith, is "in Him."

If, then, HaShem sees the believer to be "in Messiah," He sees that believer as eternally safe, and eternally the object of His unfailing and unfathomable grace and love. This is the powerful message of the gospel, and the point of Paul's exposition here.

12 Therefore do not let sin reign in your mortal body that you should obey its lusts,

Beginning with "Therefore" (οὖν, *oun*), Paul builds upon his former conclusion, that the believer no longer lives under the reign of sin but has been freed from that slavery. If, then, sin no longer reigns as undisputed master, and the old man has been crucified and in his place a new man has been created, why should Paul need to exhort the Romans not to let sin reign in their mortal bodies?

The "old man," as mentioned before, is a Pauline description of the old heart (cf. Ezek 36:26), the heart of stone, set in its ways and unresponsive to HaShem. Thus, what has changed in the life of the believer is the "will" or "volition," the desire to do what God has commanded as over against the old will which set self at the center and despised God's commandments.

But sin, while in control of the old man, resided not only in the depraved will but in the "flesh" as well, for sin characterized the very nature received from Adam. One might illustrate it by the following:

At the end of World War II, a "mopping up" operation was undertaken in the South Pacific as small enclaves of enemy soldiers, detached and isolated from their primary platoons, continued to engage in battle, not knowing that the war was over and treaties to that effect had already been signed. Since, however, all communications had been lost with these small bands of soldiers, it was impossible to convince them that the war was, in fact, over. They took such communication from the Allied forces as just another ploy to trick them into surrendering. As a result, many US soldiers were wounded and some died well after the war was officially over, as they attempted to subdue the remaining enemy forces.

This may give us a working illustration for the death of the old man yet the remaining of sin. In the WWII incident, the commander of the enemy forces had changed and the flag which flew over their fortresses was removed and replaced with the Stars and Stripes. No longer was the one making the decisions telling them to kill US soldiers. The "will" or "volition" had changed—new orders were being given by a new commander. Yet in spite of this the resolve of the enemy to continuing fighting was undiminished.

In the illustration, then, the remaining troops represent the sinful flesh which would like to usurp ruling power over the new man (even though the war has been won). Paul's admonition here, then, would be not to allow the remaining sinful nature to usurp a rule which rightly belongs now to the new man as controlled by the Spirit.

By "mortal body" (ἐν τῷ θνητῷ ὑμῶν σώματι) Paul does not mean simply the "physical part of man," for "body" (σῶμα, *soma*) can represent the whole of something (cf. v. 6), and so here it most likely speaks of the whole person dwelling as a mortal as contrasted with the immortality the believer will enjoy in the world to come. In short, "mortal body" is the whole man in his fallenness. Thus, the admonition not to allow sin to reign in the mortal body is a call to resist sin's dominion in every sphere, both physical and non-physical. This likewise applies to the lusts of the flesh in every realm.

The ability now of the new man to make a righteous, God-honoring choice, is evident in the phrase "that you should obey its lust." Here is evidence that the new man has ability to resist the demands of remaining sin, for not obeying its lust means saying "no" and refusing to follow the draw of sin.

13 and do not go on presenting the members of your body to sin as instruments of unrighteousness; but present yourselves to God as those alive from the dead, and your members as instruments of righteousness to God.

The opening μηδὲ παιστάνετε, *mede paistanete*, "and do not go on presenting" is the negative with the present active imperative, and the NASB has given the flavor of it by indicating "do not keep presenting . . . ." One could just as well translate "And stop presenting . . . ." The point is simple: if the death of the old man means now there is the actual enablement to live righteously, the ways of the flesh—the paths taken before, and the manner of life which fed the sinful nature—must stop. If indeed there remains a bent to sin in the sinful nature which we have as mortals, then it is surely wisdom to put as far away from us those activities or patterns of life which would in any way encourage the sinful nature to take control or have its way.

"Members" (τὰ μέλη, *ta mele*) means literally "limb" though it came to mean all parts of the body, including the ear and eye (cf. 1Co 12:14ff) and thus is translated "member" rather than "limb." But here it is perhaps used in an even wider sense to include any natural capacity. In fact, it may be closely equivalent to "yourselves" in the next phrase.

Why would Paul use the term, then, if it generally means "the whole person?" It may well be that he intends to have his readers focus upon that aspect of their individual lives, where they struggle in the realm of sin and righteousness. For some it may be the eyes, for others the tongue, etc. In using the term "members," then, Paul asks each of us, before HaShem, to examine where we are weak and prone to sin, and to resolve not to obey the lusts of the flesh as we strive for righteousness.

The word translated "instruments" (ὅπλα, *hopla*) can also mean "weapons," which may fit the context here, since the idea of sin "reigning" brings into the picture the idea of conflicting kingdoms and kings. Yet the idea of "slavery" may also evoke the common sense of "instrument" (= tools). The point is that the very members that once engaged gladly in unrighteousness should now willingly do the duty of the Lord who commands righteousness.

Thus, believers are to "present themselves to God as those alive from the dead." The change of status from sin-slaves to slaves of righteousness is brought about via a death and resurrection. This, once again, highlights an important fact, namely, that our salvation, like the exodus from Egypt, was not for ourselves, but so that we might serve HaShem. Even as God brought Israel out of Egypt so that she might serve Him, so He redeemed each one that each person might present to Him all one's gifts and talents for His service. Our new life is a life unto Him—that is why it was given in the first place.

14 For sin shall not be master over you, for you are not under Torah, but under grace.

The fact that sin no longer is master (κυριεύσει, *kureusei* "act as lord or master") is because the old man has been crucified and no longer has the power to direct sin within the sinful nature to deeds of unrighteousness. Left without "leadership," and with the renewed man now "in charge" and longing to follow the Lord and live righteously, the remaining sin is at a distinct disadvantage, for the inevitable course of the believer's life will be toward God and away from sin.

Does Paul, by the opening statement, make a statement of fact, or is he making an exhortation to his readers? We may sum up the interpretations as follows:

1) Paul makes a promise to his readers that never again will they yield to sin.

This is surely not possible, for Paul goes on to show that believers, while not under the reign of sin, still sin nonetheless.

2) Paul exhorts his readers not to allow sin to usurp mastery over them. This appears attractive at first, but such an interpretation would render the verse a mere reiteration of v. 12, and would therefore seem somewhat superfluous. What is more, the opening of the verse with "For" (γάρ, *gar*) as an explanation of what has been stated previously does not seem to work.

3) Paul makes a categorical statement that sin, personified as a ruler, will never again have sovereign rule over them because a new Lord has taken His rightful place over their lives. This explanation understands the opening "for" to explain why the believer should not present his members as instruments of unrighteousness—namely, because he now serves a new Master. There is no need, as it were, to appease the master of unrighteousness, for he no longer has any ruling power.

This does not mean that sin will no longer have power, for it will—in the remaining sinful nature. Thus, it also means that sin will be a constant enemy against which war will be waged. What it does mean, however, is that hope of victory is sure, because the war has already been won—the enemy's "general" has been deposed.

For you are not under Torah but under grace – Taken out of context, this phrase has regularly been interpreted by Christian commentators to mean that the authority of the Torah has been abolished for believers and superseded by a different authority, that by "law" (νόμος, *nomos*) Paul means the life of sin, and by "grace" he means the life of righteousness. Note for example, the words of Ambrosiaster (366 CE):

> If we walk according to the commandments which he gives, Paul says that sin will not rule over us, for it rules over those who sin. For if we do not walk as he commands we are under the law. But if we do not sin we are not under the law but under grace. If, however, we sin, we fall back under the law, and sin starts to rule over us once more, for every sinner is a slave to sin. It is necessary for a person to be under the law as long as he does not receive forgiveness, for by the law's authority sin makes the sinner guilty. Thus the person to whom forgiveness is given and who keeps it by not sinning anymore will neither be ruled by sin nor be under the law. For the authority of the law no longer applies to him; he has been delivered from sin. Those whom the law holds guilty have been turned over to it by sin. Therefore the person who has departed from sin cannot be under the law.[157]

Rather, the context shows clearly that Paul's point in this concluding phrase is that the reign of sin had its power or authority through the Torah, for the Torah condemns sin and the sinner. Paul has taught clearly that the power of sin to condemn is found in the Torah. Thus, when he concludes that the believer is not under the Torah but under grace, he is not putting the Torah and grace at odds with each other, but showing the means by which the believer is no longer a slave to sin but instead is alive unto God. The penalty of the Torah against the sinner, just and righteous as it was, was put entirely upon Yeshua and therefore the believer is no longer under its condemnation. In the place of condemnation has come forgiveness and grace.

Cranfield has this to say:

> [this phrase] is widely taken to mean that the authority of the law has been abolished for believers and superseded by a different authority. And this, it must be admitted, would be a plausible interpretation, if this sentence stood by itself. But, since it stands in a document which contains such things as 3:31; 7;12, 14a; 8:4; 13:8-10, and in which the law is referred to more than once as God's law (7:22, 25; 8:7) and is appealed to again and again as authoritative, such a reading of it is extremely unlikely. The fact that ὑπὸ νόμον ("under law") is contrasted with ὑπὸ χάριν ("under grace") suggests the likelihood that Paul is here think-

ing not of the law generally but of the law as condemning sinners; for, since grace denotes God's undeserved favour, the natural opposite to "under grace" is "under God's disfavour or condemnation." And the suggestion that the meaning of this sentence is that believers are not under God's condemnation pronounced by the law but under His undeserved favour receives strong confirmation from 8:1 ("There is therefore now no condemnation to those who are in Christ Jesus"), which, in Paul's argument, is closely related (through 7:1-6) to this half-verse. Moreover, this interpretation suits the context well; for an assurance that we have been set free from God's condemnation and are now the objects of His gracious favour is indeed confirmation (γάρ, "for") of the promise that henceforth sin shall no more be lord over us, for those who know themselves freed from condemnation are free to resist sin's usurped power with new strength and boldness. It is perhaps possible that in Paul's "under law" here there was also another thought present, namely, the thought of labouring (as so many of his Jewish contemporaries were doing) under the illusion with regard to the law that a man has to earn a status of righteousness before God by his obedience. Since χάρις ("grace") denotes God's free, undeserved favour, the contrast with "under law" might perhaps be not unreasonably claimed as support for this suggestion.[158]

It may be profitable for us to consider all the times the phrase "under Torah" (ὑπὸ νόμον, *hupo nomon*) is used in Paul's epistles as we attempt to understand what it means.

Rom 6:14 ἁμαρτία γὰρ ὑμῶν οὐ κυριεύσει· οὐ γάρ ἐστε ὑπὸ νόμον ἀλλὰ ὑπὸ χάριν.	Rom 6:14 For sin shall not be master over you, for you are not under Torah but under grace.
Rom 6:15 Τί οὖν; ἁμαρτήσωμεν, ὅτι οὐκ ἐσμὲν ὑπὸ νόμον ἀλλὰ ὑπὸ χάριν; μὴ γένοιτο.	Rom 6:15 What then? Shall we sin because we are not under Torah but under grace? May it never be!
1Cor. 9:20 καὶ ἐγενόμην τοῖς Ἰουδαίοις ὡς Ἰουδαῖος, ἵνα Ἰουδαίους κερδήσω· τοῖς ὑπὸ νόμον ὡς ὑπὸ νόμον, μὴ ὢν αὐτὸς ὑπὸ νόμον, ἵνα τοὺς ὑπὸ νόμον κερδήσω·	1Cor. 9:20 To the Jews I became as a Jew, so that I might win Jews; to those who are under the Torah, as under the Torah though not being myself under the Torah, so that I might win those who are under the Torah;
Gal. 3:23 Πρὸ τοῦ δὲ ἐλθεῖν τὴν πίστιν ὑπὸ νόμον ἐφρουρούμεθα συγκλειόμενοι εἰς τὴν μέλλουσαν πίστιν ἀποκαλυφθῆναι,	Gal. 3:23 But before faith came, we were kept in custody under the Torah, being shut up to the faith which was later to be revealed.
Gal. 4:4 ὅτε δὲ ἦλθεν τὸ πλήρωμα τοῦ χρόνου, ἐξαπέστειλεν ὁ θεὸς τὸν υἱὸν αυτοῦ, γενόμενον ἐκ γυναικός, γενόμενον ὑπὸ νόμον,	Gal. 4:4 But when the fullness of the time came, God sent forth His Son, born of a woman, born under the Torah,
Gal. 4:21 Λέγετέ μοι, οἱ ὑπὸ νόμον θέλοντες εἶναι, τὸν νόμον οὐκ ἀκούετε;	Gal. 4:21 Tell me, you who want to be under law, do you not listen to the Torah?
Gal. 5:18 εἰ δὲ πνεύματι ἄγεσθε, οὐκ ἐστὲ ὑπὸ νόμον.	Gal. 5:18 But if you are led by the Spirit, you are not under the Torah.

Passing by Rom 6:15 (which we will move to next), let us look individually at each of the other passages.

1Cor 9:20 – In the context Paul is arguing that as a servant of Yeshua he has every right to enjoy the fruit of his labors. Even as the farmer eats the crops he sows and harvests, and the threshing floor worker is free to eat of the grain he threshes, so Paul has a right to expect material help from those he feeds spiritually. The fact that his apostleship has come into question in the minds of some does not negate the valid ministry he has accomplished among the Corinthians. Yet just because he has been willing to minister without remuneration and support, some are saying he is less than a valid apostle. He thus explains that his decision to serve the Corinthians without remuneration was a conscious decision on his part and one he was free to make. In fact, his decision to work for his own living and not take the support of the Corinthian church was done in order to advance them in their spiritual growth. He felt, for one reason or another, that had he taken support from them, his ministry to them would have diminished.

In vv. 20-22 Paul seems to delineate 4 groups of people (or at least this seems a most natural translation): 1) Jews or Judeans, 2) those under the Torah, 3) those without the Torah, and 4) those who are weak. Many commentators want to combine #'s 1 and 2, saying that he speaks first of ethnic Jews and secondly of religious Jews, but this is a modern categorization and not something found in the ancient world.

Group #1 – It may be that by the term "Jews" (Ἰουδαίοις, *ioudaiois*) Paul refers particularly to the Jews living in or near Jerusalem (thus "Judeans"), who may have held more strictly to certain *halachic* distinctions (particularly issues of purities as related to Temple worship).

Group #2 – If we are right about Group #1, then the designation "those under the Torah" would define groups outside of the immediate vicinity of Jerusalem who were zealous for the Torah (including the Oral Torah of the Sages), yet who had rejected Yeshua as Messiah, relying upon their status as Jews to secure their covenant membership. As such, they remained under the condemnation of the Torah in Paul's view.

Group #3 must then be Gentiles whose cultural identity was not marked by Torah. This does not mean that Paul gave up obedience to God in order to win the Gentiles! What it does mean is that while in Gentile communities, he willingly let go the *halachah* of the Oral Torah when it might interfere with his primary goal of serving Yeshua in the work of the Gospel. Indeed, eating with the Gentiles in their homes would be an obvious example of how he left rabbinic *halachah* behind to accomplish his mission. But he would not have transgressed the clear command of God, as though doing so would please Him. It is never possible to honor God by disobeying Him.

Group #4 must be, in some measure, identified with the "weak" in Romans 14, i.e., those who eat only vegatables, and who fast on set days. Here once again Paul gives up his right to eat and live in a broader spectrum, but gives it up for the sake of the gospel message he is carrying, with hopes that this message will bear fruit.

In this specific case, then, being "under the Torah" would mean to "live as though the rabbinic observances and traditions of Judaism were required," even though Paul knew that for himself they were not, as he clearly states. When Paul was with those who held to various *halachot*, he would conform to these unless they compromised the gospel message or were contrary to the clear teaching of Torah. For instance, it is clear that regardless of where he was, he would not have separated himself from the Gentile believers, even if local *halachah* insisted that he should.[158a]

Gal 3:23 – We may begin first of all by discussing what Paul means in this verse by the term "faith"—"But before faith came . . . ." Now certainly Paul cannot mean here that there was no faith before the coming of Yeshua! Paul is the expounder of Gen 15:6 in Romans 4 and uses Abraham and David as the examples of what it "looks like" to have faith—saving faith. So what does Paul mean by the phrase "but before faith came . . . .?

Many commentators take the word "faith" here to be a metonym for Yeshua, i.e., the object of faith. So they would understand it to mean "But before Yeshua came we were kept in custody under the law, being shut up to the faith (in Yeshua) which was later to be revealed." But this interpretation does not work either, for the simple and obvious reason that faith, i.e., true saving faith, has always been in one object and one object alone, namely, Yeshua. Faith in the Messiah has always been the means by which God declares a sinner righteous. Surely this is proven in the case of Abraham, for Yeshua Himself declared that Abraham longed to see His day, and he saw it (Jn 8:56f). David as well understood that the promise of the Messiah was the focus of his faith, as he likewise understood the Messiah to be the hope for all mankind (2 Sa 7:19f). Therefore, to say that "faith" in this verse actually means the object of faith, i.e., Yeshua, simply cannot be sustained in the broader scope of Pauline theology (not to mention the emphasis upon faith in the Messiah throughout the scriptures).

It seems to me that the plain meaning of the text ought to be our starting point. For Paul, the concept of something "coming" is that of "understanding" or "knowing the truth." He uses this same idiom with regard to the Torah in Rom 7:9 where he writes: "And I was once alive apart from the Torah; but when the commandment came, sin became alive, and I died." The commandment was always extant, and even was very much a part of Paul's life before he came to faith in Yeshua, yet in his terminology it had not yet come. It "came" when by faith his eyes were opened to see the commandment as it actually was. That is to say, the concept of the commandment "coming" is that of knowing the truth about the commandment.

If we take Paul to be using the same concept here, in regards to faith, then the phrase "before faith came" means before Paul (or any given individual) came to understand faith as it truly is—faith as God understands it. Thus, as a Jew, living within the context of Torah observance yet without faith in the Messiah, the Torah functioned to point to the Messiah in every way—through the sacrificial system, the mo'edim (festivals), purity laws, etc. The Torah continued to function as a *pedegogue* leading to the teacher, restraining (in some ways) the natural tendencies of the flesh and directing the mind and heart to faith in Yeshua. Once Paul had genuinely placed faith in Yeshua, the Torah no longer needed to function in this convicting manner (as a *pedegogue* for an immature child) but took up the role of mentor, deepening the understanding and enlightening the willing mind.

Thus, to be "kept in custody under the Torah" is to be surrounded with the observance of Torah (as was generally true of the Jewish community of Paul's day) in contradistinction from the pagan cultures whose lives were surrounded by idolatry, etc. Paul wishes to show, then, that the Torah, while condemning the sinner, nonetheless functions to lead the sinner to Messiah, if in fact that sinner is being drawn by the Almighty—drawn to faith in Yeshua.

Here, then, we may understand "under Torah" to mean "compelled by the Torah to do those things which, though contrary to an unbelieving heart, actually point toward Yeshua." To put it another way, to be "under the Torah" in this context is analogous to being under the rule of a *pedegogue* whose primary goal is to get the student to graduation.

Gal 4:4-5 – It is easy to see why many commentators have understood Paul's use of "under the Torah" in these verses to simply mean "born as a Jew to redeem Jews." That Yeshua was born to Jewish parents, and that the first events in His life were circumcision and appearance at the Temple is emphasized by the Gospel writers (cf. Lk 2:21ff). But the parallel with 3:13-14 is so close as to warrant a continuing theme, namely, that one of the roles of the Torah as it pertains to the unbeliever is that of condemnation (cf. 2Cor 3:7ff). The Torah condemns sin and thus the sinner.

But was Yeshua born "under the condemnation of the Torah?" In one sense, He was not. As the perfect and holy Son of God, He did not partake of Adam's sin, and as such, was not born a sinner (cf. Rom 5:12f). But in another sense, He was born for the purpose of carrying the condemnation of His people, and in this sense He was born "under the condemnation of the Torah" as it pertains to their sins.

For Paul, the ministry of Yeshua was conceived of as primarily soteriological. His coming was not primarily as a teacher of Torah or of wisdom as much as it was to identify with the human condition ("born of a woman") "in order that, by His identification with the human condition . . . , His death might be the price necessary to free them from the slavery endemic to that human condition . . ."(Dunn, *Galatians,* p. 217). In this regard then, we should most likely see Paul's use of "born under the Torah, so that He might redeem those under the Torah" to be a reference to Jew and Gentile alike. Even though the Gentile has no sense that he is condemned by the Torah until such time as he hears the message of the Gospel, he is nonetheless in a state of condemnation. He is "under the Torah" in the sense of being under its condemning power. Likewise, the Jew, who may have never considered that the Torah would condemn him, is under the condemnation of the Torah until such time as he places his faith in the redemptive work of Yeshua. We may conclude that "under the Torah" in this context means "under the condemnation of the Torah."

Gal 4:21 – In this verse Paul speaks of those who "want to be under the Torah," and asks them to listen to the Torah they want to be under. In an interesting (and somewhat difficult to interpret) analogy, Paul compares the present state of Judaisms to Hagar as a slave while speaking of the "Jerusalem above" as free and analogous to Sarah (though she's actually never named). Clearly the "slave" is the one who believes his covenant membership rests upon his status as a Jew (whether native born or proselyte). In such a case, those who are relying upon the "flesh" (ethnic status) for their right standing before God are actually under the condemnation of the Torah. While on the one hand they believe that the Torah, as marking their identity as Jews, is their means of covenant membership, in actuality the Torah is the forensic means of their condemnation. Once again, "under the Torah" means "under the condemnation of the Torah."

Gal 5:18 – Here Paul is contrasting the leading of the Spirit with being "under the Torah." Note v. 16ff: "But I say, walk by the Spirit, and you will not carry out the desire of the flesh; for these are in opposition to one another, so that you may not do the things that you please. But if you are led by the Spirit, you are not under the Torah." Once again, to be under Torah means to rely upon the Torah (both written and oral) as the means of establishing covenant membership through ethnic status. For the native born, this meant maintaining Torah obedience in order not to be "cut off from one's people," while for the Gentile it meant undergoing the ritual of rabbinic conversion (becoming a proselyte). In both cases, those who are "under the Torah" are condemned by the Torah because they are trusting in "the flesh" (ethnic status) as defined by the rabbinic interpretation of Torah.

In summary, then, "under the Law (Torah)" means primarily "under the condemnation of the Torah," or may define those who are relying upon the Torah to give them a "Jewish status" which they believe is the means of covenant membership. Thus, in our text, being "under the condemnation of the Torah" is contrasted with "being under grace." Those who are "under the Torah" are those who (whether Jews or Gentiles turned proselyte) are relying upon their Jewish status (i.e., "the works of the Torah") for covenant membership, and as such, remain under the condemnation of the Torah. In contrast, those who are "under grace" have relied entirely upon God's gift of salvation as a matter of His pure and sovereign grace. Their striving to maintain (or obtain) their covenant status through the "works of the Torah" has ceased, and they have accepted the rule of grace in their lives—a rule administered by the presence of the indwelling Spirit.

15 What then? Shall we sin because we are not under Torah but under grace? May it never be!

Having looked briefly at the Pauline passages where the phrase "under Torah" is found, we are now in a better position to interpret the verse before us.

It may first appear that Paul is simply asking the same question he began the chapter with (6:1) in which he answers the false premise which some may have built upon 5:20. If where sin abounded, grace did much more abound, could it be inferred from this that one should sin all the more? The answer is an emphatic "God forbid" (may it never be). But the question which he now poses in our text is, in fact, not the same, for it poses a second false inference, namely, that if a person is no longer under the penalty of the Torah, then actions which before constituted sin are now amoral. To put it another way, if sin is only known in relationship to the Torah, and if the Torah is no longer active in its condemning function, then sin is without definition. But to this second false inference Paul answers with the emphatic μὴ γένοιτο, *me genoito*, "may it never be." For far from not making any difference to the believer, sinful acts now take on even a greater concern for they are contrary to the renewed nature of the redeemed soul.

The pains to which Paul goes in the subsequent verses to prove the premise false may well highlight the fact that some actually believed this theological error and were practicing this blantant form of anti-nomianism.

16 Do you not know that when you present yourselves to someone as slaves for obedience, you are slaves of the one whom you obey, either of sin resulting in death, or of obedience resulting in righteousness?

Paul begins with his well used phrase οὐκ οἴδατε ὅτι, "or do you not know" (cf. 1Co 3:16; 5:6; 6:2, 3, 9, 15, 16, 19; 9:13, 24, as well as Rom 11:2 and the similar ἢ ἀγνοεῖτε ὅτι, "are you unaware that" in Rom 6:3; 7:1) as a way of stating something that they, in fact, do know, but must have overlooked in the course of the discussion.

Paul draws from common life experience and offers his readers two important points. First, when one yields himself to a master and obeys that master, the obvious conclusion is that he is a slave to that master. Secondly, in the situation presently under discussion, there are only two alternatives: being slaves of sin (which results in death) or being slaves of obedience (resulting in righteousness). That both are presented as a possibility emphasizes the fact that if a believer is committing sinful acts, he is doing so voluntarily, and not as a slave to sin. But by voluntarily engaging in sin (yielding one's members as slaves to sin), he is also acting contrary to his renewed soul. Thus, the point that Paul wishes to emphasize here is a simple yet profound one: one's actions are the litmus test of one's allegience. If indeed we have been born from above so that we are no longer under the condemnation of the Torah but under the gracious work of God in our lives, then surely our lives will make this known. This harkens back to 2:13 where the "doers of the Torah" stand just before HaShem.

The end of each of the two alternatives is death and righteousness respectively. Yielding oneself to sin will yield death, and conversely, yielding oneself to obedience yields righteousness. Since the two are obvious parallels and opposites, we may rightly understand "righteousness" to be "right standing with God." For death in this context means to be under God's final judgment, and as such, righteousness must here mean acceptance by God in the final judgment.

We may also note the somewhat unexpected parallels Paul gives here. "Sin" is paralleled by "obedience" (we might have expected "righteousness") and "death" by "righteousness" (we might have expected "life"). Why? It seems most likely that Paul used these parallels because he wanted to emphasize that the life lived under God's grace is indeed a life of obedience to Him. Cranfield explains it this way:

> The question of a man's being free in the sense of having no master at all simply does not arise. The only alternatives open to him are to have sin, or to have God, as his master (the man who imagines he is free, because he acknowledges no god but his own ego, is deluded; for the service of one's own ego is the very essence of the slavery of sin). The one alternative has as its end death, but the other life with God.[159]

17 But thanks be to God that though you were slaves of sin, you became obedient from the heart to that form of teaching to which you were committed,

Paul breaks into a kind of בְּרָכָה, *b'rachah*, "blessing" language with the opening χάρις δὲ τῷ θεῷ "but thanks to God," by which he emphasizes what he knows to be true of his readers, namely, that their acceptance of the gospel as it relates to Yeshua was, without doubt, genuine.

Their obedience was not merely the perfunctory doing of deeds, but was motivated by a heart of love, first to God and then to one's neighbor. This, as I have suggested previously, marks the difference between "under Torah" and "under grace." While those under the condemnation of the Torah may go about performing ceremonies and "good deeds" as a matter of obligation without a true sense of submission to God, those under grace obey from the heart—from a relationship with HaShem. This means that being noticed by others is no concern, and true service, both to God and to man, may therefore be accomplished. It is this issue of the heart, and the Torah written on the heart, that informs Paul's upcoming use of "letter" and "Spirit" to denote merely performing religious duty on the one hand, and obedience from the heart on the other.

This is the only time Paul uses the phrase "from the heart" (ἐκ καρδίας, *ek kardias*), though in the Pastorals he uses ἐκ καθαρᾶς καρδίαν (*ek katharas karkdian*), "from a pure heart" (1Ti 1:5; 2Ti 2:22, cf. 1Pt 1:22). It's meaning, however, seems clear. It connects to the consistent notice within the Tanach that Israel's covenant relationship with God was to be a matter of the heart, soul, and strength (Deut 6:4f; 11:13ff).

to that form of teaching to which you were committed – This phrase is difficult and has received numerous suggestions by commentators. But most commentators take this phrase to mean "you were committed to that form of teaching," meaning "you readily accepted the teaching and committed yourself to obeying it."

But what is meant by "that form of teaching?" It may simply mean that teaching which accompanied the gospel as Paul presented it, namely, that the gospel entailed more than how one may have sins forgiven—that it also included a description of the manner of life demanded by the gospel as centered in Yeshua. This takes us back to 1:5 and the phrase "the obedience of the faith," for the Apostolic gospel came expecting that true faith in Yeshua would inevitably manifest itself in a changed life, a life which would be characterized by obedience to God's revealed will.

18–19 and having been freed from sin, you became slaves of righteousness. I am speaking in human terms because of the weakness of your flesh. For just as you presented your members as slaves to impurity and to lawlessness, resulting in further lawlessness, so now present your members as slaves to righteousness, resulting in sanctification.

Paul recounts the reality: they once were slaves to sin (meaning they had no recourse over it, for sin was their master) but now they have become slaves of righteousness (meaning they have not only the ability but the obligation to "live soberly and righteously in the present age" Tit 2:12).

But Paul recognizes that the metaphor of "slavery" will not fit in every way the spiritual reality he wishes to convey. He therefore acknowledges that he is speaking "in human terms," using an illustration to make his main point, recognizing that it will not "work" in every detail. Yet Paul also knows that he needs to make it plain to his readers, so he speaks to them in common terms because of the "weakness" of their flesh. This speaking according to "human terms" was common within rabbinic literature where one of the axioms of Torah interpretation is דִּבְּרָה תּוֹרָה בִּלְשׁוֹן בְּנֵי אָדָם, "the Torah speaks in the language of men."

The manner in which the illustration does not work is obvious: the believer's relationship

157

to HaShem cannot be characterized by the "unjust, humiliating, degrading, and grievous thing that slavery has always been."[160] But because Paul was fearful that his readers were prone to forget their obligations while under grace, he points to the manner of slaves who must obey their master—they have no other choice. So it is with all who profess to be followers of Yeshua: each must commit himself to obedience for it is what the Master requires.

But it was not only in ancient times that people who had come to receive God's grace errored in this notion of "no obligations." Perhaps there is no greater need in Christianity today than to understand and accept the picture of "slave" when the whole issue of "what it means to be saved" comes up. While it is important for everyone to understand the weakness in the illustration, it is equally important that we all take to heart the real picture of being a slave to righteousness. To the extent that our lives were wholly given over to sin before we were redeemed, so in like manner our lives now must be wholly given over to righteousness. Our new Master, HaShem, requires nothing less than full conformity to His will.

What is more, the effect of submitting one's members to HaShem as instruments of righteousness is that more and more the believer is set apart unto God (sanctified). Even as sin led to more sin while slaves to unrighteousness, so the life of righteousness leads inevitably to a greater degree of holiness or sanctification, which is the goal of every true believer.

The wording Paul chooses is insightful. Throughout this passage he has contrasted "death" with "righteousness" and paralleled "unrighteousness" and "sin" with "death." Here, however, he refers to sin as "lawlessness" (ἀνομία, *anomia*) and "impurity" (ἀκαθαρσία, *akatharsia*), words which both have connection to the Torah. "Lawlessness" could just as well be understood as "against Torah," and "impurity" is demonstrated in the purity laws of the Torah. The parallelism is therefore clear: "sanctification" (the result of yielding members to righteousness) is the opposite of "lawlessness"—sanctification grows through living one's life in conformity to the Torah, God's teaching about righteousness.

"Sanctification" (ἁγιασμός, *hagiasmos*) occurs 9 other times in the Apostolic Scriptures (Rom 6:22; 1Co 1:30; 1Th 4:3, 4, 7; 2Th 2:13; 1Ti 2:15; Heb 12:14; 1Pt 1:2) and denotes God's work in the believer by which he is ethically renewed—by which he, through obedience to God, becomes more and more set apart to Him. Sanctification is always considered by Paul as a process rather than a state-of-being—a process through which each believer is being more and more conformed into the image of Yeshua. The word itself is based upon the noun ἅγιος, *hagios*, "dedicated, set apart to God, holy." For Paul, this is the normal and expected result of being called into covenant relationship with God through faith in Yeshua. Thus his regular use of "saints" (ἅγιοι, *hagioi*) when addressing believers.

20 For when you were slaves of sin, you were free in regard to righteousness.

Paul puts this statement in the reverse of what we might expect. We could surely understand him saying that when we were slaves to sin we were unable to fulfill righteousness. But instead he uses the expression "free to righteousness." The dative form of "righteousness" (τῇ δικαιοσύνῃ, *te dikaiosune*), however, is clearly dative of respect, and thus the NASB and other English translations have it right when the translate "in regard to righteousness." What does it mean to be "free in regard to righteousness." It means to have no connection with it. In the same way that the believer is free from the condemnation of his sin (i.e., no longer having any connection with it), so it is true that apart from faith in Yeshua one has no real connection with righteousness as God defines it. Apart from genuine faith there is no credit of righteousness in the courts of HaShem.

What Paul is saying, therefore, is that one cannot be the slave of sin and the slave of righteousness at the same time. This accords with the words of Yeshua in Mt 6:24, "No one can serve two masters; for either he will hate the one and love the other, or he will hold to one and despise the other. You cannot serve God and mammon. "

21 Therefore what benefit were you then deriving from the things of which you are now ashamed? For the outcome of those things is death.

The manner in which this sentence is to be punctuated is debated (there were no punctuation marks in ancient Greek). Cranfield translates: "What fruit did you then obtain? Things of which you now are ashamed!" The meaning, regardless of punctuation, seems obvious. In the former life lived under the mastery of sin, lawlessness led to further lawlessness. As a result, habits of life, including "likes" and "dislikes" were formed, leading to futher lawlessness (non-Torah living). The only "benefit" derived from a lifestyle of non-Torah is death—both in this life and in the world to come. This being plain, it makes no sense whatsoever to engage in those things which only lead to death.

In point of fact, those who have been transformed by grace are ashamed to consider their former life, not because they still have some attachment to the guilt which Yeshua's blood has washed away, but because they now have hearts which beat fervently for HaShem and His will. Calvin remarks:

> Nor is what he says insignificant, Of which ye are now ashamed; for he intimates that we are possessed with extreme blind love for ourselves, when we are involved in the darkness of our sins, and think not that there is so much filth in us. The light of the Lord alone can open our eyes to behold the filthiness which lies hid in our flesh. He only then is imbued with the principles of Christian philosophy, who has well learnt to be really displeased with himself, and to be confounded with shame for his own wretchedness. He shows at last still more plainly from what was to follow, how much they ought to have been ashamed, that is, when they came to understand that they had been standing on the very precipice of death, and had been nigh destruction; yea, that they would have already entered the gates of death, had they not been reclaimed by God's mercy.[161]

Here, once again, we make an application to our times. For the Christian community is filled with those who, on the one hand, profess allegience to Yeshua, but who on the other live as though slaves to sin. Is it not very possible that they have never actually abhorred such slavery? How could they actually be ashamed of the "fruits of sin" if now, after confessing Yeshua to be their master, they willingly continue in a life marked in great measure by a disdain for the Torah (lawlessness)?

22 But now having been freed from sin and enslaved to God, you derive your benefit, resulting in sanctification, and the outcome, eternal life.

"Compare," Paul says, "the fruits of slavery to sin with the fruit of being enslaved to God." The former life yielded death, the life of faith brings life. Note carefully how the former phrase "slaves to righteousness" is here "enslaved to God." Obviously the two are synonymous, for God is the measure of righteousness, and His revealed will is the standard.

The final outcome of our having been delivered from the master of sin and transferred to the Master of righteousness is eternal life. But the intervening benefits are those of sanctification or holy living—a life which, in spite of the diligence and discipline it requires, always yields joy and contentment rather than chaos and despair. For regardless of the situation, whether painful or comfortable, the soul wrapped in faith finds a peace known only to the child of God.

We see also, as always in Paul's epistles, that sanctification is the expected norm for the believer's life. It is the inevitable result of being enslaved to God. Sanctification (ἁγιασμός, *hagiosmos*) is that work of God within the believer matched by the righteous efforts of the renewed soul by which the person is more and more separated unto God and from the world. Paul thus teaches a simple yet profound truth here, namely, that submission to God's will (i.e., being enslaved to Him) is the means by which one grows in sanctification and thus attains eternal life. It is a clear apostolic teaching that apart from holiness (=sanctification) no one will "see" God (Εἰρήνην διώκετε μετὰ πάντων καὶ τὸν ἁγιασμόν, οὗ χωρὶς οὐδεὶς ὄψεται τὸν κύριον, "Pursue peace with all, as well as the sanctification without which no one will see the Lord," Heb 12:14). Holiness, then, as the inevitable result of true, saving faith, is the surest proof of right standing with God. And to say it the other way, one who has right standing with God will surely grow in holiness.

and the outcome, eternal life – Slavery to God yields life, and ultimately, eternal life. Ζωὴ αἰωνιός (*zoe aionios*), "life eternal" is found in the Lxx of Dan 12:2, "And many of those who sleep in the dust of the ground will awake, these to everlasting life, but the others to disgrace and everlasting contempt. " Here we have a post-exilic description of what the earliest book of the Tanach portrays: "And as for me, I know that my Redeemer lives, And at the last He will take His stand on the earth. Even after my skin is destroyed, Yet from my flesh I shall see God" (Job 19:25-26).

It was vogue at the turn of the century to hold the position that only late in post-exilic Judaism did the notion of an afterlife and immortality become an accepted belief. Mowinckel, as a representative of the German schools, asserted without hesitation that a belief in the general resurrection of mankind was simply non-existent in ancient Israel.[162] Scholarship in the Tanach of more recent years, however, has shown this liberal idea to have very little substance in the texts themselves. Dahood, in his epic Psalms Commentary (*Anchor Bible*) asserts: "The opinion of Sigmund Mowinckel that neither Israel nor early Judaism knew of a faith in any resurrection nor is such a faith represented in the Psalms will not survive serious scrutiny."[163] Further studies on the symbolism of icons used in early Judaisms has reached the conclusion that the menorah, found often inscribed in tombs and on sarcophagai, is in fact a symbol of immortality, of life after death.[164]

Dahood concludes that many of the Psalms show an underlying belief in the resurrection and life after death, including Ps 1:3-6; 5:9; 11:7; 16:10-11; 17:15; 21:7; 27:13; 36:9-10; 37:37-38; 41: 13; 56:14; 73:23-24; 97:11; 116:9.

Likewise, all of the Sages of renown held to the belief that the resurrection of the righteous was a core teaching of the Tanach. So firm was this belief that in m.*Sanhedrin* 11:1, 2 (cf. b. *Sanhedrin* 99b and 105a) the first category of those excluded from the world to come is "he who says the resurrection of the dead is not taught in the Torah."[165] That the Sadduccees denied any resurrection is certain (cf. Mt 22:23; Acts 23:8 and parallel texts), but the grounds for their belief can only be conjectured. Most posit the reason to have been their strong insistance upon the "here-and-now" and a fear that belief in an "afterlife" might detract from present duties (especially those relating to the Temple and priesthood). Whatever the case, the prevailing rabbinic teaching was that one should prepare in this life for life in the world to come.

From the teachings of Yeshua it became clear to His apostles that eternal life, that is, life which never ends (=the world to come) comes not as a result of one's righteous deeds but as a result of having sins forgiven. Note the following:

> Matt. 19:16–17 And behold, one came to Him and said, "Teacher, what good thing shall I do that I may obtain eternal life?" And He said to him, "Why are you asking Me about what is good? There is only One who is good; but if you wish to enter into life, keep the commandments."

> Matt. 19:29 And everyone who has left houses or brothers or sisters or father or mother or children or farms for My name's sake, shall receive many times as much, and shall inherit eternal life.

Matt. 25:46 "And these will go away into eternal punishment, but the righteous into eternal life."

John 6:51 "I am the living bread that came down out of heaven; if anyone eats of this bread, he shall live forever; and the bread also which I shall give for the life of the world is My flesh."

John 6:58 "This is the bread which came down out of heaven; not as the fathers ate, and died, he who eats this bread shall live forever."

Most profound in this lineup of verses is the context of the "Rich Young Ruler" where it appears that Yeshua is teaching just the opposite of the Apostle Paul, namely, that one can obtain eternal life by keeping the commandments. But a reading of the whole story makes it clear that what Yeshua was actually doing was proving to a very observant Jew that performing the commandments still fell far short of keeping them all. Somehow there had to be a "heart-change," a willingness to live for God not because one expected something in return (like eternal life), but because having possessed eternal life as the free gift of the Father, one is overwhelmed by His mercy and willingly does all in his power to please Him. Indeed, that Yeshua would compare Himself to the manna of the wilderness shows that a full acceptance of Him as the Messiah (by analogy, eating the bread from heaven) was the only way to obtain eternal life. Like the children of Israel in the wilderness whose life could be sustained only by the manna, so life eternal can come only from Yeshua, for He alone is our spiritual food.

Paul therefore shows us in this passage that the ultimate goal, eternal life, is obtainable first and foremost through faith in Yeshua, and that such a faith will inevitably lead to being sanctified unto God, a condition which must certainly lead to eternal life.

23 For the wages of sin is death, but the free gift of God is eternal life in Messiah Yeshua our Lord.

Here, then, Paul draws to conclusion not only verses 21-22 but also the whole section. We may ask how the genitives should be understood in this verse. "Wages of sin" could be either 1) the wages which sin pays, or 2) the wages paid for sinning. In the context we should opt for the first suggestion, "the wages which sin pays," because sin is still personified as a slave master who pays to his slaves an allowance. Among the Romans it was normal for a slave to receive a *peculium* or "pocket-money," and according to Cicero (Phil. 8:32), a good slave could save enough in seven years to buy his freedom.[166] Thus, for those who wanted to be slaves to sin, the wages which this master pays is nothing less than death—death finally, and all of the incremental steps that lead to it.

On the other hand, God does not pay wages, for no man can put Him in his debt. Yet out of His grace and mercy He gives nothing short of eternal life! This gift of life is not a reward for proper living, but out of the free and sovereign grace of God's own eternal purpose.

What is more, as Paul has repeatedly taught, this grace finds it locus—its focal point, in no other place than in the person of Yeshua, here denoted by His full title: *Messiah Yeshua Adoneinu*, Messiah Yeshua our Lord. Nothing could be clearer: eternal life is to be found only in HaShem's Messiah, who is Yeshua, and who is therefore Adoneinu, our Lord and Master.

Chapter 7
Commentary

In the former chapter we saw how Paul emphasized the fact of our identity in Yeshua, namely, that we had died with Him and risen with Him to new life. In that dying, the penalty of the Torah was satisfied (the Torah is the revelation of God's immutable character, including His justice) and the renewed child of HaShem finds himself or herself no longer under the penalty of the Torah, but under the grace of God, that is, declared righteous, the justice of God having been satisfied by the payment of sin through Yeshua's death for His own. Striving for holiness, then, is the natural inclination of the renewed soul, for the "new man" has God's standard of righteousness as his true desire.

This change of status, from condemned to free, is the purpose of the *mikvah*, from Paul's perspective. The *mikvah* has demonstrated the move from death to life through the very media of death itself, the waters of burial. Thus, those who have confessed Yeshua as the Messiah have undergone a *mikvah* to show their union with Him in death and resurrection to newness of life. As such, the redeemed person is governed not by the volition of slavery to sin, but of the mind or heart which is bound to HaShem through faith.

What then does life look like in one who is no longer under the condemnation of the Torah but under grace? What are the practical, everyday ramifications of this change of status? It is to this question that Paul now addresses himself in the chapter before us.

The chapter may be broken down easily into two sections:

1) 7:1-6 An elucidation of 6:14, "you are not under (the condemnation of) the Torah but under grace"
2) 7:7-25 Clarifications in order to guard against possible misunderstandings regarding the nature and function of the Torah in the life of the believer

1 Or do you not know, brethren (for I am speaking to those who know the Torah), that the Torah has jurisdiction over a person as long as he lives?

Paul begins with ἢ ἀγνοεῖτε, *e agnoiete*, "do you not know," by which he means strongly to imply "surely you know!" He uses the same or similar construction in Rom 6:3; 1Co 6:2, 9, 16, 19, in which he gives an argument based upon a fact or axiom with which he knows his readers already agree.

This rhetorical use of the opening "do you not know" is confirmed by the additional parenthetical statement "for I am speaking to those who know the Torah." The early synagogues were, as described by James in Acts 15:21, engaged in teaching the Torah every Shabbat, and the believers in Yeshua were those who congregated in the synagogues. It should be no surprise to us, then, that they were conversant in the Torah and its ramifications.

that the Torah has jurisdiction over a person as long as he lives – What does Paul mean by the term "Torah" (νόμος, *nomos*) here? (Note the former discussion on 2:12 and the use of νόμος, *nomos*, "law"). The possibilities usually suggested are:

1)   law in general, i.e., the laws which exist in the universe as God's creation
2)   Roman law, particularly those laws pertaining to domestic affairs
3)   Law of Moses (= the Torah)

It is hardly possible that Paul would introduce the Roman law at this juncture without reference to it earlier, so #2 can be immediately ruled out.[167] While some may argue that natural law prescribes monogomy and the necessity of marriage, I would argue that it does not. In fact, I would argue that marriage itself, like the Sabbath, is a gift from HaShem but not something found naturally in the created universe. But even if natural law prescribed boundaries for marriage, depraved man would neglect it and live against it without judicial consequences. But for Paul, the judicial consequences are integral to his argument here, for "jurisdiction" (κυριεύει, *kurieuei*, from the root for "lord, master") means that the Torah has judicial rights and consequences. For these reasons (and others) many take it that Paul is here, once again, referring to the Torah of Moses when he uses the term "law."

2-3 For the married woman is bound by Torah to her husband while he is living; but if her husband dies, she is released from the Torah concerning the husband. So then if, while her husband is living, she is joined to another man, she shall be called an adulteress; but if her husband dies, she is free from the Torah, so that she is not an adulteress, though she is joined to another man.

Here Paul spells out the particular *halachah* to which he refers, and from which he will make his case. The point is clear and straightfoward: a woman is bound to her husband, meaning she is not free to marry another man, so long as her husband lives. If she marries another man while her husband is living, she has committed adultery. But if the husband dies, the woman is freed from the covenant with him, and she is free to marry another man, in which case she does not commit adultery.

Now Paul's main point is that which this text illustrates, namely, that the Torah has no ability to enact its penalty upon someone who has died. The Torah can only extend penalty for transgression to those who are living.

Yet though it is not Paul's main point here, (in our ongoing inquiry into Paul's use of the term "law") we may rightly ask, "where in the Torah of Moses is it written that a woman may remarry if her husband dies?" The Torah speaks directly to the issue of adultery and fornication and prescribes penalties for these transgressions (Lev 18:20; 20:10; Dt 22:22, etc.) but does not speak specifically to the issue of a woman being free to remarry after the death of her husband. One might infer this from the Levirite laws (Dt 25:5-10) though this would apply properly only to women who had no male children by their deceased husband. In point of fact, when all is said and done, the written Torah does not directly address this issue, though Paul here seems to indicate that what he is teaching is well known in the Torah.

We come to the conclusion, then, that the Torah he is describing here, which his readers are well versed in, is the written Torah as interpreted and expanded by the oral Torah of the Sages. It was not merely the written record, but the written record as studied, expounded, understood, and applied by the Jewish community of Paul's day to which he appeals.

Indeed, when we look at the Mishnah we find the law specifically spelled out:

A WOMAN IS ACQUIRED [IN MARRIAGE] IN THREE WAYS AND ACQUIRES HER FREEDOM IN TWO . . . . SHE ACQUIRES HER FREEDOM BY DIVORCE OR BY HER HUSBAND'S DEATH. As for divorce, it is well, since it is written, then he shall write her a bill of divorcement (Dt 24:1); but whence do we know [that she is freed by] her husband's death?—It is logic: he [the husband] bound her; hence he frees her . . . thus death is compared to divorce; just as divorce completely frees [permits] her, so does death completely free her.[168]

Though the written Torah never clearly defines whether or not a woman is free to remarry after her husband's death (it only gives her right to remarry if she has been given a *get*, a writ of divorcement by her husband), the Sages made a *halachic* ruling that a woman who remarries following the death of her husband is not guilty of adultery:

> If her husband's death has effect, let her be entirely free; and if not, let her remain in her original status! Why not? It [her husband's death] withdraws her from [the penalty of] death and places her under [the interdict of] an affirmative precept [as a married woman she is forbidden to others by a negative precept under pain of death].[169]

Here, then, we have yet another example of how, in some cases, the oral interpretation of the written Torah is viewed by the Apostles as bound together to form accepted *halachah*.

But Paul's point here is neither the definition of law nor the rules of marriage but the principle of law's jurisdiction relative to a person who is alive, and who then dies. But how shall we understand Paul's example of law here? Traditionally (as one would expect) this passage has been interpreted allegorically and assigned various meanings. The majority have taken the husband to represent the Torah, and the wife to represent the one who has come to faith in Yeshua. Once the Torah has died, the wife is free to be joined to another, e.g., Yeshua. But this interpretation runs into grave difficulty when in the next verse Paul makes it clear that the believer, not the Torah, was the one who died.

Paul's words here, however, must be understood in terms of the stucture of the paragraph. A key to this structure may be found in the opening word of v. 4, ὥστε, *oste*, "Therefore" rather than οὕτως, *houtos*, "in like manner," which we would have expected had v. 4 been the parallel in the allegory. Instead, v. 1 states a principle, and vv. 2-3 elucidate that principle by way of an example. V. 4, then, is Paul's conclusion drawn from vv. 1-3. To put it simply, Paul wishes to teach that there is a well established principle to which all agree, namely, that when a person dies there is an inevitable change in status to the Torah. This is then illustrated by an example from civil law (as understood by the Sages, though based upon written Torah), namely, marriage and its enduring covenant as long as both husband and wife remain alive. The conclusion Paul reaches, then, is stated in v. 4, namely:

4 Therefore, my brethren, you also were made to die to the Torah through the body of Messiah, that you might be joined to another, to Him who was raised from the dead, that we might bear fruit for God.

The death that the believer has undergone through his union with the Messiah has severed forever his connection to the penalty of the Torah, in which the wrath of God is assured against all sinners. Like the wife who is free from the bonds of the covenant with her now deceased husband, i.e., the law which bound her from marrying another has now been loosed by his death, so the believer, through his death in the Messiah, is free from the condemnation of Torah (8:1-4, to which this whole section moves), i.e., the penalty of the Torah against sinners.

I want to emphasize that I use the word "free" here in a strictly forensic sense. The Torah demands certain things of people in certain situations. In the case selected by Paul for his illustration, the Torah restricted the married woman from marrying another while the covenant with her husband remained in force. But a marriage covenant lasts only as long as both husband and wife are alive—when one dies the covenant is dissolved and the remaining spouse is "free" to remarry, i.e., the law which governed that particular situation no longer applies.

This shows, once again, that it is not the Torah that has died or changed, but the status of those over whom the Torah shed its governing power. In fact, it is the Torah itself that describes the just basis upon which the woman can remarry.

So it is with the believer in Yeshua. Having died with Him (the *mikvah* symbolizing this), the penalty of the Torah for transgressions no longer applies, for the believer has had a change of status. Having been under the rule of the flesh, he is now under the rule of Yeshua, the former having no claim upon him, the latter standing now as his rightful King and Savior.

The purpose of this change of status is directly stated: that we might bear fruit for God. Note the parallel in Eph 2:8-10:

> 8 For by grace you have been saved through faith; and that not of yourselves, it is the gift of God; 9 not as a result of works, that no one should boast. 10 For we are His workmanship, created in Messiah Yeshua for good works, which God prepared beforehand, that we should walk in them.

Our re-creation—our death and resurrection in Messiah—was for the ultimate goal of our bearing fruit unto God. As is demonstrated by the Exodus in which Israel is redeemed from slavery so that she might worship HaShem, so the sinner is, in every way, redeemed that he or she might bear fruit, that is, be worshipers (in every sense of that word) of God. In fact, it is the bearing of fruit unto God which is the seal of one's salvation, for a faith that is genuine and thus saving will inevitably bear fruit of which God approves.

(This bearing of fruit does not imply offspring as some might think, for the same term is used in the next verse with regard to "death," and the idea of a marriage which produced death is quite foreign to the context. And anyway, the metaphor of marriage used here is only to emphasize the main point, for dying with Messiah and marrying Him as well stretches the illustration itself).

Thus, the believer has died to sin (his former owner) and has become alive to Messiah (his new owner). The metaphor of marriage within the context of *halachic* Torah fits Paul's purpose perfectly.

5 For while we were in the flesh, the sinful passions, which were aroused by the Torah, were at work in the members of our body to bear fruit for death.

Here we have the contrast clearly spelled out: the believer's former life is "in the flesh," i.e., controlled by the flesh (since he was a slave to sin). That sphere of existence ceased with one's death in the Messiah—for Paul there is no such thing as a true believer who is, at the same time, a slave to sin, a servant of the flesh.

But the next phrase of our verse is astounding: how is it that the Torah aroused the sinful passions of the flesh? First, it seems that Paul must here be addressing himself primarily to the Jewish readers of his epistle, for one would presume that many of the Gentile converts had no connection to the Torah before their belief in Yeshua as Messiah. How could the Torah arouse their sinful passions[170] when they had no connection to nor knowledge of its contents? Yet we should also remember that a great many of the Gentiles in the Roman synagogue may have been "God-fearers" and thus very familiar with the Torah. In this regard, "God-fearers" would have come to the question of Yeshua in much the same way as the Jewish members of the community.

But how does the Torah stir up the sinful passions? Calvin notes:

> The work of the law, in the absence of the Spirit, . . . is to inflame our hearts still more, so that they burst forth into such lustful desires.[171]

Cranfield adds:

> Challenged by the law which claims man for God and for his neighbor, man's self-cen-
> teredness—the sinful ego—recognizes that it is being called in question and attacked, and
> so seeks all the more furiously to defend itself.[172]

Here is the key to understanding Paul's use of this concept, that the Torah actually makes
a person sin more if the Torah is held apart from the inner work of the Spirit, namely, that the
sinner's pride swells in an attempt to prove the Torah wrong—to show that he is able of his own
strength and ability to find right standing before HaShem. The Spirit brings humility, but the Torah (apart from the Spirit) fosters an attempt on the part of the guilty sinner to manufacture his
own righteousness, and in this rising pride, the passions of sin flourish.

The life lived in the flesh, then, did indeed bear fruit—but it was fruit resulting in death.
"Death" in this sense is viewed as separation from HaShem—as the inability to fulfill one's
creative purpose, i.e., to serve HaShem. It envisions setting up one's self as god and refusing to
acknowledge the One true God of Israel. This is the death spoken of in chapter One—the inevitable result of God's judgment. This death is the result of sin—the payment for acts of rebellion
against the King of kings (cf. 3:23; 6:21).

6 But now we have been released from the (condemnation of the) **Torah, having died to that
by which we were bound, so that we serve in newness of the Spirit and not in oldness of the
letter.**

In our union with the Messiah in His death and resurrection, the Torah, which rightfully
condemned us as those deserving of death, has now no more claim upon us by way of condemnation. We know that this is how Paul intends for us to understand his words because the conclusion of this thought is found in 8:1-4 in which Paul clearly states two principles: 1) we have
been released from the condemnation of the Torah, and 2) the Torah is now able to be fulfilled
in us because we no longer walk (=live) according to the flesh but in accordance with the Spirit.
Thus, far from saying the Torah has been done away with in the life of the believer, Paul teaches
clearly that what has been done away with is the condemning power of the Torah, and as a result we are free to establish the Torah by living it out through the power of the Spirit.

The contrast in Pauline literature of "Spirit" and "letter" is worthy of our further investigation. In this metaphor we find a central Pauline tenet, namely, that apart from the work of
the indwelling Spirit there is no possibility of living according to God's Torah. A study of the
passages utilizing this metaphor will reveal that for Paul, "letter" is used of the Torah when not
accompanied by the work of the Spirit, and "Spirit" is used when the Torah is combined with
the regenerating work of the Spirit.

Besides the current text, the combination "letter/Spirit" is found in our epistle at 2:29,
and twice in 2 Corinthians (3:3, 6). In the immediate text it is clear that "letter/Spirit" is parallel
to the earlier "flesh/Spirit" (v. 5). The parallels to Gal 3 are obvious, and will be insightful for
understanding the present text.

Excursus on The Letter and Spirit in Paul[173]

Gal 3

The context of Paul's rebuke in Gal 3 is clearly set within the contrasts of Spirit and flesh:
"Having begun by the Spirit, are you now being perfected by the flesh?" Whatever Paul will
condemn in the following verses, he has here identified by the label "flesh." In Rom 8, interestingly, Paul puts Spirit and flesh as opposites, concluding that those who are in the flesh cannot
submit themselves to the Torah of God, yet those who walk according to the Spirit and not the
flesh actually fulfill the requirement of the Torah in their lives.

What is more, the context as it opens in Gal 3:1-14 seems clearly to be contrasting justification by faith with those who are teaching the necessity of "works of the Torah" (i.e., the teaching that Gentiles can gain covenant status through becoming proselytes) as the means to salvation:

> Even so Abraham believed God, and it was reckoned to him as righteousness. Therefore, be sure that it is those who are of faith who are sons of Abraham. For as many as are of the works of the Torah are under a curse; for it is written, "Cursed is everyone who does not abide by all things written in the book of the Torah, to perform them." Now that no one is justified by the Torah before God is evident; for, "The righteous man shall live by faith." However, the Torah is not of faith; on the contrary, "He who practices them shall live by them." . . . . Messiah redeemed us from the curse of the Torah, having become a curse for us— for it is written, "Cursed is everyone who hangs on a tree." . . . . in order that in Messiah Yeshua the blessing of Abraham might come to the Gentiles, so that we might receive the promise of the Spirit through faith.

Rather than seeing the Torah as no longer viable, or as having no jurisdiction, Paul plainly teaches here that the Torah is very much in force, for it still has the power to curse those who have not participated in the blessing of Abraham, a blessing of redemption received by faith. If it is clear that the Torah, as Paul speaks of it here in this passage, is in force for unbelievers by way of condemning them, then it seems equally clear that the condemning aspects of the Torah are no longer in force for those who are redeemed by the Messiah. This is Paul's main issue in this text, it seems to me, namely, that one cannot have right standing before God through adherance to the Torah. The Abrahamic covenant still stands as the model of righteousness by faith, and the Mosaic covenant which came 430 years later could not overturn or annul the previous promise (Gal 3:17). The promises which God made to Abraham and to his seed were not based upon the necessity to perform stipulations. In other words, the success of the covenant depended, not upon two parties, but upon One (meaning there was no mediator of the Abrahamic covenant in constrast to the Mosaic which required a mediator, vv. 19-20). But the issue Paul stresses here is how one obtains the inheritance (v.18). The promise of blessing was to Abraham, a promise based entirely upon the faithfulness of God and not the obedience of Abraham.

Apparently there were those who were convincing the Galatians that only Jews had a place in the world to come (this rabbinic teaching was based upon Is 60:21, cf. m.*Sanhedrin* 10: 1), leaving Gentiles only one option: to become proselytes via the rabbinic ritual. Such a teaching was entirely contrary to Paul's message of justification by faith alone apart from the works of the Torah. He therefore goes to great lengths to show that the promise made to Abraham was based upon faith alone, apart from works of the Torah, and that the Torah, given as a covenant after the Abrahamic covenant was established, could not alter the blessing promised to Abraham and his seed.

Paul therefore declares that the condemning function of the Torah is abolished for all who are in Yeshua, and shows that the Torah, declaring us guilty, drove us to the Messiah as our only hope. (Paul gives his personal experience of this in Rom 7:9-12). Now that we have believed in the Messiah, this condemning aspect of the Torah no longer has jurisdiction over us. But it does not follow from this that the whole of the Torah has been abolished, for Paul immediately writes, "Is the Torah then contrary to the promises of God? May it never be!" (v. 21) And what is Paul's argument for such a statement, that the Torah is in concert with the promises of God? "For if the Torah had been given which was able to impart life, then righteousness would indeed have been based upon Torah." In other words, Paul is talking in this passage about how one obtains right standing before God, and his conclusion is that the Torah was never given for this purpose, i.e., to make a person righteous. In fact, Paul teaches that until one has right standing before God through faith in Yeshua, the only salvific function the Torah has is a condemning one, a function which God uses in the elect to shut them up to the Messiah—to faith in Him as the only means of righteousness. Like the graduate, one who has come to faith in the Messiah no longer needs the Torah as a tutor to lead to faith, for faith has become the very essence of life in the Messiah.

This is not to interpret Paul's use of "Torah" (νόμος, nomos) in this passage as "legalism" or the "wrong use of the Torah," but to understand the God-ordained condemning aspect of the Torah upon the sinner who has not yet been redeemed through faith.

So what is Paul's conclusion in Gal 3? That in the matter of obtaining righteousness before God (as Abraham did, Gen 15:6), nothing matters but faith—"there is neither Jew nor Greek," for right standing before God comes, not by works of the Torah (i.e., through one's ethnic status), but through faith alone. What is more, one can never obtain more forensic (positional) righteousness than one has already obtained through imputation of Yeshua's righteousness. Faith in Yeshua is the manner in which the blessing of Abraham is obtained: "And if you belong to Messiah, then you are Abraham's offspring, heirs according to promise." (v. 29). For Gentiles to become proselytes (i.e., be given the status of "Jewish") gains them nothing in terms of right standing before the Almighty.

Paul consistently teaches this: "For neither is circumcision anything, nor uncircumcision, but a new creation," (Gal 6:15) and this is almost perfectly paralleled in 1 Co 7:19—"Circumcision is nothing, and uncircumcision is nothing but what matters is the keeping of the commandments of God." How does one recognize a "new creation?" It is one who walks, not according to the flesh, but according to the Spirit (Rom 8:4), And what is meant by "walking according to the flesh?" ". . . because the mind set on the flesh is hostile toward God" (and what does hostility toward God look like?) " for it does not subject itself to the Torah of God, for it is not even able to do so, and those who are in the flesh cannot please God." (Rom 8:7, 8) It seems obvious to me that in the antithesis of "flesh" and "Spirit," if the life in the flesh is characterized by an inability to submit to the Torah of God, then surely life in the Spirit is the converse, a Spirit-empowered ability and desire to submit one's life to the Torah of God. In some measure, the reformer's "third use" of the Torah was grounded upon this understanding.

Various other texts are brought in to parallel Galatians 3, and I'll comment briefly upon them. First is Rom 7:1-6. The teaching here seems straightforward: the laws pertaining to marriage remain intact as long as both partners are alive. When one spouse dies, the other is free from the legal requirements of that marriage. The obvious point is this: we died in Messiah, the Torah did not die. And what is Paul's conclusion to this illustration? (vv. 5, 6) "For while we were in the flesh [i.e., without faith in Messiah], the sinful passions, which were aroused by the Torah, were at work in the members of our body to bear fruit for death. But now we have been released from the Torah, having died to that by which we were bound (i.e., we've been released from the condemnation of the Torah), so that we serve in newness of Spirit and not in oldness of the letter." Paul goes on, then, to tell in no uncertain terms that the Torah is not at fault for the condemning function, but sin. And that the Torah is holy, righteous, and good, and that it has a spiritual nature, i.e., a nature which is actually contrary to the flesh.

Romans 6:14 makes the same point: through faith in Yeshua one is released from the condemnation of the Torah and lives under the smile of God's grace. It seems to me that to understand "under Torah" in Rom 6:14 as meaning "living in observance of the Torah" is to error in two ways. First, we must seriously consider the context. Paul is not contrasting observance to the Torah with non-observance, but being a slave to sin in contrast to being a slave of righteousness. Obedience to the Torah of God (1 Co 7:19) and slave to sin are opposite in Paul's theology. Secondly, to understand "under Torah" in Rom 6:14 to mean "living in observance of the Torah" forces one to admit that in observing the Torah there is no grace. How can this possibly fit with the righteous men and women of old, such as those innumerated in Heb 11, who clearly lived in observance of the Torah and demonstrated a true faith in God, being recipients of His grace? The only consistent interpretation of "under Torah" in Rom 6:14 is to understand this phrase to mean "under the condemnation of the Torah." (Note Cranfield's comments, *Romans*, 1.319-20).

2 Cor 3

As to 2 Co 3:4-18, the contrast Paul makes is between the letter of the Torah and the ministry of the Spirit. By "letter" Paul once again focuses upon the Torah apart from faith ("ministry of death") while by the word "Spirit" (whether of the Spirit of God or man's spirit) he means the life of faith and grace. This is consistent with the other Pauline uses of the antithesis "letter/Spirit:"

1) Rom 2:28, 29 - where apparently Paul combats those who conceive the law of circumcision (becoming a proselyte) as a means of salvation, to which he attaches the phrase "having the letter."

2) Rom 7:6 (where "letter/Spirit" parallels "flesh/Spirit." It is not sufficient to equate γράμμα, *gramma*, "letter" and νόμος, *nomos*, "law/Torah" in Rom 7:6. The context makes plain enough that the Torah is not the problem but the flesh, cf. 7:14; 8:4, 7. γράμμα, *gramma* is thus the Torah apart from Messiah and apart from the Holy Spirit.

These parallels, along with the context of 2Co 3 itself, would indicate that Paul is giving an antithesis between saved and unsaved, between those who have received life and those condemned to death. The symbol of the "veil" seems to strengthen this interpretation, for in 4:3 the veil is clearly indicative of unbelievers, of the rebellious unsaved. And 3:18 makes equally clear that the absence of the veil is indicative of faith and salvation.

But Moses, in 2 Co 3, is not a representative of the "Old Testament ministry" or of the ministry of Torah as opposed to the gospel. Moses rather represents the minister whose ministry falls upon hardened hearts and deaf ears, whose message becomes an aroma of death and is received as "letter" alone. Paul's ministry, however, has resulted in true salvation of the Corinthians, so that they are his credentials even if he does not have "papers" to satisfy his opponents (3:1-2). The difference is not the message given (for Paul affirms the fact that Moses preached the same gospel of faith which he preaches, cf. Rom 10:6-8) but the hearts upon which it falls. That the Corinthians were receptive to Paul's ministry is, in Paul's mind, confirmation that God had chosen him and graced him for the work he was doing. The message is "to one an aroma from death to death, to the other an aroma from life to life" (2 Co 2:16), yet it is still the same message. The issue Paul is dealing with, then, is the antithesis of hardened hearts as over against hearts softened by the gracious work of God through His Spirit.

I would further urge that the terms "old covenant"/"new covenant" are not religio-historical in their meaning, for if they are taken as such then the text strongly suggests that righteousness and the Spirit are "New Testament" phenomena. But for Paul, righteousness (Rom 4:2ff; 10:6ff; Gal 3:6ff) and the Spirit (Gal 4:29; 2 Cor 4:13) are by no means exclusively "New Testament" phenomena. Moreover, to understand these terms as religio-historical requires Paul to be saying that before the coming of Messiah, if one were to be saved it would have been through adherance to a legal system. But this is patently opposite of all that Paul writes of the gospel, for he affirms over and over that anyone who ever obtains right standing before God does so through faith in Messiah apart from the works of the Torah.

What then is the meaning of the veil Moses wore, and the fading glory of his face? First, the reason for the veil is not specifically given in the Torah (cp. Ex 34:29ff). Some have suggested that is was to assuage the fear of the people, but this Moses did by talking to them (Ex 34:31). In fact, the text gives no reason for Moses' veil. If the shining of Moses' face was the reflection of God's glory, then it seems the people would have been ministered to by viewing his face. But in light of the sin of the golden calf, it might well be that Moses veiled his face, not as a symbol of some feature of the religion he preached or of his ministry but rather as a symbol of the condition of the people to whom he was ministering.

How would the idea of "fading" agree with this? If the fading is taken to represent the inferiority or transitoriness of the Torah and its ministry, I feel there are serious objections: First, the Ex 34 text says nothing about the shining of Moses' face fading, though this must have occurred (Paul uses δόξα, *doksa*, "glory" no doubt because the Lxx of Ex 34 employs the verb δοξάζω, *doksazo*, in 34:29, 35). Secondly, there is a contradiction between the purpose of the veil in v. 7 as contrasted with v. 13. In v. 7 it appears the veil is to shield the sons of Israel from the unbearable rays, while in v. 13 it is to keep them from seeing that the glory was fading. Thirdly, a study of the verb καταργέω, *karargew*, translated "fade, fading" reveals that regardless of voice (active or passive) the word means "to annul," "abolish," "to render ineffective," "to bring to nothing," and in the passive "to be abolished," "to render ineffective," etc. and never "to fade." Paul uses the verb 25 of the 27 times it is found in the Apostolic Writings, and never uses it in any other context where the meaning could be "to fade."

Thus, the contrast which Paul puts forward is not between the message of the Torah and the message of the gospel, but between the ministry of Moses to a nation that was hard of heart, and to the ministry of Paul to the Corinthians which had resulted in true salvation. The glory of Moses' face was veiled to show that the glory of God was not available to the Israelites (καταργέω="rendered ineffective," "done away with") while the Corinthians see the glory of God shining in the face of the Messiah (4:6). Moses put the veil upon his face for only one reason—his face was reflecting a glory that the Israelites were not permitted to see, for the glory which shone from Moses face was none other than the glory of Messiah. Paul makes this clear, for when the veil is removed, the glory of Yeshua is seen, and this results in believing faith (3:14f). The immediate connection of the glory beheld by the Corinthian believers and the glory revealed in the taking away of "that same veil" certainly suggests that the glory is the same in both cases. But then that glory can only be "the glory of the Lord" (v. 18) which is the "glory of Messiah" (4:4). In this regard, τέλος, *telos*, of v. 13 should be understood as "goal," "purpose," "fulfilment," or "ultimate significance" and not as "end." The τέλος was Messiah, the goal, the purpose, or the significance of the glory. Thus v. 13 would be rendered, "that the sons of Israel might not gaze upon the goal or signficance of the glory which he covered up with a veil." Having repeatedly rejected God's message of grace, God withholds the revelation of the glory of His Messiah from the view of Israel. In God's mysterious providence, the national awakening to the Messiah would not occur until the eschaton (Paul explains why in Rom 9-11).

This hiding of the glory of Messiah to Israel is corroborated by the message of Isaiah (6:9ff), the parables of Yeshua (Mt 13:34f) and the teaching of Paul (Rom 11:25; 2 Co 4:3). In summary of 2Co 3, I offer the following condensed commentary:

1   Are we patting ourselves on the back, or trying to build ourselves up to look impressive to you? Do we need some kind of PR package with recommendations from the elite in order to be received by you?

2   You are yourselves our letter of commendation, a letter which all can see and read,

3   because You are an epistle manifesting the Messiah, served up by us, not with ink on parchment but written by the Spirit of the living God. You as our letter of recommendation have these words written, not on stone, but on the tablets of your hearts, by which I mean that you have the reality of these things because your life shows it. Your faith is not simply a theological theory.

4   And so we are confident in your testimony for us, a confidence which rests in Yeshua and has its focus toward HaShem.

5   Not that we are able, in and of ourselves, to accomplish any ministry, but whatever we do, we do out of the strength that comes from God

6   Who has worked within us to strengthen and empower us to be those who bring the message of the new covenant, that is, as Jeremiah said, the covenant which would be a matter of faith, being written on the heart by the work of

the Spirit. This writing is not merely letters on stone, but "letters" written by the Spirit which changes one's life. For mere words on stone can only condemn and ultimately kill, but when the word of God is combined with the work of the Spirit, then there is life.

7   If you want to speak about successful ministries, and "letters of commendation," consider the ministry of Moses as he spoke the living words of God to the people of Israel. Even though he spoke God's words, it was a ministry of death because they would not believe—the message was never written inwardly by the Spirit on the hearts of all the people (though, of course, it was written upon the hearts of individuals who made up a believing remnant). Yet even though the Spirit did not write the words of God upon the hearts of all Israel, the whole event was still marked by God's evident glory. So evident was God's glory that Moses, who spoke face to face with Him, had his own face shine with God's glory. Yet this glory was hidden from the people of Israel since it was God's purpose to withhold the revelation of it from them at that time.

8   But if the giving of the Torah was attended with God's glory even though at that time He did not ordain that His word should bring about a national revival in Israel, wouldn't you think that the ministry of His word when attended by the reviving work of the Spirit would be accompanied by even greater glory?

9   For if the ministry of Moses, who spoke the same word of God and was himself a man of God, failed to bring about a national revival, yet was attended with God's manifest glory, how much more will the message of God's word when energized by the Spirit have all the more glory.

10 In fact, the glory of the ministry of God's word in the hands of Moses pales in the light of the glory of a ministry which is attended by the Spirit's work of writing the truth on the heart.

11 For if the glory of Moses' face was hidden from Israel by God's sovereign purpose, so that Israel would not behold His glory at that time, doesn't it make sense that now when God is openly displaying His glory for all to see, this ministry will be all the more glorious?

12 It's on this account that we act as ministers of the covenant written on the heart, the "new covenant," and we are very confident when we speak and preach the word. We've come to recognize that this is the time God foretold through His prophets—the time when Israel as a whole will come to see God's glory in truth.

13 We're not like Moses who put a veil over his face so that the people of Israel could not see the glory of God shining in his face, lest they should see that the goal or end to which the glory shone was none other than the Messiah. God intended at that time that Israel as a nation would not see the glory of the Messiah, which is why Moses put a veil over his face.

14 In fact, rather than writing the Torah upon the hearts of the people as a whole, their hearts were hardened, something that can be seen as true even to this day. For when they read the Torah in the synagogue, they don't read it as that which points to Messiah, in fact they don't even see Him there. It's like the veil is still hiding His glory. Indeed, it is by the Messiah Himself that the veil is removed.

15 Yes, to this very day when the nation reads the Torah, a veil covers their heart so that the glory of the Messiah cannot penetrate.

16 But just as whenever Moses would turn to speak with HaShem, he would remove the veil from his face (Ex. 34:34), so whenever a Jewish person turns to seek HaShem in faith, and honestly desires to know the Messiah, the veil is removed as well, and the glory which was hidden is revealed.

17 So in turning to the Lord, the Jew who seeks the Messiah is likewise submitting to the Spirit and His work, a work which brings liberty to the soul, for the Torah, rather than being a means of death, becomes the way of life. And this life is true liberty.

18 So all of us who have by faith confessed Yeshua to be the Messiah, we become like Moses whose face is uncovered, shining forth the glory of the Messiah. Indeed, we can see the glory of God in each other as we live out Yeshua's life—like looking in a mirror, for we all have a single identification in Him. And as we see this glory, we, like Moses, shine all the more ourselves, being transformed from one state of glory to another. This is the work of the Spirit in our hearts as He conforms us more and more to be like Yeshua.

What, then, is the meaning of Paul's use of letter vs. Spirit? Very simply, both deal with the same message, i.e., the word of HaShem. But the letter envisions no attending work of the Spirit while the term "Spirit" focuses His work of writing God's word upon the heart. The word of God apart from the Spirit of God can only kill. But the word enlivened by the Spirit brings life.

---

7 What shall we say then? Is the Torah sin? May it never be! On the contrary, I would not have come to know sin except through the Torah; for I would not have known about coveting if the Torah had not said, "You shall not covet."

As I noted before, Paul focuses these verses (vv. 7-25) upon what might be a misconception in the minds of his readers regarding the Torah. Since he has shown that the Torah, unattended by the Spirit, kills and condemns, and that the Torah, apart from the work of the Spirit, actually makes people sin more, one might come to the false conclusion that Paul thinks the Torah is somehow evil or in some ways identified with sin itself. In the present verse Paul repudiates the idea that the Torah should itself somehow be connected with sin. In vv. 8-11 he deals further with the fact that the Torah, again apart from the Spirit's direct work in writing it upon the heart via faith, can be exploited by sin and by the realm of the sinful nature of man. It is thus through the exploitation of sin that the Torah might be viewed as less than good and holy. Next, in vv. 13-23 Paul deals with the question of whether or not the Torah, which is truly good, is to be blamed for man's death. The truth is rather that sin had made use of the good thing in order to accomplish man's death. In the final paragraph (vv. 24-25) Paul describes the real anguish of severe and relentless warfare (not despair!), the earnest longing for final deliverance, thankful confidence in God, sincere commitment to God's Torah, and an honest recognition of the fact of continuing sinfulness, all brought together to describe the conflict of the believer's life. The fact that he concludes with this shows without doubt that Paul considered this extreme struggle to be characteristic of the person who is righteous by faith.

What shall we say then? – This formula is usually used by Paul to bring forward what he suspects might be a false inference drawn by his readers from something he has said (cf. 6:1; 9:14).

Is the Torah sin? May it never be! – What would have given anyone the impression that Paul felt the Torah to be sinful or somehow partaking of sin? The previous verses (7:1-6) might be so misread (as they have been by the Christian church in many cases), as might 5:20 and 6:14.

Paul's strong assertion, "may it never be" (μὴ γένοιτο, *me genoito*) is designed to put such a notion to rest immediately.

I would not have come to know sin except through the Torah – It seems clear that mankind sins without having the Torah, so Paul can hardly be teaching here (or elsewhere) that before the Torah was given on Sinai there was no sin in the world! The emphasis must be upon the meaning of "know" (γινωσκω/οιδα), for though a person may know that he or she is sinning without having direct knowledge of the Torah, what Paul appears to emphasize here is that one cannot know sin for what it truly is, i.e., direct rebellion against his Creator, unless he sees sin as God does, and therefore as the Torah describes it. Paul's example is that of coveting (the summary commandment of the Ten). One may realize that it is wrong to covet without ever knowing the Torah. But one can hardly know that coveting is wrong because God forbids it, and that deliberately disobeying God is rebellion of the highest sort, unless one has an awareness of the Torah.

At this point I should point out the obvious difference in tense between verses 7-13 and 14-25. In 7-13 the verb tenses are past, while in 14-25 they are predominantly present tense. In both sections, Paul is speaking in the first person singular, and this also must enter into the discussion of how we are to interpret his words. Do these sections describe Paul's own experience, past and present?

As to 7-13, we may offer the following possibilities:

1) the passage is strictly autobiographical, Paul describing his own experience as illustrative of his present teaching;
2) Paul uses the first person singular to depict the experience of the typical Jewish individual or even of the Jewish people as a whole;
3) that he uses the first person singular in a generalizing way without intending a specific reference to any particular individual or group, in order to depict vividly the situation of mankind in the absence of the Torah and in its presence.

It seems to me that number 1 above is the most obvious and fits the passage best. Yet his own experience in faith is, for Paul, not unique but common, and therefore may be brought forward as illustrative of the general truth for all men, i.e., 1) that the Torah leads one to Messiah and is only rightly understood in light of Him being the goal of the Torah, 2) that apart from Messiah and the Spirit He sends, the Torah will inevitably be misunderstood and misinterpreted, and 3) that any attempt to live out the Torah apart from faith in Yeshua and the enabling of the Spirit, ends in futility, not life.

The fact that vv. 14-25 are cast in the present tense as contrasted to the past tense of the verbs in 7-13 have led to some difficulty in the history of interpretation of this passage. Since the section seems to cast too dark a picture of the "Christian life," many have posited the view that though verses 14-25 are cast in the present tense, Paul has transported himself back to his "pre-conversion" days, and is describing the struggle of a pious Jew attempting to keep the Torah without true faith in the Messiah Yeshua. Yet this theory falls into grave difficulty when Paul's own words regarding his life before Yeshua are considered:

> Phil. 3:6 as to zeal, a persecutor of the church; as to the righteousness which is in the Torah, found blameless.
> Gal. 1:14 and I was advancing in Judaism beyond many of my contemporaries among my countrymen, being more extremely zealous for my ancestral traditions.

Here Paul, reflecting upon his life before Yeshua and how he viewed himself at that time, makes the contrast obvious. While our text (Rom 7) describes a struggle with sin and righteousness, between the bent of the flesh to sin and the desire of the soul to please God, the verses quoted above picture Paul as one who felt quite secure in his "Torah observance," giving himself high marks both for intent and duty. Surely the Paul we see in Romans 7 is a man whose heart has been softened by the Spirit and who has come to accept God's view of himself, not his own.

Here, as difficult as it may be, we have Paul describing his current life of faith, a life which is filled in one measure or another with struggle, defeat, and victory.

Most object to this viewpoint for the simple reason that Paul has described the believer as liberated from the mastery of sin (6:6, 14, 17f, 22; cf. 8:2) yet here speaks as though he is still enslaved to it, not being able to do what he wills, and yielding to the draw of sin even though he wishes not to. Furthermore, the phrase πεπραμένος ὑπὸ τὴν ἁμαρτίαν, "bondage under sin" (v. 14) as descriptive of a believer seems too incredible in light of the change Paul has previously described in terms of the "new man" and the life of those who are "in the Messiah."

We may note, however, how Paul describes an unregenerate person in contrast to what he says of himself here. Here Paul says of himself that he wills the good and hates the evil (vv. 15, 16, 19, 20) and that he delights after God's Torah in his inward man (v. 25b). Paul has described the unregenerate man as a slave to sin, not able to serve God at all, and not wanting to serve Him (6:17-20). The unregenerate does not seek after God (3:11) and is unable to be subject to God's Torah (8:7). What becomes clear after these comparisons are considered is a true yet frightening fact, namely, that the born again soul has come into a cooperation with God in the battle of overcoming sin, and this battle will continue until the time when mortal puts on immortality.

Indeed, it seems clear that the reason some Christian commentators have been unable to accept Paul as speaking here of events in a believer's life is simply because they have overlooked (or refused to accept) the biblical teaching that one's sanctification (i.e., being more and more set apart unto God and from the world in one's own thoughts and actions) is a cooperative effort with God and not a monergistic work on His part. How nice it would be if after coming to faith in Yeshua, God, by a miraculous and instantaneous work of His power, made us all into people who no longer sin and who are conformed in every way to His will and word. But He does not. What is more, He requires that we strive to put to death the deeds of the flesh and to live more and more within the realm of the Spirit. While it surely is true that the strength for our striving is entirely derived from His Spirit in connection with His word and will, nonetheless the "willing" is our part, and we are able to grieve the Spirit and to neglect those "means of grace" by which HaShem intends that our sanctification should be realized.

It is equally true that within the whole scope of God's providence He has decreed that all those whom He has chosen should, in the course of time, become conformed to the image of His Messiah, Yeshua, and that they can therefore never stand the risk of becoming anything other than fully sanctified. This is clearly His doing and its inevitability rests upon His sovereign ordination. Even here, however, He has decreed that the means by which our sanctification should be accomplished is none other than the personal application of His Torah within the context of obedience. Surely He supplies all of the power (for in our flesh we are nothing) and secures the inevitability of our sanctification by His sovereign will, yet He also decrees that we, as re-created after the image of His Son (Col 3:10), must apply ourselves to growing in the grace which He offers. That our final sanctification should be a cooperative effort while at the same time giving all glory to Him seems the clear intent of His purposes.

In this light consider once again 1:5, descriptive of Paul's ministry to the Gentiles at Rome, ". . . we have received grace and apostleship to bring about the obedience of faith among all the Gentiles, for His name's sake." The "obedience of the faith" (see comment on 1:5 above) is the obedience which faith enjoins upon the redeemed sinner—an obedience which is an intregal and necessary part of his salvation. For though a sinner's transgressions are entirely atoned for by the blood of the Messiah, appropriated via the gift of faith, the holiness which he must possess if ever he should stand in God's presence (cf. Heb. 12:14) is not only forensic (i.e., decreed in the "court" of God) but also practical in the sense of one's everyday living. This practical holiness or sanctification is the result of the cooperation between the renewed child of God and the Almighty's own divine work.

It is this work of cooperation between the redeemed child of God and the indwelling Spirit that Paul describes in our passage. Here he shows us that the possession of true holiness (=conformity to the image of Yeshua) comes through a battle waged between the new man and the flesh, a battle which engages the efforts of the renewed soul strengthened by the Spirit against the remaining sin of the flesh (sin nature). As the battle is engaged, the believer comes to understand more and more how terrible his sin is, and decries it all the more. It is in this growing awareness of the hideousness of sin in light of the ever-growing understanding of God's utter holiness that the child of God struggles to become sanctified. Cranfield notes:

> With regard to the objection that it is incredible that Paul should speak of a Christian as πεπραμένος ὑπὸ τὴν ἁμαρτίαν [bound under sin], we ought to ask ourselves whether our inability to accept this expression as descriptive of a Christian is not perhaps the result of failure on our part to realize the full seriousness of the ethical demands of God's law (or of the gospel). Are we not all of us too prone still to understand them legalistically, as did the young man who could say: 'Master, all these things have I observed from my youth' (Mk 10.20)? And is it not true that the more the Christian is set free from legalistic ways of thinking about God's law and so sees more and more clearly the full splendor of the perfection towards which he is being summoned, the more conscious he becomes of his own continuing sinfulness, his stubborn all-pervasive egotism, and also of the fact that there is none among his Christian acquaintance—even among those whose real sincerity shines most brightly—of whom it would be untrue to say: 'but I can see his pride peep through each part of him'? [quote from Shakespeare, King Henry the Eighth 1.1.68f][174]

Paul now sees the Torah in a new light—in light of God's holiness as displayed in the sacrifice of Yeshua. Rather than sinful, the Torah has become an understandable revelation of God's holiness and a joy to the one who has set himself to please the Almighty. "Coveting," chosen by Paul as perhaps the summary of all the 10 Words, can now be understood as first and foremost a rebellion against the Almighty, for in coveting one has evidenced his inability to believe God for all his needs. The Torah, rather than being sinful, has actually revealed the true nature of sin as rebellion against the Most High—as the idolatry it actually is. But until one sees the Torah through the eyes of faith, and understands the Torah through the person of Yeshua, this revelation of God's holiness is veiled.

8 But sin, taking opportunity through the commandment, produced in me coveting of every kind; for apart from the Torah sin is dead.

What is meant by "opportunity" here? The Greek word is ἀφορμή (*aforme*) and means "a starting-point, the origin, occasion or pretext of a thing, the means with which one begins a thing, resources, or the capital of a banker."[175] It is used twice in this chapter (7:8, 11) as well as in 2Co 5:12; 11:12; Gal 5:13; 1Tim 5:14. Does he mean to say here that the commandment is the means by which sin took opportunity, as though without the commandment the sin of coveting never would have existed? One hardly thinks so, for surely Paul was convinced of the fact that sin existed in the world well before the giving of the Torah at Sinai. Rather, the commandment offered a "platform" for sin as an act of rebellion against the Creator, for the commandment came as the direct revelation from the Creator.

It will not suffice, either, to interpret Paul's meaning here as merely the psychological explanation that "forbidden fruit is the sweetest of all." Rather, the giving of the commandment revealed in the selfish motivations of mankind the true and more terrible sin of rebellion, for the sin was no longer nor even primarily against one's neighbor but first and foremost against God. "Against You and You alone have I sinned" was the realization of David (Ps 51:4) regarding his sin as he reckoned it in light of God's Torah.

Thus, the commandment "you shall not covet" calls upon man to find his true freedom in HaShem by submitting to His kingship, but is inevitably misinterpreted and misrepresented by depraved man as an infringement upon his own freedom and dignity, and thus can be an occasion for resentment and rebellion against his true Lord. In this way sin, now heightened and enhanced by rebellion, has found in the commandment a means for arousing all manner of covetousness.

for apart from the Torah sin is dead – even without the giving of the Torah at Sinai, sin existed in the world. But relatively speaking sin did not have the power of conviction and sentencing until the Torah prescribed the curses for rebellion against HaShem. "Dead" here may be understood as "inactive" (cf. James 2:17, 26). In the absence of the Torah, sin is relatively powerless (cf. 1Co 15:56). If we compare the Genesis narrative, the serpent was only able to attack Adam and Eve because the commandment of Gen 2:17 had been given.

We may also note an interesting shift in Paul's terminology here. Consider his use of "the commandment" — is it synonymous with "the law / Torah?" It seems apparent that when he writes ". . . sin, taking opportunity through the commandment . . .," we should understand him as saying that sin took opportunity through the Torah. Can there be any explanation for his use of "the commandment" here?

The other times where Paul uses the expression "the commandment" (singular with article) are:

Rom 7:8 ἀφορμὴν δὲ λαβοῦσα ἡ ἁμαρτία διὰ τῆς ἐντολῆς κατειργάσατο ἐν ἐμοὶ πᾶσαν ἐπιθυμίαν· χωρὶς γὰρ νόμου ἁμαρτία νεκρά. 9 ἐγὼ δὲ ἔζων χωρὶς νόμου ποτέ, ἐλθούσης δὲ τῆς ἐντολῆς ἡ ἁμαρτία ἀνέζησεν, 10 ἐγὼ δὲ ἀπέθανον καὶ εὑρέθη μοι ἡ ἐντολὴ ἡ εἰς ζωήν, αὕτη εἰς θάνατον· 11 ἡ γὰρ ἁμαρτία ἀφορμὴν λαβοῦσα διὰ τῆς ἐντολῆς ἐξηπάτησέν με καὶ δι' αὐτῆς ἀπέκτεινεν. 12 ὥστε ὁ μὲν νόμος ἅγιος καὶ ἡ ἐντολὴ ἁγία καὶ δικαία καὶ ἀγαθή. 13 Τὸ οὖν ἀγαθὸν ἐμοὶ ἐγένετο θάνατος; μὴ γένοιτο· ἀλλὰ ἡ ἁμαρτία, ἵνα φανῇς ἁμαρτία, διὰ τοῦ ἀγαθοῦ μοι κατεργαζομένη θάνατον, ἵνα γένηται καθ' ὑπερβολὴν ἁμαρτωλὸς ἡ ἁμαρτία διὰ τῆς ἐντολῆς.	Rom. 7:8 But sin, taking opportunity through <u>the commandment</u>, produced in me coveting of every kind; for apart from the Torah sin is dead. 9 And I was once alive apart from the Torah; but when <u>the commandment</u> came, sin became alive, and I died; 10 and this commandment, which was to result in life, proved to result in death for me; 11 for sin, taking opportunity through <u>the commandment</u>, deceived me, and through it killed me. 12 So then, the Torah is holy, and the commandment is holy and righteous and good. 13 Therefore did that which is good become a cause of death for me? May it never be! Rather it was sin, in order that it might be shown to be sin by effecting my death through that which is good, that through <u>the commandment</u> sin might become utterly sinful.
1Tim. 6:14 τηρῆσαί σε τὴν ἐντολὴν ἄσπιλον ἀνεπίλημπτον μέχρι τῆς ἐπιφανείας τους κυρίου ἡμῶν Ἰησοῦ Χριστοῦ,	1Tim. 6:14 that you keep <u>the commandment</u> without stain or reproach until the appearing of our Lord Yeshua Messiah.

The use of singular "commandment" with article (הַמִּצְוָה, *hamitzvah*) is common in the Tanach to denote the entire Torah or a particular body of commandments:

> Deut. 6:1 Now this is the commandment, the statutes and the judgments which the LORD your God has commanded me to teach you, that you might do them in the land where you are going over to possess it,
> Deut. 7:11 Therefore, you shall keep the commandment and the statutes and the judgments which I am commanding you today, to do them.
> Deut. 17:20 that his heart may not be lifted up above his countrymen and that he may not turn aside from the commandment, to the right or the left; in order that he and his sons

may continue long in his kingdom in the midst of Israel.
2Kings 17:37 And the statutes and the ordinances and the law and the commandment, which He wrote for you, you shall observe to do forever; and you shall not fear other gods.
2Chr. 14:4 and commanded Judah to seek the LORD God of their fathers and to observe the law and the commandment.

The same usage is standard within the Rabbinic literature (e.g., b.*Berchot* 5a), where the singular "the commandment" is used as a synonym for the Torah as a whole.

We may be confident, then, that Paul is not talking about a specific commandment here, but of the Torah in general. Of course, the term "the commandment" can refer to a specific commandment within the Torah if the context so warrants. But where there is no specific commandment in mind, the term "the commandment" should most likely be understood as a synonym for the "Law/Torah."[176]

9 And I was once alive apart from the Torah; but when the commandment came, sin became alive, and I died;

The interpretations of this verse vary widely, as one might expect. Shulam considers it possible that Paul speaks of living "apart from the Torah" as the time before his bar mitzvah![177] Others, including Cranfield[178], consider it possible that Paul is using the first person ("I") in a general sense and referring to man's situation before the giving of the Torah, including the description of Adam and Eve before Gen 1:28f.

But both of these explanations seem weak to me, for a number of reasons. First, Paul's strong teaching throughout Romans thus far is that man is born into a state of sin, having inherited a sin nature as well as condemnation from Adam (cf. 5:12). He certainly could not have thus believed that before his bar mitzvah he was alive. Secondly, as to Cranfield's suggestion, the so-called "general use of the 1st person singular" in the Greek to denote a universal application is not substantiated generally nor as something which Paul utilized. We should understand his use of the 1st person as autobiographical unless something else in the context clearly points a different direction.

Calvin, it seems to me, has understood the passage according to its historical-grammatical sense, and I quote him here at length:

> He means to intimate that there had been a time when sin was dead to him or in him. But he is not to be understood as though he had been without law at any time, but his word I was alive has a peculiar import; for it was the absence of the law that was the reason why he was alive; that is, why he being inflated with a conceit as to his own righteousness, claimed life to himself while he was yet dead. That the sentence may be more clear, state it thus, "When I was formerly without the law, I was alive." But I have said that this expression is emphatic; for by imagining himself great, he also laid claim to life. The meaning then is this, "When I sinned, having not the knowledge of the law, the sin, which I did not observe, was so laid to sleep, that it seemed to be dead; on the other hand, as I seemed not to myself to be a sinner, I was satisfied with myself, thinking that I had a life of mine own." But the death of sin is the life of man, and again the life of sin is the death of man.
>
> It may be here asked, what time was that when through his ignorance of the law, or as he himself says, through the absence of it, he confidently laid claim to life. It is indeed certain, that he had been taught the doctrine of the law from his childhood; but it was the theology of the letter, which does not humble its disciples, for as he says elsewhere, the veil interposed so that the Jews could not see the light of life in the law; so also he himself, while he had his eyes veiled, being destitute of the Spirit of Christ, was satisfied with the outward mask of righteousness. Hence he represents the law as absent, though before his eyes, while it did not really impress him with the consciousness of God's judgment. Thus

the eyes of hypocrites are covered with a veil, that they see not how much that command requires, in which we are forbidden to lust or covet.[179]

What could Paul mean by the phrase "alive without the Torah?" If we take it that the first person must be interpreted as autobiographical, then there must have been a time in the life of Paul when, for him personally, the Torah (in one sense) did not exist.

We may gain some help from the following phrase "but when the commandment came." Here we have an action metaphor, the coming of the commandment. Paul recognizes that there was a time in his life when the Torah did not function to bring about true repentance and faith in the goal of the Torah, even Yeshua. In terms of its greatest work, the Torah was, for all practical purpose, nonexistent in Paul's life before he was given faith to believe.

The coming of the commandment, then, in this context, must be the activity of the Torah whereby sin is known for what it really is, i.e., rebellion against HaShem, and more specifically, rebellion against His Messiah, Yeshua. For Paul, this function of the Torah did not come until by faith, he understood the goal to which the Torah moves, that is, Yeshua. Once having seen Yeshua through the eyes of faith, the Torah functioned as it was intended to, in the hands of the Spirit, and showed Paul's sinfulness to be what it truly was—rebellion against HaShem. What is more, by the illumination of the Spirit, the Torah left Paul without hope apart from Yeshua, for it clearly described a standard of righteousness which no one, including Paul, could hope to attain by one's own efforts. Before Paul was granted faith to believe, the Torah existed as "letter," and God did not give the Torah to be "letter." The divine purpose of the Torah (to show Messiah) was nonexistent for the unbelieving Paul, and he thus arrogantly felt he had no problem with sin or death. But when faith was granted him, he saw (for the first time) the Torah through the eyes of the Spirit, and the unveiled glories of Messiah, and this exposed his own sin as utter rebellion and made him see the death penalty under which he stood guilty.

10 and this commandment, which was to result in life, proved to result in death for me;

The covenant at Sinai, in which the Torah came to Israel as the treaty of the Great King, was made with the "redeemed" nation, for Israel had just been brought out of Egypt with the outstretched arm of HaShem. As such (and within the metaphor of salvation which these great events portray), the Torah was given as a means by which the redeemed people should find true covenant life within the realm of obedience. For those who had the faith of Abraham (and thus participated in the covenant HaShem made with him), the Torah at Sinai was received as the loving protection of the King, and as a means of expressing to Him (through obedience) one's love and loyalty.

Note these verses which indicate this function of the Torah:

Lev. 18:5 So you shall keep My statutes and My judgments, by which a man may live if he does them; I am the LORD.

Deut. 30:15 –20 See, I have set before you today life and prosperity, and death and adversity; in that I command you today to love the LORD your God, to walk in His ways and to keep His commandments and His statutes and His judgments, that you may live and multiply, and that the LORD your God may bless you in the land where you are entering to possess it. But if your heart turns away and you will not obey, but are drawn away and worship other gods and serve them, I declare to you today that you shall surely perish. You shall not prolong your days in the land where you are crossing the Jordan to enter and possess it. I call heaven and earth to witness against you today, that I have set before you life and death, the blessing and the curse. So choose life in order that you may live, you and your descendants, by loving the LORD your God, by obeying His voice, and by holding fast to Him; for this is your life and the length of your days, that you may live in the land which the LORD swore to your fathers, to Abraham, Isaac, and Jacob, to give them.

But the very fact that the Torah contains both blessings and curses indicates that its further function was to expose those among the nation who had no faith, and who would, then, attempt on their own merits to gain the life that only faith could bring. For these, rather than life, the Torah was a means of their condemnation, for in attempting to gain life from the Torah (rather than have the life they already possessed defined and directed) they only heaped up condemnation for having believed they could accomplish what only the Messiah could do. Though the unbeliever may not realize it in his unbelief, the Torah he thinks is a source of life is actually the source of condemnation and death.

While it is surely true that the Torah provides no source of life apart from faith, we should not take this to mean that the Torah has no life value for the believer. The Sages reference Prov 3:16ff as descriptive of the Torah (cf. b.*Berchot* 32b):

> 16 Long life is in her right hand;
>   In her left hand are riches and honor.
> 17 Her ways are pleasant ways
>   And all her paths are peace.
> 18 She is a tree of life to those who take hold of her,
>   And happy are all who hold her fast.

This accords with the words of Deut 30 quoted above, which considers clinging to HaShem through obedience to His word as one's "life and the length of your days." However, the source of eternal life is God Himself, and the Torah is but one means (though surely a primary one) for bringing about the life of holiness which He intends for all who are His.

11 for sin, taking opportunity through the commandment, deceived me, and through it killed me.

We may first ask how the sentence is to be structured. The NASB has included commas so as to link "through the commandment" (διὰ τῆς ἐντολῆς, *dia tes entoles*) with "taking" (λαβοῦσα, *labousa*), though another possibility exists. We could read the sentence this way: "For sin taking opportunity, through the commandment deceived me, and through it killed me." The question is, should "through the commandment" be linked to "taking opportunity" or "deceived me?" Cranfield likes the latter, though most of the modern translations (NASB, NIV, NRSV) opt for the former. Did sin find an opportunity in the commandment (=Torah) or did the commandment deceive? The NEB has combined the possibilities in an interesting way:

> because in the commandment sin found its opportunity to seduce me, and through the commandment killed me.

Sin does indeed have a partner in the flesh, for the flesh seeks independence from God, and pridefully attempts to create its own righteousness. Seeing the Torah through faithless eyes, the Torah is misunderstood and misinterpreted and appears to the unbeliever as a means by which he or she can actually acquire life through good deeds. Each attempt to stockpile good deeds in order to earn one's righteous standing before HaShem only results in piling up sin and future judgment. Deceived by the mirage before the eyes of the flesh, the Torah appears to be a well of water springing forth to life, when in fact it is, apart from Yeshua, the unchangeable and unrelenting death warrant against all unrighteousness.

This surely must be Paul's perspective, for he immediately goes on to express the glory and value of the Torah lest anyone should misunderstand his words.

12 So then, the Torah is holy, and the commandment is holy and righteous and good.

So then (ὥστε, *hoste*) — this is Paul's conclusion, and his final word on the question of v. 7, as to whether the Torah is sinful because it condemns sinners.

the Torah is holy and the commandment is holy and righteous and good. – Surely the Torah is holy (קָדוֹשׁ, *kadosh*) because it is God's Torah! (Rom 7:22, 25; 8:7; 1Co 7:19; Mt 15:3, 6; Mk 7:8ff, etc.). Since it derives from Him, it bears the unmistakable marks of its origin and authority from Him. But not only is the Torah holy as a body of revelation, each commandment—each part, is holy, righteous and good. "Righteous" means "just," and the commandments are so because they require just conduct of mankind, and being merciful and not burdensome, they bear witness of God's own justice. They are "good" because they are given by God Who is good (Ps 25:8; 34:8; 52:9; 86:5; 100:5; 106:1; 119:68) and because they are intended for man's benefit.

In light of this bold statement, how could anyone think Paul labels the Torah as bad? How could the Church begin, early on in her history, to teach that the Torah was a source of condemnation only, and that once a person is redeemed from the curse of the Torah, it serves no further function? Surely these words of Paul were overlooked, and before anyone can accuse Paul of abandoning the Torah as unworthy of the believer's attention, he must reckon with this bold statement of the Apostle. Would that preachers everywhere would boldly proclaim the message about the Torah which our Apostle here asserts.

13 Therefore did that which is good become a cause of death for me? May it never be! Rather it was sin, in order that it might be shown to be sin by effecting my death through that which is good, that through the commandment sin might become utterly sinful.

Having just stated that the Torah is "good,"[180] Paul now asks the obvious question. "Has that which is good actually caused evil?" Is the Torah a source of evil? His direct and clear answer is "may it never be" (μὴ γένοιτο, *me genoito,* one of the strongest refutational terms). The "good thing" (the Torah) is not to be blamed for my death.

Rather it was sin – The sentence seems to be incomplete, or perhaps Paul has jumped ahead assuming the reader would finish the thought. The sense is surely "Rather it was sin which caused my death." Thus, it was not the Torah's purpose to condemn, but sin made use of that which was good in order to accomplish the demise of God's creation. Yet sin will not win the day ultimately, for the Torah shows sin for what it really is—rebellion against God, and thus sheds its light upon sin in a way only God's revelation can. The very fact that sin could utilize the Torah as an ally shows the deceitfulness of sin, but does not tarnish the glory of Torah. Paul therefore affirms that when the Torah causes the sinner to sin all the more, it is because it is being misused.

But though we can see that Paul is laying the entire blame upon sin and not upon the Torah when it comes to producing death, we must also reckon with the fact that within the Divine purpose for the Torah was this function of showing sin to be utterly sinful. God, Who is the God of distinction and dividing, for He always separates between the holy and profane, so fashioned the Torah that it would likewise mark the distinction between the righteous and the unrighteous—between deeds of holiness and deeds of wickedness. So while we must affirm that the Torah was given so that God's people might live by it (Lev 18:5), we must also reckon with the fact that the Torah is a double-edged sword, protecting and guarding on the one hand, but slaying all who rise up against it on the other. While it comes to the believer as a revelation of God's holiness and thus of his standards for His children, it also displays in stark reality the inability of any mortal to keep the Torah as God intends. That the rabbinic interpretations and additions made the Torah "manageable" was, in fact, to attempt to remove this aspect from it and to fortify the pride of those who were attempting to find covenant membership through the identity which the Torah afforded. How else could the rich young ruler exclaim, "all these things I have kept from my youth?" Without the inner working of the Spirit of God, the unregenerate heart takes a view of the Torah that wrests it from its God-given purpose.

Sin, then, is seen to be more than bad behavior or unkind actions. Sin, because of the commandment, is seen to be outward rebellion against the Almighty—it is seen for what it truly is—idolatry, an attempt to replace the Almighty with one's own ideas and desires. Sin attempts to overcome the clear revelation of God, as seen in Satan's initial lie: "you surely will not die" (Gen 3:4).

Thus, the Torah, which is "good" by its very nature as God's revelation, had come to cause no small alarm in the person of Paul, for having his eyes now opened by the Spirit, he was able to see what the Torah was actually saying (that it pointed to Yeshua as the necessary atonement for sin) and what it required, and thus he saw himself as utterly without holiness. What a shock this must have been for the pious Paul who could describe himself as blameless before the Torah.[181] So shocked was he by the manner in which the Torah condemned him as utterly without righteousness, that I think it was easy for him, as new believer, to question the value of the Torah. "How could the Torah be good if for so many years it allowed him to blindly assess himself as righteous?" Yet upon further reflection and learning, Paul came to realize that it was not the deficiency of the Torah that contributed to his self-righteousness, but rather the sin of his fallen nature. The Torah itself was good and righteous, but it was weak in its inability to overcome the sin nature. Paul had come to realize that the Torah apart from the Spirit was insufficient to bring about repentance. Yet in the hands of the Spirit the Torah was the divinely ordained tool to lead sinners to Yeshua. Paul had come to realize that the "letter" was not enough. The letter must be combined with the Spirit if the Torah should be a means of leading to Yeshua. Left as the "letter" only, the Torah could fulfill only one of its divinely ascribed functions: condemnation.

14 For we know that the Torah is spiritual; but I am of flesh, sold into bondage to sin.

Paul begins a thought with "for we know"[182] when he wants to bring to light something with which he is confident his readers have already agreed, cf. 8:22; 2Co 5:1; Rom 2:2; 3:19; 8:28; 1Ti 1:8.

No one will argue with the statement that the Torah is spiritual in nature, for it surely was divine in it origins. This must be what Paul intends to convey by the term "spiritual" (πνευματικός, *pneumatikos*). Except for 1Pt 2:5 (where the word is used twice), Paul alone uses the word in the Apostolic scriptures (Rom 1:11; 15:27; 1Co 2:13, 15; 3:1; 9:11; 10:3; 12:1; 14:1, 37; 15:44, 46; Gal 6:1; Eph 1:3; 5:19; 6:12; Col 1:9; 3:16). Taken as a whole, these passages would indicate that the term, in its broadest sense, means that which is connected to the eternal as over against the temporal, that which pertains to righteousness as over against sinfulness. The "spiritual gift" (χάρισμα πνευματικὸν, *charisma pneumatikon*) which Paul desired to impart to the Romans (1:11) was a gift of teaching which would "establish" them in the truth. No doubt this sense of "spiritual" also adheres here as well. The Torah, in the hands of the Spirit, is "spiritual" because it imparts to the believer the message of HaShem Himself, and thus establishes that person in the faith that saves. The Torah, then, was for Paul the word of God which leads to salvation (cf. 10:16-17) because it is the revelation of the Messiah ("the word of Messiah").

That everyone would agree that the Torah is "spiritual" is obvious, and makes Paul's case. In listing those things by which a person may forfeit a place in the world to come, the Talmud lists the following:

AND HE WHO MAINTAINS THAT THE TORAH WAS NOT DIVINELY REVEALED.

Our Rabbis taught: Because he hath despised the word of the Lord, and hath broken his commandment, that soul shall utterly be cut off: this refers to him who maintains that the Torah is not from Heaven.[183]

The reasoning is obvious: since the Torah came directly from the hands of the Almighty, it must have a divine purpose, and that purpose must ultimately be good, since God Himself is good. But the use of the term πνευματικός, *pneumatikos*, "spiritual," must also indicate that Paul intended us to understand that the Torah, in functioning within the scope of God's salvific plan, was also to be vitally connected to the Spirit as passages like the following indicate: Mt 22: 43; Mk 12:36; Acts 1:16; 4:25; 28:25; 2Pt 1:21. Indeed, the giving of a "new heart," or a "heart of flesh" is a repeated motif in Ezekiel (11:19; 18:21; 36:26), and the new heart is that mind or soul which has been enlivened by the Spirit. Thus those who do not have the Spirit grasp only the letter, and the letter without the Spirit kills.

but I am of flesh, sold into bondage to sin. – What does it mean to be "of flesh" (ἐγὼ δὲ σάρκινός εἰμι)? The use of the pronoun with the verb is one of emphasis, "I myself am of flesh." Here Paul uses the present tense (ellipsis) for the first time in this autobiographical section. How could he describe himself as "of flesh" and "sold into bondage of sin" while at the same time reckon his position by faith in Yeshua as one of freedom, not bondage? Some, therefore, with this tension before them, resolve to interpret this passage as describing Paul's situation before faith in Yeshua, contrasted to Chapter Eight which, they say, describes his life in Yeshua.

But I have already mentioned that Paul's own description of his pre-faith life is not one of "bondage to sin." Paul, before he came to faith in Yeshua, considered his life to be one of righteousness and holy living.

The key must be in understanding "flesh," not as comprising the physical body (contra Shulam[184]), but as describing that bent toward sin which remains in the believer as long as he or she remains in this mortal life. This connection with sin is the inevitable result of being related to Adam, the one who sold himself and all of his descendants into sin. While it is surely true (and one central aspect of the gospel) that in Messiah we have been crucified and the "body of sin" is being done away with, we must reckon with the fact that still remaining within us is that inherited sinful nature, a nature we will war against until we leave this mortal life and "put on" immortality.

The phrase "sold into bondage to sin" is literally "sold under sin." The word "sold" (πεπραμένος, *pepramenos*, from πιπράσκω, *piprasko*) is in the passive, and can be demonstrated to mean "sold as a slave," thus the translations of the NASB and NIV ("sold as a slave to sin"). The point seems to be that if in Adam all died, and all received the sin nature, then until the mortality inherited from Adam is done away (i.e., when death gives way to eternal life), there remains a sense of being connected to sin which one simply cannot finally eradicate. This produces the "groaning" of which Paul speaks (8:22-23) and the longing expectation of leaving this life and enjoying the eternal freedom in the world to come. Thus, though we must war against the flesh (cf. Gal 5:17), and though we are promised ultimate victory (cf. Phil 1:6), the fact remains that in this life we must resolve within ourselves that the fight against sin will be a constant one.

Cranfield sounds this warning:

> Understood in isolation from the teaching of chapters 6 and 8 and 12ff, these words would certainly give a thoroughly wrong impression of the Christian life; but, taken closely together with it, they bring out forcefully an aspect of the Christian life which we gloss over to our undoing. When Christians fail to take account of the fact that they (and all of their fellow Christians also) are still "sold into bondage to sin," they are specially dangerous both to others and to themselves because they are self-deceived. The more seriously a Christian strives to live from grace and to submit to the discipline of the gospel, the more sensitive he becomes to the fact of his continuing sinfulness, the fact that even his very best

acts and activities are disfigured by the egotism which is still powerful within him—and no less evil because it is often more subtly disguised than formerly. At the same time it must be said with emphasis that the realistic recognition that we are still indeed "sold into bondage to sin" should be no encouragement to us to wallow complacently in our sins.[185]

15 For that which I am doing, I do not understand; for I am not practicing what I would like to do, but I am doing the very thing I hate.

Paul opens this verse with "for" (γάρ, gar) to tie it back to the previous phrase, "sold in bondage to sin." Indeed, vv. 15-23 go on to explain what Paul means by this phrase in v. 14 and how his own personal experience in faith demonstrates that what he has said is true.

There are three different verbs used in this verse for "doing": κατεργάζομαι (katergazomai), πράσσω, (prasso) and ποιῶ (poio). While κατεργάζομαι (translated "doing" in the opening clause of the verse) and ποιῶ (translated "doing" in the last clause of the verse) may be synonyms, πράσσω (translated "practicing") is never found in the Apostolic Scriptures with God or Messiah as the subject, and in every case the action described by this word is an activity that is disapproved of. Yet it seems most likely that he uses the three terms as generally synonymous, except that he may subtly be distinguishing between a description of his general struggle, and specific instances which highlight that struggle.

I do not understand – Literally the Greek has "I do not know (γινώσκω, ginosko). How is it that Paul can say he acts, not knowing what he is doing? Surely he knows full well about his actions, the proof being that he's disturbed by them. It furthermore cannot mean "I do not understand," for his words here surely describe a fairly in-depth understanding of the struggle against sin. Most likely the word "know" here means "acknowledge" (as the word is used at times in classical Greek) in the sense of "approve"—"what I am doing I do not condone," which seems to be reiterated in the final clause, "I am doing the very thing I hate."

for I am not practicing what I would like to do, but I am doing the very thing I hate – The conflict is between the new man, brought to life by the Spirit, and the remaining sin nature inherited from Adam. The renewed man concurs with the Torah (cf. v. 22), thus loving righteousness and hating evil, but the flesh strives against God and His teaching, making for the spiritual battle of sanctification.

16 But if I do the very thing I do not wish to do, I agree with the Torah, confessing that it is good.

The fact that there is a conflict within the soul of a believer, a conflict between what God teaches (the Torah) and what the sinful nature desires—the very presence of this struggle proves that the redeemed soul has a love and loyalty for God's Torah. The struggle comes because of the presence of the Spirit, for before coming to faith in Messiah, Paul had no struggle as regards the Torah! It was when his eyes were opened to see the Messiah as the goal of the Torah, and the standard by which righteousness would be measured, that he recognized his sorry state and his need for redemption. If this knowledge, then, led to the struggle against sin, and if the knowledge came by the Spirit's use of the Torah, then surely the Torah is good.

17 So now, no longer am I the one doing it, but sin which indwells me.

Paul does not make this statement as an excuse for his sin, but rather as an acknowledgment of the extent to which sin, dwelling in the believer, usurps control over his life. The hope which the believer has is that he or she has become a new creature in Yeshua, and that this "new man" (=new person) is the true stature of the believer. This centers on hope—eschatological hope of eternally becoming in fulness what God has declared me to be in this temporal life.

Since "I" am grieved by my sin, it is clear that sin is contrary to my renewed self. As such, sin in my life is not the norm but is incongruous and must eventually be eradicated.

The opening words of the verse, νυνὶ δὲ οὐκέτι (*nuni de ouketi*, "but now no longer") can be taken either logically (indicating a logical conclusion in the argument) or temporally (detailing when the action took place). The context would favor the logical use, making the opening words equivalent to: "But, this being so (that is, in the circumstances indicated by v. 16), it is then not I who is doing it, but sin which indwells me."

18 For I know that nothing good dwells in me, that is, in my flesh; for the wishing is present in me, but the doing of the good is not.

Paul is not disagreeing with the word of God when He pronounced all that He had created as "good." The fact that Paul knows nothing good dwells in his flesh is further defined by the final clause, "for the wishing is present in me, but the doing of the good is not." In other words, the "good thing" which Paul lacks in his flesh is the *ability* to obey God in doing of His will. This is not a fault of God's creative power, but is the result of the sinful nature inherited from fallen Adam. Each of us, in our fallen natures, participates in Adam's rebellion against God.

For Paul, the term "flesh" indicates that sinful bent of mankind inherited from Adam (5: 12) and which, apart from the gracious work of the Almighty in the awakening and regenerational work of the Spirit, can do nothing but please self. This, of course, is not the natural thinking of a sinner! It is bound up in the flesh to think that one is able not only to overcome evil, but also to produce righteousness. Such deception is brought to light by the regenerational (making alive) work of the Spirit, by which the sinner comes to see himself as he truly is—guilty and helpless. Paul here makes it clear that the pursuit of holiness is an effort carried out, not by the efforts of one's fallen nature, but through the strength that comes by the Holy Spirit.

So Paul adds the necessary qualification to the statement of helplessness, "that is, in my flesh." Paul as a believer in Yeshua recognized that the Spirit dwelt within him (cf. 1Co 6:19-20) and that it was through Him that the desire for holiness was present, as well as the recognition of sin as contrary to the Torah of HaShem. This is why he describes the Torah as "spiritual" (v. 14), for it is only via the Spirit that one is able to acknowledge the rightness of the Torah and, in contrast, the sinfulness of sin.

for the wishing is present in me, but the doing of the good is not – We should not understand Paul to be saying that the believer in Yeshua is unable to ever do what he intends. Rather, as Calvin has explained,

> He does not mean that he had nothing but an ineffectual desire, but his meaning is, that the work really done did not correspond to his will; for the flesh hindered him from doing perfectly what he did. So also understand what follows, The evil I desire not, that I do: for the flesh not only impedes the faithful, so that they cannot run swiftly, but it sets also before them many obstacles at which they stumble.[186]

Thus, Paul's dilemma is that though his desire is to please God fully and always, the presence of sin within him brings him short of this desired goal.

19–20 For the good that I wish, I do not do; but I practice the very evil that I do not wish. But if I am doing the very thing I do not wish, I am no longer the one doing it, but sin which dwells in me.

Here Paul reiterates what he has just taught (v. 19 being a restatement of 15b, and v. 20 a restatement of vv. 16a and 17) and then draws the logical conclusion. If I am unable to do what I actually want to do, but rather do what I honestly do not want to do, then it seems apparent that there is some other force or influence operative within me. This "other force" is the presence of indwelling sin, or the sin nature.

Once again, it is not that the believer in Yeshua is never able to do what is holy and always ends up sinning! That, obviously, cannot be Paul's point, since he has everywhere made it plain that the life of the believer is one of holiness, conforming more and more to the very image of Yeshua (cf. 6:1ff; Gal 5:17, etc.). What he therefore teaches us here is that the longing of the "new man," the regenerate soul, is to live fully and wholly unto God without any lapse of self-centeredness and sin. Yet what one finds in this pursuit of holiness is that though the old man has been crucified (6:6), there remains a sinful bent that, try as one will, cannot fully be overcome in this lifetime. Always, then, there is the necessity for continual forgiveness and cleansing from sin (cf. 1Jn 1:9). For until "this mortal puts on immortality," the sinful nature remains and causes conflict.

21 I find then the principle that evil is present in me, the one who wishes to do good.

One of the difficulties in the final verses of this chapter is Paul's use of the term "Torah" (translation of νόμος, *nomos*) and especially νόμος with the article (ὁ νόμος, *ho nomos*).

21 εὑρίσκω ἄρα τὸν νόμον, τῷ θέλοντι ἐμοὶ ποιεῖν τὸ καλόν, ὅτι ἐμοὶ τὸ κακὸν παράκειται· 22 συνήδομαι γὰρ τῷ νόμῳ τοῦ θεοῦ κατὰ τὸν ἔσω ἄνθρωπον, 23 βλέπω δὲ ἕτερον νόμον ἐν τοῖς μέλεσίν μου ἀντιστρατευόμενον τῷ νόμῳ τους νοός μου καὶ αἰχμαλωτίζοντά με ἐν τῷ νόμῳ τῆς ἁμαρτίας τῷ ὄντι ἐν τοῖς μέλεσίν μου. 24 Ταλαίπωρος ἐγὼ ἄνθρωπος· τίς με ῥύσεται ἐκ τοῦ σώματος τοῦ θανάτου τούτου; 25 χάρις δὲ τῷ θεῷ διὰ Ἰησοῦ Χριστοῦ τοῦ κυρίου ἡμῶν. Ἄρα οὖν αὐτὸς ἐγὼ τῷ μὲν νοΐ δουλεύω νόμῳ θεοῦ τῇ δὲ σαρκὶ νόμῳ ἁμαρτίας.	21 I find then the principle that evil is present in me, the one who wishes to do good. 22 For I joyfully concur with the Torah of God in the inner man, 23 but I see a different law in the members of my body, waging war against the Torah of (in) my mind, and making me a prisoner of the law of sin which is in my members. 24 Wretched man that I am! Who will set me free from the body of this death? 25 Thanks be to God through Yeshua Messiah our Lord! So then, on the one hand I myself with my mind am serving the Torah of God, but on the other, with my flesh the law of sin.

Many interpreters and commentators have simply taken the references of νόμος, *nomos*, "law," here to mean the Torah, and have suggested (in general) that the meaning of these verses is that Paul, in his attempts to keep Torah, only found himself unable and condemned.

Cranfield rightly considers such explanations as "incredible."[187] Surely Paul has introduced a second entity which he describes as νόμος, *nomos*, but which is different from the Torah, and in fact, contrary to it. This may be seen by the simple fact that he adds τοῦ θεοῦ (*tou theou* "of God") in some instances in order to differentiate it from that which he eventually describes as "another law" (ἕτερος νόμος, *heteros nomos* v. 23).

How then should we understand νόμος in our verse? Most have suggested a translation such as "principle" or "rule," but it appears more likely that Paul is referring to what he calls in v. 23 "another law." This "other law" is identified as the "law of sin" (τῷ νόμῳ τῆς ἁμαρτίας, *to nomo tes hamartias*) in v. 23. In 8:2, the word θάνατας (*thanatas*, "death") is added, "the law of sin and death." This must mean "the law in which sin always produces death."

For Paul, then, the presence of sin means the inevitable presence of death. In a spiritual sense, this means a less than full, 100% life of holiness. Yet Paul indicates to us the truth that for the believer in Yeshua, nothing less than full and complete holiness is one's desire—one's will.

Paul has proven by his own experience in faith (which is how we most likely should understand the idea of "I find") that though his heart is fully desirous of holiness unto HaShem, there is a continuing presence of indwelling sin which prevents living out completely his holy desires.

One might think, then, that there exists within the believer's life a kind of "hopelessness" to ever overcome sin and to live fully according to God's teaching of righteousness (the Torah). Yet this is where we must remember that Paul asks us to consider the life we live now in light of the eschatological hope. Now we struggle to overcome sin, and to grow steadily in holiness before God. Yet in that growth we never cease to battle with the evil that remains within us, and we sometimes fall and disobey. But there is coming a time when the groaning of this battle—the longing for holiness in full comformity to the will of HaShem—will be a reality. This is the hope we have of the world to come, when mortal puts on immortality, and when we will be like Him, for we shall see Him as He is (Rom 8:23; 1Jn 3:2). Thus, our striving is not in vain, nor is it with a sense of futility. For we prepare now in our struggle for holiness to become finally what we have already been declared to be—righteous before HaShem.

One might wonder at the need for this stuggle. If, as Paul teaches, we will one day be fully conformed to the image of Yeshua through the transformation of mortal to immortality, why strive now? Of course, Paul's answer is two-fold (at least): 1) because our struggle is the inevitable outflow of who we are. We have been made new creatures, therefore, we long to do the will of God. As such, anything in our lives that is less than, or contrary to, the Torah of HaShem, grieves us and causes us to strive against it; 2) because in our struggle holiness takes on a greater value. That for which we must strive becomes to us the treasure it truly is.

22 For I joyfully concur with the Torah of God in the inner man,

That our verse begins with the common "for" (γάρ, *gar*) reminds us that what Paul states here and in the following verse (the continuation of the sentence) is his substantiation for the statement in v. 21. He does not want his readers to think that his inability to live in full accordance with what is "good" comes from a lack of desire.

The NASB has translated the Greek word συνήδομαι, *sunedomai*, "joyfully concur." When used with the dative (as it is here) the word generally means "to rejoice with" or "rejoice in." Indeed, this is, for Paul, the normal response of any believer to God's Torah. He ". . . delights in God's law, embraces it with gladness, loves it as the revelation of God's good and merciful will."[188] Such a perspective corresponds with the words of the Psalmist:

> 19:8 The precepts of the LORD are right, rejoicing the heart; The commandment of the LORD is pure, enlightening the eyes.

> 119:14 I have rejoiced in the way of Your testimonies, As much as in all riches.
> 16 I will delight in Your statutes; I shall not forget Your word.
> 24 Your testimonies also are my delight; They are my counselors.
> 35 Make me walk in the path of Your commandments, For I delight in it.
> 47 And I shall delight in Your commandments, Which I love.
> 70 Their heart is covered with fat, But I delight in Your Torah.
> 77 May Your compassion come to me that I may live, For Your Torah is my delight.
> 92 If Your Torah had not been my delight, Then I would have perished in my affliction.

Delighting in the Torah which God has given means finding honest and personal pleasure in the doing of the *mitzvot* (commandments) themselves. Those who delight in the Torah, therefore, find satisfication in the obedience itself—the joy coming from the mere doing of the commandment, knowing that such doing is pleasing to the Lord.

The Rabbinic view of the Torah as beautiful and a delight in and of itself is often expressed. Note the following from Midrash Rabbah *Shir HaShirim* (Song of Songs):

"Thou art beautiful, my love" (Shir HaShir. 1:15). Thou art beautiful through the commandments, both positive and negative, beautiful through loving deeds, beautiful in thy house with the heave-offerings and the tithes, beautiful in the field by the commands about gleaning, the Forgotten Sheaf and the Second Tithe; beautiful in the law about mixed seeds and about fringes, and about first fruits, and the fourth year planting; beautiful in the law of circumcision, beautiful in prayer, in the reading of the Shema, in the law of the door-posts and the tefillin, in the law of the lulav and the Citron; beautiful, too, in repentance and in good works; beautiful in this world and beautiful in the world to come.[189]

Note once again that Paul includes the defining adjectival genitive τοῦ θεοῦ (*tou theou*, "of God") since he has just in the previous context spoken of a "law" which is not "of God."

The phrase "in the inner man" qualifies the "I" as subject of the sentence. We may compare Paul's similar phrases in the following texts:

2Cor. 4:16 Therefore we do not lose heart, but though our outer man is decaying, yet our inner man is being renewed day by day.
Eph. 3:16 that He would grant you, according to the riches of His glory, to be strengthened with power through His Spirit in the inner man;
Col. 3:10 and have put on the new self who is being renewed to a true knowledge according to the image of the One who created him
Eph. 4:24 and put on the new self, which in the likeness of God has been created in righteousness and holiness of the truth.

The meaning of the phrase here in our context must be similar to Paul's use of "mind" (νοῦς, *nous*) in v. 23 and v. 25 (cf. 12:2, "the renewing of the mind"). The renewed mind for Paul is that heart (place of moral and ethical decisions) which is bound on the one hand to God's Torah, and is therefore, on the other hand, open and submissive to the work of the Spirit in sanctification and spiritual growth. For Paul there had come a dynamic change within his soul–a change of what he desired—what he longed for. No longer were the visions of power, authority, prestige, and notoriety at the heart of his longings. Now he longed to do God's will—to live out the perfection of His Torah. This is the result of a true regeneration—a true rebirth or re-creation after the image of the One Who created (cf. Col 3:10).

23 but I see a different law in the members of my body, waging war against the Torah of my mind, and making me a prisoner of the law of sin which is in my members.

Paul speaks of "another law" (ἕτερον νόμον, *heteron nomon*) in contrast to the "law (Torah) of God," a law which he finds located "in the members of my body," i.e., in my being as attached to humanity—as related to and thus corrupted by the sinful nature inherited from Adam. By using the same term, "law" (νόμος, *nomos*), Paul intends for us to understand metaphorically that what resides within the fallen nature is an exercised power, authority, or control by which sin gains a foothold within and over the sinner. But the fact that Paul uses the same word is also to emphasize that such a control or exercise of authority by indwelling sin is a "hideous usurpation of the prerogative of God's law" (Cranfield, *Romans*, 1.364). What rightly belongs to God (through His creative act) has been usurped by sin, so that allegience which ought to be His and His alone has been captivated by the "sin that dwells within me." As those created in the image of God, we ought to have one King, and thus one Torah by which we live. That a "law of sin" exists within us shows full well that another ruler has attempted to usurp the place of authority over us which rightfully belongs only to HaShem.

The military language employed by Paul in this verse highlights once again that the battle in which we are engaged is far greater than our own selves—indeed, it is cosmic, for it is the battle of authority between the Almighty Himself and Satan, who would attempt to usurp His place. We may rightly presume that by "law of my mind" (τῷ νόμῳ τοῦ νοός μου) Paul means "that which my mind acknowledges" and thus to identify it with "Torah of God" or that Torah with which Paul joyfully concurs "in the inner man." When it comes to what Paul longs for in terms of life's decisions, it is in alignment with the Torah. His dilemma, of course, is that doing all that he desires is hampered by the presence and hostility of the "law of sin." Thus, the doing of righteousness constantly requires engaging in the battle for righteousness.

As such, Paul recognizes that in this mortal life he never will escape the battle for righteousness. This he characterizes as being a "prisoner," for what is a prisoner (in this metaphorical sense) but someone who is restrained from fully accomplishing his will? If Paul were fully free (in that eschatological sense of the world to come and the realm of immortality), then all that he willed (or joyfully concured with) would always flow out in his actions. On the contrary, in this fallen world, and while sin remains within the realm of mortality, there will be a constant battle for living righteously.

Paul does not shrink back from this inevitable and constant battle, but he does wish that the fight would end, for he is confident that in the end, the battle will be won, and righteousness (full conformity to the image of Yeshua) will be the possession of every believer.

24 Wretched man that I am! Who will set me free from the body of this death?

Many have come to this verse and felt compelled to adopt the view that Paul could not be uttering such words as a believer—particularly not after stating so eloquently that those who are in the Messiah have been declared righteous before HaShem, and are free from the condemnation which the Torah prescribes upon those who sin.

Yet such a view fails to grasp the full seriousness of the believers obligation to express his gratitude to God by obedience of life.

> The farther a person advances in the life of faith, and the more mature their discipleship, the clearer becomes their perception of the heights to which God calls them, and the more painfully sharp their consciousness of the distance between what they ought, and want, to be, and what they are. The assertion that this cry could only come from an unconverted heart, and that the apostle must be expressing not what he feels as he writes but the vividly remembered experience of the unconverted man, is, we believe, totally untrue. . . . the man, whose cry this is, is one who, knowing himself to be righteous by faith, desires from the depths of his being to respond to the claims which the gospel makes upon him.[190]

What is more, the term "wretched" (ταλαίπωρος, talaiporos) can indicate "distress, affliction, suffering," without in any way implying hopelessness. Indeed, the question which Paul asks "who will set me free" surely looks forward to 8:23 and the eschatological redemption not only of the individual believer but of the whole universe.

Thus, "this body of death" must once again refer (as "members" did in the previous verse) to the fallen, sinful nature which everyone related to Adam shares, and which wages war against the renewed mind—the redeemed soul characterized by Paul as "joyfully concurring with the Torah of God." In the believer, this sinful nature is doomed, for the body will die, and in the resurrection will put on newness in immortality.

> That from which the speaker longs to be delivered is the condition of life in the body as we know it under the occupation of sin which has just been described, a life which, because of sin, must succumb to death.[191]

25 Thanks be to God through Yeshua Messiah our Lord! So then, on the one hand I myself with my mind am serving the Torah of God, but on the other, with my flesh the law of sin.

The exultation in this statement is an indirect answer to the question of the previous verse. Such an expression indicates that Paul has full knowledge that God will deliver him from the sinful nature, and that though it remains to be realized in the future, by faith he is able to lay hold of it as though it were present.

Here, once again, we find a crux issue: that of sin and how it is dealt with. Paul, the Pharisee, has come, through the eyes of faith, to see the righteous requirements of the Torah as well above his present ability. Yet, through the regeneration of his soul by the Spirit, he has come to long for nothing less than this full righteousness. All his attempts at keeping *mitzvot*, as important as his obedience is, has proven to him that he cannot match the righteousness which he now knows to be required, and for which he longs. His hope rests, not merely in his growing ability to keep the Torah, but in his hope which lies in the Person and work of Messiah, through Whom he is not only growing in holiness now, but has complete assurance he will fully put off the flesh with all of its abiding corruptions, and will be fully renewed after the image of the Creator. His hope, then, is in the person of the Messiah. He finds in the Messiah not only One who would teach and explain the Torah perfectly—not only One who would capture the heart of the nations and turn them to the One and only true God, but he sees in Yeshua the only One able to finally and eternally transform his sinful nature into a completely righteous one—a nature which will in every way live out what has become his inward delight—even the righteousness prescribed in the revelation of God's own person, and revealed in the written Torah of Moses, and especially the Living Torah, Yeshua Messiah Adoneinu (Yeshua Messiah our Lord).

Chapter 8
Commentary

The obvious theme of chapter 8 is the presence and indwelling ministry of the Holy Spirit. In chapters 1 - 7, πνεῦμα, *pneuma* the Greek word which most often translates רוּחַ, *ruach,* Spirit, in the Tanach, is found only five times. In chapters 9 - 16, the same word occurs only eight times. But in chapter 8, "Spirit" shows up 21 times, and the majority of these obviously refer to the Spirit of God. Twice, the word clearly refers to something other than the Holy Spirit, and in some instances there is debate as to how the word should be understood. Nevertheless, it is clear even to the casual reader that for Paul, the life of one who is justified by faith is a life lived in and by the Spirit.

1 There is therefore now no condemnation for those who are in Messiah Yeshua.

Paul is taking his thought back to 7:1-6, not to 7:25, for 7:7-25 is a clarification of 7:1-6. Having made the clarification (lest any should think the Torah to be evil since it causes sin to have its power), Paul reiterates the general truth of 7:1-6, i.e., that since a death has occurred (the death of the believer in union with Yeshua), the condemnation of the Torah against sin is assuaged and can never again claim rightful authority over the child of God.

Paul has already shown conclusively that mankind carries the penalty of sin inherited from Adam (chapter 5), that as sinners mankind does not seek for God (3:10ff), and that in man's weakness to overcome sin, he stands condemned by the righteous Torah (5:16). This state of condemnation in which mankind exists can be overcome only through the just payment of sin by a substitute, illustrated time and time again by the sacrificial victim within the Temple, and fulfilled by the One to whom the sacrifices pointed, Yeshua our Messiah. Paul's perspective is that only the person who is in union with Yeshua, who is "in" Him, having thus undergone death and resurrection in union with Him—only this person stands as uncondemned in the eyes of Heaven.

Modern Judaisms (by this I mean those of so-called "rabbinic Judaism" following the destruction of the Temple and foundational for the growth of what today is generally referred to as "orthodox Judaism") have, on the one hand, much to say about sin, yet in another sense, consider it almost in a peripheral way.

> . . . the concept of sin in and of itself is never fully developed or clarified in Judaism. . . . concern with sin itself occupies an insignificant place in Jewish thought. . . . Sin is viewed as a correlate of mitzva; it is treated not as a separate independent entity but rather as a shadow-essence or even, at times, a reverse image of mitzva. [192]

> . . . In every case, that is to say, it [sin] is conceived as the negation of something else, and not as an independent entity in its own right. [193]

Steinsaltz goes on to show that Judaism defines sin as essentially a lack of doing *mitzvot*, which may be conceived in several ways:

1) The *mitzvot* are essentially Divine command, so that doing the *mitzvot* is an act of obedience, and thus sin would be viewed primarily as disobedience or rebellion.

2) The *mitzvot* are essentially Divine counsel, or the path best for man, and thus sin would be straying from this path or deviation from that which would be the creative order for mankind.

3) The *mitzvot* are essentially an act of rectification or completion of the world (*tikkun olam*), so that sin is when man as keeper or guardian of the world does not fulfill his creative purpose and instead blemishes reality or allows it to deteriorate.

Steinsaltz's conclusion is thus:

> Nevertheless, a deeper look will show that all these approaches [to defining the *mitzvot*] have a common denominator: they do not see evil as a concrete subject or entity existing in and of itself. Even in these descriptions that view the history of the world or the inner spiritual life of man as a battle between good and evil, evil is not grasped as an essence to be defined independently. It is but the "other side" (*sitra achra*, in the terminology of the kabbalah) of reality, which is good, and it has no existence or essential definition of its own.[194]

If, then, "sin" is defined as the neglect or distortion of the *mitzvot*, punishment for sin is viewed not as "revenge but rather as the natural consequences of distortion or error."[195] Sin may therefore be overcome through study and appreciation of the *mitzvot*, and personal commitment to their performance. In fact, "the higher mankind's level of consciousness, the less possibility there is for sin."[196]

Taking sin in this definition, the obvious conclusion is that one is able, within his own being, to overcome sin through obedience to God and the doing of the *mitzvot*. But what about atonement for sins already committed? In the ancient times the Sages taught that the bringing of the sacrifice itself was accepted by God as atonement for sins:

> The offering of sacrifices was conjoined to the duty of confession; and it was implied that the sacrificer was ready to repent, for the confession was the sign of penitence. With regard to the early Chasidim [pious men] R. Judah said: 'Seeing that the Holy One, blessed be He, does not allow an offence to be perpetrated by them, what did they do? They arose and made a free-will vow of naziriteship to the Omnipresent, so that they should be liable to bring a sin-offering to the Omnipresent.[197] R. Nathan testified that R. Ishmael had written in his account book: 'Ishmael b. Elisha tilted the lamp on the Sabbath. When the Temple will be rebuilt, he will be liable to bring a sin-offering."[198] The sacrifices only expiated iniquities between man and God, for which it was not in the power of an earthly court to impose punishment. Transgressions that were liable to punishment by a court were not atoned for by sacrifices, and only the penalty brought with it atonement for the sin. Those who were sentenced to death were told to make confession, 'For such is the way of those condemned to death to make confession, because every one that makes confession has a share in the world to come . . . and if he does not know to make confession, he is told: "Say, May my death be an atonement for all my iniquities"'.[199] Similarly, it is stated regarding the penalty of lashes: 'Lashes are precious, for they atone for sins, as it is said: 'according to [כדי] the measure of his wickedness.'[200] The Sages even said, "For all who are liable to extinction, if they have received lashes, are exempted from their penalty of extinction."[201]

As one can imagine, with this view of sin and atonement for sin, the destruction of the Temple (which caused the sacrificial system to cease) and the removal of capital punishment from the hands of the Jewish court, caused a sense of despair and the feeling that Israel had been deprived of the possibility of atonement.

> It once happened that Rabban Yochanan b. Zakkai was leaving Jerusalem and R. Joshua was walking behind him, when the latter saw the Temple in ruins. Said R. Joshua: "Woe to us that this is in ruins—the place where the sins of Israel were expiated!" Rabban Yochanan b. Zakkai replied: "My son, be not grieved, we have a means of atonement that is commensurate with it. Which is this? It is the performance of acts of lovingkindness, as it is said, 'For I desire lovingkindness and not sacrifice'" (Hos 6:6).[202]

This teaching, after the destruction of the Temple, that the doing of *mitzvot* atoned for sin was taken up by later Sages:

> R. Eliezer b. Jacob said: 'Whoever entertains a scholar in his house and lets him enjoy his possessions it is accounted to him by Scripture as if he had offered up the daily burnt-offerings.[203]

According to the normal understanding by the Sages, the atonement of sins depends on the sacrifice of the daily burnt-offerings and the Scripture 'he-lambs' of the first year (Num 28:3), which was expounded by the School of Shammai thus:

> Kevasim (he-lambs) are so called because they suppress [כובשים] the sins of Israel. The School of Hillel said: Kevasim (are so called) because they cleanse [כובסין] the sins of Israel.[204]

Indeed, it was reckoned by the Sages that the death penalty itself atoned for the sin of the guilty, and after the death penalty was removed from the hands of the Sanhedrin, natural death itself atoned for sin.[205]

Other acts of piety were added to the list of means of atonement:

> Rev Sheshet said: Sovereign of the universe, it is known to Thee that when the Temple was in existence, if a man sinned he would bring a sacrifice, of which only the fat and the blood were offered up, and he would be granted atonement. Now I have observed a fast and my own fat and blood have been diminished. May it be Thy will that my diminished fat and blood be accounted as though I had offered them up before Thee on the altar, and do Thou show me favor.[206]

All of this is a logical and reasoned conclusion if sin is defined as the absence of *mitzvot*. If, however, sin is understood to be fundamentally a rebellion and disobedience against God Who is infinitely holy, and He exacts payment from mankind which he cannot, of his own "afford," then sin surely has a condemning power, and one which man is hopeless to overcome. This primary difference between modern or so-called "rabbinic" Judaism and the teachings of Yeshua and Paul as to the definition and consequences of sin is fundamental to the correlated understanding and definition of atonement.

Paul's exclamation that those who are in Messiah Yeshua are no longer under the condemnation of sin comes forth rather flat if, in fact, no one ever need fear condemnation from sin! Furthermore, from the viewpoint of rabbinic Judaism, the need for a suffering Messiah to atone for sin becomes the invention of the Christian church who, having left her roots in the *mitzvot*, seek rather to have atonement the "easy way," by mere confession apart from careful and disciplined keeping of Torah. Unfortunately, the "dumbing down" of the modern Christian church has made them vulnerable to this line of thinking, and the occasional trickle of people back into the orthodox synagogues of our day is the result on the one hand, while the overwhelming flood of people out of the church into so-called "secularism" (better called paganism) is the more obvious consequence. After all, if "sin" is simply human weakness, then its remedy can be found in any concerted effort to "be a better person." But, of course, the Scriptures speak otherwise.

Jeremiah writes: (13:23) "Can the Ethiopian change his skin or the leopard his spots? Then you also can do good Who are accustomed to doing evil." And again the prophet affirms: (17:9) "The heart is more deceitful than all else and is desperately sick; Who can understand it?" Here we find a principle—the inability of sinners to overcome their sin nature, while at the same time overtaken by it. And Paul has already made this clear by the quoting of passages (3:10ff) from the Psalms.

There is one thing the Sages have right in their view of sin and atonement, and it is this: sin by its very nature requires payment. If they saw the doing of *mitzvot* or the bringing of sacrifice, or personal suffering (even death) as this payment, they were wrong. But they recognized that payment had to be forthcoming, for God is a God of justice and payment is required to satisfy justice.

How then, one might ask, does the Psalmist regularly ask for forgiveness on the basis of God's mercy?

> Psa. 25:7 Do not remember the sins of my youth or my transgressions; According to Your lovingkindness remember me, For Your goodness' sake, O LORD
> Psa. 25:11 For Your name's sake, O LORD, Pardon my iniquity, for it is great.
> Psa. 25:18 Look upon my affliction and my trouble, And forgive all my sins.
> Psa. 39:8 Deliver me from all my transgressions; Make me not the reproach of the foolish.
> Psa. 51:1–3 Be gracious to me, O God, according to Your lovingkindness; According to the greatness of Your compassion blot out my transgressions. Wash me thoroughly from my iniquity, And cleanse me from my sin. For I know my transgressions, And my sin is ever before me.
> Psa. 51:9 Hide Your face from my sins, And blot out all my iniquities.
> Psa. 79:9 Help us, O God of our salvation, for the glory of Your name; And deliver us, and forgive our sins, for Your name's sake.
> Psa. 85:2 You did forgive the iniquity of Your people; You did cover all their sin. Selah.
> Psa. 103:10 He has not dealt with us according to our sins, Nor rewarded us according to our iniquities.
> Psa. 103:12 As far as the east is from the west, So far has He removed our transgressions from us.

Here we have only a few of the examples which abound in the Tanach, of the penitent sinner asking for God's mercy and grace in forgiving of sins. If, in fact, the forgiveness of sins is brought about by the daily sacrifice, or (later) by the doing of the *mitzvot*, why doesn't the Psalmist simply apply himself to these means? Why plead for forgiveness of sins on the basis of God's character (faithfulness, loyalty to the covenant, etc.)? Furthermore, could God be just in forgiving of sins without exacting the penalty/payment He Himself has decreed?

> Ezek. 18:4 "Behold, all souls are Mine; the soul of the father as well as the soul of the son is Mine. The soul who sins will die.
> Ezek. 18:20–21 The person who sins will die. The son will not bear the punishment for the father's iniquity, nor will the father bear the punishment for the son's iniquity; the righteousness of the righteous will be upon himself, and the wickedness of the wicked will be upon himself. But if the wicked man turns from all his sins which he has committed and observes all My statutes and practices justice and righteousness, he shall surely live; he shall not die.

What is meant by "die" (מוֹת, *mot*) here (Ezek 18:4)? Are we to make the assumption that the person who repents and lives righteously (Ezek 18:21) will never experience physical death? If so, how are we to explain a verse like Ps 116:15, "Precious in the sight of the LORD is the death of His godly ones." No, Ezekiel is not speaking merely of physical death here, but of that eternal death to which physical death points. The one who repents, that is, seeks the forgiveness of God and the cleansing He offers, and through returning to Him receives from Him the power to live righteously—this one receives eternal life because he has been cleansed of his sin through the eternal mercies of HaShem, through the means God Himself ordained for forgiveness. Thus God's mercy is not devoid of justice! His mercy is based upon the known fact and reality of Messiah's sacrifice—His death on behalf of sinners. It is only when God's justice is satisfied that He is able to receive the repentant sinner and forgive his sins.

Here we return to one of Paul's basic tenets, namely, the example of Abraham in Gen 15:6, "And Abraham believed God and it was reckoned to him for righteousness." This statement is, interestingly, reserved by Moses for the very time and place when the promise of the "seed" is made explicit. The object of Abraham's faith was none other than the seed by Whom all the nations would be blessed. The text does not say that it was Abraham's obedience or doing of good deeds (and he did both) that was reckoned by God as righteousness, but his faith. Surely his faith was the fountain out of which flowed his obedience—but it was the satisfaction of HaShem's justice by the sacrifice of the Messiah that Abraham laid hold of by faith, and it was this that rendered him righteous before the Holy God with Whom he conversed.

Indeed, why must the Servant of HaShem suffer (Is 53) in order to justify the sinners? Why must the innocent suffer for the guilty if, in fact, the guilty are able to atone for their own transgressions through the doing of *mitzvot* and the acceptance of due punishment—even death? Why must "Messiah son of Joseph"[207] suffer though surely he is righteous?

The obvious answer, gleaned from the sacrificial system itself, is that God intends that sin be paid for through death, for sin, in any of its various forms, is a spit in the face of the God Who is eternally holy, and cannot remain unaccounted for. The innocent animal in the sacrificial ritual metaphorically takes the sin of the guilty, and carries it away (so to speak) through the expiation of sacrifice. The Giver of Life requires a life for the payment of sin in His universe. When John declared, "Behold the Lamb of God. . ." (Jn 1:29) he simply took the obvious metaphor and applied it to the obvious anti-type. The Messiah had come—the atoning Lamb of God was there.

If we, then, take sin for what it truly is—an infinite transgression against an infinitely Holy God, and see how utterly impossible it is to ever pay that infinite debt out of our own resources—then we are able to understand as Paul did that our sin leaves us in the position of condemnation. Brought before the tribunal of God's court we are pronounced "guilty"—and we're not surprised. Our sin lies before us as the obvious evidence of our rebellion against God, and the verdict is therefore anticipated: "Guilty!" "Sentenced to eternal death"!

Somewhere in those moments and days of darkness experienced by Saul of Tarsus as he was blinded by the Shekinah of God's glory, he came to realize the terrible and awful reality of his sin. All of his "righteous deeds" had amounted to nothing, and he sat, condemned before the very God he desired to serve. Deceived by the darkness of man-made religion, he had come now to understand the dire state of affairs surrounding his own soul, and one can speculate that he labored under the "death" that he was now shrouded with as the "commandment" came, and shined its light upon the darkness of his soul. Condemnation without hope of reprieve; damnation without the hope of recovery.

It was out of this experience, no doubt, that Paul sings forth his triumphant refrain: "There is therefore now no condemnation to those who are in Yeshua the Messiah!" Paul, Pharisee of Pharisees, disciple of Gamiliel, Hebrew of Hebrews, zealous for his ancestral traditions—this Paul had come to understand and agree with God's assessment of sin. He had come to appreciate firsthand that he stood as a condemned sinner before the throne room of God, and that his only hope was the mercies that HaShem might extend to him on the basis of Messiah's death and resurrection. This he had come to understand, not from some body of Scripture owned by the "Christian church" (i.e., the New Testament, which, of course, did not exist at the time of his coming to faith in Yeshua) but from the pages of his own Bible—from the Tanach. From these pages the Spirit had taken the inspired word and penetrated his mind and soul with the truth of the Good News. Emerging from his darkness, with eyes renewed to see, Paul began his life's mission of heralding forth the "no condemnation" message of the Gospel of Yeshua. This would become his theme—his hallmark, for it was for Paul the central core revelation of God's faithful, lovingkindness. The blessing promised upon the nations through the seed of Abraham was a blessing of "no condemnation." God had revealed His way of declaring sinners just, and it rested entirely upon the Messiah.

Far from a meaningless statement of systematic theology, Paul's opening jubilation of 8:1 is the core of the Gospel and central pillar of our salvation.

As stated above, the opening verse in our chapter attaches to 7:1-6, drawing the conclusion that (6:14b) those who have placed their faith in Yeshua are no longer under the condemnation of the Torah because the condemnation which they deserve has already been fully borne for them by Him.

The emphasis upon "now" (νῦν, *nun*) is either logical (i.e., within the scope of the argument Paul is able to declare the axiom) or temporal (i.e., that this statement can be categorically affirmed since Yeshua has died and risen, fulfilling completely the necessary sacrifice for the salvation of sinners.) I rather think the "now" is best understood within the scope of Paul's polemic—having explained the manner in which the Torah condemns sin, and how Yeshua stood as the substitute for sinners, he is "now" able to make the sweeping and summary statement of no condemnation.

The Textus Receptus (Authorized text which was the basis for the King James Version of 1611) has a longer reading:

> There is therefore now no condemnation to them which are in Messiah Yeshua, who walk not after the flesh, but after the Spirit.

The manuscripts which have the longer reading are ℵᶜ, Dᶜ, K, P, 33, 88, etc., itᵃʳ, syrᵇ, and some of the church fathers. Some manuscripts add "who do not walk according to the flesh," leaving off "but according to the Spirit."

Here we have an excellent example of scribal activity in attempting to "fix" what they saw as a possible error. Since 8:4 has these words and since some no doubt took Paul's bold and forthright statement as "too dangerous" to stand by itself, they added the words from v. 4 to hopefully "balance" the Apostle's message. Apparently it was felt that to simply declare one's eternal salvation to be based entirely and only on the work of Yeshua would lead to undisciplined living and the rise of sin in the confessing community. In order to guard against such a thing, the scribes simply took the words of v. 4 and copied them into v. 1 as well.

But the shorter reading is surely original, as all of the major and older manuscripts agree with the shorter reading. What are the ramifications of this textual issue?

First, it highlights once again that salvation by God's grace, obtained through the means of faith, is contrary to our natural way of thinking and seems at odds with the way things normally work. In the everyday course of life, if I make a mistake or otherwise cause harm, I'm obligated to make it right. Would it not seem logical, then, to assume that if I have sinned against God I must, in some way, make it right? Yet this is the very point that even the later scribes missed: salvation must be based upon God's grace because it is impossible any other way. Apart from God's grace all are doomed to be eternally condemned. To add the phrase "who walk not according to the flesh but according to the Spirit" is, in the scope of Paul's argument, to possibly "muddy" the waters of justification with the subsequent reality of sanctification. Surely the two are bound together, and one follows the other as day follows the sunrise. This is affirmed in vv, 2-4. But the point Paul wishes to stress in the opening verse is that our justification—our escaping condemnation is fully and in every way resting upon what He did in the Messiah, not what we do. So pervasive was the idea that sin was not something in and of itself, but that it was merely the absense of the *mitzvot*, and thus it could be overcome through their performance—so pervasive was this idea within the teachings of the Sages[208] that Paul needed to state without hint of reservation or possible misunderstanding that salvation from sins was first and forever grounded in the atoning work of the Messiah, not on the pious lives lived out by His true disciples.

2 For the Torah of the Spirit of life in Messiah Yeshua has set you free from the law of sin and of death.

Having stated clearly that the one who, like Abraham, had believed was no longer under the condemnation which the Torah prescribes as payment for sins, Paul goes on to give further substantiation why this is true: another "law," another aspect of the Torah now takes precedence. Even as the established *halachah* of marriage lawfully allows a woman to marry after the death of her husband, so the Torah provides freedom for those who have escaped condemnation through the death of Messiah. (Indeed, James considers the Torah the Royal Torah of Liberty, James 1:25; 2:12.)

The opening "For" (γάρ, *gar*) surely hearkens back to verse 1, and substantiates why there is no longer any condemnation for those who are in Yeshua the Messiah. Since verse one itself is a regathering of the thoughts initially stated in 7:1-6, we might wonder if v. 2 does not likewise pick up a theme from that section—and it does. 7:6 ends with ". . . so that we serve in newness of the Spirit and not in oldness of the letter." Coupled with this is Paul's strong assertion that the Torah is "spiritual" (7:14) and we see a consistent theme which Paul now desires to stress, namely, that when the Torah is seen through the eyes of faith, it is because the Spirit has opened the eyes and has illumined the text, and has thus opened the Torah to the believer as the pattern for life it was intended to be (cf. 7:10).

Furthermore, the phrase "law of sin and of death" must be speaking of the same thing as "the law of sin" (7:23, 25) and "another law" (7:23), that is, the existing sin nature which wars against the Spirit and the regenerated soul—against which the regenerate heart (which longs for obedience to God's Torah) must constantly be engaged in battle.

But how shall we understand the words "Torah of the Spirit of life?" First, we need to understand the basic thrust of the sentence and then ask some obvious questions. Diagramming the sentence will help us see its primary import:

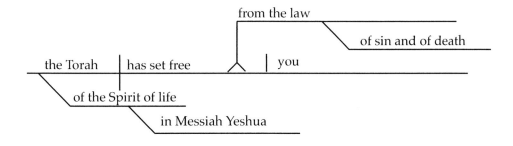

When we diagram the sentence we see the primary point: "The Torah has set you free" is the core sentence. Of course, there are decisions which must be made in the diagram:

1) does "life" attach to "Spirit" or to "Messiah Yeshua?" Is it "the Spirit" who brings "life in Messiah Yeshua" or is it "the life producing Spirit" Who works in connection with all that Messiah is and has done?

2) Does the phrase "in Messiah Yeshua" go with "the Spirit of life" or with what follows, i.e., the realm (so to speak) in which the freedom exists, i.e., ". . . has set you free in Messiah Yeshua?"

I think that in light of the preceding context, and the identification of the Torah as good, holy, and just, as well as spiritual, what Paul is saying here is that the Spirit of God, Who does the work of regeneration in the heart of the sinner, does His work always in concert with, and on the basis of, the death and resurrection of Messiah. He is therefore identified as the Spirit of life, i.e., the Spirit Who gives life. But the phrase "in the Messiah Yeshua" identifies the realm and covenant in which the Spirit works—it is always in concert with the outworking of God's plan of redemption in His Son, Yeshua.

The Torah of life, then, is the living Torah (Heb 4:12) which, energized by the Spirit in connection with the work of Yeshua, enables the word of God to become active in the life of the believer, changing him and conforming him to the image of Yeshua Himself. This work of the Spirit in connection with Torah ("so that we serve in the newness of the Spirit," cf. 7:6) in the life of the believer is evidence that a true saving work has been done, and that condemnation is no longer to be feared.

Note well the verb tense of "has set free" (ἠλευθέρωσεν, *eleutherosen* from ἐλευθερόω, *eleutheroo*)—it is aorist active indicative, indicating that as far as Paul is concerned the "setting free" has already been accomplished in the sense that it is as good as finished. The very fact that the believer has a genuine love for God and for His Torah is proof that the sinful nature is being overcome, and will, eventually, be fully subdued by the same power which saved us—the power of resurrection—victory over sin and death (cf. Phil 3:10).

One might rightfully ask how a believer could, at the same time, be both a "prisoner of the law of sin" (7:23) and "free from the law of sin and death" (8:2). The answer is twofold: First, the "prison" of which Paul speaks is the sin nature, which, apart from full glorification in immortality, will always be a foe with which to reckon. Thus, though our efforts may be valiant and our victories over sin sure, we know that the struggle will always be ongoing until "this mortal puts on immortality."

Secondly, the freedom consists in the fact that the regenerate soul actually is able to wage war against the sin nature and to gain victories over it. While dead in trespasses and sins, the unregenerate is powerless to affect honest strides toward righteousness, the death of the old man and the presence of the new man indicates a foretaste of the inevitable freedom awaiting us in the world to come. Our freedom now is to fight against the sin that remains within us. And the very fact that we both want to fight and are able to engage the battle means that eventually we will be completely free. Our freedom is thus an "already/not yet" entity, real in the present, but full in eternity.

3–4 For what the Torah could not do, weak as it was through the flesh, God did: sending His own Son in the likeness of sinful flesh and as an offering for sin, He condemned sin in the flesh, in order that the requirement of the Torah might be fulfilled in us, who do not walk according to the flesh, but according to the Spirit.

The translation of verse 3 is difficult, and the translators have inevitably needed to add words to give the sense they believe was Paul's intention. But the overarching point Paul is making is clear:

1) The Torah was weak, not in and of itself, but because it could not, on its own strength, bring to life those dead in sin. (Of course, the Torah was never intended to initiate life in the sinful soul. The Torah only benefits those who are

already endowed with life.)

2) God accomplished the work of giving life to those dead in sin, not through the Torah, but through the work of His Son, Yeshua.

3) It was thus through the life-giving Spirit, in connection with the work of Yeshua, that the sinner is made new and given both the will and ability to live life in accordance with the Torah. (This points back to 2:13, "for not the hearers of the law [are] righteous before God, but the doers of the law shall be declared righteous"). Thus, since the "requirements" of the Torah are actually accomplished in the life of the believer, this is proof of a position of righteousness before God.

For what the Torah could not do, weak as it was through the flesh – Here, as in chapter 7, Paul affirms that the fault does not lie with the Torah, but with the flesh. The Torah was never given to bring to life that which was dead. The order of the covenants (Abrahamic, followed by Mosaic) is a graphic illustration that the Torah, given on Sinai, expected the faith of Abraham to be intact.

God Himself His Son sent – I have given the literal translation to show the emphasis, first in the addition of the pronoun ἑαυτοῦ, *eautou,* and then in the word order in which "Son" (υἱος, *huios*) is thrust forward before the verb so as to receive the emphasis. The remedy for the inability of the Torah to affect life where there was death is the sending of Yeshua, something that only the Father could have accomplished. Here we have the heart of the gospel, for had there been any other way for the sinner to be brought to life, then surely God would have preferred it to the agony of His own Son's death. But if the Torah, as eternal and wonderful as it is, could not affect life in the dead soul of the sinner, then only that which was greater than the Torah could accomplish the task—even the Law-giver Himself.

Note well the emphasis upon God's activity in the salvation of sinners. Too often the emphasis is put on the work of the Son to the near exclusion of the Father. But constantly the Scriptures portray the Father Himself as intimately involved in the saving of sinners.

in the likeness of sinful flesh – In the course of the theological debate over the mystery of the incarnation, this phrase (and the similar terms in Phil 2:5ff) have given rise to a number of interpretations. The following are representative:

1) the term "likeness" is used because Paul did not wish to imply the reality of Messiah's human nature.

2) the term "likeness" is used to avoid implying that the Messiah assumed a fallen human nature.

3) the term "likeness" is used to avoid implying that Messiah ever sinned.

4) the term "likeness" means "form" rather than "likeness" in order to convey the idea that Yeshua took on the actual "form" of the sinful nature, but was always able to overcome the temptations of sin.

5) that the term "likeness" is used to convey the idea that while Yeshua took on a human nature (sinful flesh), He nonetheless remained Himself, the eternal Son of God.

Of all of these suggestions, #1 can be ruled out immediately. This was the view of the docetic doctrines, which denied that the Messiah actually came in the flesh. The fact that the text indicates that He actually took on flesh administers a death blow to this explanation. #2 has its difficulties, because though the Scriptures give full evidence that Yeshua never sinned, it does teach us that He experienced other aspects of a fallen, human nature (pain, agony, anguish, sorrow, etc). The explanation of #3 is difficult because it fails to explain how Yeshua was "like" sinful flesh. #4 has a valid approach, but the term "likeness" (ὁμοίωμα, *homoioma*) usually means just that, and not a change of "form." Perhaps #5 is thus best, since it fits with the meaning of "likeness," that is, Yeshua "assumed the self-same fallen human nature that is ours, but that in His case that fallen human nature was never the whole of Him—He never ceased to be the eternal Son of God."[209]

and as an offering for sin – The Greek phrase περὶ ἁμαρτίας, *peri hamartias*, "concerning sin" is often found in the Lxx in connection with the sin-offerings, and thus the NASB adds this idea in italics. While it is true that Yeshua is our sin-offering, the idea seems remote in Paul's mind at this point, and we are probably better to translate literally, "and concerning sin," giving the primary focus of Yeshua's mission in being sent by the Father. He came to deal with sin in His first appearing (cf. Heb 9:28) but will come a second time to reign.

He condemned sin in the flesh – "in the flesh" must refer to the flesh of Messiah, so that we are to understand that God condemned sin in the death and sacrifice of Messiah. But in what way did He "condemn" it (κατέκρινεν, *katekrinen*, aor. indic. from κατακρίνω, *katakrino*)? What did Yeshua in His death do that the Torah could not do? Did not the Torah effectively condemn sin? Surely what Paul teaches here is that the death of Yeshua condemned sin for all those for whom He died in a way that the Torah was unable to. The term "condemn" may likewise be translated "render ineffective," so that while the Torah surely points out what sin is, and gives a penalty for sin (and in that way "condemns" it), what the word here must convey is that God, in the death of Yeshua for sinners, rendered sin finally and eternally ineffective. He broke the power of sin to condemn by condemning sin itself in the infinitely worthy sacrifice of Yeshua. Thus, "in the flesh," meaning "in the flesh of Yeshua" substantiates the utter necessity of the incarnation if God were both to be Just and the Justifier of sinners.

in order that the requirement of the Torah might be fulfilled in us – Here is described the purpose of God's having condemned sin, namely, that the requirement of the Torah might be fulfilled in the lives of His people. But since God inevitably gains the purpose of His actions, we should also understand Paul's sentence here to describe the sure outcome of the condemnation of sin through the death of Messiah, namely, that the Torah would be lived out in the lives of God's people, and thus His righteous ways would be manifest. This is what we have been set free for, to manifest the righteousness of God in how we live. Even as Israel of old was liberated from the slavery of Egypt so that she might serve HaShem, so sin is condemned in the death of Yeshua for the believer that he might live righteously. But note well that for Paul, this "living righteously" is defined openhandedly as fulfilling the "requirement" of the Torah.

The word translated "requirement" is δικαίωμα (*dikaioma*) and is used 4 other times in Romans (1:32; 2:26; 5:16, 18). While it can be understood as "righteousness" (cf. the KJV), in the context it ought to be understood (as it is in 2:26) to mean "righteous requirement." Note well that it is singular, not plural, highlighting the fact that the requirements of the Torah are essentially a unity. As Cranfield notes,

> . . . the plurality of commandments being not a confused and confusing conglomeration but a recognizable and intelligible whole, the fatherly will of God for His children.[210]

Here we have a good illustration of what the word "fulfill" means in the context of the Torah. If God's purpose in condemning sin in the death of Yeshua was so that the righteous requirement of the Torah should be realized in the lives of believers, then what the word "fulfill" must mean is that He has established the means by which His Torah might be truly and sincerely obeyed—where it might actually be lived out in daily life as God intended. This is the fulfillment of Jeremiah 31:33ff and Ezekiel 36:26ff (the prophecies of the "New covenant"). Here we see the Torah written on the heart, the effect being that the Torah becomes the template upon which life is lived, and thus the righteous ways of God (for the Torah is the verbal revelation of

God's character) are known through the lives of His people.

But how do those who are "in Yeshua Messiah" fulfill the righteous requirement of the Torah when, obviously, no one is able to obey the Torah fully and continually? Once again Cranfield has said it well:

> They fulfill it in the sense that they do have a real faith in God (which is the law's basic demand), in the sense that their lives are definitely turned in the direction of obedience, that they do sincerely desire to obey and are earnestly striving to advance ever nearer to perfection. But, so long as they remain in this present life, their faith is always in some measure mixed with unbelief, their obedience is always imperfect and incomplete. And this means of course that there can never be any question of their being able to make their new obedience a claim on God. Grace was indeed given, in order that the law might be fulfilled . . . .[211]

Some have wanted to translated the phrase "in order that the requirement of the Torah might be fulfilled *among us*" (italics for emphasis), with the idea that the Torah is fulfilled in community rather than in the individual life. Surely ἐν, *en*, with the dative can have the sense of "sphere" (=among), but an attempt to make the fulfillment communal in order to avoid saying the Torah is fulfilled in the life of the individual believer is wrong-headed. "Community" is nothing more nor less than the cumulative reality of individual lives. The point which Paul wishes to make here is clear: even as the individual's sin was condemned in the death of Yeshua, so the individual believer is enabled through this condemning of sin to live in accordance with the Torah and thus to glorify God in righteous actions.

who do not walk according to the flesh, but according to the Spirit – These words can easily be misconstrued if not carefully studied. Some might, from a surface reading, understand them to mean that the Torah is fulfilled in us when we walk according to the Spirit and not according to the flesh. But the grammar is against this. Had Paul intended such a meaning, he would have used some such words as "when" or "if"—some aspect of conditionality. But of course there is no hint of this. Rather, the phrase is given to more fully define how the Torah is fulfilled in those for whom sin has been condemned. The Torah is fulfilled in the manner in which we "walk," a term obviously chosen by Paul to convey the manner in which life's choices are made—the outworking of *halachah*. We may paraphrase the sentence this way: "God's purpose in sending His Son and condemning sin was that the requirement of the Torah might be fulfilled by our walking not according to the flesh but according to the Spirit." Thus, these words serve to clarify what is meant by the word fulfill. Note well that the direction in which the Spirit leads us is the direction of Torah-submissiveness—to obedience of God's revealed will. Thus, the Torah is fulfilled in us the more we decide for the Spirit and against the flesh. What is more, this living according to the Spirit (which results in living out the requirement of the Torah) is a life of freedom and liberty, for in the hands of the Spirit, the Torah is the Royal Torah of Liberty (James 1:25; 2:12).

5 For those who are according to the flesh set their minds on the things of the flesh, but those who are according to the Spirit, the things of the Spirit.

Paul now goes on to explain in greater detail what he means by "who do not walk according to the flesh, but according to the Spirit." Though the word "For" (γάρ, *gar*) attaches primarily to verse five, we should understand verses 5-11 as a unit, and as being introduced by this opening "For," and thus as describing what Paul means by walking not according to the flesh but according to the Spirit.

Before we look closely at the various characteristics Paul is describing in these verses, we need to determine what he means by the contrary terms "flesh" and "Spirit." Some have suggested that Paul is contrasting an "obedient" believer as over against a "disobedient" one. Or, to use other language, that Paul is describing the difference between the so-called "carnal Christian" and the "Spirit-led Christian." However, a quick look at what Paul teaches in this section indicates clearly that he is contrasting believers and unbelievers—those who have the Spirit and those who do not.

walk according to the flesh	walk according to the Spirit
mind set on the things of the flesh	mind set on the things of the Spirit
mind set on the flesh is death	mind set on the Spirit is life and peace
mind … is hostile toward God	*mind … is at friendship with God*
mind … does not subject itself to God's Torah	*mind … is subjected to God's Torah*
mind … unable to submit to God's Torah	*mind … is able to submit to God's Torah*
those in the flesh cannot please God	*those in the Spirit are able to please God*

While the list of characteristics for those who walk according to the Spirit is not explicit, it would seem most likely that Paul expects us to understand that the contrast he expresses in the first two elements is a contrast he expects to be carried throughout (thus the italicized phrases). When considered in this way, it becomes clear that those who Paul characterizes as walking according to the flesh have an innate inability to obey God, and thus are characterized as those who cannot please God (Rom 3:10-18) for they, without the Spirit, have no ability to obey Him out of a heart of faith. What we have, then, is Paul's descriptive contrast of believer and unbeliever; one who is led by the Spirit, in contrast to one who lives by the flesh.

set their minds on the things of the flesh – The first issue which Paul addresses is the "mind" (φρονέω, *phroneo*, "to think"), for in his understanding the issue of the volition—the ability to make decisions pleasing to God—is the beginning point of the regenerate heart. Paul had come to recognize that before coming to faith in Yeshua, his zeal for Torah observance was tainted with self-centeredness, though at the time he was deceived into thinking that his zeal was entirely righteous. Having come "face-to-face" with the Messiah, Paul, though physically blinded, had his spiritual eyes opened to see that true righteousness comes as the fruit of faith in the Messiah. He had come to know firsthand that the desire and ability to decide for righteousness was the immediate fruit of God's work of regeneration by the Spirit.

Before coming to faith, Paul saw himself as having a mind "set on the flesh," for all of his striving in regard to the Torah produced nothing which pleased HaShem. In contrast, the self-serving observance was actually fighting against God ("Saul, why do you persecute Me?"). The flesh has no power to please God, for it has itself always in view, and makes all choices relative to itself, even those which appear to be "other-oriented."

but those who are according to the Spirit, the things of the Spirit – We must understand the words "set their mind upon" as intended to be supplied. The thinking process—where all actions (*halachah*) begin (cf. Prov. 4:23), is, for those who have the Spirit, controlled by the Spirit. That is to say, the characteristic of their lives is that they live in accordance with the Spirit and His leading—their lives take on a spiritual dimension so much so that in every realm of life He is the One who leads and from Whom guidance is sought. Thus, since the Spirit leads always in accordance with God's righteous ways, the Torah is lived out in the lives of those who, walking according to the Spirit, set their minds upon the things which the Spirit designs and desires.

This is not to say that the task of following the Spirit is an easy one! Chapter seven should not be lost sight of here—there is a struggle, a war, as it were, going on and the believer is engaged in it. But it is the desire of the believer ("I joyfully concur with the Torah of God in the inner man," 7:22) to live as God commands, and it is the work of the Spirit to lead the believer in this obedience. Waging war against the flesh, the believer is assured of victory through the indwelling Spirit.

6 For the mind set on the flesh is death, but the mind set on the Spirit is life and peace,

The first constrast between believer and unbeliever, or those who have the indwelling Spirit and those who do not, is that of the inner desire, the "thinking process" which initiates actions. Now, in this verse, Paul notes the fruit or end of this contrast: the one leads to death, the other to life and peace.

The literal translation of this verse is: "For the mind of the flesh is death, and the mind of the Spirit is life and peace." The NASB has interpreted the genitive ("of") by the words "set on." The NIV does it this way: "The mind of sinful man is death, but the mind controlled by the Spirit is life and peace." The obvious point is that the phrases "mind of the flesh" and "mind of the Spirit" describe the mind controlled or in some way persuaded by the flesh or the Spirit.

The contrast is clear in the fruit of each: the flesh yields spiritual death, and thus an inability to please HaShem. In contrast, the Spirit yields spiritual life and peace. Here, as often in the Scriptures, spiritual "death" is viewed as a separation from God, while spiritual "life" is characterized by communion with Him.

"Life and peace" may be a hendiadys (literally "one-through-two"), describing a single thought or idea by combining two terms (cf. 1Sa 25:6; Prov 3:2; Mal 2:5). If this is the case, then the idea would be "life as it should be," "life as God intends it." Note that in the Mal 2:5 text, the terms are used in a covenant setting. For "life," note Rom 7:10; 8:2, 10, 11. For "peace," note 1:7; 2:10; 5:1; 14:17; 15:13, 33.

7 because the mind set on the flesh is hostile toward God; for it does not subject itself to the Torah of God, for it is not even able to do so;

Why does the mind set on the flesh result in death? Because (διότι, *dioti*) it is hostile toward God. It is good logic that anyone who wages war against God is sure to fail! Such a battle can only result in death. Here, once again, Paul characterizes those who live according to the flesh as "enemies" of God (the word "hostile" [ἔχθρα, *echthra*] is from the root ἔχθρος, *echthros* meaning "enemy"). This metaphor of "enemy" is descriptive of the unbeliever (cf. 5:10; 11:28).

But if such is the case, why would any one be so foolhardy as to engage in such an obvious losing battle? The second clause is Paul's explanation: "for it does not subject . . . ."

> Fallen man's fierce hostility to God is the response of his egotism (which is the essence of his fallenness) to God's claim to his allegiance. Determined to assert himself, to assert his independence, to be the center of his own life, to be his own god, he cannot help but hate the real God whose very existence gives the lie to all his self-assertion. His hatred of God and his rebellion against God's claim upon him expressed in God's law are inseparable from each other. As a rebel against God he hates God, and as one who hates God he rebels against Him.[212]

Not only is the unregenerate soul unwilling to submit to God's Torah, it is also unable to submit. This statement of inability (οὐδὲ γὰρ δύναται) may sound similar to what Paul has said of himself in chapter seven (cf. 7:15ff). However, there is an important difference. In chapter seven Paul describes the battle that rages between the regenerate soul and the sinful flesh, and the lost battles of the soul to live as the heart desires. But there is no statement of inability. The reason that the flesh wins over the regenerated soul is because of weakness, not inability. God has enabled the believer, through the death of the old man and the indwelling Spirit, to grow in holiness and in righteous living. In fact, the struggle which Paul describes here is one borne out of a renewed realization of God's utter holiness, something the unregenerate mind neither knows of nor cares about.

Thus, Paul's assertion that the mind set on the flesh, that is, the unregenerate soul, cannot subject itself to God is the basic statement of inability usually called "depravity" by the theologians. The teaching that man is "depraved" or "totally depraved" means "totally unable to please God on his own." Sinful mankind simply does not have it within himself to "pull himself up by the boot straps" and find a position in which he will be viewed favorably by God. In contrast Paul simply says that the reason the unregenerate soul engages in hostility toward God in an obviously "no-win" battle is because it is unable to do anything else. Apart from the work of regeneration done by the Holy Spirit, there is no ability of the soul to submit to HaShem in truth. Indeed, submitting to HaShem involves, first and foremost, a death of the self-centered flesh. Apart from such death, the mind set upon the flesh (which takes its cue from the flesh) is simply unable to submit to God's Torah. It is evident from this that one mark of life lead by the Spirit is submission to God's Torah. Far from being abolished as that which is contrary to God's ways, Paul upholds the Torah as the very litmus test for the life lead by the Spirit!

8 and those who are in the flesh cannot please God.

This is a logical conclusion from what has just been stated. "Those in the flesh" are those who, without the Spirit, live life in accordance with the fallen nature—who have the "old man" in control of life's decisions. Such decisions will, inevitably, be contrary to the Torah of God which points to, and finds its ultimate meaning in, Yeshua.

We can see from this restatement (in personal terms) of the previous verse that from Paul's perspective the goal of the life lived in righteousness is to "please God." We know that this same language was used when the heavenly voice (בַּת קוֹל, *bat kol*) declared: "This is the Son of My love, with Him I am very pleased" (Mt 3:17; 17:5, and parallels). What is it that "pleases God?" We can see the answer in the life of our Messiah:

> Matt. 7:21 Not everyone who says to Me, 'Lord, Lord,' will enter the kingdom of heaven; but he who does the will of My Father who is in heaven.

> John 8:29 And He who sent Me is with Me; He has not left Me alone, for I always do the things that are pleasing to Him."

Here in these juxtaposed verses we see a basic principle, stated by Yeshua and repeated by Paul (cf. 2:13), that the characteristic of those who have true faith (who will commune with the Father in the world to come) are those whose lives are characterized as doing the Father's will (=what pleases Him). Yeshua Himself states that He always did the things that pleased the Father, meaning He lived a complete Torah-submissive life, because He lived, in every way, by the leading of the Spirit.

We must be careful to distinguish between several Pauline meanings attached to the phrases "in flesh" (ἐν σαρκί, *en sarki*), "in the flesh" (ἐν τῇ σαρκί, *en te sarki*) and "according to the flesh" (κατὰ σάρκα, *kata sarka*). It is clear that in some cases Paul simply uses the idea of "in the flesh" to denote "living in this world" (e.g., Gal 2:20). Other times, however, Paul uses the phrase to mean "life before faith in Messiah," and such is the case in vv. 4 and 5 of our chapter, as well as in our present verse and the next (vv. 8 and 9). Interestingly, 2Co 10:3 demonstrates these two uses:

> For though we walk in the flesh, we do not war according to the flesh…

Here, "walking in the flesh" means "living in this fallen world." But "according to the flesh" means "in one's own strength" or "apart from faith."

When, in our verse, Paul therefore makes the proclamation that "those who are in the flesh cannot please God," he means that those who are not born from above and who, therefore, are not endowed with the indwelling Spirit, and who live in their own strength and do not walk by faith—these simply cannot please God.

What exactly are we to understand by the phrase "please God?" Interestingly, the one other time where Paul uses this exact phrase is 1Thess 4:1—

> Finally then, brethren, we request and exhort you in the Lord Yeshua, that, as you received from us instruction as to how you ought to walk and please God (just as you actually do walk), that you may excel still more.

The emphasis in this text is that how one "walks" (i.e., *halachah*) determines whether or not the Lord is "pleased." The application is obvious: those who truly love God desire to walk in His ways—to do what He wants. But how do we know what He wants? How can we walk in His ways if we have no communication from Him as to how He intends us to conduct our lives while upon this earth? The point, once again, is obvious: He has communicated to us His will, for He has taught us what is right and what is wrong, and His gracious teaching is called Torah.

9 However, you are not in the flesh but in the Spirit, if indeed the Spirit of God dwells in you. But if anyone does not have the Spirit of Messiah, he does not belong to Him.

Here Paul addresses the congregation in Rome directly and affirms that (by and large) they were not in the flesh (i.e., without faith in the true Messiah and therefore unable to please God) but in the Spirit (ἐν πνεύματι, *en pneumati*) and thus able to please the Holy One. "The direction of their life is determined not by the flesh but by the Spirit of God."[213]

The phrase that now follows appears to make the opening one conditional, as though it says: "You are in the Spirit, if you have the Spirit, but some of you may not have the Spirit." But in fact this is not the intent of the grammar. The Greek conditions may be either real, in which case the clause states what is actual, or unreal, in which case the clause refers to what could be or might be actual. When the particle εἰ (*ei*, "if") is used with the indicative (as it is here), it often denotes a real condition.[214] Thus we should understand the sentence in this way: "However , you are not in the flesh but in the Spirit, for indeed the Spirit of God dwells in you."

Here, then, is the proof which Paul gives for the fact that they are not in the flesh but in the Spirit, namely, that the Spirit of God dwells within them. This proof is confirmed by the negative which follows: "But if anyone does not have the Spirit of Messiah, he does not belong to Him."

Several issues/questions follow from this assertion: 1) How did Paul know that the Spirit of God indwelt those who made up the Roman congregation? Or to put it another way, what is the evidence of the indwelling Spirit? 2) Why does Paul change to the designation "Spirit of Messiah" in the last clause of the verse? Are we to equate the Spirit of God and the Spirit of Messiah?

1) *How did Paul know that the Spirit of God indwelt those who made up the Roman congregation?*

Apparently Paul had been given reports of those who made up the congregation in Rome, that their faith was evident through their deeds, deeds which are the product of the Spirit and simply cannot be accomplished apart from His enabling. Whether these were the gifts which had been displayed in the congregation (cf. chapter 12) or simply the manner in which the congregation as a whole had conducted itself in the face of persecution for the faith, one cannot be certain. But it seems clear that Paul must affirm the presence of the Spirit in them because of their life which was consistent with the outworking of the Spirit. Here we may be reminded of what Paul indicates is the "fruit of the Spirit" (Gal 5:22-23):

> But the fruit of the Spirit is love, joy, peace, patience, kindness, goodness, faithfulness, gentleness, self-control; against such things there is no law.

The fact that Paul concludes with the notification that "against such things there is no law" relates to the metaphor of "fruit." Even as the charity of leaving the corners of the field or the gleanings of the vine could not be measured because there was no law defining its parameters (thus one was to leave as much as possible, cf. m.*Peah* 1.1f), so in the harvest of spiritual fruit one should strive for as much as possible, without thinking that some measurement could define "enough."

2) *Why does Paul change to the designation "Spirit of Messiah" in the last clause of the verse? Are we to equate the Spirit of God and the Spirit of Messiah?*

It seems evident that Paul uses both designations ("Spirit of God" and "Spirit of Messiah") to denote the Spirit, the Spirit of revelation, illumination, and regeneration, the third designation in passages such as Isaiah 48:16; Matt 28:19, etc. (It is possible that we should take the genitive "of" to be a genitive of source, i.e., the Spirit Who comes from God or the Spirit Who comes from the Messiah.) He thus is making a clear statement that one who does not have the indwelling Spirit is not to be counted as "belonging to Him," which must mean "not redeemed," "not purchased by the Father." We have here, then, a remarkable statement of Pauline theology—indeed, of Biblical theology, namely, 1) that all who are redeemed are, by the very nature of the redemption, owned by God and belong to Him (cf. 1Co 6:19), 2) that the presence of the indwelling Spirit is proof God's ownership, 3) that the Spirit is also known as the Spirit of Messiah (πνεῦμα Χριστοῦ, *pneuma Christou*) because the seal of ownership was purchased, as it were, with the blood of Messiah, 4) that therefore the work of the Spirit is in every way in concert with and on the basis of the Messiah's work of redemption, and 5) there is no middle ground in one's relationship with HaShem. Either one is indwelt by the Spirit and belongs to Him, or one is not indwelt by the Spirit and does not belong to God—no "gray area" exists.

Excursus on Whether We Should Attribute "Personhood" to the Spirit of God

The question of "personhood" constantly arises whenever the Spirit of God is spoken of in some circles. Should we approach the Spirit of God as the expression of God Himself, or is the Spirit a kind of "force" or "presence" without personal attributes? Furthermore, why does this question come up, and what do we intend to gain by answering it?

"Personhood" in the Hebrew Scriptures

Our English word "person" comes from the Latin *persona* which, at its base, means "mask," as that worn by actors in a play. Hence, the word came to mean "role," "part," "character," and "personality." In English, the word has generally come to mean "an individual person with his or her distinctions."[215]

Theologically, the term "person" has usually been defined as possessing 1) will (including the ability to make ethical choices), 2) intellect, and 3) individual subsistence (a person can be identified individually as distinct from other persons and other entities).[216] It is the common and standard procedure of the systematic theologians, upon the basis of this definition, to proceed by showing that the Scriptures surely attribute to the Spirit of God all three of these attributes.

> Acts 13:2 And while they were ministering to the Lord and fasting, the Holy Spirit said, "Set apart for Me Barnabas and Saul for the work to which I have called them."
> John 15:26 When the Helper comes, whom I will send to you from the Father, that is the Spirit of truth, who proceeds from the Father, He will bear witness of Me,
> John 16:13–14 But when He, the Spirit of truth, comes, He will guide you into all the truth; for He will not speak on His own initiative, but whatever He hears, He will speak; and He will disclose to you what is to come. He shall glorify Me; for He shall take of Mine, and shall disclose it to you.
> 1Cor. 2:10–12 For to us God revealed them through the Spirit; for the Spirit searches all things, even the depths of God. For who among men knows the thoughts of a man except the spirit of the man, which is in him? Even so the thoughts of God no one knows except the Spirit of God. Now we have received, not the spirit of the world, but the Spirit who is from God, that we might know the things freely given to us by God,

Of course, these same characteristics can be found attributed to the Spirit in the Tanach as well:

> 2Sam. 23:2 The Spirit of the LORD spoke by me, And His word was on my tongue.
> Job 33:4 The Spirit of God has made me, And the breath of the Almighty gives me life.
> Mic. 2:7 Is it being said, O house of Jacob: 'Is the Spirit of the LORD impatient? Are these His doings?' Do not My words do good To the one walking uprightly?
> Psa 104:30 You did send forth Your Spirit, they are created; And You renew the face of the ground.
> Psa. 106:33 Because they were rebellious against His Spirit, He spoke rashly with his lips.
> Psa. 143:10 Teach me to do Your will, For You are my God; Let Your good Spirit lead me on level ground.

The fact is obvious that in the Tanach as well as in the Apostolic Scriptures, the Spirit is viewed and spoken of with the same language as God. Furthermore, that which is ascribed to the Almighty (creation, sovereignty, omnipresence, righteousness, holiness) is equally ascribed to His Spirit.

1) Isa 6:9, revelation to the prophet ascribed to Adonai, cf. Acts 28:25, where it is ascribed to the Holy Spirit.
2) Jer 31:31ff is said to be the words which Adonai spoke, but in Heb 10:15 the words are attributed to the Spirit.
3) Creation is attributed to the Spirit, Jb 33:4, but is equally attributed to Elohim (Gen 1:1) as well as to the Messiah, Isa 48:12ff; Jn 1:3; Col 1:16f.

There is no doubt that the Scriptures, when taken as a whole, speak of the Spirit as though He is a person, and attribute to Him works and characteristics ascribed to Adonai in other places. It is also of interest that in the Greek Scriptures, πνεῦμα, pneuma, though usually neuter, when speaking of the Spirit of God is regularly referred to by masculine pronouns (e.g., John 16:13, 14). This fact, coupled with the fact that He leads, teaches, sanctifies, and comforts the individual believer as well as the community of the faithful, would indicate His individual personality. He equips for specific ministry and duty (as Bezelel in the construction of the Tabernacle, or Barnabas and Paul in outreach ministries) and appoints those who should lead the congregation.

Believers in Yeshua are said to be the Temple of God because the Spirit dwells within them (Eph 2:22; 1Cor 6:19). To lie to the Spirit is the same as lying to God (Acts 5:1-4).

Interestingly enough, the issue of the "personhood" and divinity of the Spirit was never an issue until the Greek fathers grappled with the composition of the godhead. The issue of the divinity of the Spirit was a major agenda item for the Council of Nicea (325 CE) as well as the Council of Constantinople (381 CE). These, along with individual fathers (such as Tertullian and Athanasius) formulated the final orthodox statement on the person and work of the Spirit, more fully defining what was already contained in the so-called "Apostolic Creed"—"I believe in (on) the Holy Spirit." This was expanded by the councils with "I believe in the Holy Spirit, the divine (τὸ κύριον, *to kurion*), the life-giver, who proceeds from the Father, who is to be worshipped and glorified with the Father and the Son, and who spoke through the prophets." Athanasius (in the Creed named after him) added that the Spirit was of the same "substance" as the Father and the Son, that He was uncreated, eternal, and omnipotent, equal in majesty and glory, and that He (the Spirit) proceeds from the Father and the Son. The Athanasian Creed became the accepted creed of the Church.

The issue of "personhood" as relates to God in general is entirely missing in the Jewish debates and dialogs. While God is surely outside of the realm of creation in terms of His eternal existence, He is, nonetheless, regularly referred to by anthropological terminology (e.g., He has hands, eyes, feet; He rejoices, grieves, sorrows; He sees, touches, feels, walks, desires, etc.). One's relationship with HaShem is couched in human terms—the same terms we use for interpersonal relationships with each other.

What is more, there is no single word in the Hebrew that captures the idea of "person." אָדָם (*adam*, "man") or נֶפֶשׁ (*nefesh*, "soul") can be used to denote an individual (but these are never applied to God) and this is as close as one can come to the idea of "person" in the Hebrew. Particularly נֶפֶשׁ emphasizes the unique qualities that give individuality and uniqueness to each person. Thus, loving God with all of one's soul (נֶפֶשׁ) means to love Him with all of one's unique gifting—the various talents and attributes which separate one person from all others.

The Hebrew mind was grounded in the natural balance of unity and diversity. The year as a unit was always made up of the *mo'edim* (festivals), yet the component parts are so bound together as to be indispensable and thus a clear unity. Indeed, the Torah is one, but its teaching many. It can be entirely contained in the first letter of Bereshit (Genesis), yet even the universe cannot contain it all. Israel is one but made up of the tribes. Indeed, all of Israel can be subsumed in the Messiah. This strong idea of corporate solidarity, in which the actions of one affects the many, no doubt gave a sense of unity in the midst of great diversity. Seeing the characteristics, even the sins of the fathers passed on to the next generation gave a clear understanding of generational solidarity within the scope of clear temporal and physical diversity. There seems to be no problem or question aroused by the enigmatic statement of Moses, "the two shall be one" (Gen 2:24). Apparently then, unlike the Greeks and Romans, the ancient Hebrew could allow a pure unity within the context of diversity without asking the questions of composition. There was no need to posit the manner in which each component part made up its unique part of the whole. Each part is the whole yet the whole consists of each part. This outlook or mindset not only allowed diversity within the sphere of absolute unity, but even required and thrived on such a perspective.

It is not, then, until the Hellenized Gentiles began to stream into the synagogues through the preaching of Yeshua by the Apostles, that the need to find an answer to the question of composition of the godhead surfaces. It is not surprising, either, to find that the Greek answer to this Greek question was cast in very Greek or Western terms. How each "part" functioned and how these "functions" overlapped or cancelled each other out became essential questions requiring precise answers. In attempting to describe the mystery of God, the Greek and Latin fathers gave formulations which, though they may describe biblical truth, are nonetheless often interpretive of it and clearly additional to it. Surely the Hebrew Scriptures describe the activity of God and His Messiah, along with the Spirit, as activities of distinct individuals Who nonetheless work in perfect and concise harmony. Such unity in the sphere of diversity was good enough for the Hebrew as he accepted the mystery of God in general. He accepted God's multiple "faces" all the while affirming His uniqueness as the only God and as the only Sovereign or King. He never considered that though Adonai is invisible, it would be impossible for Him to reveal Himself and to appear in time and space, to make known His will and to come into relationship with His chosen people. Nor did His eternal and infinite "otherness" conflict with the fact that He dwelt "in the midst of Israel" and "walked in her camp." He could appear as a man (Gen 18) but never lose His essential character as the One Who is not a man (Jb 9:32); He could seek for Adam without ever diminishing the fact that He is the All-Knowing One; He could "argue" with Abraham, or with Moses without ever giving up the clear fact that He is the One Who controls the outcome of all things.

That the Hebrew/Oriental mind could allow these kinds of categories to exist, yea, need them to exist, without attempting to explain how they could exist in the same sphere is, to the Western mind, an anomaly. But the argument against receiving the Scriptural perspective also falls prey to a Western way of thinking, for the arguments against the clear, distinctive persons of the godhead proceed from the linear logic that prohibits diversity to exist in absolute unity.

The somewhat "modern" position that the Spirit did not "indwell" believers in ancient Israel, but only believers following the "initiation of the New Covenant," is common and widely held. Generally, such a belief is based upon various passages of the Apostolic Scriptures, of which the following will serve as examples:

> John 7:39 But this He spoke of the Spirit, whom those who believed in Him were to receive; for the Spirit was not yet given, because Yeshua was not yet glorified.

> John 14:17 that is the Spirit of truth, whom the world cannot receive, because it does not behold Him or know Him, but you know Him because He abides with you, and will be in you.

> Acts 19:1–7 And it came about that while Apollos was at Corinth, Paul having passed through the upper country came to Ephesus, and found some disciples, and he said to them, "Did you receive the Holy Spirit when you believed?" And they said to him, "No, we have not even heard whether there is a Holy Spirit." And he said, "Into what then were you baptized?" And they said, "Into John's baptism." And Paul said, "John baptized with the baptism of repentance, telling the people to believe in Him who was coming after him, that is, in Yeshua." And when they heard this, they were baptized in the name of the Lord Yeshua. And when Paul had laid his hands upon them, the Holy Spirit came on them, and they began speaking with tongues and prophesying. And there were in all about twelve men.

The examples given above are often misunderstood because they appear to teach that the Spirit did not actually begin His work until the time of Yeshua. The fact that the Spirit had not yet "been given" might seem to imply that His presence had not yet been made known. Furthermore, Yeshua appears to teach His disciples that while the presence of the Spirit may have been theirs, the intimate fellowship of the indwelling Spirit was something still future for them. Finally, that the disciples of John, apparently living in the desert, had not received the Spirit when they believed (in Yeshua?), and further were not even sure about the existence of the Spirit (or so the sentence seems to imply), is often taken as proof that the indwelling work of the Spirit did not begin until the "Christian Church" was fully established.

There are, of course, obvious flaws in this kind of interpretation. First, we should understand that fundamentally what Yeshua promised in the "giving" of the Spirit (Jn 14) is not the beginning of the Spirit's work but the continuation of His work in bringing the realization of the Abrahamic promise/covenant, i.e., that all the nations of the earth would be blessed through his seed, Yeshua. That the disciples were supposed to wait in Jerusalem until the "power from on high" would come upon them (Lk 24:2) speaks to the fact that they were to receive special power/gifting to accomplish the work of worldwide evangelism, i.e., the ingathering of the nations. Surely the fact that the Spirit was "given" on Shavuot emphasized that He was empowering the believers for the specific work of harvesting the nations. That the Spirit can be "given" in a special empowering does not in any way preclude His normal (and wonderful) work of indwelling all those who "belong to God," nor that He might enable others at other times for specific works and ministries.

When John writes (John 7:39) that "the Spirit had not yet been given" (οὔπω γὰρ ἦν πνεῦμα, ὅτι Ἰησοῦς οὐδέπω ἐδοξάσθη, literally, "For [the] Spirit was not yet, because Yeshua was not yet glorified"), the language of the original (as presented by the translators who insert the word "given") would indicate that what John means is simply that the special work of the Spirit in empowering the disciples to gather the nations to faith in Yeshua had not yet been initiated because this would require the glorification of Yeshua (i.e., the return of Yeshua to the Father, implying that the work of the Spirit in empowering believers to witness worldwide is based upon the intercessory work of Messiah).

John 14:17 seems to imply that the indwelling nature of the Spirit is clearly future from the time frame of the narrative. But first, we should consider the language itself and a more careful understanding of the terms used:

Greek Text	Literal Translation
τὸ πνεῦμα τῆς ἀληθείας, ὃ ὁ κόσμος οὐ δύναται λαβεῖν, ὅτι οὐ θεωρεῖς αὐτὸ οὐδὲ γινώσκει· ὑμεῖς γινώσκετε αὐτό, ὅτι παρ' ὑμῖν μένει καὶ ἐν ὑμῖν ἔσται.	The Spirit of truth, whom the world is unable to receive, because it is neither able to comprehend (see) nor know Him. You (pl) know Him, because He remains with you (pl) and will be in (among) you (pl).

The first thing to notice is that the preposition translated "with" (παρά, *para*) carries the idea of "assisting," "alongside of" in the sense of support or help (though in terms of spacial relationship, παρά followed by the accusative indicates "alongside of"). Secondly, the 2nd person pronouns throughout the verse ("you") are plural, thus speaking in the context of the group rather than to a given individual. Thirdly, the two prepositions παρά and ἐν (*en*) are sometimes synonyms, as Col 4:16 would show:

> Col. 4:16 And when this letter is read among (παρά) you, have it also read in (ἐν) the assembly of the Laodiceans; and you, for your part read my letter that is coming from Laodicea.

Fourthly, the statement of Yeshua confirms that the Spirit was already abiding with the disciples, because the Greek word which carries the meaning "abide" is present tense, so that one might accurately translate "because He keeps on remaining with you . . . ." Finally, the preposition ἐν can just as well mean "among" or "near" (in the sense of close relationship). For example, the common "sit at the right hand" (Eph 1:20; Heb 1:3; 8:1) employs the preposition ἐν where the English has "at." We surely would not want to translate the phrase "sit in the right hand." Thus, for Yeshua to say that the Spirit would be "in you (pl)" would mostly likely speak of an abiding presence in the community of the disciples as they travelled to accomplish Yeshua's work of witnessing, beginning in Jerusalem, then going to Judea, Samaria, and to the farther reaches of the world.

We should therefore understand a text like Acts 19:1ff in the same manner, i.e., that the disciples of John had not heard of the extraordinary gifting of the Spirit enabling believers to evangelize the world, nor had they received such gifting. They may well have known that Yeshua promised such "power from on high" to His disciples, but since they were separated from Jerusalem and the work of the Spirit there, they had not participated in His special outpouring. As such, Paul lays hands upon them and they receive the Spirit, evidenced by speaking in tongues and prophecying, the two primary gifts needed for the evangelism of the pagans (ability to speak in foreign languages, and boldness to proclaim the gospel).

Thus, the work of the Spirit in ancient Israel in which He "entered in" (בוא, *bo'*, "came" Ezek 2:2; 3:24), "overpowered" (צָלַח, *tzalah,* Jud 14:6, 19; 15:14; 1Sa 10:10; 11:6), "clothed" (לָבֵשׁ, *libesh,* Jud 6:34; 1Chron 12:18; 2Chron 24:20), "filled" (מָלָא, *mala',* Ex 31:3; 35:31), and "fell upon" (נָפַל, *naphal,* Ezek 11:5) people, would continue among the disciples as they carried out Yeshua's mission to the nations.

The "newness" of the Spirit's work after the ascension of Yeshua, then, centers primarily in quantity not quality of expression. Through His empowering, everyone who was truly born from above would be a witness of Yeshua in order that the world would come to know Who He is and what He has accomplished within the scope of the Father's plan of redemption. The establishment of the "new covenant" surely involves the work of the Spirit (note Is. 44:3; Joel 2:28-29; Zech. 12:10 which promises the pouring out of the Spirit upon Israel in the last days) in an expanded and evident way. Indeed, every time the covenant was renewed in the history of Israel, the group to which it was renewed was larger than before. Since at the initiation of the covenant to Abraham the Gentiles are specifically mentioned as those who would benefit from its blessings, we should not marvel that in the unfolding of the covenant, God Himself would assure the ingathering of the nations through the infallible work of His Spirit.

This is not a new work in "kind," only new in "scope," for never before had the worldwide application of the covenant become a reality. Beginning with the outpouring of the Spirit on the Shavuot following Yeshua's death, the Spirit has empowered believers to bring in the final harvest of the nations.

---

10 And if Messiah is in you, though the body is dead because of sin, yet the spirit is alive because of righteousness.

Paul immediately "switches" to "Messiah in you" after speaking of the indwelling Spirit. Some have suggested that he did not make a difference between the Spirit and the Messiah, but the language both here and in 2Co 3:17f is against this. If the two designations are to be equated, why would Paul use the term "Spirit of Messiah" (πνεῦμα Χριστοῦ, *pneuma Christou*) in v. 9? (Note also the use of "Spirit of the Lord" [πνεῦμα κυρίου, *pneuma kuriou*] in 2Cor 3:17 as well). Rather, what we see in this type of language by the apostle Paul is the presumed unity of the godhead. Far from beginning from a debate of the essential unity of the godhead, Paul, like the other apostles, speaks as though this is a given—an accepted presupposition not needing proof. Thus, Paul can speak of the πνεῦμα θεοῦ (*pneuma theou,* "Spirit of God") and πνεῦμα Χριστοῦ (*pneuma Christou,* "Spirit of Messiah") as referring to the one Spirit, for the Father, Messiah, and Spirit are mysteriously one. I say "mysteriously one" because while the unity of the godhead is affirmed by the Scriptures, so is the individuality of each in terms of function or execution of the divine will. It is natural for the "western mind" to seek to find ways to explain this mystery rather than allowing it to remain as a necessarily unexplained reality of the eternal Almighty. Paul, of course, sees no need for such an explanation.

We must confess, then, that Messiah is with us and in us and that the "manner of Messiah's dwelling in us"[217] is via the Spirit—He, i.e., the Spirit, again mysteriously, is the executor, if you will, of the presence of the Messiah in us.

A *crux interpretum* for this verse is the understanding of πνεῦμα, *pneuma*, "spirit"—should we understand Paul to be speaking of the immaterial part of man, i.e., his spirit, or of the Spirit of God? The key to this question is the phrase πνεῦμα ζωή, *pneuma zoe*, "Spirit is life" (not, as the NASB and NIV, "spirit is alive" but as the KJV "Spirit is life") which is paralleled in 1Co 15:45:

> So also it is written, "The first man, Adam, became a living soul." The last Adam became a life-giving spirit.

Since Paul's primary subject in vv. 1-11 is the Holy Spirit, it seems most warranted to understand the word in our verse as also referring to the Spirit of God. What is more, v. 11 makes it clear that this is Paul's intention here. Thus, we are now in a position to understand the contrasting aspects of the verse:

"And if the Messiah is in you,

on the one hand the body is (destined to bring) death because of sin	but on the other hand the Spirit (is destined to bring) life because of justification (being declared righteous)

Since as humans we are connected to Adam and thus the sin of our race, we are destined to die: "it is appointed unto man to die once and afterward comes the judgment" (Heb 9:27). This is the inevitable result of sin and the carrying out of the punishment promised to Adam.

On the other side of the parallel, however, is the glorious reality of our justification (declared to be righteous). And since the indwelling Spirit is the fruit of Messiah's work on our behalf (cf. 5:5, cp. Jn 14:16ff), it is His presence in our lives that assures us of our justification and therefore of our eternal life, i.e., that the death of the body is not the end but the beginning of life with God. Thus, in the very next verse the Spirit is spoken of in His resurrecting ability.

What Paul is therefore contrasting is the inevitable fruit of the sinful nature of man, i.e., death, and of the Spirit's purifying presence upon those who have been declared righteous, which brings life. The wages of sin include not only eternal death but also physical, temporal death, of which Paul here speaks. The result of being declared righteous, and of the work of the Spirit in the life of the believer is both temporal and eternal, for righteous living becomes the mark of the believer, and he is likewise assured of life forever.

11 But if the Spirit of Him who raised Yeshua from the dead dwells in you, He who raised Messiah Yeshua from the dead will also give life to your mortal bodies through His Spirit who indwells you.

The ease with which Paul moves between the various designations for the Spirit is amazing! Here we have not the "Spirit of God" nor the "Spirit of Messiah" but the "Spirit of Him who raised Yeshua . . . ." This should be compared to the phrase in 4:24, ". . . those who believe in Him who raised Yeshua our Lord from the dead . . . ." Interestingly, the Father is given credit as the One who raised Yeshua, but so is the Spirit (1Pt 3:18 if ἐν πνεύματι, *en pneumati* should be taken as instrumental), as well as Yeshua Himself (Jn 10:18).

The resurrection of Yeshua is thus brought into the discussion as the necessary fountainhead from which the resurrection of all believers flows (cp. 1Co 6:14; 15:20, 23; 2Co 4:14; Phil 3:21; 1Thess 4:14). Since the Spirit is the One who gives life to the dead, and since He proved the glory of His work via the resurrection of Yeshua, all who believe may rest assured that they too will rise in triumph over the grave and will live forever with the Lord.

The Spirit, then, by virtue of His indwelling, has come to possess the believer, i.e., to lay claim of ownership. That His ownership extends to the physical as well as the non-physical realities is proven by the resurrection. The Ruach Who dwells within is jealous of the whole person and thus lays claim to the whole person, for Yeshua died to redeem the chosen one. We are thus reminded that from God's perspective the material reality of creation is good and not to take second place to the non-physical realities.

"mortal body" is τὰ θνητὰ σώματα ὑμῶν in the Greek, literally, "your dying bodies." Our English "mortal" is based upon the Latin *mortalis*, "subject to death" and *mors*, "death." Once again the above interpretation of v. 10 (that "death" and "life" refer to the temporal death of the body and the eternal life of the believer) is strengthened.

12 So then, brethren, we are under obligation, not to the flesh, to live according to the flesh–

The opening "So then" (Ἄρα οὖν, *ara oun*) alerts us to the fact that Paul has begun a new section or paragraph and is drawing upon the conclusions reached in the previous section. Since the flesh or sin nature is moving inevitably to death (and in fact we are putting the sin nature to death more and more), then it is clear we are under no obligation to follow or obey its lusts.

The NASB has translated the sentence more directly from the Greek, leaving it "dangling" as it were, in need of some completion (which we might look for in the ongoing context, but in vain). Indeed, the Greek sentence would read in such a way as to presume that Paul had in mind to finish with something like ". . . but to the Spirit, to live according to the Spirit." If this was in his mind, it never become part of the Epistle! The NIV solves the issue this way:

> Therefore, brothers, we have an obligation — but it is not to the sinful nature, to live according to it.

Though this is not exactly as the Greek has it, the NIV does give the obvious sense: we do have an obligation to pursue righteousness and to live according to the will of HaShem, but we have no obligation to fulfill the desires of the flesh.

But why would Paul even think that the Roman believers would consider an obligation to the "flesh?" Here we must understand "flesh" to be more than the individual psyche or inner wrestlings. "Flesh," while primarily connoting the sinful nature, takes into its context the culture and traditions of culture which lead to sin or are themselves sinful. We should remember that in the pagan cultures, religion and clan involvement were hand in hand, so that a believer in Yeshua in the context of 1st Century Rome would constantly be faced with decisions pertaining to what, in God's point of view, was clearly immoral and wrong, but to the culture was accepted and even praiseworthy. It is surely conceivable that believing Gentiles would face the dilemma of family/cultural issues which would ask them to compromise their faith and not walk in righteousness. Here Paul makes it clear that one has no obligation to the sinful ways of the flesh, whether they originate from within one's own soul, or come from without. As those who are learning what submission to the Torah actually is in everyday life, we must remember where our obligations lie.

13 for if you are living according to the flesh, you must die; but if by the Spirit you are putting to death the deeds of the body, you will live.

These two contrasting clauses present the two possible conditions offered in the covenant (Dt 11:26ff; 30:15ff): blessing and cursing, life and death. To "live according to the flesh" is to live in bondage to the sinful desires and passions which Paul represents by the term "flesh," a condition which is true of unbelievers, not believers. Such a living makes it clear that the Spirit is not in control and that such a person exists always at the point of death as the punishment of sin. The Greek is periphrastic: μέλλετε ἀποθνήσκειν, literally "about to die" (NASB = "must die;"

NIV = "you will die"), emphasizing the inevitable connection between living according to the flesh and death.

by the Spirit – "Spirit" is instrumental, i.e., the only means by which the believer may in fact put to death the deeds of the flesh is the Spirit of God. But in order to dissuade anyone from viewing the Spirit as a mere tool in the hands of the believer, Paul goes on in the next verse to describe Him as πνεύματι θεοῦ ἄγονται, "led by the Ruach Elohim."

putting to death – note the continual aspect (pres. act. indicative) of "putting to death." Though death may be viewed as a onetime occurrence, Paul uses the metaphor as a radical dealing with the multitude of sinful lusts which are characteristic of the sinful flesh. Thus, the chore of putting the deeds of sin to death is a continual one for the child of God.

"deeds of the body" must be equivalent to "deeds of the flesh" (σάρξ, *sarks*) and in fact in a few manuscripts (D G latt Ir Tert) "flesh" is written in place of "body." Thus it is not the normal functions of the body which Paul refers to here but the sinful, human self-centeredness and self-assertion which must be mortified.

you will live – this phrase helps us to understand and define the opposite of "death" already referred to. Since the believer is putting to death the deeds of the flesh/body, he or she is assured of not only life in this world, but eternal life in the world to come. In the same manner, then, the person characterized by the deeds of the flesh will die in the sense of eternal separation from HaShem. That Paul, along with Yeshua, understood the punishment of the wicked to be both conscious and eternal seems apparent (Mt 10:28; 13:42; Mk 9:48; Rom 2:6ff; 2Thess 1:5-10). Some scholars (particularly those of the Seventh-day Adventists) have challenged this viewpoint, however. See Samuele Bacchiocchi, *Immortality or Resurrection?* (Biblical Perspectives, 1997).

14 because those who are led by the Spirit of God are sons of God.

Paul's point in this summary statement (which is restating what was said in the previous verse) is obvious: putting to death the deeds of the flesh is accomplished by following the lead of the Spirit. Even as those who by the Spirit put to death the deeds of the body will live, so it may be categorically stated that all who are led by the Spirit truly belong to God, i.e., are the sons of God.

Here we have, once again, that enigma of the cooperative work of the believer with God to accomplish His purposes in one's life. For the former verse makes the child of God active in this process ("put to death the deeds of the body") but here the Spirit is acting ("those who are led by the Spirit") and the believer merely follows (thus the passive ἄγονται, *agontai*, "are led"). We may explain it this way: the work of sanctification is both initiated and prompted by the Spirit, enabling the believer to do what he otherwise could not. But it is the believer, having been renewed in soul by the regeneration process of salvation, who actively engages in the process of sanctification (i.e., the putting to death of the deeds of the flesh). As Cranfield puts it:

> The daily, hourly putting to death of the schemings and enterprises of the sinful flesh by means of the Spirit is a matter of being led, directed, impelled, controlled by the Spirit.[218]

Yeshua is our prime example of what it means to be lead by the Spirit (Lk 4:1). And Paul writes in similar language to the Galatians (5:16-18)

> But I say, walk by the Spirit, and you will not carry out the desire of the flesh. For the flesh sets its desire against the Spirit, and the Spirit against the flesh; for these are in opposition to one another, so that you may not do the things that you please. But if you are led by the Spirit, you are not under the *(condemnation of the)* Torah.

Note that "under the Torah" must correspond to the idea of "death" (i.e., "condemnation") in the Romans parallel. Thus, to be "led" by the Spirit is to "walk" by the Spirit—the phrases convey the same idea. Likewise, to live according to the flesh is "death," i.e., being under the condemnation of the Torah.

sons of God – this interprets what Paul means in the previous verse by "shall live." Members of God's family are assured of His blessing and good pleasure, and need never fear His condemnation. "The life which God promises is not a mere not-dying: it is to be a son of God, to live as a son of God, both now and hereafter."[219]

Here then is yet another description of our freedom: even as we were redeemed from Egypt to serve the Almighty, so we have been redeemed from our sin to be led by the Spirit, to do His bidding, not our own. Our freedom consists in pleasing our Father by Whose grace and election we have obtained our place as sons. (On the phrase "sons of God," cf. Mt 5:9; Lk 20:36; Rom 8:19; Gal 3:26 and note the idea of immortality which is attached to or latent in the terminology.)

15 For you have not received a spirit of slavery leading to fear again, but you have received a spirit of adoption as sons by which we cry out, "Abba! Father!"

Our verse begins with the word "For" (γάρ, *gar*) which most likely informs us that this verse is intended as confirmation of the statement just made in v. 14 (that those who are led by the Spirit are the sons of God).

The contrast is obvious: "spirit of slavery" (πνεῦμα δουλείας, *pneuma douleias*) vs. "spirit of sonship (adoption)" (πνεῦμα υἱοθεσίας, *pneuma huiothesias*). But various options have been given for explanations of each of these phrases. We may summarize the various interpretations as follows:

1) Some feel that since the same verbiage is used for both ("received" and "spirit") that "spirit" must be the same in both. Thus, if "spirit of adoption" is referring to the Holy Spirit (capital S) then so must the phrase "spirit of slavery." Since the Holy Spirit cannot be the "spirit of slavery," then it is reasoned that "spirit of adoption" is likewise not referring to the Spirit of God. Thus, according to this view "spirit" in each case refers to the human spirit, and is interpreted to mean that the believer has a spirit of adoption (a spirit which responds to a Father-son relationship with HaShem), albeit, moved upon by the Spirit of God. The spirit of slavery, then, would be the heavy, burdensome spirit of the unbeliever, and particularly the unbeliever under the condemnation of the Torah.

2) Others do not feel that the word "spirit" is necessarily to be equated, so that the "spirit of slavery" speaks of the disposition of the unbeliever, while "Spirit of adoption" refers to the Holy Spirit.

3) A third option, and one which seems most likely to me, is that the sentence itself does not necessarily affirm the existence of a "spirit of slavery," but simply that the Holy Spirit is not the kind of spirit Who would bring slavery, but would rather confirm and strengthen the relationship to HaShem of His children. Compare also the following parallels:

1Cor. 2:12 Now we have received, not the spirit of the world, but the Spirit who is from God, that we might know the things freely given to us by God,

2Tim. 1:7 For God has not given us a spirit of timidity, but of power and love and

215

discipline.

The fact that the aorist (final, past tense) is used of the word "to receive" (ἐλάβετε, *elabete*, from λαμβάνω, *lambano*) would point to the once and for all giving of the Spirit at the time of initial belief.

Paul's primary point here is that the Spirit is the One Who indwells the believer and unites him or her to God through the eternal work of the Son. He does not bring them back under the bondage of sin, whether in the sense of striving to gain one's own salvation through status gained through the Torah, or in the senseless rituals of paganism.

"Fear" (φόβος, *phobos*) here must, then, be anxiety or despair, not the kind of "fear of God" which we are told is the beginning of wisdom and an essential ingredient of a holy life. Here we understand the difference between those who live under the mistaken impression that one can actually gain right standing before God through one's ethnic status (Jewish by identity, whether native born or proselyte), and those who have come to rest in the finished work of Yeshua. The indwelling Spirit reminds and constantly teaches us that our security—our safety from the wrath of God against sin—is to be found in the completed and perfect work of Yeshua the Messiah. He does this through the word of God, the inspired record of HaShem's purposes and accomplished deeds.

How important, then, for us to understand the difference between "adoption" and "fear." The two are mutually exclusive, for to understand what it means to be a child of God—this understanding leaves no room for fear. For God makes promises to His children, promises He will inevitably keep. And even His chastening is a sign of His love (Heb.12:6). Thus, to labor under the fear of condemnation is to fail to understand and/or believe the reality of our identity as "sons of God" (cf. Dt 14:1; Mt 5:9; Gal 3:26).

What exactly does the word "adoption" mean here? The Greek term υἱοθεσία (*hiothesia*) occurs only a few times in the Apostolic writings: Rom 8:23; 9:4; Gal 4:5; Eph 1:5. It is not found in the Lxx. We know that in the Hellenistic world adoption in a legal sense was common, and this word was the primary word denoting such an occurrence. While an exact parallel to adoption within the Hellenistic world is lacking in the Jewish culture of ancient Israel, the fact that orphans were raised by guardians is a given. David uses this metaphor (Ps 27:10) of a person abandoned by mother and father but sustained by God. The idea of "guardian" (הָאֹמֵן, *ha'omein*) is found in a number of texts in the Tanach (Num 11:12; Ruth 4:16; 2Ki 10:1; Is 49:23) and Yeshua reminded His disciples that He would not leave them as orphans (Jn 14:16-18) but would send the Spirit to act as their "guardian." One finds, therefore, in this term, the clear teaching of one's relationship with God as a familial one. And that He should be known as the believer's Father is taught by Yeshua (Mt 6:9f) and the Apostles (1Co 8:6, etc.) as well as by the prophets of the Tanach (Is 64:8, etc.). We might also note an example from the midrashim:

> Another explanation of 'But now, O Lord, Thou are our Father' (Is 64:8). The Holy One, blessed be He, said: 'You have ignored your own fathers, Abraham, Isaac, and Jacob, and Me do you call father?" To which they [Israel] replied: 'Thee do we recognize as our Father.' It can be compared to an orphan who was brought up with a guardian [אפוטרופוס] that was a good and trustworthy man, and brought her up and looked after her most carefully. Later he wished to marry her, and when the scribe came to write the marriage document he asked her: 'What is your name?' To which she replied: 'So-and-so'; but when he asked her: 'What is the name of your Father?' She was silent. Whereupon her guardian asked her: 'Why are you silent?' And she replied: 'Because I know of no other father save you, for he that brings up a child is called a father, and not he that gives birth' . . . . Similarly, the orphan is Israel, as it says, 'We are become orphans and fatherless (Lam 5:3). The good and faithful guardian is the Holy One, blessed be He, whom Israel began to call 'Our Father', as it says, 'But now, O Lord, Thou are our father' (Is 64:8). God said: 'You have ignored your own father, and now call Me your father'; as it says, 'Look unto Abraham your father,

etc. (Is 51:2). They replied: 'Lord of the Universe! He who brings up children is called the father, not he who gives birth,' as it says, For Thou art our father; for Abraham knoweth us not (Is 63:16).[220]

Thus, here as well as in 9:4, Paul's use of the idea of "adoption," while no doubt embracing the Hellenistic legal "adoption," may still have had in mind the general situation lived out in the ancient Israelite community of the orphan being cared for by a guardian.

by which we cry out, "Abba, Father – Some translations (such as the RSV) connect this phrase with the next verse:

> 15 For you did not receive the spirit of slavery to fall back into fear, but you have received the spirit of sonship. When we cry, "Abba! Father!" 16 it is the Spirit himself bearing witness with our spirit that we are children of God,

The NIV has isolated the phrase so that it goes with verse 15, but as a separate sentence:

> 15 For you did not receive a spirit that makes you a slave again to fear, but you received the Spirit of sonship. And by him we cry, "Abba, Father." 16 The Spirit himself testifies with our spirit that we are God's children.

While the grammar could allow either, it seems best to take the traditional understanding as represented by the NASB, and make this the final phrase of v. 15. As such, the point Paul is making is an important one, namely, that it is by the work of the indwelling Spirit that we are able to approach HaShem as Abba and call out to Him with this relationship in mind (cp. Gal 4:6). This being the case, "Spirit of adoption" refers to the Holy Spirit in His work of making the believer a son or daughter in the family of God, and of teaching that child of God about his or her identity—so much so that one is able to call out "Abba."

The use of the verb "cry out" (κράζειν, *krazein*) seems to suggest a calling out to God at times of distress or need (cf. 1Co 14:15). Others, suggesting that the word simply denotes a loud proclamation, feel it refers to public prayer or the opening of a liturgical section. Still others have suggested that it speaks of open public prayer in full voice as over against the whispered prayer common in the ancient Jewish congregation. But if we look at the use of κράζειν in the Lxx, we discover the most obvious sense, that being of urgent prayer, a use often found in the Psalms (cf. Ps 3:4[5]; 4:3[4]; 18:6[17:7]; 22:2, 5[21:3, 6]; 34:6[33:7]). As Cranfield notes:

> It is used to represent several different Hebrew words. So here it is best taken to denote an urgent and sincere crying to God irrespective of whether it is loud or soft (or even unspoken), formal or informal, public or private.[221]

"Abba" (אַבָּא) is, of course, an Aramaic word whose origin was an exclamatory form of "father" used by small children, but by the time of Yeshua was used more extensively, no longer something thought of as child's speech. It's origin, however, was never lost, and it evoked a homey and affectionate sense of the father-child relationship, so much so that it is never used in ancient Judaism to address HaShem (used as a vocative. Its non-vocative use with reference to God is very rare).[222] That Yeshua addressed HaShem this way (Mk 14:36) expressed His unique relationship to God. That He instructed His disciples to use the title "Abba" as well would indicate that He wanted them (and us) to know that a unique relationship likewise exists between each believer and the Father.

If we are to look at the general argument of Paul in this section we can see that it is to this point he wishes to move—here is his primary emphasis—the addressing of God as "Abba." For he wishes his readers to know that our slavery to sin has been broken, and that our freedom to live unto God is now the reality. We no longer are slaves to sin because we have become sons of God. The proof of our sonship is that we are putting to death the deeds of the flesh through the power of the Spirit, we are being led by the Spirit in our daily *halachah*, and it is by the presence of the Spirit and His work in our lives that we are confident in our acceptance before the Father, causing us to cry out to Him, "Abba."

> This then is what it means to live after the Spirit, to mortify by the Spirit the deeds of the
> body, and to be led by the Spirit of God—simply to be enabled by that same Spirit to cry,
> 'Abba, Father.' And it is here expressed not as an imperative but as an indicative: Chris-
> tians do as a matter of fact do this. The implicit imperative is that they should continue to
> do just this, and do it more and more consistently, more and more sincerely, soberly and
> responsibly. This is all that is required of them. It is what the whole law of God is aimed
> at achieving. All that must be said about the Christian's obedience has been already said
> in principle when this has been said. Nothing more is required of us than that we should
> cry to the one true God 'Abba, Father' with full sincerity and with full seriousness. That
> this necessarily includes seeking with all our heart to be and think and say and do what is
> well-pleasing to Him and to avoid all that displeases Him, should go without saying. In
> the accomplishment of this work of obedience the 'righteousness of the law' is fulfilled (cf.
> v. 4) and God's holy law established.[223]

16 The Spirit Himself bears witness with our spirit that we are children of God,

This is the means by which we are willing and able to cry out, "Abba, Father," because the Spirit is witnessing with our spirit about the realities of who we are–our true identity. Thus, the means by which we gain our adoption as sons, and by which we call out "Abba," is nothing less than the authority of God Himself in His Spirit assuring us that we are His children. This work of the Spirit comes before our calling out "Abba," and is independent of our own efforts and abilities. For Paul, the working out of the righteousness of the Torah in the lives of the believers is the ongoing work of the Spirit as He witnesses to the spirit of the believer.

There is a question whether the word συμμαρτυρεῖν, *summarturein*, "witness with" should be understood as "witness together with" or "witness to," and thus "assure." In light of the position taken above that the Spirit is the means by which one calls out to HaShem as "Abba," it seems best to understand this not that the Spirit witnesses together with the spirit of the be-liever, but that the Spirit witnesses to the spirit of the believer. It is this work of the Spirit, apart from anything we do, that assures us that we are, indeed, the children of God.

What is the means by which the Holy Spirit assures us in our spirits that we are, indeed, the child of God? The means is the knowledge we gain from the very revelation of God in His word, a knowledge which could never be imparted to us apart from the work of the Spirit. It is, then, the work of the Spirit to illumine our minds both to receive and understand the signifi-cance of the Scriptures for our lives. In this knowledge we come to know the method by which God declares sinners righteous (i.e., faith in the sacrificial work of His Son) and thus the man-ner in which we stand justified in His sight. It is likewise by this knowledge, gained through the avenue of faith, that we are enabled to cry out to Him in the language of family, calling Him "Abba." The assuring work of the Spirit, then, is not one of subjectivity (in which He subjec-tively witnesses together with our spirit) but is objective in the sense of unfolding the truth of Scripture to our spirits or minds, and by this divine revelation assuring us of our status as sons.

17 and if children, heirs also, heirs of God and fellow heirs with Messiah, if indeed we suffer with Him in order that we may also be glorified with Him.

In this concluding sentence Paul has moved us from sonship to the concept of heirship, by which he moves us to the whole concept of "hope," the primary subject of this paragraph (vv. 17-30), as well as the work of the indwelling Spirit. For the Spirit, in assuring us of our position as children of God, likewise causes us to cast our gaze forward to the day of our final and full redemption—the day when we will receive the inheritance reserved for us by our Father (cf. 1Pt 1:3-4).

The language of inheritance in Paul is found primarily in two other places: Rom 4 and Gal 3 & 4. In Rom 4:13 the fact that Abraham was promised to inherit the world (τὸ κληρονόμον αὐτὸν εἶναι κόσμου) is linked to the covenant which God made with him, a covenant which required Abraham's faith in the "promise" (Gen 15:6) and was not based upon works of the Torah. That is, Abraham did not first gain acceptance through obedience, and then was granted covenant membership. Rather, he was granted covenant membership through faith, which resulted in his obedience. Furthermore, those who are members of that covenant, i.e., who have righteousness by faith in the Messiah, are likewise heirs with Abraham (4:17).[224] Here, then, the heirship afforded the believers in Yeshua is clearly traced through their relationship with Abraham (as those who likewise participate in the same faith that Abraham exercised) and the covenant God made with him and his heirs.

The other Pauline passage which touches on heirship is Gal 3 & 4. Here, as in Rom 4, the distinction is made between those who would think their inheritance is based upon Torah (ἐκ νόμου, *ek nomos*, "flowing from Torah") and those who have inheritance based upon faith, i.e., who are heirs "according to promise" (κατ᾽ ἐπαγγελίαν κληρονόμοι), on the basis of faith and not of righteous deeds. Furthermore, while the text of Rom 8 has the phrase "heirs of God" (κληρονόμοι μὲν θεοῦ), Gal 4:7 uses the language "heir through God" (κληρονόμος διὰ θεοῦ). What may we make of these similarities and differences in the language?

First, we should consider the very real possibility that Paul speaks on two levels: one is the level of the direct redemption which God has accomplished for each of His chosen ones through the death and resurrection of Messiah. From this point of view there is only the mediator Yeshua between God and the redeemed sinner (cf. 1Tim 2:5). This level considers the individual member of the covenant. The second level, however, is corporate and is thus one of history—of the history of redemption and of the covenant made with Abraham and his seed. At this level, the redemption is seen as the covenant benefit for all who may rightly claim family ties with Abraham. Thus, while from one point of view the believer is an "heir of God," from the other standpoint he is an "heir through God," i.e., through the covenant which God made with Abraham.

We should consider the obvious fact that neither level or point of view is more valuable than the other, but both work together in the overall picture of redemption. For the redemption which God has accomplished through His Son Yeshua is in every way tied to the covenant made with Abraham, yet is applicable to each individual within the covenant. There is thus both a corporate identity ("heirs of promise") as well as an individual identity as an "heir of God" and "joint heir with Messiah."

This heirship language of Paul may also be considered from the standpoint of covenant. For whereas a mortal dies and leaves his wealth to his children as their inheritance, HaShem lives for ever, and will never die. In what way, then, can His children inherit His wealth?

It is an interesting fact that in the ancient Near East kings would often adopt their vassals in order to strengthen the vassal's credibility and warn off any who might try to usurp his position. As the adopted son of the Great King, he was far more untouchable than merely as an appointed ruler. Thus, adoption, and the heirship which went with it, became connected with the whole matter of covenant between Great Kings and their vassals. In fact, the Greek word διαθήκη, *diatheke*, which is the word used in the Apostolic Scriptures for "covenant," likewise could be used of a "last will and testament" (cf. Heb 9:16-17). Thus, "inheritance" came to be connected with the whole matter of "covenant"—inheritance being, in this way, the very fruit of the covenant promises enjoyed by those it embraced.

and fellow-heirs with Messiah – This additional phrase is not a condition but rather gives further substantiation for the claim that the believer is an "heir of God." The Greek begins with εἴπερ, *eiper*, which here (as in v. 9) means "seeing that" and is roughly equivalent with Greek γάρ, *gar*, "for." Cranfield paraphrases this way:

> "for the fact that we are now suffering with Him, so far from calling the reality of our heir-ship in question, is a pledge of our being glorified with Him hereafter."[225]

if indeed we suffer with Him – The suffering which Paul alludes to here is not the suffering undergone for us vicariously in the death of Messiah, nor the metaphoric "suffering" drama-tized in our baptism (*mikvah*), for if either of these would have been in the Apostle's mind he doubtless would have used the past tense. In using the present tense however (συμπάσχομεν, *sumpaschomen*) he emphasizes the

> "element of suffering which is inseparable from faithfulness to Christ in a world which does not yet know Him as Lord."[226]

The life of the truly redeemed is a life of conformity to Yeshua, and this conformity will bring suffering as He taught it would (Lk 6:22; cf. 1Pt 2:21). This suffering for righteousness sake is, in one sense, a true test of genuine faith, for often those who possess only spurious "faith" fail when the times of testing come (cf. James 1:2ff).

in order that we may also be glorified with Him – The sense of "in order that" (ἵνα, *hina*) is not the subjective motive of the sufferers ("if I suffer more I'll gain eternal glorification") but, as is often the case with this Greek particle, indicates the inevitable result of the action or condition previously described. Thus, the sure reward for all who suffer as a result of being followers of the Messiah is that they will be glorified with God for all eternity. It is this promise of sure reward that constitutes the hope of all true believers (cf. 1Jn 3:2-3).

18 For I consider that the sufferings of this present time are not worthy to be compared with the glory that is to be revealed to us.

The actual Greek word order puts the emphasis upon the idea of "compared": ἄξια, *aksia*, from ἄξιος, *aksios*, means "weighing as much," "of like value," "of equal worth." Thus, the NASB "not worthy to be compared" translates οὐκ ἄξια (*ouk aksia*) which stands at the beginning of the verse. We might translate, then, "For not even worthy of comparison are the sufferings of this present time with the glory that is to be revealed to us."

Paul speaks similarly in 2Cor 4:16-17:

> Therefore we do not lose heart, but though our outer man is decaying, yet our inner man is being renewed day by day. For momentary, light affliction is producing for us an eternal weight of glory far beyond all comparison,

In accordance with the previous verse, the "sufferings of this present time" are no doubt those which come as a result of publically proclaiming one's faith in Messiah. The coming glory is the full realization of that which we now only possess in part, i.e., as the foreshadowing of what the full glory will be. As sons and heirs we now possess the presence of the Spirit in our lives, and He is the "down payment" (עֲרָבוֹן, ἀρραβών, *arrabon,* cf. 2Cor 1:22; 5:5; Eph 1:14) assuring us of the full inheritance. But as wonderful and real as the "down payment" (NASB = "pledge") is, the full reality of the glory we are to possess is not yet known nor can it be.

revealed to us – The Greek is ἀποκαλυφθῆναι εἰς ἡμᾶς, literally "revealed unto us." We might have expected the simple dative to be used (rather than the preposition εἰς, *eis*) or even ἐν ἡμᾶς (*en emas*), "in us." Perhaps the preposition εἰς ("unto") is used to emphasize that the glory, though possessed by those who are redeemed, is actually not their doing, but is given in every way by the hand of God. Thus, the "agent" of the glory event is the Almighty and no one else.

19 For the anxious longing of the creation waits eagerly for the revealing of the sons of God.

Having set forth the idea of the glory that awaits the redeemed, Paul launches into a section (vv. 19-30) in which he initially supports the statement of v. 18, but also therefore expands on the whole concept of the world to come as compared with this present world. The world to come represents a locus of hope for the redeemed as it is compared with the present world of pain and suffering, a pain and suffering which goes well beyond what can be casually observed by anyone. For to understand the true despair of the fallen world one must view the whole situation with eyes of faith.

The Greek word ἀποκαραδοκία (*apokaradokia,* "anxious longing") is found only one other time in the Apostolic Writings, at Phil 1:20 where it is also connected to the concept of "hope." The basic idea of the word is that of "stretching the neck," "craning forward."[227]

The word "creation" has been variously interpreted through the centuries, with one of the following: 1) whole creation, including mankind both believing and unbelieving as well as angels; 2) all of mankind; 3) unbelieving mankind only; 4) believers only; 5) angels only; 6) subhuman nature together with the angels; 7) subhuman nature together with mankind in general; and 8) subhuman nature only. Most of these fail to fit the context, and may be discarded. It seems most likely that Paul uses the term "creation" to speak of all that is created in the world in contrast to mankind. Not that mankind is not created, obviously, but that mankind stands, in one sense, as the pinnacle of creation, and as such, distinct from all creation as the object of God's redemption. Using the personification of creation so often encountered in the Tanach, Paul here attributes to the subhuman creation (both animate and inanimate) those attributes usually reserved for mankind. Yet in doing so he also agrees with the Tanach in which the creation is portrayed as a partner in HaShem's overall plan of revealing His glory.

> With poetic boldness and with a penetrating prophetic insight Paul sees the whole splendid theatre of the universe together with all subhuman life within it as eagerly awaiting the time when the sons of God will be made manifest in their true glory. [228]

the revealing of the sons of God –

> Believers are already sons of God in this life, but their sonship is veiled and their incognito is impenetrable except to faith.[229]

Indeed, even those who have true faith must believe in their sonship against the loud evidence of much in their circumstances and condition which seems to cry out against their position in Yeshua! We know that we are indeed sons by faith, yet all too often our weaknesses bring a ready platform for doubt. Yet in that day when mortal puts on immortality, the reality of the redeemed and their status as sons will be known by all, and evident to all.

20–21 For the creation was subjected to futility, not of its own will, but because of Him who subjected it, in hope that the creation itself also will be set free from its slavery to corruption into the freedom of the glory of the children of God.

Here, the creation, as personfied, is nonetheless not the cause of her subjugation, but is subjected passively, as it were, as the inevitable result of the entrance of sin into the world through mankind's disobedience.

The word "futility" (ματαιότητι, *mataioteti*) is the word used in the Lxx of Qohelet for the Hebrew הֶבֶל, *hevel*, often translated "futile" or "futility," but actually means "vapor." Here the Greek word itself helps to explain the use of הֶבֶל, for the idea of a "vapor" is not, in and of itself, negative. Rather, in terms of the creation, the goal to which it was created, i.e., to constantly give glory to HaShem, cannot be realized with a vapor that is transitory—here today and gone tomorrow. Thus, the Greek term (ματαιότητι) used both here and in Qohelet denotes the ineffectiveness of that which does not attain its goal. Like a vapor (הֶבֶל), the creation is subjected to "futility," i.e., the inability to effectively reach the goal for which it was created.

not of its own will – (οὐχ ἑκοῦσα, *ouks ekousa*) can also be understood as "not through its own fault." It was not the subhuman creation that made the fatal decision to disobey her Creator—no, this was the action of mankind.

but because of Him who subjected it – The subject is obviously HaShem (so the NASB and most translations capitalize the pronoun) and speaks of the fact that as a result of mankind's disobedience, the creation, given to support him and to enhance his life upon the earth, was also negatively affected so as to make life difficult and to, at the same time, wrest mankind's attention from the creation to the Creator upon Whom he must constantly rely for his life and sustenance.

in hope – The first question we must ask is to what "in hope" (ἐφ᾽ ἐλπίδι, *eph elpidi*) should be attached: to the closest verb, ὑποτάξαντα, *hupotaksanta*, "subjected" (i.e., subjected it in hope) or to the initial verb in v. 20, "was subjected" (ὑπετάγη, *hupetage*)? It would seem to make better sense to understand the basic sentence this way: "For the creation was subjected . . . in hope that the creation itself also will be set free . . ." If this is the manner in which the sentence is structured, then we can say that God subjected the creation to His curse with its final redemption and freedom fully in sight. The divine judgment upon the creation included the promise of a better future, indeed, of the Messiah Himself (Gen 3:15, cf. Rom 16:20).

that the creation itself also will be set free – The opening word translated "that" in the NASB and the NIV is the Greek διότι (*dioti*) which normally has the meaning "because." There is a variant in the Greek manuscripts, ὅτι, *hoti*, the normal word for "that," but this seems no doubt to have found its way into the manuscripts as an attempt to explain the more difficult διότι. We should most likely retain the normal meaning for διότι and translate the phrase "because the creation itself also will be set free . . ." Thus, we learn that the creation was subjected to futility but always with its full redemption in view.

Here we come, once again, face to face with the Hebrew mind of the Apostle, for he sees the need not only for the redemption of sinful mankind, but also of the whole creation, for the material universe is not evil of itself, nor is it morally inferior. Indeed when HaShem created the world He declared the works of His hands to be good, and even very good. The Platonic viewpoint that somehow things material are inferior in worth to the nonmaterial realm finds no place in the perspective of the Apostles.

It is in this reality that we find a biblical prescriptive for ecology. In the same sense that as redeemed individuals we strive to put away from us the effects of our falleness in order to glorify our Creator, so it is our desire to restore to the physical world the glory it had before it was subjected to futility through mankind's sin. We are careful with the world God has created because we want it, in every way, to bring Him the glory He deserves.

from its slavery to corruption – This could also be translated "from its bondage to decay" (NIV). The subhuman creation is subject to the slavery of corruption and decay, and thus transitoriness, which is the very opposite of "glory." Whether we reflect upon the simple reality of entropy in the world, or categorize it under the second law of thermodynamics (that energy flows from potential to kinetic, and not *vice versa*), the decay of the universe as we know it is obvious.

into the freedom of the glory of the children of God – The creation will be freed from its position of slavery to corruption, and will enter into the realm of freedom which it enjoyed before the fall, a freedom here characterized by that which the children of God possess.

How are we to understand the phrase "the freedom of the glory of the children of God?" There are three genitives (possessive forms) linked together. Some have taken the first one ("of the glory") to function as an adjective, giving the sense "the glorious freedom or liberty." While the genitive does have an adjectival function at times, this particular construction would not favor such an interpretation. It is better to note the parallelism with the former "slavery to corruption" (literally "slavery of corruption") and understand this to mean "the liberty that results from the glory" which the children of God will enjoy. In this case, the word "glory" acts as the opposite of the former "corruption" or "decay." The natural decay of the world and of mankind does not match the creative purpose and goal of God, a purpose or goal which is best described by the term "glory." God created for His glory and for the glory of mankind as His image-bearer. Thus, the glory which will be restored in the world to come (to those who are His) is the entire reversal of the present corruption brought about by sin.

There may be a sense also that Paul here alludes to the fact that the creation, made to be ruled by mankind, is unable to achieve its full glory while its "lords" (i.e., mankind) remain in disgrace by sin. Such passages as Gen 1:26, 28; Ps. 8:6 might have been in his mind as he considered the current corruption and the promised freedom realized in redemption.

22 For we know that the whole creation groans and suffers the pains of childbirth together until now.

The metaphor of birth pangs is commonly used by the Sages to refer to the troubles that will proceed the coming of the messianic age.

> Ulla said; Let him [The Messiah] come, but let me not see him. Rabbah said likewise: Let him come, but let me not see him. R. Joseph said: Let him come, and may I be worthy of sitting in the shadow of his ass's saddle. Abaye enquired of Rabbah: "What is your reason [for not wishing to see him]? Shall we say, because of the birth pangs [preceding the advent] of the Messiah? But it has been taught, R. Eleazar's disciples asked him: "What must a man do to be spared the pangs of the Messiah?" [He answered,] "Let him engage in study and benevolence; and you, Master, do both."[230]

Paul likewise uses the idea of birth pangs to describe the process through which the present creation travails in its expectation of the final and full redemption promised by her Creator. The fact that Paul begins this verse with his common "For we know" shows that this concept was well recognized by the community to which he writes, having been taught in the Tanach (as early as Gen 3:17), "reinforced by the apocalyptic tradition, and confirmed and sharpened by the gospel."[231]

Even as the travail and pain of child bearing must be endured in order to receive the blessing of the child himself, so the present groaning of the creation is considered by the Apostle as a birthing experience which will eventuate in the revelation of glory for which the creation was originally made.

The Greek words for "groans" and "suffers" (συστενάζω, *sustenazo* and συνωδίνω, *sunodino* respectively) both have the συν (*sun*, "with") prefix for which the translations appropriately add the word "together." The question, then, is together with what or whom is the creation groaning and suffering? It cannot be with believers, for this would be inappropriate in view of v. 23. Nor is it with Messiah, seeing that Messiah no longer suffers, having suffered once for all. Furthermore, Messiah has not been named in our text since v. 17. It is not mankind in general either that groans and suffers together with the subhuman creation, for the groaning of mankind is spoken of separately. While the συν prepositions could be perfective (i.e., intensive), the evidence that these verbs function in such a way is lacking. The best suggestion is that the "together" means "with one accord." That is, the creation altogether with one accord has been groaning and suffering the effects of sin within its realm from the fall until the present. Thus, Paul adds ἄχρι τοῦ νῦν, "until now" indicating that the creation has altogether or with one accord suffered ever since the entrance of sin.

23 And not only this, but also we ourselves, having the first fruits of the Spirit, even we ourselves groan within ourselves, waiting eagerly for our adoption as sons, the redemption of our body.

And not only this – This phrase indicates that Paul separates the subhuman creation from mankind. Not only does the subhuman creation groan, but even mankind groans, and specifically believers.

but also we ourselves – This same phrase is repeated again ("even we ourselves") giving the highest level of emphasis. Not only does the subhuman creation groan, and mankind in general, but most specifically even believers also groan. Faith in this world is not a promise of exemption from the pain and woes of a fallen world. All too often modern Christianity has taught that faith nullifies the effects of the curse upon the creation, and expects that a "life of faith" ought to be a comfortable life of joy and pleasure. Paul sees it differently! Even the believers, including the apostle himself, groan and suffer the travail of this "birthing" process.

Paul identifies the believers as those who possess the Spirit and the work of His presence. He describes this with the phrase "first fruits of the Spirit." The word "first fruits" is ἀπαρχη, *aparche*, found in the Apostolic writings at Rom 11:16; 16:5; 1Co 15:20, 23; 16:15; 2Th 2:13; James 1:18; Rev. 14:4 and is used in the extra-biblical Greek of firstlings or first fruits for sacrifice or offering and used throughout the Lxx to translate בְּכוֹר, *bichor*. Here it is used, not of something which man gives to God, but that which comes from God to man, and the sense seems to be that the

> Spirit is the gift of a part as a pledge of the fuller gift yet to come. What the believer has already received is a foretaste and a guarantee of what he has still to hope for.[232]

In what way may we say the Spirit, given freely to us as the inevitable first fruits of Yeshua's death and resurrection on our behalf, is a "foretaste and a guarantee of what is still hoped for?" We may simply say that the manner in which the Spirit is working sanctification within us is part and parcel of our identity as children of HaShem, so what we may expect in the world to come is nothing less than the full realization of this sanctification—full holiness unto HaShem.

That the first fruits are "of the Spirit" means in general that they are His doing, His activity, indeed, His very presence. Because we so much appreciate and love the presence of the Spirit in our lives, we groan to realize that His activity is limited by our fallenness—even by our mortality. His work is one of constant repair, of calling to repentance and of grief in the presence of sin. We therefore long for the time when, mortal "putting on" immortality, the Spirit is free to change us forever into those people we were always intended to be—a people for His own possession, zealous for righteous deeds (cf. Tit 2:14, cf. Ex 19:5; Dt. 14:2).

waiting eagerly for our adoption as sons – The tension that this phrase causes rests upon the present tense of it. Are we not already "children of God?" Certainly. Then in what manner do we currently "wait eagerly for our adoption as sons?" The key may be found in the following phrase, "the redemption of our body" which Paul appends as explanatory.

> We are already sons of God but our sonship is not yet manifest. We have been adopted, but our adoption has yet to be publically proclaimed.[233]

the redemption of our bodies – It is not until we are "raised incorruptible" and receive our inheritance which is "imperishable and undefiled and will not fade away, reserved in heaven for you" (1Pt 1:4) that we are seen for what we truly are. For now, though we live our lives in righteousness unto the Lord, we still fail and sin, and must constantly seek forgiveness and repentance both from our Creator and from our fellowman. But in the resurrection of the body to eternal life and glory it will be manifest beyond doubt that we have been fully redeemed and that we will never again be subjected to futility.

Once again, Paul is as concerned with the restoration of the physical aspects of mankind as he is about the nonphysical, for he fully believes that God's work of creation is extolled in both.

24 For in hope we have been saved, but hope that is seen is not hope; for why does one also hope for what he sees?

Salvation, by its very nature, is in one respect future. If we live in the realm of trouble and fear, then the realization of one's salvation is at that time when trouble and fear are no more. Paul, nonetheless, uses a past tense (aorist) to speak of our salvation, writing "we have been saved" (ἐσώθημεν, *esothemen*, aorist of σώζω, *sozo*). The point is simply that we are fully assured of our ultimate and final salvation yet at the present we have not fully possessed it in actuality. Since, however, our hope for final salvation rests firmly upon the immutable and infinite word of God, we know that we will fully possess it.

Thus, it is in the sphere or realm of hope that we have been saved. We recognize that our salvation, while surely having present realities, is yet future, and that our focus is on what will come as much as upon the present reality of our membership in God's covenant. Thus, even though we have the first fruits of the Spirit, we still groan and wait for what we do not yet fully possess.

but hope that is seen is not hope – Here Paul objectifies "hope" as something hoped for, and thus if one is waiting and hoping for a given object, when that object arrives, there is no longer any need for hope. What Paul is clearly teaching us here is that our present experience through faith in the Messiah is not a complete one, and we should not therefore be surprised when life is filled, to one measure or another, with the effects of this fallen world. All to often new believers in Yeshua have the mistaken notion that the life of faith is one without struggles. But the Apostle here gives us a clear warning that as we pursue a life of faith in Messiah, we will experience the groaning of spirit which results from not yet attaining the full salvation we rightfully own as adopted sons and daughters.

for why does one also hope for what he sees? – This explains and supports the previous sentence, namely, that if the object upon which one has placed his hope has arrived, then there is no more need for hope (in the sense of "anticipation").

25 But if we hope for what we do not see, with perseverance we wait eagerly for it.

Here, then, is the conclusion of Paul's short discourse on "hope": if we are saved within the sphere of hope, i.e., salvific "hope" is an integral part of our faith experience, then we will naturally (or shall we say supernaturally) persevere until we receive that for which we hope.

Here "hope" is combined with "perseverance" or "steadfast patience." The Greek term ὑπομόνω, *hupomono*, translated "perseverance" is used also in 2:7 and 5:3. "Perseverance" is one of the true marks of saving faith, for the hope which is shed abroad in our hearts is a hope generated by the Spirit. As such, the sincere desire to persevere and not give up hope is the sure work of the Spirit in the life of the believer. Conversely, failure to persevere by faith in the ways of righteousness is a sure sign of a spurious faith (cf. 1Jn 2:19 [where "persevering" is characterized as staying within the believing community]; Jms 1:12; Rev 2:10).

The addition in the NASB of the adverb "eagerly" simply interprets the compound ἀπεκδέκομαι (*apekdekomai*, "to wait," the preposition ἄπο, *apo*, taken as perfective), thus to "really wait" or "wait eagerly." The NIV leaves this out here, but inconsistently includes the idea of "eager" in 8:19, 23 where the same word is used. Does the word contain the idea of "eagerness?" Its other occurrences in the Apostolic Scriptures are 1Co 1:7; Gal 5:5; Phil 3:20; Heb 9:28; 1Pt 3:20. That the verb itself (in its compound form) can be perfective, i.e., somewhat intensive, is attested.[234] The context here, furthermore, would warrant such an interpretation of the word, for the "waiting" here is one in the context of "groaning" and strong anticipation. The NASB has most likely pointed us in the right direction, then, by adding the word "eagerly."

26 And in the same way the Spirit also helps our weakness; for we do not know how to pray as we should, but the Spirit Himself intercedes for us with groanings too deep for words;

The verse begins with the comparison "And in the same way . . ." (ὡσαύτως, *hosautos*), but to what is the comparison being made? It cannot mean that in the same way as we wait patiently the Spirit helps us, nor as we are sustained by "hope" so the Spirit sustains us. Rather, it appears that Paul has returned to the idea of "groaning," so that the comparison is between our "groaning" (vv. 22, 23) and the "groaning" of the Spirit as He intercedes for us.

Paul says that the Spirit "helps" us. The word is συναντιλαμβάνομαι, *sunantilambanomai* found only here and in Lk 10:40 in the Apostolic Scriptures. It is found in the Lxx at Ex 18:22; Num 11:17; Ps 89:21 [88:22]. The compound verb is most likely perfective or intensive[235] so that the idea is not so much that the Ruach combines His strength with ours (the συν prefix suggesting the idea of "with") but simply that He gives real and relevant help.

The context is that of prayer, and thus our weakness here is that which is in the sphere of prayer. It is here that the Spirit helps our weakness.

for we do not know how to pray as we should – Here our weakness is directly defined by the Apostle—we lack knowledge of how we ought to pray. What is entailed in this "how we ought to pray?" Two possibilities present themselves: 1) we do not know what to pray for, or 2) we do not know the manner in which we should pray. The fact that Yeshua specifically gives an outline of prayer to His disciples (commonly called the "Lord's Prayer") would indicate, it seems to me, that He taught a general manner for prayer. What seems most reasonable, then, is that the weakness we experience in prayer is that we do not fully know the mind of God, and thus we are not always certain what His will is, and for what we should pray. For example, is the difficulty I'm encountering (and what therefore prompts me to pray) actually sent by God Himself for my spiritual growth? Then I dare not ask Him to take it away. But if the difficulty is actually the enemy's attack against me, I surely must ask God to intervene and remove it. And the same may be true as I pray for others: wisdom dictates that my prayers for others be in accord with the will of God. Thus, my weakness is in knowing God's mind—here the Spirit is able to take the intent of my prayer and, with groanings, intercede on my behalf and present it to the Father appropriately.

but the Spirit Himself intercedes [for us] with groanings too deep for words – The manner in which the Ruach helps our weakness in the realm of prayer is through His interceding on our behalf.

Some in ancient times,[236] as well as some in the present, have seen in this phrase a reference to *glossolalia* (tongues), so that the Spirit causes the one praying to break into ecstatic utterances as a method for conveying what otherwise could not be expressed. A telling issue against such an interpretation is that *glossolalia* are never described as a "groaning" and in fact were usually associated with praise and worship within the congregation. But even more decisive is the argument that, coming after the words "the Spirit Himself intercedes . . . ," the "groanings too deep for words" are the Spirit's own groanings, and not of those praying. It seems that what Paul is indicating here is that the Spirit intercedes with groanings that even the praying believer could never know or understand in his current state of weakness. The meaning of "too deep for words" (ἀλαλήτοις, *alaletois*) could mean "that which cannot be expressed in ordinary human speech" or simply "unspoken." Verse 27 would favor the latter. The Spirit's groanings are not uttered because they do not need to be, since God knows the Spirit's intention without it being expressed. Thus, the "groanings" of the Spirit are outside of the human experience and exist in the realm of silence.

27 and He who searches the hearts knows what the mind of the Spirit is, because He intercedes for the saints according to the will of God.

Apparently Paul's logic is this: since it is a well known fact that God searches and knows the secrets of men's hearts (1Sa 16:7; 1Kgs 8:39; Ps 7:9; 17:3; 26:2; 44:21; 139:1, 2, 23; Prov 15:11; Jer 17:10; Ac 1:24; 15:8), it is a given that He knows the unspoken desires of His own Spirit.

The "because" (ὅτι, *hoti*) should be taken in the sense of "and the proof is" or "for," since the last clause tells us not what He knows, but what He does in relationship to the believers, i.e., He intercedes according to the will of God. The fact that He intercedes according to the will of God proves that the Father and Spirit are one in knowing the mind of the Spirit and the purpose of His intercession on behalf of the praying saints.

according to the will of God – literally, "according to God" (κατὰ θεόν, *kata theon*) which no doubt means "according to the will of God," "according to what God determines."

Note that those who are true believers are characterized as "holy," i.e., "saints" (ἅγιοι, *hagioi*).

28 And we know that God causes all things to work together for good to those who love God, to those who are called according to His purpose.

The fact that Paul begins with "and" (δὲ, *de*) clearly ties this verse with that which precedes. The fact that the Spirit must interceed for us with silent groanings only highlights the fact that we are engaged in a life of struggle—a life which anticipates the rich future promised by God but must, for the present, bear up under the sorrows of fallenness. Yet in spite of this inevitability, the Apostle wants us to know that this groaning which we experience as we hope for the future is not the result of chaos or indetermined randomness, but is, in fact, a part of the Master's plan as He providencially guides our lives to His appointed purpose.

we know – Paul uses this opening four other times (2:2; 3:19; 7:14; 8:22) and in each case is introducing something he is sure his readers are both well aware of and with which they are in agreement. That God "causes all things to work together for good" is a well substantiated teaching of the Tanach and throughout the entire Scriptures.

The manner in which God controls the events of history, however, is something upon which there has not been universal agreement, and thus the interpretation of this verse has been varied. In addition to the theological viewpoints which differ, (and in some cases because of these theological differences), our verse contains several variant readings which contribute to the difficulty of arriving at a consensus interpretation. The primary variant in the text is whether or not to include the words ὁ θεός (*ho theos*, "God") after the verb συνεργεῖ, *sunergei*, "work together." Without the addition, the sentence would read "and we know that all things work together for good . . ." while with the addition it would read "and we know that God causes all things to work together . . . ." In other words, the additional word settles the theological issue of whether or not God is active in providence, or whether it is possible that He is (in one manner or another) more passive.

Interestingly, while some of the major witnesses (ℵ C D G K P etc) attest the shorter reading, the longer reading has some equally strong support (𝔓⁴⁶ B A sa sy^pal arm). In terms of textual criticism, it is therefore difficult to make an objective judgment based upon manuscript strength. We might think that the longer reading came from the need on the part of some scribes to emphasize the sovereign role of God in the affairs of man, but a similar argument can be made regarding the shorter reading—that some wanted to expunge the clear, direct mention of God as "controller" of all things.

An additional factor in the interpretation of our verse is the subject: if the shorter reading is accepted, then the question of the subject of the sentence arises. Some have suggested that the subject must be the Spirit Who is the subject of the previous verses. Since v. 28 is joined to the previous context with the particle δέ ("and"), one might presume that the subject remains the same. There is, however, a clear objection to this proposal, namely, that vv. 29ff are clearly linked to v. 28, and the subject of the following verses is God. To make such an abrupt change of subject from v. 28 to vv. 29f without any notice in the text itself seems unduly harsh, far more difficult than seeing a change of subject (from "Ruach" to "God") from v. 27 to v. 28.

Finally, a question relates to the use of "all things" (πάντα, *panta*) in our verse: is it the object of the verb (thus, "works all things together") or should it be understood as the sphere in which the action is done (thus, "works together in all things" or "in all respects")? Though this second alternative is possible (as an accusative of respect), we would expect ἐν πᾶσιν, *en pasin*, the normal manner of conveying "sphere." Thus, it seems best to take "all things" as the object of the verb, meaning "He (i.e., God) works all things together for the good."

Furthermore, while the longer reading (the inclusion of "God" as the definite subject of the verb "works together") may, on text critical grounds, have slightly less weight (since it can be explained as a scribal gloss or addition on theological grounds), it nonetheless seems to me to accurately explain the meaning of the verse. For the subject must certainly be "God," not "Spirit," and the object of the verb is "all things," so that the meaning is that God actively works all things together for good. In the midst of this life's struggles and groanings (vv. 26-27), we may take full assurance that all matters of life, particularly those which are burdensome, are fully within the preview of God's providence as He sovereignly works the events of history together to accomplish His purposes of each of His children.

The fact that the Apostle presumes all are in agreement with this ("And we know") is also telling. In an era of theological drift, where biblical illiteracy is the norm rather than the exception, it is no wonder that people who claim faith in Yeshua are driven this way and that by the tyranny of life's worries. We have learned to live life from one care to another, unable to "cast all our cares" upon the One Who alone is able to control all things by the word of His power. And we have done this because we have never owned as our personal possession the glorious gift of God's sovereignty. We have not practiced the faith-exercise of placing into the hands of the Almighty the events of our lives which are out of our control. Yet for Paul's audience, he presumes that they are not only well aware of this truth, but that they likewise live with this reality in mind.

Therefore Paul, at the beginning of this great crescendo of praise, emphasizes the all-controlling, merciful hand of God in ordering the affairs of our lives.

The actual order of the words in the Greek is this: "And we know that to those who love God all things He (or God) works together resulting in good, to those who according to His purpose are called." The phrase "to those who love God" identifies Paul's target audience in the statement of this verse. Placed at the beginning of the verse, "to those who love God" is emphasized as the normal characteristic of those who have come into a covenant relationship with Him. The whole idea of "loving" God is a common thread in the Tanach and early Jewish literature.[237] It speaks, not so much of the emotional aspects so associated with our English word "love," but of covenant loyalty and obedience—of covenant relationship based upon a commitment to honor and sanctify HaShem in one's life and actions. "Loving God" means keeping His commandments[238] and demonstrates covenant membership through faithfulness to the King.

to those who are called according to His purpose – Paul ends the verse by adding an additional phrase by which he further characterizes and identifies those he first designates as "those who love God." A number of questions are presented by this phrase: 1) why did Paul feel the need to further identify "those who love God?" 2) Why did he qualify "called" with the words "according to His purpose" (can anyone be called other than "according to His purpose?") 3) To what does "purpose" refer?

The word translated "purpose" is πρόθεσιν (*prothesin*) and is understood by the early Greek commentators (Chrysostom, Theodoret, etc.) to mean "choice" and to refer to the action of man's will in "choosing" to believe. Augustine, of course, took the opposite view, referring the word to God's choice, not man's.

If we look where the Greek word is used elsewhere, we find it only one other time in the Apostolic Scriptures, namely, at Rom 9:11— "for though the twins were not yet born, and had not done anything good or bad, in order that God's <u>purpose</u> according to His choice might stand." Here Paul surely has God's choice in mind, not that of mankind. And this is also the thrust of Paul in our own context as vv. 29-30 show, in which the verbs "foreknew" and "predestined" clearly put the emphasis upon God's sovereign choice, not man's.

Why does Paul add the term "according to purpose?" It seems clear that his reason is to emphasize the effectual nature of the "call" to which he refers, for the words of Yeshua, "many are called but few are chosen" (Mt 22:14) may have been understood by some (as they were by later fathers in the church) to imply a non-effectual calling by the Father, i.e., a call which could be refused. However, in John 10 Yeshua teaches that His sheep hear (=obey) His voice and follow Him, so that when He calls, they come. Thus, we find that in the Scriptures the context determines whether the divine "call" to salvation is that of the general proclamation of the gospel (which can be refused) or the divine call of the Father drawing His own to Himself (Jn 6:44). It is to the latter that Paul refers here, for the unbreakable chain of salvation in vv. 29-30 begins with the divine call of the elect to salvation.[239]

So why was it that Paul added this final phrase to the verse, an additional characterization of those who "love God?" It seems clear now to see that the additional phrase puts the love the elect have for God in correct perspective. Behind the love which those who are righteous by faith have for God is God's own prior choice of them.

> So Paul in a way corrects himself (cp. Gal 4:9): 'to those who love God'—that is, 'to those who are called according to his purpose.' Their love for Him is a sign and token of His prior love for them. The certainty of the hope, of which Paul has spoken, rests on nothing less than the eternal purpose of God.[240]

29–30 For whom He foreknew, He also predestined to become conformed to the image of His Son, that He might be the firstborn among many brethren; and whom He predestined, these He also called; and whom He called, these He also justified; and whom He justified, these He also glorified.

Verses 29-30 form a five-fold chain, linked together and unbreakable. A literal (or somewhat wooden) translation of the core sentence brings this out:

"For those He foreknew, He predestined . . . and those He predestined, these also He called. And those He called, these He also declared righteous. And those He declared righteous, these He also glorified."

Thus, all those gathered together under one action of God are inevitably moved to the next group—none are lost in the process, for everyone that is foreknown ends up in the group designated by the term "glorified." That Paul begins the verse with "For" alerts us to the fact that he is here giving further substantiation of the stated fact, that God works all things together for good.

whom He forknew – The Greek προέγνω (*proegno*) has the common word for "know" as its base (γινωσκω, *ginosko*) and should be understood in the context of Hebrew יָדַע, *yada'*, which denotes that special relationship between God and a chosen individual, which is the result of God's electing grace.[241] That He is said to "foreknow," should be understood as "have relationship (=know) before" in the sense of having been chosen and brought into the covenant even before the world was created.[242] The verb in its present context is surely the action of God and results in ultimate and final salvation. To attempt to bring into this context the "decision" of the individual as simply "seen in advance by God" is to miss the thrust which Paul desires, namely, that God is the One who is in control and working everything out according to His purpose. (See the Exursus below on "God's Foreknowledge").

He also predestined to become conformed to the image of His Son – This is the second link in the five-fold chain of God's salvific work on behalf of sinners. Whereas "foreknow" denoted God's gracious election or choice of those who would be His, the term "predestined" envisions the means by which this choosing would affect the individual. God has determined each and every event through which He, in His kind intentions, will bring the elect to faith. And, the ultimate goal of this predestination is the full realization of mankind's creation, i.e., the full outshining of the image of God in which he was created. Since Paul sees Messiah as the focal point of all creation (cf. Col 1:16) as well as the perfect revelation of the Father (cf. 2Co 4:4; Col 1:15), it is obvious that those who realize their creative purpose will have become conformed to the image of God as seen in the incarnate Son. Thus, becoming "like Messiah" is the inevitable end of God's providence as worked out by His grace.

Now in the context Paul certainly intends that his readers recognize that the present "groaning" is part of this providence, so that suffering for righteousness in this life is part of the means by which God conforms His children into the very image of His Son, Yeshua.

On the idea of predestination, cf. Ac 4:28; Eph 1:5, 11. Also cp. Acts 14:38.

that He might be the firstborn among many brethren – Here we have, as often in Paul, the purpose given for God's salvation of the elect. It is not, in the first case, for their own comfort or safety, but rather for the glory of Messiah. God has determined that Messiah be seen not as the only One who enjoys the blessings and privileges of sonship, but as the Head of a multitude of brothers who, through Him, have come into that familial relationship with the Father. Even as the former context spoke of the groaning with regard to the adoption as sons, so here we see that the enjoyment of this adoptive privilege and the status of "sonship" awaits (at least in its full expression) the time when the elect will be fully conformed to the likeness of Yeshua.

The word "firstborn" (πρωτότοκος, *prototokos*) is found in Col 1:15, 18; Heb 1:6; Rev 1:5, and conveys first a "priority" or "pre-eminence," as the firstborn son was allotted a double portion in matters of inheritance. That Yeshua should receive the "double-portion" (as it were) from creation is at least one primary intent of God's willingness to save sinners.

But the term "firstborn" also denotes the idea of "unique" for the simple reason that there could be only one "firstborn" in the family. Yeshua as the "only begotten" (cf. Jn 3:16, μονογενής, *monogenes*) is the unique Son of God. In this position of unique pre-eminence, Yeshua is willing to share His privileges of sonship with all of His brethren.

and whom He predestined, these He also called – This is the third link in the five-link chain and brings us into the realm of history. Here we have, not the general call of the gospel, but the specific and individual event in which God, through the means of the gospel, effectually calls the sinner to repentance, giving him or her faith to believe in the Lamb of God as a substitute for the punishment of sin rightfully deserved. Thus, when God so works upon the heart of the elect as to call him or her to faith, the elect individual always responds with the obedience of faith (cf. Rom 1:5).

> Indeed, calling in this sense and in the salvation experience might be likened to the obverse and reverse of the same coin: they are the same event seen from two different points of view.[243]

This is usually labelled the "effectual call" by systematic theologians.

and whom He called, these He also justified – Each and everyone summed in the group labeled "predestined" is likewise "called" with an effectual call. The reason we know this calling is effectual is because the chain continues forward with the word "justified" (declared righteous). All those who are called become part of the group labeled "justified" or "declared righteous." The calling of the gospel upon the heart of the elect is energized by the Spirit in such a way as to always lead to an acceptance of Yeshua, a repentance of sin, and a turning to live unto HaShem through the power of the Spirit. Having placed faith in the Lamb of God, His death is accredited to the elect, and their sin is therefore expunged. He is declared "justified" (not guilty) in the courts of heaven.

and whom He justified, these He also glorified – The use of the same past tense (aorist) in the word "glorified," as with the former verbs, is significant. In a very real sense the glorification of the elect is still future, and in fact, is that upon which the believer has laid his hope (cf. vv. 25ff; 5:2). And this future aspect is not to be lost sight of, for we cannot expect that in this fallen world the righteousness which characterizes the very dwelling of God should be the norm. Rather, recognizing that the making-right of all things is still future, we wait with anticipation.

But the fact that Paul has cast the glorification of the elect in the same aorist tense as their justification only highlights the fact that for Paul, the glorification of the elect is equally as sure as their justification, for it has, like justification, been ordained of God.

> Moreover, Messiah, in whose destiny their destiny is included, has already been glorified, so that in Him their glorification has already been accomplished.[244]

Its accomplished fact, then, need only be applied in the course of time at the appearing of Yeshua for His bride.

What is more, the fact that sanctification is not mentioned as an intermediate link between justification and glorification should in no way be construed to say that sanctification is relatively unimportant to Paul. On the contrary, Paul has spent a good deal of time (chapters 6-7) speaking to the very issue of sanctification. Rather, it seems most likely that for Paul glorification was viewed as the final aspect of sanctification, which culminates in a full conformity to the image of the Messiah which will only take place at the time when mortal puts on immortality. In this way, glorification is the final step of sanctification for the believer.

Excursus on God's Foreknowledge

The great dilemma in the minds of some is the simple fact that "free will" cannot exist in a universe where there is Divine determination. To admit that events are predetermined is, in the minds of some, at the same time to dismiss the possibility of a valid choice by mankind. Either there is determinism, in which case all events are set in place and thus man's choice is excluded, or there is free will, which, if it does exist, must preclude Divine determinism.

The problem with this either/or position, however, is that the Scriptures surely speak as though both are true (i.e., valid choice and Divine determinism) yet do not attempt to reconcile what, to our minds, may seem a blatant contradiction. Note, for instance, a verse like Proverbs 16:4—

> The LORD has made everything for its own purpose, Even the wicked for the day of evil.

Or the wide-sweeping statement of Paul in Rom 11:33-36:

> Oh, the depth of the riches both of the wisdom and knowledge of God! How unsearchable are His judgments and unfathomable His ways! For who has known the mind of the Lord, or who became His counselor? Or who has first given to Him that it might be paid back to him again? For from Him and through Him and to Him are all things. To Him be the glory forever. Amen.

How can "all things" come from God, be sustained by God, and return to God, if in fact He has not determined the events which govern "all things?"

Or consider 1 Peter 2:6-8 which has the Apostle Peter teaching us that the wicked were "appointed" to their punishment of doom:

> For this is contained in Scripture: "Behold I lay in Zion a choice stone, a precious corner stone, And he who believes in Him shall not be disappointed." This precious value, then, is for you who believe. But for those who disbelieve, "The stone which the builders rejected, This became the very corner stone," and, "A stone of stumbling and a rock of offense;" for they stumble because they are disobedient to the word, and to this doom they were also appointed.

On the other hand, those who come to faith in Yeshua and are therefore given an eternity of bliss are likewise appointed to this end: Acts 13:48

> And when the Gentiles heard this, they began rejoicing and glorifying the word of the Lord; and as many as had been appointed to eternal life believed.

Note well in this description by Luke that believing is the result of being appointed, not *vice versa*.

B. B. Warfield sums up the issue this way:

> That the acts of free agents are included in the "productive foreknowledge" or rather in this all-inclusive plan of the life of the universe, created for the Old Testament writers apparently not the least embarrassment. This is not because they did not believe man to be free,—throughout the whole Old Testament there is never the least doubt expressed of the freedom or moral responsibility of man,—but because they did believe God to be free, whether in His works of creation or of providence, and could not believe He was hampered or limited in the attainment of His ends by the creatures of His own hands. How God governs the acts of free agents in the pursuance of His plan there is little in the Old Testament to inform us; but that He governs them in even their most intimate thoughts and feelings and impulses is its unvarying assumption: He is not only the creator of the hearts of men in the first instance, and knows them altogether, but He fashions the hearts of all in all the changing circumstances of life (Ps 33:15); forms the spirit of man within him in all its motions (Zech 12:1); keeps the hearts of men in His hands, turning them withersoever He will (Prov 21:1); so that it is even said that man knows what is in his own mind only as the Lord reveals it to him (Amos 4:13). The discussion of any antinomy that may be thought to

arise from such a joint assertion of the absolute rule of God in the sphere of the spirit and the freedom of the creaturely will, falls obviously under the topic of Providential Government rather than under that of the Decrees: it requires to be adverted to here only that we may clearly note the fact that the Old Testament teachers, as they did not hesitate to affirm the absolute sway of God over the thoughts and intents of the human heart, could feel no embarrassment in the inclusion of the acts of free agents within the all-embracing plan of God, the outworking of which His providential government supplies.[245]

Surely we see the revealed truth of God calling His people to obedience and offering them rewards for submission to His will, and punishment for disobedience. But there is a further question: do the Scriptures teach that each person has both the responsibility and the ability to choose what is right, so that rewards for obedience and punishment for disobedience rests upon the individual choice? Do the Scriptures indicate that man has a "free will" and that as a result of this "free will" he is able and therefore responsible to choose the good and to shun evil? A brief reflection upon the Pauline letters makes it clear that, in fact, fallen mankind does not have the ability to choose what is good. Paul has gone out of his way in Romans 3 to show us that (based upon the Tanach) sinful man will always and inevitably choose the evil and run from God. Even his "best" choices are not those which please HaShem. If Paul is right that "there is none righteous, not even one" and that "none seek for God," then it seems patently clear that left to himself, man will never choose to submit to God's rule, and to receive from Him the salvation that comes through faith alone.

Here, then, is the myth of "free will." Mankind's will is naturally bent to sin and to hostility against God (Rom 8:7). His will is not free—it is bound by sin to which he is a slave. He is totally depraved, by which I mean, he is totally unable of his own strength either to find God or to lay hold of Him for salvation, because fallen man's nature is such that he inevitably runs from God, not toward Him. What is more, this fallen nature would much rather "make a god" than submit to the One, True God.

How then can sinful man ever be saved? How can a fallen soul, bent to sin and against God, ever come to honest contrition and repentance, and find in God the salvation that comes through faith apart from the works of the Torah?

The answer lies in God's sovereign work of redemption, a work which He initiates, accomplishes, and applies to those He has chosen as His own. From all that the Scriptures teach us, we may come to the understanding that sometime in eternity past, God, of His own free will, unencumbered by any outside influence, chose to commit Himself in covenant faithfulness to a host of people He would create. This covenant faithfulness was determined in light of these people's sin and rebellion, and included the means by which their salvation should be wrought. If we should put this transaction of eternal, covenant faithfulness into a single word, it would be the term the Apostle uses in this text, the term "foreknow."

All too often the term "foreknow" (προγινώσκω, proginosko and πρόνωσις, pronosis) is read with our Western worldview to mean "know in advance" or what the Christian theologians called "prescience." But this is to overlook the use of the word "know" (primarily the Hebrew verb יָדַע, yada') in the Tanach. We are all familiar with the fact that the euphemistic "know one's wife" means to have sexual relations. This use of the word "know" doubtlessly gave rise to the sense of "have close relations with" and thus the term became standard terminology in covenant language. Thus, to "not know" means "to be faithless to the covenant maker" (Is 1:3; 45:4). On the other hand, "to know the Lord" means to be loyal to the covenant maker, and to live within the boundaries of the covenant (Jer 31:34). For the Lord "to know" Israel means to establish His covenant relationship with her (Amos 3:2, "You only have I known….").

Indeed, even in the covenants and treaties of the Ancient Near East the use of the term "know" is found. In a Hittite treaty between Hugganas and the Great King (referred to as the "Sun") we read:

And you, Hugganas, know only the Sun regarding lordship: also my son of whom I , the
Sun, say, "This one everyone should know . . .
you, Hugganas, know him! . . . . Moreover, any other do not know![246]

This single example could be duplicated multiple times as the ancient texts reveal the covenant
use of the term "know."

The implications for our study are obvious: "foreknowledge" has nothing to do with
"knowing something in advance" when the term is used in a covenant sense. And surely redemption throughout the Scriptures is cast in the context of covenant. It seems obvious to me
that "foreknow" must be understood to mean "enact a covenant relationship beforehand." This
is what God has done for His chosen ones. He has "foreknown" them in the sense that He has
established covenant relationship with them from before the world began.

**31–32 What then shall we say to these things? If God is for us, who is against us? He who
did not spare His own Son, but delivered Him up for us all, how will He not also with Him
freely give us all things?**

"What shall we say" is a way for Paul to introduce his own conclusion on the matter (cf. 3:
5). But to what does he refer with "these things?" It seems clear that the direct reference is to
verses 28 or 29 through 30, but the breadth of material contained in this section shows that Paul
has in mind the whole of the epistle up to this point, not merely the last three verses. By "these
things," then, we should understand Paul to be referring to his entire treatise on how God saves
sinners—the means by which God declares a sinner righteous.

If God is for us (εἰ ὁ θεὸς ὑπὲρ ἡμῶν) – We should compare Ps 23:4, "I will fear no evil, for
You are with me" or Ps 56:9, "This I know, that God is for me" (ἰδοὺ ἔγνων ὅτι θεός μου εἶ σύ)
and 56:11 "In God I have put my trust, I shall not be afraid. What can man do to me?" (ἐπὶ τῷ
θεῷ ἤλπισα οὐ φοβηθήσομαι τί ποιήσει μοι ἄνθρωπος). Indeed, throughout the Tanach the presence of God with Israel was the assurance of her success and victory over her enemies. On the
other hand, if God withdrew from Israel, she was left vulnerable and subdued by her enemies.

Once again, the "if" of this clause should be understood as a real condition and suggesting
that there exists a possibility that God is not for us. We could as well translate it "Since God is
for us . . . ."

The phrase "God is for us" (ὁ θεὸς ὑπὲρ ἡμῶν) is to be understood as "God is on our side."
Mark 9:40 (=Luke 9:50) uses the same preposition (ὑπέρ, *huper*) as in our text, clearly giving it
the meaning "on the side of": "For he who is not against us is for us."

The declaration that God is "for" us or "on our side" forms a concise summary of the gospel. What is meant, simply, is that God is for us in the way indicated in all of the gospel events:
in His own sovereign desire to rescue us from the damnation of our sins, and His willingness
to pay the necessary "costs" which our redemption would require. He is "for us" in foreknowledge, predestination, calling, justification, and glorification. He is "for us" in all those things
necessary to bring us to Himself, and to make us whole and fit for His kingdom.

who is against us? – Like the former "for" (ὑπέρ) means "on the side of," so "against" (κατά,
kata) means "against us" in the sense of "not on our side," and should be understood to convey the idea in a rhetorical way, i.e., that we need not fear those who may be our enemies. For
though they may wage war against us, their power is no match for that of the Almighty Who
is "for us" and will therefore protect us with His divine power and presence. Though enemies
of this world may cause us no little pain and distress, they are not able to "snatch us from the
Father's hand," for our lives are secured there by His omnipotence.

He who did not spare His own Son – The language is very similar to the Lxx of Gen 22:12, 16:

Lxx (Gen 22:12, 26)	Paul (Rom 8:32)
καὶ οὐκ ἐφείσω τοῦ υἱοῦ σου τοῦ ἀγαπητοῦ δι' ἐμέ and on My account have not withheld your beloved son	ὅς γε τοῦ ἰδίου υἱοῦ οὐκ ἐφείσατο He who did not spare his own Son

The contrast, however, is also obvious: Abraham, in actually putting Isaac upon the altar and binding him with every intention to slaughter him, is viewed by God as having actually given Isaac. Isaac, however, was spared the death of sacrifice, and the ram was slain in his place. (Some rabbis believed Isaac was actually slain and offered as a sacrifice, cf. *Sifra,* ed. Weiss, p. 102c; y.*Taanit* 65a; b.*Ta'anit* 16a; Mid. Rab. *Gen* xlix.11; xciv.5; Mid Rab. *Lev* 36:5; *Tanchuma Vayyera,* §23; *Mechilta,* 1.57, 87-8). Not so for the Messiah, the son of God. Like Abraham, God put forward the Son of His love, but there was no substitute to be found.

But delivered Him up for us all – The word order of the verse throws the "for us" to the front of the sentence, emphasizing it: "But for us all He delivered Him up." The clear meaning of the Apostle is that the death of the Messiah was purposeful, and that by His death that purpose was realized. This goes together with the language of sacrifice in the verb "deliver up" (see below), for the sacrificial ritual involved the placing of the sinner's hands upon the head of the sin offering as symbolically transferring his sin to the innocent victim. This vicarious, one-for-one representation is surely in the mind of the Apostle as He considers Yeshua the sin offering. He was delivered up for us, i.e., with our sins placed upon Him.

The verb "deliver up" (παραδίδωμι, *paradidomi*) was used in 4:25 (in the passive voice) of Yeshua's sacrifice, and echoes the language of the Lxx of Isaiah 53:6, 11-12, which is somewhat different than the MT. (See notes on 4:25 above). The Greek verb παραδίδωμι in Isaiah 53 surely pictures the sacrificial ritual of "delivering up" the animal to the altar (note the opening motif of a "lamb" led to the slaughter), and this central text among the early Messianics most likely attached this more technical meaning to the word which otherwise has its primary meaning within the context of war or agression (i.e., to be delivered/not delivered into the hands of one's enemies).

how will He not also with Him freely give us all things? – The argument is *kal v'chomer*: if God gave the greatest of gifts, i.e., His Son Yeshua, in order to redeem us from our sins and to constitute us holy before Him, how much more will He be willing to give us those things necessary to walk in the ways of grace and sanctification in order to be conformed to the image of His Son? All other matters of our salvation are far less costly than the high cost of His own Son's life.

"Freely give" translates χαρίσεται (*charisetai* from χαρίζομαι, *charizomai*) which could also be understood as "forgive" (cf. 2Co 2:7, 10; Eph 4:32). But the context as well as the prepositional phrase "with Him" (σὺν αὐτῷ, *sun auto*) would rather opt for the meaning "give," (cf. Phil 1: 29; 2:9; Philemon 22), and with the sense of χάρις, *charis,* "grace," the NASB is justified in adding "freely." God, Who delivered up the supreme gift of His Son for us, can be expected to do all things necessary to assure the full success of His Son's saving work.

all things – Comparing this passage to 1Co 3:21-23 might suggest that the phrase "all things" means a share in the reign of Messiah in the eschaton. Some have seen this idea hinted at as well in the phrase "fellow heirs with Messiah" found in Rom 8:17. However, the immediate context would rather suggest that what Paul means by "all things" is "all things necessary for our salvation" or "all things necessary to secure our eternal and final salvation."

One thing that is obvious from this verse (among others) is that for Paul, the full realization of salvation is the inevitable end or result of the cross. Those for whom the Messiah dies are assured all aspects of God's grace necessary to bring about their full and eternal salvation.

It seems clear, then, that the Apostle did not envision the work of Messiah in His death, resurrection, ascension and intercession as anything but efficacious. That is to say, since the death of the Messiah was a vicarious, substitutional death (foreshadowed by the sacrificial system of the Tabernacle and Temple), and since it was in every way accepted before the Father, the outcome must be that those sins for which He died are, in fact, paid for and will never require payment again. It is, in fact, this view of the Messiah's atonement that corresponds to the words of Scripture in which those for whom He died are assured eternal peace and life.

Excursus on the Purpose of Messiah's Death

We may speak of Messiah's death as encompassing not only His death but also His resurrection, ascension, and intercession, for the Apostles clearly meld all aspects of Yeshua's salvific work together as a unit, as Rom 8:32 itself suggests. We may therefore ask an all-important question: for what purpose did the Father require the Son to die, and was that purpose realized?

When we ask ourselves regarding the purpose of the cross, numbers of Scriptures immediately supply the answer. We may begin with the high point of the Tanach on the subject, Isaiah 53:

> 5 But He was pierced through for our transgressions, He was crushed for our iniquities; The chastening for our well-being fell upon Him, And by His scourging we are healed.

> 10–11 But the LORD was pleased To crush Him, putting Him to grief; If He would render Himself as a guilt offering, He will see His offspring, He will prolong His days, And the good pleasure of the LORD will prosper in His hand. As a result of the anguish of His soul, He will see it and be satisfied; By His knowledge the Righteous One, My Servant, will justify the many, As He will bear their iniquities.

In each of these passages from Isaiah 53 the language itself is cast in the nuance of "purpose:" He was pierced *for* our transgressions, He was crushed *for* our iniquities. . . . The reason He was pierced was *on account of* our sins—thus, the purpose of the piercing/crushing (which was done by the Father in the final analysis, cf. v. 10) was to pay for sins. Furthermore, in vv. 10-11 the purpose of the Father in cursing the Messiah was so that He would be rendered a guilt offering (אָשָׁם, *'asham*), and thus, by bearing the iniquities of His people, He would "justify the many." Clearly the purpose of the Messiah's sufferings here is pinpointed in the term "justify."

This same motif is repeated over and over again in the Apostolic Scriptures. Note the following:

> Luke 19:10 For the Son of Man has come to seek and to save that which was lost."

> John 10:10 The thief comes only to steal, and kill, and destroy; I came that they might have life, and might have it abundantly.

> 2Cor. 5:21 He made Him who knew no sin to be sin on our behalf, that we might become the righteousness of God in Him.

> 1Tim. 1:15 It is a trustworthy statement, deserving full acceptance, that Messiah Yeshua came into the world to save sinners, among whom I am foremost of all.

> 1Pet. 3:18 For Messiah also died for sins once for all, the just for the unjust, in order that He might bring us to God, having been put to death in the flesh, but made alive in the spirit;

In each of these passages the purpose for the very coming of Messiah is clearly spelled out: He came in order to save sinners—to bring them to God. The question which must then be asked is obvious: did He fulfill the purpose for which He came? As far as the Apostle Paul is concerned, the answer is an emphatic "yes." The work of the Messiah in all of His saving acts assures that there will be a great host of people of every kindred and tongue who are redeemed and who, because of the sacrifice Yeshua made for them, will spend all eternity in the presence of God. None for whom the Messiah suffered can ever run the risk of being anything other than fully redeemed and fully guaranteed eternal life in God's presence.

This inevitability is not the result of the sinner's repentance nor of his "good works." It is rather the result of the efficacious work of the Messiah—the value of His saving work (death, resurrection, ascension, and intercession) secures the safety of the sinner, for He has purchased the sinner with the necessary price (life for life) and has secured his eternal shalom.

Thus, even as Rom 8:32 indicates that one's justification and glorification are linked via the unbreakable chain of God's sovereign decrees, so Paul makes it clear that each and everyone for whom Messiah has suffered will also receive the necessary graces ("all things") to cause him to persevere in the ways of God's grace. And the inevitable reward for perseverance is nothing short of eternal redemption.

This understanding of the efficacious nature of Messiah's death, however, is not normally taught in the Christian, mainline denominations. What used to be the standard understanding of the purpose of Messiah's death has given way to a perspective that can best be identified by the word "potential." Instead of seeing that the death of Yeshua secures the inevitable and eternal salvation of the elect, this view holds that the death of Messiah simply made salvation (in all of its facets) possible, not actual. No one is actually saved by the death of Messiah, but rather the death of the Messiah makes salvation possible. What then is required to be added to the death of the Messiah in order to turn this potential salvation into actual salvation? It is the choice of the sinner to take the redemption which is offered. Thus, the death of Messiah makes no absolute claim upon sinners. The salvation is simply made available, and the the choice of the sinner is the final issue which either appropriates the salvation (resulting in eternal life) or despises it (resulting in condemnation).

The interesting thing, however, is that the Scriptures do not speak about the death of Messiah in any kind of "potential" or "possible" terms. Rather, the death of Messiah is constantly understood by the Apostles to make salvation inevitable, not possible. Note the following:

> Acts 20:28 Be on guard for yourselves and for all the flock, among which the Holy Spirit has made you overseers, to shepherd the church of God which He purchased with His own blood.

> 1Cor 6:19–20 Or do you not know that your body is a temple of the Holy Spirit who is in you, whom you have from God, and that you are not your own? For you have been bought with a price: therefore glorify God in your body.

> Col 2:13–14 And when you were dead in your transgressions and the uncircumcision of your flesh, He made you alive together with Him, having forgiven us all our transgressions, having canceled out the certificate of debt consisting of decrees against us and which was hostile to us; and He has taken it out of the way, having nailed it to the cross.

> Rev. 5:9 And they sang a new song, saying, "Worthy art Thou to take the book, and to break its seals; for Thou wast slain, and didst purchase for God with Thy blood men from every tribe and tongue and people and nation."

In each of these the death of the Messiah does not make salvation possible, but makes it inevitable or actual for those for whom He died. There is no sense of "potential" language here, but clear and concise language of "actuality." The Scriptures, when considered as a whole, clearly teach that Messiah's death upon the cross as the substitute sacrifice for sinners was nothing short of efficacious, meaning that His death actually purchased doomed sinners and redeemed them from the penalty of sin, securing their eternal salvation. This makes the cross infinitely powerful, not potential, for it is the basis for the victory of God over sin, and thus makes the future salvation of an innumerable host a reality.

Moreover, it is this knowlege, that the saving work of Messiah actually redeems sinners, that becomes the greatest motivation for telling others the good news of the cross.

33–34 Who will bring a charge against God's elect? God is the one who justifies; who is the one who condemns? Messiah Yeshua is He who died, yes, rather who was raised, who is at the right hand of God, who also intercedes for us.

Since the Greek text does not have any punctuation marks, there has been, in the history of the interpretation of Romans, varying suggestions on exactly how these verses should be punctuated. The NASB and NIV, along with all major English translations follow the punctuation suggested by Nestles Greek text. Other possibilities include:

> Who will bring a charge against God's elect? Is not God the one who justifies? Who is the one who condemns? Is not Messiah Yeshua He who died? Yes, rather who was raised? Is He not at the right hand of God? Does He not also intercede for us?

> Who will bring a charge against God's elect? Is not God the one who justifies? Who is the one who condemns? Is not Messiah Yeshua He who died, yes, rather who was raised, who is at the right hand of God, who also intercedes for us?

The primary difference, of course, is in making rhetorical questions out of what the NASB and the rest cast as statements of fact. But in the end, the result is nearly the same, for rhetorical questions presume a positive answer, and this would surely be the case here as well.

Who will bring a charge against God's elect? – Beginning in v. 28 Paul has laid out for us a very tight argument regarding the inevitable salvation of God's children. Since God causes all things to work together for good to those who love Him, that is, to those who are called by His purposes, we can be assured that He will accomplish all of His will. Paul then goes on in verses 29-32 to show that God has determined to save His people from their sins through a plan of salvation which He both initiated and maintains, a plan which assures the eternal safety of all who are His. This begins with His predetermined plan, and includes all the events, both eternal and historical, necessary to bring His chosen to dwell with Him forever. He will equip them in everything necessary to bring them to glory.

Paul has, in these verses (28-32) taken every obstacle out of the way, both in the realm of God's intentions as well as in the believer's position in Messiah. God will never change His mind, and the elect are the object of God's determined, saving actions.

In our present verse, however, Paul now turns his attention to those forces outside of the believer, and other than God. Is it possible that someone, somewhere would be able to make a charge against one of God's children, a charge that would render them unfit for an eternity with the Master? Paul, in stating this as a rhetorical question, makes the answer emphatic. No one could ever bring a charge against someone for whom Messiah died, and make that charge "stick." The death of Yeshua on behalf of His own chosen ones is a death which in every way answers the charge of God's justice and righteousness. If, therefore, the Father's justice is fully satisfied by the death of Yeshua for His chosen ones, then surely no other being in the universe could ever think to make a legal claim against one of God's children.

God is the one who justifies – Here Paul, for the last time in Romans, pens the word "justify," a term that has been used often in the first eight chapters. How fitting it should be in a statement so categorical and direct: God is the one who justifies! Here, in his final statement on justification, Paul once again reminds us that being declared righteous is the work of God toward the sinner, and not anything the sinner does himself.

Obviously, in the context, the emphatic statement that "God is the one who justifies" is given to show how totally absurd it is to think that after God has declared a sinner righteous, anyone could think to bring a charge against the justified one. For if God, the supreme Sovereign and Judge of the universe has declared a particular sinner to be "without guilt," who would dare call into question His declaration?

In this we find our true assurance. If our justification were, in any way, dependent upon our own work or strength, we would often be sure that we were doomed. For no matter how we may long to be righteous before HaShem—no matter how much we strive for and attain righteous living, when we are compared to the infinite holiness of God Himself, we always find ourselves falling short. And since He is the standard for holiness, anyone who falls short of His infinite holiness is in need of "cleansing," of being justified.

Furthermore, if our justification were dependent upon a "church" or some other governing authority, we would be just as hopeless as trusting in our own strength. For regardless of how mature and pious leaders may be, they cannot themselves attain the stature of God's holiness for themselves—how much less could they attain it for someone else? In the final analysis, then, only the justification that God Himself both accomplishes and proclaims can ever hope to stand in the light of His infinite holiness. That God is the one Who justifies is the only hope for sinners. And Paul affirms that this is true for all upon whom, from eternity past, God showered His mercy and love in the Messiah.

Who is the one who condemns? – Once again, Paul raises his challenge to the extent of the universe, asking anyone to bring a condemning charge against the sinner whose sin has been covered by the blood of Yeshua. His question, once again rhetorical, is an emphatic way of saying: "no one is able to condemn!"

Paul then proceeds to outline four "pillars" which support the categorical statement that no one would ever be able to condemn the child of God: 1) the death of Yeshua, 2) the resurrection of Yeshua, 3) the ascension of Yeshua, 4) the intercession of Yeshua on behalf of His people. We might look at these four as the legs of a chair. While three legs can be somewhat stable, two legs, or even one, cannot work. But if one wants full stability, four legs are the best. Here Paul gives the platform of our salvation a full compliment of "legs," bringing forth the essential work of Yeshua on behalf of His people, work which assures their full salvation.

When these four aspects of Yeshua's work are considered, if most believers were to be asked how the death and resurrection of Yeshua provide the foundation for their salvation, many would be able to give fairly adequate answers. When asked, however, how the ascension of Yeshua constitutes a foundation for salvation, a greater number of people are left in a quandary, and even more when the task is to explain how the intercessory work of Yeshua as our High Priest secures our salvation. Yet Paul does not consider the death of Yeshua sufficient for salvation, nor even the death and resurrection of our Messiah. Paul envisions the saving work of Yeshua as encompassing His death, resurrection, ascension, and intercession, because Paul recognizes the essential part each of these play in the overall scope of redemption.

We may begin by discussing the term "condemns." The Greek word is κατακρίνω, *katakrino,* found in 2:1; 8:3; and 14:23. Paul uses it to describe eternal condemnation (as here) as well as temporal (2:1). The primary meaning is to "judge as worthy of death," the word being made up of the common term for "judge" with a perfective preposition, thus, "thoroughly or completely judged." Paul's question, then, comes to the "bottom line:" when the dust clears and the final judgment has past, who will stand as righteous, and who will be condemned?

Paul's confidence that those who are "in Messiah" will not be condemned (cf. 8:1) is based upon his understanding that salvation for an individual sinner rests not only upon the grace of God, but equally upon His justice or righteousness. For in the same way that God's infinite grace has reached out to unworthy sinners; in the same way that His unflinching justice has demanded the punishment of sinners—in this same way His holiness and justice demand that He fulfill His promises. Moreover, it is His very justice which demanded the payment for sin in the first place, and thus required that His own Son, Yeshua, make payment for the sins of His people. In that Yeshua paid the penalty in full, and since God is just and right in all His ways, it stands that He must accept the work which Yeshua has accomplished, and that as a result those who are "in Messiah" are assured of their eternal well-being. Never will anyone be able to judge us as worthy of eternal condemnation, for the penalty for our well-being fell upon Him and by His stripes we are healed.

Messiah Yeshua is He who died – The language is emphatic and to the point. The death of the Messiah was in every way sufficient to pay the penalty of our sins. Some manuscripts have only "Messiah" (Χριστός, *christos*) without the following "Yeshua," (Ἰησοῦς, *iesous*) and it may well be that it was added by later scribes who regularly associate the name "Yeshua" with the death of the Messiah.

Why is the mere stating of the fact that Yeshua died sufficient to begin the answer of "Who is the one who condemns?" Once again we see that Paul viewed the death of Yeshua as having actually accomplished salvation because His death was worthy of such aims. And why was His death worthy? The only answer which can be formulated is that His person—His character, demands that His death be worthy. If Yeshua was, as some would have us believe, simply the best of men but in no way divine, then it follows that His death is no better than the death of any one else. For in order for His death to have efficacious benefit for others, He must Himself be without sin. Who, however, is without sin? What man or woman, born into the race of mankind, can honestly claim sinlessness? But if Yeshua's death for us is that which can be argued by the Apostle as sufficient safeguard against our condemnation, then His death must have not been for His own sin, but for the sin of others. Like the sacrificial lamb of old, Yeshua, in order to be a worthy sacrifice, must have been without spot or blemish.

But not only must He have been perfect in terms of righteousness, that is, without sin—He also must be infinite in His being. If the sacrificial system describes for us the manner in which each offense required yet another sacrifice, then it stands to reason that if Yeshua's life was finite, He could have acted as substitute for only one other sinner. On the contrary, however, Yeshua is Himself infinite in His being, and thus as the sacrifice lifted up to the Father, He, the eternal One, was able to give His life as ransom for the many. Thus, in Paul having written "Messiah Yeshua is He who died," the emphasis is first and foremost upon the character of the One who died, not the act of dying. Only after one reckons with the infinite and sinless nature of the Messiah can one understand that His death, and His death alone is sufficient to bring about the salvation of sinners.

That the Messiah should suffer on behalf of sinners is not an idea newly conceived in the Apostolic era. The later rabbinic literature gives evidence that early Sages believed the Messiah, son of Joseph, would suffer. Note Mid. Rab. *Genesis* xcv where the phrase in Genesis 46:28, "And he sent Judah before him unto Joseph" is being expounded:

> BEFORE HIM: to him [Joseph] who will receive the kingdom before him [Judah]. Now when an ox attacks, a lion can come and rescue; but if a lion attacks, an ox cannot come and rescue. Thus of Judah and Joseph, let Joseph receive [power first], because his is temporary; and then Judah, because his is forever.

"Joseph," in this case, refers to Messiah son of Joseph who will suffer and die, while "Judah" refers to Messiah son of David, Who will reign.[247]

Note as well the reference to Zechariah 12:10 in the comments of the Talmudic Sages:[248]

> What is the cause of the mourning [mentioned in the last cited verse]? R. Dosa and the Rabbis differ on the point. One explained, The cause is the slaying of Messiah the son of Joseph, and the other explained, The cause is the slaying of the Evil Inclination.
>
> It is well according to him who explains that the cause is the slaying of Messiah the son of Joseph, since that well agrees with the Scriptural verse, And they shall look upon me because they have thrust him through, and they shall mourn for him as one mourneth for his only son; but according to him who explains the cause to be the slaying of the Evil Inclination, is this [it may be objected] an occasion for mourning? Is it not rather an occasion for rejoicing? Why then should they weep? [The explanation is] as R. Judah expounded: In the time to come the Holy One, blessed be He, will bring the Evil Inclination and slay it in the presence of the righteous and the wicked. To the righteous it will have the appearance of a towering hill, and to the wicked it will have the appearance of a hair thread. Both the former and the latter will weep; the righteous will weep saying, "How were we able to overcome such a towering hill!" The wicked also will weep saying, "How is it that we were unable to conquer this hair thread! And the Holy One, blessed be He, will also marvel together with them, as it is said, Thus saith the Lord of Hosts, If it be marvellous in the eyes of the remnant of this people in those days, it shall also be marvellous in My eyes.

Another mention of Messiah son of Joseph in the rabbinic literature is found in the Midrash on Song of Songs:[249]

> THE FLOWERS APPEAR ON THE EARTH: the conquerors have appeared on the earth. Who are they? R. Berekiah said in the name of R. Isaac: As it is written, And the Lord showed me four craftsmen (Zech. II, 3), namely, Elijah, the Messiah, Melchizedek, and the War Messiah.

Once again, the first Messiah mentioned is understood by the Sages to be Messiah son of Joseph who suffers and dies, while the "War Messiah" is the conquering Messiah, often called "King Messiah," who is Messiah son of David. That the suffering Messiah preceeds the reigning Messiah was a presumption of the early Sages.

Interestingly, even Rashi seems to agree with the early Sages' interpretation of Zechariah 12:10, or at least he gives them mention in his own notes:

> They shall look to me because of those who have been thrust through. Jonathan renders: And they shall look to Me to complain about those of them whom the nations thrust through and slew during their exile. And they shall mourn over it. Over that slaughter, as one mourns over an only son. As a man mourns over his only son. And our Sages expounded this in tractate Sukkah 52a as referring to the Messiah, son of Joseph, who was slain.[250]

The question of whether or not the Qumran scrolls envisioned a suffering Messiah has been hotly contested. One fragmentary text in particular, 4Q285, seemed by some scholars to contain references to a "messiah" who suffers and dies, but who returns to life. Eisenman and Wise made this initial assessment:

> Here, the key question is whether Fragment 7 comes before or after Fragment 6. If after, as we have placed it in our reconstruction, then the Messianic Nasi or 'Leader' would be alive after the events described in Fragment 6 and could be the one 'put to death'.[251]

The text is quite fragmentary, but does use "messianic imagery" (branch, root of Jesse, etc.) and prophesies that "they will put to death the Leader (Nasi) of the Community, the Branch of David." Nasi is used in a messianic way in Ezekiel 37:25, where "My servant David" describes the nasi. Others, however, have questioned whether or not this text actually refers to a dying Messiah who also raises from the dead.[252]

The Gospels also record the words of Caiaphas, the High Priest at the time of Yeshua, who seemed to understand that the death of One for the many was a possible reality: (John 11:47-52)

> Therefore the chief priests and the Pharisees convened a council, and were saying, "What are we doing? For this man is performing many signs. "If we let Him go on like this, all men will believe in Him, and the Romans will come and take away both our place and our nation." But a certain one of them, Caiaphas, who was high priest that year, said to them, "You know nothing at all, nor do you take into account that it is expedient for you that one man should die for the people, and that the whole nation should not perish." Now this he did not say on his own initiative; but being high priest that year, he prophesied that Yeshua was going to die for the nation, and not for the nation only, but that He might also gather together into one the children of God who are scattered abroad.

Moreover, the early Sages understood Isaiah 53 to be speaking of the suffering Messiah as well, not of the nation of Israel as the suffering Servant of God (an interpretation made popular by Rashi):

> Rab said: The world was created only on David's account. Samuel said: On Moses account; R. Johanan said: For the sake of the Messiah. What is his [the Messiah's] name? The School of R. Shila said: His name is Shiloh, for it is written, until Shiloh come. The School of R. Yannai said: His name is Yinnon, for it is written, His name shall endure for ever: e'er the sun was, his name is Yinnon. The School of R. Haninah maintained: His name is Haninah, as it is written, Where I will not give you Haninah. Others say: His name is Menahem the son of Hezekiah, for it is written, Because Menahem [the comforter], that would relieve my soul, is far. The Rabbis said: His name is "the leper scholar," as it is written, Surely he hath borne our griefs, and carried our sorrows: yet we did esteem him a leper, smitten of God, and afflicted. (b. *Sanhedrin* 98b; cf. also Mid. Rab. *Ruth* on 2:14; *Yalqut* ii.571; ii.620)

There is plenty of evidence, then, that there existed a 1st Century expectation for a messiah who would come and die, not as a result of his own sins, but for the sins of the people (note further comments in this regard in Hegg, *The Letter Writer* [FFOZ, 2002], pp. 160-167). That this "messiah" was referred to as the "Messiah son of Joseph" fits the picture of Joseph who, though chosen, was forsaken by his own and mistreated by foreigners. Yet the fact that Joseph excelled and was, in the end, both the "savior" of the then known world as well as the second in command of Egypt, took the illustration to its obvious conclusion: the suffering messiah would, in the end, win over his enemies and rule and reign as the King Messiah, Messiah ben David.

yes, rather, who was raised – The Apostle Paul cannot speak of the death of Messiah without immediate reference to His resurrection. By the opening words of this phrase, "yes, rather . . ." (μᾶλλον δὲ, *mallon de*), Paul insists that the death and resurrection of Messiah be viewed as an inseparable unity. The reason is obvious: apart from the resurrection one could never be sure that the sacrifice had been accepted by the Father. Had Yeshua died and not risen again, one could have argued sufficiently that He died for His own guilt—that He deserved to die.

This necessity of the resurrection is illustrated in the Tabernacle and Temple rituals, particularly in the picture of the Cohen HaGadol (High Priest) on Yom Kippur. According to the Torah,[253] the skirt of the Cohen HaGadol was to have embroidered pomegranates on its hem, separated by golden bells. We know that pomegranates were an ancient symbol of life, shaped as they are like a woman's womb, and full of seeds. The bells also signalled life, for any movement of the priest would cause them to chime. On all ordinary days of the year, the activity of the High Priest would be known by the sound of the bells on his garment. On Yom Kippur, however, the High Priest laid aside his beautiful outer garments, and was robed only in the white linen tunic. He entered silently into the domain of God's glorious presence, there to present the blood and incense upon the Mercy Seat. Only when he reemerged to the waiting throngs were they assured that the atonement had been accepted. Had his service been unacceptable, he would have died as did Nadav and Avihu, the sons of Aaron, who presented strange fire to the Lord. It was therefore the reappearance of the High Priest on the Day of Atonement that was the assurance of an accepted sacrifice.

In the same way the resurrection of Yeshua guaranteed that the Father had fully received and accepted His sacrifice on behalf of sinners. This idea is found in the language of Isaiah 53:11:

> As a result of the anguish of His soul, He will see [light] and be satisfied; By His knowledge the Righteous One, My Servant, will justify the many, As He will bear their iniquities.

The MT and most English translations have "He will see it and be satisfied." However, in the MT there is no object for the verb "see." Interestingly, the Lxx has φῶς, *phos*, "light," a reading that was corroborated by the Dead Sea Scrolls. What does it mean "He will see light?" More than likely it is a reference to the resurrection, for in the Hebrew mind darkness can be associated with the grave, while light is indicative of life. Note, for instance, Luke 1:79

> To shine upon those who sit in darkness and the shadow of death, To guide our feet into the way of peace."

Here, "sitting in darkness" is parallel with the "shadow of death," an expression which means "deepest darkness," because it uses "death" as a superlative. The same is true in Psalm 23, "valley of the shadow of death" (בְּגֵיא צַלְמָוֶת, *b'gei' tzalmavet*), where "death" is viewed as the absence of light.

On the other hand, "light" is associated with life. Note these obvious examples from Job:

> Job 33:28 'He has redeemed my soul from going to the pit, And my life shall see the light.'

> Job 33:30 To bring back his soul from the pit, That he may be enlightened with the light of life.

Here, then, in Isaiah 53, the great chapter outlining the death of the Messiah on behalf of His people, we see the prophet speaking of the resurrection via the metaphor of "light," and associating the concept of "satisfy" with it as well. The point is clear: the resurrection, in the mind of Isaiah, is the clear proof of the value of the Messiah's death, a value which the Father has received and which has satisfied divine justice.

But the resurrection is also an essential aspect of our salvation for yet another reason. Not only does the resurrection proclaim the acceptance of Yeshua's sacrifice before the throne of divine justice, it also proves to all that death can be conquered. If, as we read in Scripture, death is the result of sin, then if Yeshua's death purposed to overcome sin, life must be the result, not death. This is Paul's reasoning in 1Cor 15:16–19:

> For if the dead are not raised, not even Messiah has been raised; and if Messiah has not been raised, your faith is worthless; you are still in your sins. Then those also who have fallen asleep in Messiah have perished. If we have hoped in Messiah in this life only, we are of all men most to be pitied.

Indeed, that Yeshua is the "first fruits from the dead"[254] is the assurance that we who are in Him will follow, one day being raised from the dead and living forever with the Lord. The resurrection is essential because the life which we have in Messiah is eternal life, not merely life in this temporal sphere.

Like the idea that the Messiah would suffer for the unrighteous deeds of the nation, so the belief that He would resurrect from the dead may also have been affirmed in early rabbinic thinking. The second benediction of the *Shemonei Esrei*, called the אַתָּה גִבּוֹר, *'ata gibor*, "You are mighty . . ." affirms the ability of God to raise the dead from the grave, and this ancient prayer is, by most scholars, believed to have been in existence in the 1st Century, and surely by the time of Yavneh in the early 2nd Century CE. M.*Sanhedrin* 10:1 notes that anyone who denies the resurrection forfeits his place in the world to come.

But beyond that clear fact of the resurrection of the righteous in the rabbis, there may likewise be a hint at the resurrection of one who suffers to atone for the sins of others. The *Akedah*, the story of the binding of Isaac, was understood by some rabbis to teach that Isaac was actually offered as a sacrifice by Abraham. In the Yom Kippur liturgy, it is noted that the ashes of Isaac atone for the sins of Israel every year (Artscroll Machzor [nusach sefard] for Yom Kippur, p. 392: זְבוּחוֹ וְדִשׁוּנוֹ לְפָנֶיךָ יְתְיַחַד, "may his [Isaac's] slaughter and his ashes be one before You.") Though the Sages were not unified on the idea that Isaac was actually slaughtered, the theme of his sacrifice and ashes is found throughout the rabbinic literature (see comments on 8:31-32 above for additional references). This interpretation is partly based upon the fact that, at the end of the *Akedah* narrative (Gen 22), the text states (v. 19): "So Abraham returned to his young men, and they arose and went together to Beersheba; and Abraham lived at Beersheba." Conspicuously missing is any mention that Isaac actually returned. Yet the fact that Isaac obviously reappears in the later narrative presumes that if he was slaughtered on Mt. Moriah, he was likewise resurrected. It may be that the writer of Hebrews had this same teaching in mind when he wrote (Heb 11:17–19):

> By faith Abraham, when he was tested, offered up Isaac, and he who had received the promises was offering up his only begotten son; it was he to whom it was said, "IN ISAAC YOUR DESCENDANTS SHALL BE CALLED." He considered that God is able to raise people even from the dead, from which he also received him back as a type.

Thus, Isaac is portrayed in the rabbinic literature as one whose death atones for sins, and who also is resurrected. It is hardly proper, then, to suggest (as many liberal scholars have), that the death and resurrection of the Messiah is an entirely "new" idea of the later, Christian Church. (On the subject of the *Akedah*, its use in rabbinic literature, and the foundation it provided for Apostolic teaching on redemption, see Geza Vermes, *Scripture and Tradition in Judaism* [Brill, 1983], pp. 193ff).

Who is at the right hand of God – The figure of Messiah sitting at the "right hand of God" is taken primarily from Psalm 110:1 in midrashic connection with Psalm 80:17 [Hebrew 80:18]:

> Psalm 110:1 The LORD says to my Lord: "Sit at My right hand, Until I make Thine enemies a footstool for Thy feet."
> Psalm 80: 17 Let Thy hand be upon the man of Thy right hand, Upon the son of man whom Thou didst make strong for Thyself.

There is some allusion to Psalm 110 by the Sages as being Messianic,[255] but its regular use by the early followers of Yeshua caused later rabbinic authorities to interpret it differently. Regardless, the "right hand" was considered the place of power and authority[256] and to sit at the right hand of the Almighty is to sit in a place of sovereign power and authority.

The author of Hebrews considered this position of the Messiah, being at the right hand of God, to be significant indeed, for such a position showed two things: one, that He had been exalted to a name above every name for He had, indeed, been given all authority in heaven and earth, and two, that He had finished His work, for the posture of "sitting" is one of service completed. Noteably there were never any chairs in the Tabernacle or Temple proper, for the work of the priests was never finished. Thus, when he makes his assertion that Yeshua "sat down" at the right hand of God, he is clearly telling us that Yeshua is in a place of supreme authority, and that He sits, having completed His work.

That Stephen reveals a vision of Yeshua "standing at the right hand" (Acts 7:55) does not contradict this metaphor of "sitting." Each is metaphoric language to convey an aspect of Yeshua's work. As sitting upon the right hand, we are to understand that Yeshua has accomplished all of His work in death and resurrection, and that never again will He need to undergo the pangs of death. His standing posture, however, reveals that Yeshua is still active in His priestly duties, and that in His exalted position He is undertaking everything necessary to assure our ultimate and final redemption. That He stands at the death of Stephen indicates a posture of readiness to receive each and everyone who, through death, enters into His presence.

Now Paul makes an explicit statement regarding Yeshua's position "at the right hand" (what the systematic theologians refer to as His "session") which implies His ascension. Paul uses the final aspect to include the ascension, for surely Yeshua would have to ascend to the Father in order to obtain His position at the "right hand." That the ascension was an intregal part of the early confession of the Messianic Jews is evidenced by the wording of 1Timothy 3:16:

> And by common confession great is the mystery of godliness: He who was revealed in the flesh, Was vindicated in the Spirit, Beheld by angels, Proclaimed among the nations, Believed on in the world, Taken up in glory.

"Taken up in glory" forms the final member of this early confessional. Why? Why is the ascension so important? There are two primary reasons. First, the ascension once again assures all who are in the Messiah that they too, as Yeshua is now, will be ushered into the presence of the Father. In the model of Yeshua's prayer in John 17, one of the requests we see Yeshua making is that His own would be with Him where He was, that they might behold His glory.[257] The fact that Yeshua ascended to the Father means that all those who are in Him will likewise ascend.

Secondly, it was of absolute importance that the Messiah ascend because of the issues involved in the making of atonement. The picture of the Tabernacle/Temple and the activities on Yom Kippur will make this clear.

Yom Kippur is viewed by the Apostolic authors as the most detailed picture of the sacrificial/redemptive work done by God on behalf of His people. Proof of this may be seen in the book of Hebrews, where Yom Kippur forms the basis for the author's exposition of atonement. Since the yearly cycle of festivals (mo'edim) is a mini-picture of the entire scope of God's redemptive work, one of the emphases of Yom Kippur is the once-for-all-time work of the High Priest in affecting atonement for God's chosen people.

In the Tabernacle/Temple, the arrangement of the necessary articles (brazen altar, laver, altar of incense, etc), as well as the Tabernacle/Temple itself are all illustrative of God's plan of redemption. The sacrifice is slain and offered upon the brazen altar which is outside of the Tabernacle. However, on Yom Kippur, no atonement is affected by the slaying and offering of the sacrifice. It is not until the blood of the sacrifice has been taken by the High Priest and applied to the mercy seat of the Ark of the Covenant in the Most Holy Place that atonement is accomplished. Now this activity of the Cohen HaGadol, taking the blood from the altar which is outside of the Tabernacle and bringing it into the Holy Place, then into the Most Holy Place— foreshadowed the very work of Yeshua. For He was slain outside of the Heavenly Tabernacle and ascended in order to make atonement in the eternal, heavenly Tabernacle (Heb 9:11-12). Even as the picture of atonement in the earthly Tabernacle would never have been complete without the priest entering the Most Holy Place with blood and incense, so the sacrifice of Yeshua would have been without consequence if He had not ascended to the Father and the heavenly Tabernacle there to apply (as it were) His blood to the "mercy seat." It is Yeshua's very presence before the Father, and (if we can speak in these terms) before His bar of justice that confirms and makes effectual His death and resurrection on the behalf of His people. Thus, His presence before the Father corresponds to the application of the blood to the mercy seat in the earthly Tabernacle.

Note the following verses:

> 1John 2:1 My little children, I am writing these things to you that you may not sin. And if anyone sins, we have an Advocate with the Father, Yeshua Messiah the righteous;

> Heb. 7:25 Hence, also, He is able to save forever those who draw near to God through Him, since He always lives to make intercession for them.

> Heb. 9:24 For Messiah did not enter a holy place made with hands, a mere copy of the true one, but into heaven itself, now to appear in the presence of God for us;

Here we find this theme of Yeshua's presence before the Father as a necessary aspect of His atoning work. And of course, His presence before the Father necessitates the ascension. To deny His ascension is likewise to deny His work of intercession, an integral and necessary part of our redemption.

Who also intercedes for us – This, then, is the fourth of the pillars which Paul enumerates in our verse, and one which is most important. As the Cohen HaGadol of old, Yeshua carries out the work of intercession on behalf of His people.

There are several points I would like to make regarding the intercessory work of Yeshua:

1) the intercessory work of Yeshua corresponds directly to His sacrificial work.

That is to say (using the metaphor of sacrifice), Yeshua's intercession consists of the application of His blood, shed on the "altar" of the cross, to the mercy seat in the Most Holy Place. The application of the blood corresponds directly to the sacrifice, that is, those represented in the sacrifice are those for whom the blood is applied. In the symbol of Yom Kippur, for instance, the sacrifice made by the Cohen HaGadol was for the nation of Israel, not for all of the nations. Thus, those represented in the sacrifice are those represented by the Cohen HaGadol in the application of the blood to the mercy seat. In like manner, we find clear evidence that Yeshua's intercession is not for all, but specifically for His chosen ones, those for whom He died.

John 17 records the prayer of Yeshua as He unburdened His soul to the Father before the cross. Yet there is every indication in this chapter that what we have before us is a glimpse of the kind of prayer Yeshua offers in His intercessory work now. Notice that the language appears to transport Yeshua beyond the cross, beyond the resurrection and ascension, to the very work of intercession.

> John 17:4–5 I glorified You on the earth, having accomplished the work which You gave Me to do. And now, glorify Me together with Yourself, Father, with the glory which I had with You before the world was.

> John 17:11 And I am no more in the world; and yet they themselves are in the world, and

I come to You. Holy Father, keep them in Your name, the name which You gave Me, that they may be one, even as We are.

As such, we should understand the prayer of Yeshua, recorded in John 17, as a model of the intercession in which He now engages on behalf of His people. One such characteristic is that His prayer—His intercession—is not for everyone, but specifically for those who believe in Him:

John 17:9 I ask on their behalf; I do not ask on behalf of the world, but of those whom You have given Me; for they are Yours;

Here we see that the pattern of Yeshua's intercession follows exactly the pattern foreshadowed in the Tabernacle: the Priest's intercession corresponds directly with those represented in the sacrifice. Even as Yeshua would die for those who were His, so He would live to intercede for them as well.

The connection of the sacrifice and the intercession carried out by the Cohen HaGadol on Yom Kippur is explicitly seen in the commandment that he take both blood and incense into the Most Holy Place. What is more, the incense is not secondary—he must take it in with him "lest he die":

And he shall take a firepan full of coals of fire from upon the altar before the LORD, and two handfuls of finely ground sweet incense, and bring it inside the veil.
And he shall put the incense on the fire before the LORD, that the cloud of incense may cover the mercy seat that is on the ark of the testimony, lest he die.
Moreover, he shall take some of the blood of the bull and sprinkle it with his finger on the mercy seat on the east side; also in front of the mercy seat he shall sprinkle some of the blood with his finger seven times.   (Leviticus 16:12-14)

Thus, the blood, representative of the sacrifice, is combined with the incense in the Most Holy Place ceremony, giving an illustration of Yeshua's work whereby the sacrifice which He underwent for His people is combined with His intercessory work in the application of it to His people. The extent of the sacrifice equals the extent of the intercession, for the two are combined inextricably. The conclusion is obvious: if Yeshua does not intercede for all (cf. John 17:9) it is because He does not intend His sacrifice to be for all. This corresponds to the fact that the death of Yeshua is in every way efficacious, meaning it actually atones for sin. The purpose of Yeshua's death is realized in the salvation of those for whom He died.

2) The intercessory work of Yeshua is absolutely necessary for the salvation of sinners.

Even as the blood of the sacrifice, slain on the altar, makes no atonement on Yom Kippur until the blood has been applied to the mercy seat of the Ark of the Covenant, so the death which Yeshua died upon the cross has no value for redemption until it is applied (as it were) at the bar of the Father's justice. In the same way that the incense is symbolic of prayer, so Yeshua's intercession (prayer) on behalf of His chosen ones is the means by which He applies the value of His death to the account of those for whom He died. It is by His intercession that He "pleads the merits of His blood" (to use a Puritan term) before the Father, and therefore His intercession on behalf of the elect is an essential element of their final and eternal redemption. Apart from the intercessory work of Yeshua, no one could have their sins covered by His blood, for the blood (the death as payment for sin) would not be applied.

3) The intercessory work of Yeshua makes active what is both historical and eschatological.

Our salvation has several dimensions: it is something that is eternal in the plan and mind of God, for He determined to save us from eternity past. It is also historical in the sense that our salvation rests upon events which occurred in time and space (the life, death, resurrection, and ascension of Yeshua). But it is also future in the sense that we have not yet fully apprehended the salvation which is ours in Yeshua, nor has the fullness of the salvation which He purchased for us been made active in our lives.

When I say that the intercessory work of Yeshua makes active what is both historical and eschatological, I am focusing upon the "here and now" of our existence. If our salvation was secured in the past by the death and resurrection of Yeshua; if our future, eternal salvation is secured by His "ever living to make intercession for us," is there any aspect of our salvation that is present—current, in the here and now? The answer, of course, is an emphatic "yes." And the current aspects of our salvation are the direct result of Yeshua's intercession.

How might we characterize the current aspects of our salvation? First, we are saved from sin, not only in an eternal sense, but in an immediate one. That is to say, we find ourselves in a battle against the flesh (the evil inclination), a battle that before our faith in Yeshua we were powerless to win. The characteristic of our lives, now, however, is that we regularly and progressively in greater measure win over the temptations of sin, and live righteously before HaShem. To put it in a positive construction, we are able to obey God's loving commandments in an ever increasing and significant way.

Now this ability to overcome sin and to live unto righteousness (i.e., our sanctification) is the direct result of Yeshua's intercession on our behalf. For it is by the means of His prayers for us that we are enabled to grow in the grace and knowledge of God. It is by His intercession before the Father that we are able to persevere in the "ways of grace." Now we may glean this truth from the requests that are outlined for us in the "high priestly prayer" of Yeshua as glimpsed in John 17. Note the precise requests and the obvious application of each to our own lives:

Request 1 - (John 17:1) "glorify Your Son, that the Son may glorify You."

Here we have Yeshua requesting that the glory which He had with the Father before the world began be restored to Him as the conquering victor of sin and death. We see from the very beginning of this prayer that the glory of the Father is the ultimate goal of the Son. But the Father is best glorified by the salvation of sinners, which is the result or outcome of the Son's work. To be glorified, then, means to be shown victorious in His saving acts. The final and eternal salvation of those He has chosen is therefore co-terminus with His glory. Their salvation is just as secure as is the very glory of God.

Request 2 - (John 17:11) "keep them in Your name, which You have given Me, that they may be one, even as We are."

The second request is that those who belong to Yeshua (whom He purchased with His own blood) should be "kept," that is "guarded" from anything that might separate them from the salvation which is theirs. The context makes it clear that this "keeping" or "guarding" is seen in the sphere of unity—oneness. He is asking that they be kept as safe and secure in their relationship with the Father as the Son and Spirit are secure in their oneness with Him. Thus, this "keeping" has as its primary focus the issue of covenant, for the request is "keep them in Your name," i.e., in the Name which is attached most closely to the giving and keeping of the covenant (cf. Ex 3:14ff). It therefore has a corporate dimension as its primary focus. This prayer of Yeshua secures the inevitable presence of the people of God (קְהִלָּה, k'hilah, "congregation"; ἐκκλησία, ekklesia, "assembly") upon the earth until the "end of the age" (cf. Mt 28:18ff).

Request 3 - (John 17:15) "keep them from the evil one"

The third request is specific in regard to the warfare in which the follower of Yeshua is engaged, a warfare not "against flesh and blood" but against wicked spirits and demonic forces (Eph 6:12). Such a request signals to us the harsh reality that, apart from the sustaining power of Yeshua's intercession, the battle with Satan would be lost. That is to say, the spiritual battle we fight against Satan is one which, left to our own strength, even the strength of the renewed man, would be lost apart from the ongoing application of Yeshua's sacrifice to our lives. It is important to see that our warfare against evil is not only based upon the historical, past event of the cross, but equally to the present reality of Yeshua's intercession for us. Through His intercession, He constantly secures in the life of each believer what He purchased by His death. This includes the ability to successfully wage war against the enemy of the soul.

Request 4 - (John 17:17) "Sanctify them in the truth; Your word is truth"

Here we have the fourth request—one which secures the application of the word of God to the heart and soul of the believer. "Sanctify" means to "set apart," "to make holy." Thus, the inevitable outcome of Yeshua's intercession—His prayer on our behalf, is that we will be set apart from the world of unrighteousness through the application of the truth of His word. It is the truth that becomes the agent of sanctification, a truth that comes to the heart and soul of the believer as the direct result of Yeshua's intercession. Thus, the work of the Spirit in illumining the truths of Scripture, and making application to the heart of the redeemed is the direct result of Yeshua's intercession.

Request 5 -(John 17:20-21) "I . . . ask . . . that they may all be one, even as You, Father, are in Me and I in You . . . that the world may believe."

This fifth request has a slightly different point of view than the earlier request to "keep them in Your name" (Request 2). There, the issue was the mere existence of the *kehilah* or community of believers. Here, the focus is on their ability to be in unity as an expression of their love for each other, and thus as a witness of God's love in which they live. For the outcome of their unity is that "the world may believe." This recalls the words of the former context of John (13:35) where it is written, "By this all men will know that you are My disciples, if you have love for one another." If the prayer of Yeshua is being worked out in any given community of faith, then love for each other will be an evident reality.

Request 6 - (John 17:24) "Father, I desire that they also whom You have given me be with Me where I am . . . "

The sixth request secures the resurrection and life in the world to come for all those who are His, a world in which Yeshua will be seen as the glorious Messiah He truly is. This particular prayer of Yeshua makes our being with Him throughout eternity a reality. Even as He ascended to the very presence of the Father, so we too will stand one day in the glory of His presence and be welcomed in as true brothers and sisters.

Request 7 - (John 7:26) ". . . that the love wherewith You did love Me may be in them
and I in them."

This seventh and final request secures that those who have been justified will be conformed to the image of Yeshua. The "love" of God is unparalleled and unmatched, and it is
demonstrated in the mystery of the godhead. The eternal and mysterious relationship between
the Father, His Messiah, and the Spirit is marked by absolute unity, while at the same time an
interdependence and mutuality that is the essence of love. It is eternal, omnipotent, unchang-
ing, and pure. It is this love which forms the model for loving each other within the multifaceted relationships of mankind. What is more, it is a love well displayed in the actions and life
of Yeshua, for this "love" which is requested to be "in them" is followed by the words "and I in
them." That is to say, this kind of love manifests the very life of Yeshua lived out through His
disciples.

**35 Who shall separate us from the love of Messiah? Shall tribulation, or distress, or persecu-
tion, or famine, or nakedness, or peril, or sword?**

Paul begins this sub-paragraph with yet another rhetorical question, emphasizing the obvious answer: "no one will separate us from the love of Messiah!"

What exactly does Paul mean by using the term "separate?" The word "separate" (χωρίζω,
chorizo) means "to leave" or "to separate." It is used most often regarding the marriage covenant, e.g., in the well-known phrase "what God has joined together let no man separate" (Mt
19:6). When an unbelieving spouse "leaves," (i.e., separates, a legal term for divorce), the remaining spouse is no longer under covenant obligation (1Co 7:15). It seems quite possible that
the covenant language of marriage is in the mind of the Apostle as he writes, envisioning the
relationship of the believer to Messiah as endowed with all of the sanctity of the marriage vow.

The covenant between the believer and Messiah is secure because it is guaranteed by the
Spirit (Rom 5:5; Eph 1:14). Furthermore, the phrase "love of Messiah" must be a subjective
genitive, meaning Messiah's love for us. Since the covenant is secure because of His love, and
because His love is unwavering and eternal, nothing can separate us from Him.

The list that Paul gives of those things which, one might think, could separate a believer
from the covenant with Messiah, are experiences which he had undergone himself—except for
the last one, of course. On "tribulation and distress," cf. Rom 2:9; for "persecution," cf. 1Co 4:
12; 2Co 4:9; 12:10; Gal 5:11; for "famine and nakedness," cf. 1Co 4:11; 2Co 11:27; for "peril" cf.
1Co 15:30; 2Co 11:26. Of course, many believers did face the sword, cf. Acts 12:2; Heb 11:34, 37.
The point is obvious: the worst of conditions upon this earth can never take from the believer
the salvation which is secure in Yeshua, nor can they rob the child of God of the riches of the
world to come.

We see as well in this verse yet another subtle marker of Paul's "christology." Here, Paul
puts the love of Messiah as the decisive factor in the maintenance of the covenant, while in v. 39
as well as 5:5 it is the "love of God." For Paul, the "love of God" and the "love of Messiah" for
the believer is one and the same. For the Father and the Son are One.

**36-37 Just as it is written, "For Your sake we are being put to death all day long; We were
considered as sheep to be slaughtered." But in all these things we overwhelmingly conquer
through Him who loved us.**

Paul now quotes from Psalm 44:22 (Lxx, 43:23) as an expression of his own experience and
to show that a life of trials is nothing new for the people of God. This verse was used by the
Sages to refer to martyrs, and it was so applied to the mother who suffered the loss of her seven

sons during the Hasmonean revolt, and then was herself killed (2 Macc 7). It was also applied to those who live righteously and suffer for it.[258] For Paul, the Psalmist has described the suffering of the righteous but not their defeat. In the end, the righteous prevail.

But in all these things – This phrase might well be understood to mean "But in spite of all these things."

Overwhelmingly conquer – This translates ὑπερνικῶμεν (*hupernikomen*, from ὑπερνικάω, *hupernikao*, the prefixed preposition being perfective, and in this case, emphatic), thus "over-whelmingly" = "conquer in every way."

Through Him who loved us – This phrase gives, without ambiguity, the source of the victory. We are more than conquerors not because of our own courage, endurance or determination but through Messiah, and not by our hold upon Him, but His hold on us. This "love" is nothing less than covenant faithfulness and loyalty of our Savior, an eternal promise forever kept.

38-39 For I am convinced that neither death, nor life, nor angels, nor principalities, nor things present, nor things to come, nor powers, nor height, nor depth, nor any other created thing, shall be able to separate us from the love of God, which is in Messiah Yeshua our Lord.

Paul now adds his own, first person singular to the crescendo of this doxology, making his own personal declaration of the conviction he personally owns.

I am convinced (or persuaded) – On this phrase, cf. 14:14; 15:14; 2Tim 1:5, 12. It is used by Paul to show a firm and settled conviction, a confident certainty.

The list of powers seems to be in pairs except for the term "powers" (δυνάμεις, *dunameis*) in the middle of the list and "things created" (τις κτίσις ἑτέρα, *tis ktisis hetera*) at the end of the list.

death nor life

nor angels nor principalities

nor things present, nor things to come,

nor powers,

nor height nor depth,

nor any other created thing

death nor life – In human experience death is the great "separator." It might appear from some contexts that death also separates man from God (Ps 6:5; 30:9; 88:5, 10-12; 115:17; Is 38:18), but the reality is that the righteous, always having the hope of the resurrection, know that death is actually a means by which we come into the very presence of our Creator. In contrast, though in "life" we are "absent from the Lord" (2Co 5:6), we know that "whether living or dying we are equally the Lord's" (2Co 14:8) since He is both the Lord of the living and the dead (2Co 14:9). It may well be that Paul also hints at martyrdom, and the fact that when called upon to face death for one's faith, the grace of God would sustain the believer to prove and strengthen his covenant ties in Messiah.

angels nor principalities – The Greek is ἄγγελοι οὔτε ἀρχαί (*angeloi oute archai*) which could be translated "angels or magistrates," but when ἀρχή (*arche*) is coupled with "angel," it inevitably means a rank of angelic beings. Lists of angelic beings usually contain both of these terms (1Co 15:24; Eph 1:21; 3:10; 6:12; Col 1:16; 2:10, 15). The terms used for the angelic creatures were not invented within the Messianic community, but were extant in other Jewish sources as well (cf. 1 Enoch 61:10; 2 Enoch 20:1). The common angelic designations seem to be applied both to those who uphold God's righteousness as well as to those who are enemies of the Most High. The obvious point of the Apostle here is to disavow to any cosmic power the ability to separate the believer from the covenant relationship he has with Messiah.

things present, things to come – Current events can almost inevitably be 'trumped' by one's imagination of what the future might hold. Regardless, in Paul's mind neither events of the present nor of the eschaton can sever the covenant God has made with His people, nor cause them to be bereft of His presence and sustaining love. For the believer, the future holds nothing but the hope of eternal life.

nor powers – This term can denote "miracles" or "angelic beings." True miracles are from God and could not therefore be contrary to His promises. It seems unlikely that Paul considers miracles to be against the believer and his standing in grace. Most likely, then, the word "powers" refers to angelic beings, perhaps particularly tied into the eschatological events. We know that the apocalyptic literature (such as the Revelation) employed the imagery of angels as the messangers of God to carry out His purpose in the eschaton. As such, they are often messangers of doom. Yet even in the Day of the Lord, when judgment will fall upon the earth, the believer is assured of his standing in God's grace and in the Messiah.

nor height nor depth – In ancient times this doublet was often understood to mean "things above the heaven, and things under the earth." Some have connected the terms with astrology and occult. More than likely, however, the terms are hyperbolic and simply mean "the highest and the lowest," i.e., heaven and hell, cf. Ps 139:8ff.

nor any other created thing – This is a final "catchall" phrase, and is a fitting conclusion to the poetic list the Apostle has crafted. While all of the things mentioned certainly appear to threaten our standing with Messiah, the truth is that nothing of this created universe is able to overturn the promises given to us by HaShem in His Messiah. And, outside of the created universe only God exists. So once again we are left up to His all-encompassing love and power.

shall be able to separate us from the love of God which is in Messiah Yeshua our Lord – Here Paul is very specific. The love of God, the attribute whereby He remains utterly and eternally faithful to His word and His people, is fully demonstrated and carried out in the Messiah Yeshua Who is our divine Master. The love of Messiah is not fully and accurately known until it is recognized as the love of the eternal God Himself, and it is only in Yeshua that the love of God is fully manifested in all of its truth and greatness.

Endnotes

1   1Sa 10:20, cp. Rom 11:1; Phil 3:5.

2   Acts 13:9

3   See the comments of Louis Feldman, *Jew & Gentile in the Ancient World* (Princeton, 1993), 70-72.

4   e.g., b.*Sanhedrin* 43a.

5   cf. C. F. D. Moule, *An Idiom-Book of the New Testament* (Cambridge,1959), p. 118f.

6   C.E.B. Cranfield, *Romans* in *The International Critical Commentary*, 2vols. (T&T Clark, 1975), 1.66. [Hereafter Cranfield, *Romans*]

7   b.*Kiddushin* 73a; cf. Mid. Rab. *Gen.* 70:5.

8   though Cranfield considers the real possibility that the emphasis is not the Gentile majority, but rather upon the geographical location in the midst of the Gentile world, p. 1.68.

9   Cranfield, *Romans*, 1.70.

10 In the Greek there exists a particle, μέν, which the English translations do not translate. The Greek particle is often used to introduce the protosis, or opening statement, to which is later added the apodosis, a parallel statement. In English we might use a phrase such as "on one hand . . . " to which "on the other hand" would inevitably be appended. Some have suggested that the use of the particle μέν with πρῶτος ("first") forms a peculiar case in which the second member (δέ) is not required. Others, however, suggest that Paul intended to add a second clause beginning with δέ but simply decided not to or omitted it.

11 For other places where Paul uses similar oath terminology, cf. 2Co 1:23; 11:31; Gal 1:20; Phil 1:8; 1Thess 2:5, 10; cp. Rom 9:1; 2 Co 2:17.

12 "What Does πληρωσαι Mean in Matthew 5:17?," delivered at the NW Regional ETS Meeting, Feb. 28, 1998. The full text of this paper is available at www.torahresource.com

13 Mid. Rab. *Ruth* vii. §6, on 3.18.

14 C. G. Montefiore, *Rabbinic Literature and Gospel Teachings* (KTAV, 1970), p. 49.

15 b.*Shavuot* 36a.

16 *Mechilta* on Exodus 20:1, 2.

17 Chrysostom, in his comments on this text, considers "spiritual" to denote Christian in contrast to Jewish. (cf. notes of Cranfield, *Romans*, 1.76).

18 Note the various suggestions for punctuation in the UBS text, ad loc.

19 Mark Nanos, *The Mystery of Romans* (Fortress, 1996), p. 211.

20 Zech 3:9; 14:16; Mal 3:12; Ps 86:9; note Rom 15:10-12 and the quotes there, and cf. Rev 15:4

21 for so I take the term συμπαρακληθῆναι (*sumparaklethenai*), from παρακαλέω (*parakaleo*), to mean "encourage," "comfort" here rather than "exhort," though the word does have this meaning in other contexts.

22 Note other instances where he uses this same opening line: 11:25; 1Co 10:1; 12:1; 2Co 1:8; 1Th 4:13.

23 The other two are θέλειν (*thelein*) and βούλεσθαι (*boulesthai*).

24 Paul uses the technique known as "asyndenton" here, which is to leave out the word "and" between the two clauses, which tends to add weight to the statement as a whole.

25   Cranfield, *Romans*, 1.91. *BDAG* (ad loc πρῶτον, *proton*, p. 734) has: "of degree in the first place, above all, especially" and lists Rom 1:16 accordingly.

26   *TDOT*, 1.317.

27   γνῶστος (*gnostos*) in other parts of the Apostolic Writings is used to mean "known," but in Classical Greek and in the Lxx it often has the meaning "knowable," which fits this context best.

28   the Greek term is καταφρονέω, (*kataphroneo*) which usually means "despise," cf. Mt 6:24; 18:10; Lk 16:13; 1Co 11:22; 1Ti 4:12; 6:2; Heb 12:2; 2Pt 2:10.

29   Sandy & Headlam, *Romans* in *The ICC* (T & T Clark, 1902), p. 58. Apparently this point of interpretation goes back as far as Origen.

30   Cranfield, *Romans*, 1.848.

31   Interestingly, the modern Hebrew translation of the New Testament (1976) uses חֲלִילָה, *chalilah* (from חָלַל, *chalal*, "that which is profane") to translate μὴ γένοιτο, (*me genoito*) every time it occurs in Romans (3:4, 6, 31; 6:2, 15; 7:7, 13; 9:14; 11:1, 11).

32   cf. Cranfield, *Romans*, 1.182, n. 1.

33   Martin Hengel, *Judaism & Hellenism* (Fortress, 1974), 1.200.

34   Mark Nanos, *The Mystery of Romans*, p. 129.

35   "4QMMT C27, 31 and 'Works Righteousness' at Qumran," read at the SBL 1998 Annual Meeting by Martin G. Abegg.

36   contrary, in part, to Sanders, *Paul and Palestinian Judaism* (Fortress, 1977).

37   Cranfield, *Romans*, 1.199-200.

38   Ibid., 1.201.

39   The textual variant in this verse may be noticed by comparing NASB or NIV with the NKJV. An added phrase "and on all" (καὶ ἐπὶ πάντας) is found in the Byzantine manuscripts (אᶜ D G K) and the papyri (33 181 326 330 etc.) which is a conflated reading with the old Italian and Vulgate. It is most likely to be considered added by later hands.

40   John Murry, *Romans* in the *NICNT*, 1.114.

41   Note that the term is based upon the root כָּפַר, *kaphar*, so that the כַּפֹּרֶת, *kaporet* is the result or outcome of the activity denoted by כָּפַר.

42   *Mekilta de Rabbi Ishmael* 3 vols. (JPS, 1933), 1.220.

43   Ibid., 1.253.

44   Cranfield, *Romans*, 1.229.

45   Ibid., 1.233.

46   Ibid., 1.234, n. 4.

47   b. *Sukkah* 55b.

48   Note the compilations of Mattis Kantor, *The Jewish Timeline Encyclopedia* (Aronson, 1992).

49   Cranfield, *Romans*, 1.237.

50   That some would interpret the anarthrous νόμου (*nomos*) as meaning "law in general" and not the Mosaic Torah in particular is simply without support. The following verses (14-16) surely identify the Torah to which Paul refers as the Torah given to Moses.

51   Cranfield, *Romans*, 1.241.

52   Ibid., 1.242.

53   מוֹן (*mon*) may mean "kind, species" and is found in the Palestinian Syriac to mean "nations" (cf. BDB, p. 568). The translation could rightly be "Father of various kinds of nations." The point may well be that the group which would call Abraham "father" would indeed be a diverse group.

54   *Tanhuma*, Lek Lecha, § 6.

55   Quoted from Louis H. Feldman, *Jew & Gentile in the Ancient World* (Princeton, 1993), p. 339.

56   b.*Baba Metzia* 59b.

57   Mid. Rab. *Ruth* Zuta 1.12.

58   Philip Blackman, *Mishnaot.* 7 vols. (Judaica Press, 1983), 1.469.

59   This, again, was standard Rabbinic teaching, cf. *Mekilta* Ex 18:3 (65b); 21:37 (95a); 22:22 (101b).

60   The translation of אֵל שַׁדַּי (*el shaddai*) as "God Almighty" is based upon the root of שַׁדַּי being שָׁדַד, (*shadad*) "destroyer," thus "God who destroys" or "God who is a fearful destroyer." Others have suggested the root שָׁדָה, *shadah,* from the Akkadian *shadu,* "mountain," and thus considered the meaning "mountain God." Still others point to the root שַׁד, (*shad*) "breast," and derive the meaning "breasted God" = "God who nourishes" or "God who gives suck," thus, "God who opens the womb." It should be noted that every use of אֵל שַׁדַּי in Genesis is in the context of those who are barren and seeking God's mercy for children or those who have been bereaved of children (17:1; 28:3; 35:11; 43:14; 48:3).

61   Calvin, cf. Cranfield, *Romans,* 1.248.

62   John Calvin, *Commentaries,* 22 vols (Baker Book House, 1984 reprint), 19:180.

63   John Piper in a sermon on 1Co 10:31.

64   Calvin, *Commentaries,* 19.182.

65   Cranfield, *Romans,* 1.257, n. 1

66   Ibid., 1.258

67   Ibid., 1.259.

68   Note the use of ἵστημι (*histemi*) in other Pauline letters: 1Co 7:37; 15:1; 2Co 1: 24; Eph 6:11, 13, 14; Col 4:12; 2Tim 2:19; 1Pt 4:12.

69   Rom 1:23; 3;23; 15:7; 1Co 10:31; 11:7; 2Co 4:6, 15; Phil 1:11; 2:11; 1Ti 1:11; Tit 2: 13.

70   b.*Shabbat* 88b.

71   *Tanchuma*, quoted from Montefiore & Loewe, *Rabbinic Anthology* (Schoken, 1974), p. 543.

72   *Midrash Psalms* on 73:1, p. 167a, §1.

73   cf. Rom 6:9; 13:11; 1Co 15:58; 2Co 4:14; 5:6, 11; Gal 2:16; Eph 6:8, 9; Col 3:24; 4: 1; 1Pt 1:18.

74   Calvin, *Commentaries,* 19.191.

75   Note the use of δόκιμος (*dokimos*) in 1Pt 1:7, "that the proof (refined residue) of your faith, being more precious than gold which is perishable, even though tested by fire, may be found to result in praise and glory and honor at the revelation of Yeshua the Messiah."

76   Cranfield, *Romans,* 1.261.

77   Ps 22:5; 25:3, 20; 119:116 (Lxx= 21:6; 24:3; 118:116) all of which contain the verb καταισχύνη (*kataischune*) preceded by the negative: "not ashamed," the exact construction found here. Cf. Is 28:16 as well.

78   The textual variants substitute a number of different readings since this is a less than common Greek construction. Alford opted for εἴ γε (*ei ge*) which is read by B and the Coptic, though he suggests a possible confusion with a liturgical phrase χριστὸς ὄντων ἡμῶν ἀσθενῶν ἔτι ("Christ, when we were weak, still . . ."); Henry Alford, *The Greek Testament.* 5 vols. (Moody, 1958) 2.357.

79   I am aware of the textual variants in this verse, some of the Byzantine manuscripts having κύριος (*kurios*, "Lord") rather than θέος (*theos*, "God") but the

clear weight of manuscript evidence is on the side of reading θέος, and in addition, this is surely the more difficult reading.

[80] The ἐν (en) most likely denotes "by means of" or "by virtue of," not sphere.

[81] quoted from Cranfield, *Romans*, 1.274.

[82] *Ben Sira* xxv.28[24].

[83] for a thorough discussion of this topic, i.e., a rabbinic understanding of sin, see the comments of Ephraim Urbach, *The Sages* (Harvard, 1979), pp. 422ff.

[84] Mid. Rab. *Eccl.* vii.13.

[85] Mid. Rab. *Gen.* xiv.6.

[86] b.*Sanhedrin* 102a.

[87] b.*Mo'ed Qatan* 28a; m.*Eduyot* ii.9, and Urbach's comments, *The Sages*, pp. 264-266.

[88] though evil deeds can hasten death, showing the ambiguity which the sages were willing to live with when it came to the intersection of providence and free will.

[89] cf Rom 8:3 "For what the Torah could not do . . ."

[90] b.*Bava Batra* 16a.

[91] *Sifre Deut.* §45, p. 103. cf. b.*Berechot* 61a.

[92] Mid. Rab. *Cant.* i.2, cf. b.*Sukka* 52a; b.*Sanhedrin* 92b.

[93] *Avot de-R. Nathan*, Version I, xvi, 32a

[94] b.*Berechot* 61b.

[95] Hans-Joachim Kraus, *Psalms 1-59* (Augsburg, 1988), p. 503.

[96] Cranfield, *Romans*, 1.282.

[97] Mid. Rab. *Gen.* xii, 2.

[98] b.*Zevachim* 116a. The figure of 974 is derived from the following calculation: The Torah existed a thousand generations before the Creation (Ps 105:8). There are 26 generations between Adam and Moses: 1000-26 = 974.

[99] b.*Shabbat* 89b.

[100] i.e., this book belongs to the generations of Adam. Mid. Rab. *Gen.* xxiv.5.

[101] Cranfield, *Romans*, 1.283.

[102] Calvin, *Romans*, 19:206.

[103] Cranfield, *Romans*, 1.284.

[104] Ibid., 1.288.

[105] Ibid., 1.290.

[106] Ibid.

[107] Sandy and Headlam, *Romans* in the *ICC* (Edinburg, 1895), p. 139.

[108] Barrett, *Romans* (London, 1957), p. 110.

[109] Leenhartdt, *Romans* (London, 1961), p.149.

[110] Cranfield, *Romans*, 1.292.

[111] Ibid., 1.293.

[112] Ibid., 1.296.

[113] Ibid., 1.300.

[114] See the article "proselyte" in *Encyclopedia Judaica*, 16 vols. (Macmillan, 1971), 13:1182ff.

[115] Num 19.

[116] Lev 15.

[117] Lev 15:19ff.

[118] b.*Yevamot* 47a; b.*Gittim* 1 [*Gittim* is one of the 14 minor tractates found in some editions of the Mishnah and Talmud attached to the fourth order, *Nezikin*.]

[119] b.*Yevamot* 46.

[120] *Yad, Mikva'ot* 11:12.

[121] Epictetus, *Dissert.*, II.9.9-21, as noted in Beasley-Murray, *Baptism in the New Testament* (Eerdmans, 1973), p. 23. A passage, found in the fourth Sibylline Oracle, dated about 80 CE, deals with proselyte baptism in the opinion of most scholars. The Rabbinic discussions in the Mishnah most certainly represent earlier traditions, and evidence a practice well in place by the end of the 1st Century CE.

[122] Solomon Zeitlin, "The Halaka in the Gospels and its relation to the Jewish Law at the Time of Jesus", *HUCA*, (I, 1924), p. 360.

[123] Jn 18:28; Acts 10:28; 11:12; and possibly Mt 8:7.

[124] J. Jeremias, "Der Ursprung der Johannestaufe", *ZAW*, 1929, p. 313. Quoted from Beasley-Murray, *Baptism*, 21, n. 2.

[125] *Wars*, II, viii.10.

[126] See Daube's remarks in *The New Testament and Rabbinic Judaism* (London, 1956), pp. 106ff.

[127] Daube, (ibid.) bases his argument on the fact that women, who could not undergo circumcision in the proselyte ritual, were left with nothing if baptism was not administered. Since, he argues, the vast majority of proselytes were women, baptism became the most common public ritual connected with proselytism as a whole. G.F. Moore, a recognized scholar in 1st Century Judaisms, agrees with Daube (though on slightly different basis) as did Büchler, who wrote: "There is no evidence for the assumption that the immersion prescribed for the proselyte was instituted to wash off symbolically his numerous sins." A. Büchler, *Studies in Sin and Atonement in the Rabbinic Literature of the First Century*, (1928), p. 373.

[128] This is based on the wording of Ex 12:26-27, which envisions the future generations asking about the Passover seder and its meaning. The parent is to tell the child, "It is a Passover sacrifice to the Lord who passed over the houses of the sons of Israel in Egypt when He smote the Egyptians, but spared our homes." Thus, each generation may rightly say that the Lord redeemed us out of Egypt, and that we passed through the Sea to safety.

[129] Num 19:16ff.

[130] Beasley-Murray, *Baptism*, p. 29.

[131] Cp. also 1Co 12:13. Both Cranfield (*Romans*) and Murray (*Romans* in NICNT) recognize that Paul is speaking about the actual ritual of baptism, but emphasizing that its import is essentially union with the Messiah.

[132] 1Co 10:2, ". . . all were baptized into Moses . . ."

[133] 1Co 1:13-16.

[134] Mt 3; Mk 1; Lk 3.

[135] Beasely-Murray's remarks (*Baptism*, p. 33, n. 1) are unfortunate. He accepts uncritically the notion that 1st Century Judaisms embraced a belief that no circumcised person would be punished by God. This misunderstanding of the Judaistic theology of the 1st Century may be traced back to Strack-Billerbeck, and their misquoting of the Mishnah and Talmud. The two most often quoted citations to substantiate this teaching are Mid. Rab. *Exodus*, 19, "The circumcision do not go down to Gehinnom" and b.*Shabbat* 128a, "All Israelites are sons of kings (=patriarchs)." Both of these, when read in context, show that a Jew who acted corruptly, even if circumcised, would feel the anger and justice of HaShem, and could even descend to Gehinnom.

[136] See Beasley-Murray's remarks, *Baptism*, pp. 38-9.

137 Jn 3:22, 26; 4:2.

138 The Hebrew concept of בַּת קוֹל, *bat kol*, as the Divine voice, would favor the 3rd person, since the divine voice must be heard by objective parties, and more than one person. See the comments of Geze Vermes, *Jesus the Jew* (Fortress, 1973), pp. 205-6.

139 Mt 3:13-17; Mk 1:9-11; Lk 3:18-22.

140 Mt 3:14.

141 Mt 3:15.

142 Mk 10:38, 39.

143 Wise, Abegg, Cook, *The Dead Sea Scrolls* (HarperCollins, 1998), p. 129. The quote is from 1QS 2.25ff.

144 Cranfield, *Romans,* 1.305.

145 Ibid., 1.308-9.

146 Joseph Shulman, *Romans* (Lederer, 1997), p. 217.

147 Godet, *Romans* (Zondervan, 1956), p. 244. This is merely representative of many commentators who hold that the "old man" terminology refers to the old sin nature.

148 Cranfield, *Romans,* 1:309.

149 John Murray, *Romans,* (Eerdmans, 1968), p. 220.

150 Note the grammatical comments of Eadie, *Ephesians* (James & Klock, 1977 reprint of the 1883 edition), pp. 338-39.

151 b.*Shabbat* 30a; 151b.

152 Mid. Rab. *Exodus,* 51.8.

153 Outside of Romans, cp. 2Co 4:14; 13:4; Gal 2:19; Eph 2:5; Col 2:13, 20; 3:3, 4; 1Th 4:14, 17; 5:10; 2Ti 2:11f.

154 For other references regarding the once-for-all nature of Yeshua's death, cf. Heb 7:27; 9:12, 26, 28; 10:10; 1Pt 3:18.

155 Ex 30:2; Lev 16:2.

156 Cranfield, *Romans,* 1.315.

157 Gerald Bray, ed. *Romans: Ancient Christian Commentary on Scripture* (IVP, 1999), p. 165.

158 Cranfield, *Romans,* 1.319-20.

158a An interesting scenario to propose is this: what would Paul have done when in Jerusalem with some of his Gentile brothers? Suppose they were going to the Temple to offer a thanksgiving offering. As Paul and his fellow believers entered the Temple precincts, they would have come to the place where Gentiles could go no farther. Would Paul have left his brothers there and continued into the court of the Jews? One could speculate that he may have remained with his Gentile brothers in the court of the Gentiles, even though he would have normally gone into the court of the Jews had he been by himself or with other Jewish acquaintances. This would be a case where, when with those who were reckoned as "without the Torah" by the leading authorities of his day, he would have identified himself with them, likewise being viewed as "without the Torah," and remained in the court of the Gentiles.

159 Ibid., 1.323.

160 Ibid., 1.325.

161 Calvin, *Romans,* 19.241-42.

162 S. Mowinckel, *He That Cometh* (Oxford, 1959), p. 205. Cf. also Mowinckel, *The Psalms in Israel's Worship,* 1.240.

163 Mitchell Dahood, *Psalms* 3 vols in the *Anchor Bible* (Doubleday, 1970), 1.xxxvi.

[164] Cf. M. F. Thelen, "Jewish Symbols and 'Normative' Judaism", *JBL* 83 (1964), 361-63; W. Wirgin, "The Menorah as Symbol of After-Life," *IEJ* 14 (1964), 102-4.

[165] It appears that the debate on this issue was so heated that some manuscripts were altered to leave this phrase out, cf. C. G. Montefiore and H. Loewe, *A Rabbinic Anthology* (Shocken, 1974), p. 600.

[166] cf. Cranfield, *Romans*, 1.329, n. 2.

[167] Some have suggested that Paul has been referring to Roman Law throughout the epistle (Sanday and Headlam, *Romans*), but this seems highly unlikely since he quotes from the Tanach as examples of what he means by "law", cf. 3:10ff; 4:7-9. What is more, the "law" Paul refers to in the "law"/"letter" metaphor, is paralleled in 2Co 3, in which place the Torah of Moses is clearly in view.

[168] m.*Kiddushin* 1.1; b.*Kiddushin* 13b.

[169] b.*Kiddushin* 13b.

[170] τὰ παθήματα, *ta pathemata* from the root πάθημα, *pathema*, used of "desires" or "emotions" and is itself neutral (neither moral nor immoral). The context must therefore decide whether or not the "desires" prescribed are godly or not. Cf. Gal 5:24.

[171] Calvin, *Romans*, 19.250.

[172] Cranfield, *Romans*, 1.338.

[173] The following excursus is taken from a paper written for a symposium on "The Believer and the Law." Some statements may therefore be repetitive of material already in the preceding commentary.

[174] Cranfield, *Romans*, 1.346-47.

[175] cf. Liddell and Scott, ad. loc.

[176] This being the case, the meaning of 1Tim 6:14 must be that Paul is admonishing Timothy to "keep the Torah" until the coming of Messiah.

[177] Shulam, *Romans*, p. 245.

[178] Cranfield, *Romans*, 1.350-351. Cranfield also thinks that in this whole section Paul has Genesis 1-3 primarily in his mind, and that "the commandment" he refers to is the prohibition to eat of the tree of the knowledge of good and evil. While there are obvious parallels and even some verbal similarity, it seems to me to be a bit of a stretch, especially since "coveting" is Paul's at-hand example, a commandment which surely has Sinai in mind, not the garden of Eden.

[179] Calvin, *Romans*, 19.255.

[180] Note *Pirkei Avot* 6:3, ". . . 'the perfect shall inherit good' and good is nothing but Torah, as it is said, 'For I give you good doctrine, forsake not My Torah' (Prov 4:2)."

[181] Phil 3:6.

[182] The variant οἶδα μέν (*oida men*, "on the one hand he knows," separating οἴδαμεν, *oidamen*, "we know," into two words), adopted by Jerome, does not have sufficient manuscript evidence to be a viable option.

[183] b.*Sanhedrin* 99a.

[184] p. 250.

[185] Cranfield, *Romans*, 1.358.

[186] Calvin, *Romans*, 19.268.

[187] Cranfield, *Romans*, 1.362.

[188] Ibid.

[189] Mid. Rab. *Cant.* 1, §15.

190 Cranfield, *Romans*, 1.366.

191 Ibid., 1.367.

192 Adin Steinsalz "Sin" in *Contemporary Jewish Religious Thought*, ed. Arthur A. Cohen and Paul Mendes-Flohr (Free Press, 1987), p. 881.

193 Ibid., p. 882.

194 Ibid, p. 883.

195 Ibid., p. 885.

196 Ibid.

197 y.*Shabbat* i,3; b.*Nedarim* 10a.

198 y.*Shabbat* i,3; b.*Nedarim* 12b.

199 m.*Sanhedrin* vi.2.

200 b.*Shavuot* 21a.

201 *Sifre Deut* §286.

202 *Avot d'R. Natan* Version 1, iv. ed. Schechter, 11a.

203 b.*Berakot* 10b.

204 *Pesiqta de-R. Kahana*, (trans. by Braude and Kapstein [Routledge & Kegan Paul, 1975]), p. 120.

205 Urbach, *The Sages* (Harvard, 1987), p. 434.

206 b.*Berachot* 17a; cf. b.*Ta'anit* 27b; b.*Megillah* 31b; *Tanchuma* Tzaw, 14.

207 cf. b.*Sukkot* 52a where Zech 12:10-12 is understood by some of the Sages as referring to Messiah son of Joseph who must suffer before the coming of Messiah son of David.

208 I recognize the work of E.P. Sanders in this arena, in which he has shown that "salvation by works" was not a prominent theme of 2nd Temple Judaisms, and I actually agree with much he has done. But what he fails to address is that the concept of "salvation by works" is an innate reality of the fallen nature, and does not need an organized theology to exist. Mankind believes in his fallen state that somehow he can "pull himself up by the bootstraps" or that in some measure he deserves God's grace. This innate belief in one's own ability to atone for sins played out beautifully in the 1st Century Judaisms, as both the teachings of Yeshua and Paul affirm, and the DSS give witness. Granted, the primary understanding of 1st Century Judaisms seems to be that Jewish status guarantees God's favor (m.*Sanhedrin* 10:1). But maintaining this covenant status required Torah obedience for the Jew. Moreover, the Gentile could only gain "Jewish status" through becoming a proselyte, which entailed "taking upon oneself the yoke of the Torah." Thus, by rabbinic standards, a Gentile gained covenant membership through the "works of the Torah" (=submitting to the rabbinic ritual of proselytism). In the rabbis view, covenant membership, based upon "Jewish status," whether for the native born Jew or the proselyte, was dependent to one measure or another upon one's righteous deeds.

209 Cranfield, *Romans*, 1:382.

210 Ibid., 1.384.

211 Ibid.

212 Ibid, 1.386.

213 Ibid., 1.387.

214 Note the discussion in *BDAG*, p. 217-18; Maximilian Zerwick, *Biblical Greek* (Scripta Pontificii Instituti Biblici, 1963), pp. 102ff.

215 *Complete Oxford Dictionary*, ad loc.

216 Hodge, *Systematic Theology* 3 vols. (Scribners, 1883), 1.523.

[217] Calvin, *Romans*, 19.291.

[218] Cranfield, *Romans*, 1.395.

[219] Ibid., 1.396.

[220] Mid. Rab. *Exodus* 46:5.

[221] Cranfield, *Romans*, 1.399.

[222] Ibid., 1.400.

[223] Ibid., 1.402.

[224] Note comments above on 4:13ff.

[225] Cranfield, *Romans*, 1.408.

[226] Ibid. cf. Mt 5:11f; Mk 8:34f, 38; Jn 15: 18-20; 16:33; Acts 14:22.

[227] Note the words used in the Fathers for ἀποκαραδόκια (*apokaradokia*, "eager expectation"): ἀποκαραδοκεῖν (*apokaradokein*), καραδοκεῖν (*karadokein*), καραδοκία (*karadokia*), none of which occur in the Apostolic Scriptures. It seems clear that the prefixed preposition ἀπο of ἀποκαραδοκία is perfective.

[228] Cranfield, *Romans*, 1.412.

[229] Ibid.

[230] b.*Sanhedrin* 98b.

[231] Cranfield, *Romans*, 1.416.

[232] Ibid., 1.418.

[233] Ibid., 1.419.

[234] *BDAG*, ad loc.

[235] So Cranfield, *Romans*, 1.421.

[236] Origen and Chrysostom both took this view, cf. Cranfield, *Romans*, 1.423.

[237] Ex 20:6; Dt 5:10; 6:5; 7:9; 10:2; 11:1, 13, 22; 13:3; 19:9; 30:6, 16, 20; Josh 22:5; 1Kgs 3:3; Neh 1:5; Ps 31:23 [Lxx 30:24]; 97:10 [Lxx 96:10]; 116:1 [Lxx 114:1]; 145:20 [Lxx 144:20]; Dan 9:4; cf. in Qumran texts CD 3:2ff; 1QH 15:9; in other Apostolic texts, Mt 22:37 (cf. Mk 12:30); Mk 12:33; Lk 10:27; 1:42; Jn 5:42; 1Co 2:9; 8: 3; Js 1:12; 2:5; 1Jn 4:10, 20f; 5:1f.

[238] Ex. 20:6; Dt. 5:10; 7:9; 11:1; 11:13; 30:16; Josh. 22:5; Neh. 1:5; Ps. 119:47,127; Dan. 9:4; Jn 14:15; 14:21; 15:10; 1Jn 5:2; 2Jn 1:6. All of these combine the idea of "love" with that of "keeping commandments."

[239] For the concept of an effectual call, cf. Rom 9:24; 1Co 7:17ff as examples.

[240] Cranfield, *Romans*, 1.431.

[241] Cp. Gen 18:19; Jer 1:5; Amos 3:2.

[242] Cf. Eph 1:4; 2Ti 1:9; 1Pt 1:20.

[243] Cranfield, *Romans*, 1.432.

[244] Ibid., 1.433.

[245] B. B. Warfield, *Biblical and Theological Studies* (Pres & Reformed Pub., 1968), pp. 282-83.

[246] H. B. Huffmand and S. B. Parker, "A Further Note on the Treaty Background of Hebrew ידע", *BASOR* 184(1966), 36-38.

[247] Note the comments in the reference in the Soncino Edition of *Midrash Rabbah*, 2:916.

[248] b.*Sukkah* 52a.

[249] Mid. Rab. *Song of Songs*, ii.33.

[250] Rashi on Zech 12:9-10.

[251] Robert H. Eisenman and Michael Wise, *The Dead Sea Scrolls Uncovered* (Element, 1992), p. 24.

[252] Martin Abegg, "4Q285", address delivered at the 1991 annual meeting of the SBL in Kansas City. Note also the remarks of Hartman Stegemann, *The Library*

of Qumran (Brill/Eerdmans, 1998), pp. 102ff.

253 Ex 28:33; 39:25.

254 1Cor 15:20-23.

255 Cf. Mid. Rab. *Genesis* 85.9 (on Gen 38) where Psalm 110:2 is considered to be speaking of the Messiah.

256 Note that David had a throne placed 'at his right hand' for Bat Sheva, 1Kings 2:19.

257 Jn 17:24.

258 According to Cranfield, *Romans*, 1.440.